Cities and Society

Edited by

Nancy Kleniewski

Blackwell
Publishing

BLACKWELL PUBLISHING
350 Main Street, Malden, MA 02148-5020, USA
108 Cowley Road, Oxford OX4 1JF, UK
550 Swanston Street, Carlton, Victoria 3053, Australia

The right of the Nancy Kleniewski to be identified as the Author of the Editorial Material in this Work has
been asserted in accordance with the UK Copyright, Designs, and Patents Act 1988.

First published 2005 by Blackwell Publishing Ltd

Library of Congress Cataloging-in-Publication Data

Cities and Society / edited by Nancy Kleniewski.
    p. cm.—(Blackwell readers in sociology; 13)
   Includes bibliographical references and index.
   ISBN 1-4051-0231-4 (hbk : alk. paper)—ISBN 1-4051-0232-2 (pbk. : alk. paper)
   1. Sociology, Urban. 2. Cities and towns. 3. Urban economics. 4. Urban policy.
5. Globalization. I. Kleniewski, Nancy. II. Series.

HT108.C523 2005
307.76—dc22
                                                                    2004050167

A catalogue record for this title is available from the British Library.

Set in 10 on 13pt Sabon
by Kolam Information Services Pvt. Ltd, Pondicherry, India
Printed and bound in the United Kingdom
by TJ International, Padstow, Cornwall

The publisher's policy is to use permanent paper from mills that operate a sustainable forestry policy, and
which has been manufactured from pulp processed using acid-free and elementary chlorine-free practices.
Furthermore, the publisher ensures that the text paper and cover board used have met acceptable
environmental accreditation standards.

For further information on
Blackwell Publishing, visit our website:
www.blackwellpublishing.com

Contents

Preface

This volume represents some of the major research in urban sociology during the past 25 years. I selected the readings with three tensions or balances in mind:

- to include a broad range of topics but focus on the most significant issues for scholars and policymakers;
- to emphasize works by sociologists but incorporate work from other disciplines; and
- to be accessible and interesting to undergraduates but include enough scholarly substance to engage graduate students.

The works included here are by no means a comprehensive survey of urban sociology. Space limitations forced me to make some difficult choices, including the omission of many important writings that are available in other collections.

The intent behind this volume is to collect the original work of contemporary scholars in slightly abbreviated versions. Of the 20 readings in this collection, 16 are excerpts from books and 4 are articles from scholarly journals. Although they are recent works, they are likely to stand the test of time because of their solid contributions to central questions in the field of urban sociology.

Many people assisted with this project. Malcolm Crystal recruited me to take on the project for Blackwell. My editors, Ken Provencher and Justin Vaughan, helped shape my approach to the contents. Their professionalism and good cheer made working with them a delight. In addition, several anonymous reviewers gave thoughtful comments on the prospectus. I owe a debt of gratitude to my assistants at Bridgewater State College, Sandy Christoun and especially Kelly Duarte, for their active help in preparing the manuscript. I am fortunate to have such capable and caring colleagues. As always, I am grateful to Bill Davis for his understanding and support.

In recent weeks, one of my most important teachers and mentors passed away. Sister Marie Augusta Neal, SND, was a creative thinker, innovative instructor, scrupulous researcher, and champion of social justice. I dedicate this book to her memory.

Nancy Kleniewski, March 2004

Acknowledgments

The editor and publisher gratefully acknowledge the permission granted to reproduce the copyright material in this book:

Bonacich, Edna and Richard P. Appelbaum, "The Return of the Sweatshop." From *Behind the Label: Inequality in the Los Angeles Apparel Industry* (Berkeley: University of California Press, 2000), pp. 1–14, 16–23, 25, notes. © 2000 by the Regents of the University of California. Permission granted by the Regents of the University of California and the University of California Press.

Davis, Mike, "Fortress L A" From *City of Quartz: Excavating the Future of Los Angeles* (New York and London: Verso Ltd, 1992), pp. 224, 226–36, 244, 246, 248, 250–3, 257–8, 260–3. © 1990 by Verso. All rights reserved.

Dear, Michael, "Los Angeles and the Chicago School: Invitation to a Debate." From *City & Community* 1(1) (2002): 5–6, 14–19, 21–5, 29–32. Reprinted by permission of the American Sociological Association.

Fainstein, Susan S., "Economic Restructuring and Redevelopment" From *The City Builders: Property, Politics, and Planning in London and New York* (2nd edn), (Lawrence, Kansas: University Press of Kansas, 2001), pp. 1–8 and 16–26. © 1994, 2001 by the University of Kansas Press.

Gilbert, Alan and Josef Gugler, "The Urban–Rural Interface and Migration." From *Cities, Poverty, and Development* (Oxford: Oxford University Press, 1992), pp. 62–4, 66–73. © Oxford University Press.

Jargowsky, Paul A., "Chaos or Community? Directions for Public Policy." From Chapter 7 of *Poverty and Place: Ghettos, Barrios, and the American City* (New York: Russell Sage Foundation, 1997), pp. 185–6, 193–5, 197–213. © 1997 Russell Sage Foundation, 112 East 64th Street, New York, NY 10021. Reprinted with permission.

Lin, Jan, "Community, Ethnicity, and Urban Sociology." From *Reconstructing Chinatown: Ethnic Enclave, Global Change* (Minneapolis: University of Minnesota Press, 1998), pp. 7–15. © 1998, Regents of the University of Minnesota. All rights reserved.

Lloyd, Richard, "Neo-Bohemia: Art and Neighborhood Redevelopment in Chicago." From *Journal of Urban Affairs* 25(5) (2002): 518–32. Copyright © 2002 Urban Affairs Association and Blackwell Publishing Ltd.

Logan, John R. and Todd Swanstrom, "Urban Restructuring: A Critical View." From *Beyond the City Limits: Urban Policy and Economic Restructuring in Comparative Perspective,* eds. John R. Logan and Todd Swanstrom (Philadelphia:

Temple University Press, 1990), pp. 3–21. Reprinted by permission of Temple University Press. © by Temple University Press. All rights reserved.

Massey, Douglas S. and Nancy A. Denton, "The Missing Link." From *American Apartheid: Segregation and the Making of the Underclass* (Cambridge, MA: Harvard University Press, 1993), pp. 1–16, notes. Copyright © 1993 by the President and Fellows of Harvard College. Reprinted by permission of the publisher.

Molotch, Harvey, "The City as a Growth Machine: Toward a Political Economy of Place." *American Journal of Sociology*, 82 (1976): 309–18, 326–32. © 1976 by the University of Chicago Press. All rights reserved.

Sassen, Saskia, "Overview of Global Cities." From *The Global City: New York, London, Tokyo* (New Brunswick, NJ: Rutgers University Press, 1991), pp. 3–12. © Princeton University Press. Reprinted by permission of Princeton University Press.

Savage, Mike and Alan Warde, "Modernity, Post-modernity, and Urban Culture." From *Urban Sociology, Capitalism, and Modernity* (London: Macmillan, 1993), pp. 138–46. © 1993 by Mike Savage and Alan Warde.

Spain, Daphne, "Space and Status." From *Gendered Spaces*, (Chapel Hill: University of North Carolina Press, 1992), pp. 3–7, 10–21, 25–6. Copyright © 1992 by the University of North Carolina Press. Used by permission of the publisher.

Swanstrom, Todd, Peter Dreier and John Mollenkopf, "Economic Inequality and Public Policy: The Power of Place." From *City & Community* 1(4) (2002): 349–57, 359–72. Reprinted by permission of the American Sociological Association.

Urry, John, "Gazing on History." From *The Tourist Gaze: Leisure and Travel in Contemporary Societies* (Thousand Oaks, CA: Sage Publications, 1990), pp. 104–10, 112–16, 120–2, 123–6, 129–32, 134. © 1993 by Sage. Reprinted by permission of Sage Publications Ltd.

Waldinger, Roger, "The New Urban Reality." From *Still the Promised City? African-Americans and New Immigrants in Postindustrial New York* (Cambridge, MA: Harvard University Press, 1996), pp. 1–7, 21–6, 27–32. Copyright © 1996 by the President and Fellows of Harvard College. Reprinted by permission of the publisher.

Williamson, Thad, David Imbroscio, and Gar Alperovitz, "The Challenge of Urban Sprawl." From *Making a Place for Community: Local Democracy in a Global Era* (New York: Routledge, 2002), pp. 71–85, 89–98, notes. Copyright © 2002 from *Making a Place for Community: Local Democracy in a Global Era* by Thad Williamson, David Imbroscio, and Gar Alperovitz. Reproduced by permission of Routledge/Taylor & Francis Books, Inc.

Wolch, Jennifer and Michael Dear, "Understanding Homelessness: From Global to Local." From *Malign Neglect: Homelessness in an American City* (San Francisco: Jossey-Bass, 1993), pp. 1–14, 20–2, 24–43. Reprinted by permission of the authors.

Zukin, Sharon, "Gentrification, Cuisine, and the Critical Infrastructure: Power and Centrality Downtown." From *Landscapes of Power: From Detroit to Disney World* (Berkeley: University of California Press, 1991), pp. 187–95, 206–8, 214–15, notes. © 1991 by the Regents of the University of California. Permission granted by the Regents of the University of California and the University of California Press.

Every effort has been made to trace copyright holders and to obtain their permission for the use of copyright material. The publisher apologizes for any errors or omissions in the above list and would be grateful if notified of any corrections that should be incorporated in future reprints or editions of this book.

Introduction: Contemporary Issues in Urban Sociology

Nancy Kleniewski

"Ford to City: Drop Dead!" was the headline in New York's *Daily News* the day after President Gerald Ford's 1975 speech refusing to assist the nearly bankrupt city with a loan guarantee. Although its social and economic problems were extreme, New York was not alone in its plight. Cities in the United States, United Kingdom, and other industrialized nations began to face massive problems in the 1970s caused by worldwide economic changes. In this volume we explore these ongoing global changes, their impacts on cities, and responses by policymakers.

The readings in this book are divided into four sections exploring four major approaches to cities. The first section addresses theoretical perspectives and debates among urban scholars. The second section explores the impact of the global economy on cities. The third section describes the changing urban economy and its impact on different groups of people. The final section describes some key issues and choices for public policy. This Introduction sets the stage for the readings by discussing the overall context of urban sociology in the four areas that make up the collection. It is followed by a list of key references for further reading.

Recent Theoretical Perspectives on Cities and Society

During the past 30 years, our sociological understanding of cities has undergone a major change. From the early days of urban sociology until the 1970s, the dominant paradigm (or way of understanding) in urban research was the theory of *human ecology*. This theory, developed at the University of Chicago, interpreted city life and form as an extension of the processes of the natural world. The most important assumption of human ecology was that the city was like a living organism that consisted of interdependent parts. The parts (or natural areas) of the city, according to the theory, were arranged in a regular pattern with a central business district surrounded by concentric rings of other land uses. Changes in patterns of land use or residential location were thought to be driven by a competition for space in which groups that could bid more for space were able to obtain better locations. The patterns of social norms that differentiated urban life from rural life were presumed to be the result of the larger, denser, and more heterogeneous population of the city in contrast with the smaller, less dense, and relatively homogeneous populations of rural areas.

Human ecology produced a large body of research, exploring many urban issues and processes. By the 1970s, however, new urban problems and new realities prompted researchers to question the continued usefulness of human ecology as a research tool. Some of those new issues included declining populations in the central cities, increasing racial polarization, government intervention in the real estate market, economic instability, and the growing differences between cities in the rich and poor nations. Human ecology theory was unable to explain these phenomena, prompting the search for alternative theoretical perspectives.

The emergence of political economy

In the 1970s, several French sociologists turned their attention to urban studies, and some of this early work was translated for an English-speaking audience. The French sociologists were trying to understand the relationships between the real estate market, the government, and social policy that resulted in major urban upheavals. Another source of innovation was the work of British geographers and sociologists, whose studies helped reinterpret urban issues. These new writings set off a series of conferences and publications that brought scholars together around a common research agenda and a theoretical perspective known as political economy. (Other labels for the emerging perspective included neo-Marxist, neo-Weberian, and the new urban sociology.)

The rise of the political-economy approach in the United States can perhaps be dated from 1976, when Harvey Molotch published the article that begins this collection, "The City as a Growth Machine: Toward a Political Economy of Place." Its appearance was highly symbolic, since the journal in which it appeared, *The American Journal of Sociology*, was founded by University of Chicago-based human ecology theorists. While Molotch was using political economy to explain urban growth, a number of other scholars were using political economy to explain urban population decline, urban redevelopment, the persistence of poverty, and racial inequality. Various streams of research converged on two principles: that the capitalist economy structures opportunities that result in differential access by social group and location; and that economic changes influence political and social life. The research agenda that emerged from these studies pinpointed the phenomenon of economic restructuring as the key to understanding other urban issues.

To grasp why economic restructuring was so important in the late twentieth century, we must understand the global context in which nations and cities are situated. From the late nineteenth century to the middle of the twentieth century, manufacturing was the engine driving economic and urban growth. In the latter part of this period, from the end of the Second World War in 1945 until the early 1970s, the industrialized nations of the world experienced a period of sustained economic growth and a rising standard of living. As the suburban middle class grew, it demanded (and industry provided) mass-produced consumer goods such as automobiles and appliances. Strong labor unions were able to win increased wages and benefits in return for an atmosphere of labor peace and few strikes. Despite social and racial inequality, real wages were rising, unemployment was relatively low, and the middle class was expanding. At the same time, national governments in Europe and North America instituted comprehensive social welfare systems including education, healthcare, old age pensions, and child welfare support.

Gradually during the postwar period the world economy changed in ways that destabilized the industrial economies. These changes, generally known as *economic restructuring*, involved three trends that changed the economies and social structures of industrial nations. They are: a *shift from manufacturing to services* as the engine of the economy, *changes in the process of production* due to new technologies and forms of organization, and *globalization* and the spread of industrialization around the world. We will explore the first two trends here and address globalization in detail in the next section.

The Growth of the Service Economy: Economic historians generally agree that up to the 1880s, agriculture, mining, and other extractive industries were the core of the US economy. From the 1880s to the 1950s, manufacturing was the engine for economic growth. By the 1960s, however, the service sector grew to employ more workers than manufacturing. The shift to services opened up many new jobs, for example in information technology, communications, financial services, legal services, hospitality, and other nonmanufacturing employment. Because wages in the service sector tend to be divided into very high-paying jobs (physicians and attorneys) and very low-paying jobs (fast food, security guards), the growth of service jobs had a profound effect on the distribution of income, which we will explore below.

New Technologies and Forms of Organization: Capitalist economies are characterized by economic and political systems that analysts call *regimes of accumulation* (after Aglietta 1976). From the 1940s to the 1970s, at the height of the manufacturing economy, the regime of *Fordism* was dominant. Fordism involves vertical integration of manufacturing, standardization of products for mass consumption, unionized labor forces with generally good wages, and a social safety net of government services. Picture a vast Ford plant with iron ore going in at one end and new cars coming out the other end; with unionized employees who work for the company until retirement, with high pay and good benefits. The plant, representing a huge investment, is built to produce millions of standardized cars, and the workers repeatedly perform specialized functions on an assembly line.

The regime of Fordism was gradually replaced by the regime of *flexible production* (sometimes called post-Fordism). Instead of large, vertically integrated companies, flexible production fosters networks of small companies producing parts for each other. Picture an electronics company that subcontracts with small providers to have circuits made and delivered for assembly into several different products. The amount of investment in the plant is relatively small, and the computerized equipment can easily be converted to make different products. The production schedule at the assembly site varies constantly depending on the number of orders being placed. Parts are shipped to assembly points from half a dozen contractors whose workforce is hired on an as-needed basis at relatively low wages with no job security.

Although analysts differ on the long-run effects of flexible production, they generally agree that in the short run it caused dislocation of many workers who were beneficiaries of the Fordist system. In addition, because many communities in the North American and European industrial heartlands were built around large manufacturing plants, the shift from Fordism to flexible production affected entire communities and regions.

Gender and urban research

Urban sociologists traditionally saw cities through the lenses of race, ethnicity, and social class. Until the 1980s they seldom discussed or studied the ways in which men and women lived different lives or experienced different realities. Early studies of gender, especially coming from feminist geographers in the United Kingdom and Canada, investigated the empirical differences in the daily rounds of the two sexes. They focused on such issues as housing needs, job location, transportation, recreational opportunities, unpaid household work, and community involvement. Researchers began to discuss the ways in which city planners made assumptions about "proper" household composition, laid out transportation routes that favored male work patterns, and encouraged the separation of homes from schools, shops, and other daily needs.

Building on these empirical studies, urban research began to address the broader literature on gender, including women's work, changing family patterns, and women's political and economic status. As an example, Daphne Spain's contribution in this volume (chapter 3) addressed the intersection of three variables: gender, space, and status. It thus contributed not only to how we understand women in cities but also to our understanding of how gender works as a key factor in social life. These important contributions laid the foundation for a growing body of research on gender and urban life.

Postmodernism and urban theory

Are cities of the twenty-first century fundamentally different from those of the twentieth century? Some urban analysts think that there has been a rupture from the past of such significance to have ushered in a new era: the *postmodern era*. There are several scholarly definitions of postmodernism existing on a number of levels, from the concrete to the abstract. The first level is that of architecture: postmodernism is the practice of mixing a number of dissimilar architectural styles in a single building. In the 1980s, this eclectic style largely replaced the modernist style of simple glass-and-steel boxes. The second level is that of the city itself: postmodern cities are thought to consist of many centers without apparent spatial organization (e.g., Los Angeles), as opposed to the modern industrial cities with their central business districts and surrounding suburbs (e.g., Chicago). The third level is that of theorists's thought processes: whereas modernists use a linear thought process, believe in progress, and try to understand why things happen, postmodernists use a cut-and-paste thought process (or pastiche), see multiple, conflicting realities simultaneously, and do not believe that explanations of reality (or metanarratives) have any objective meaning distinct from the meanings given to them by individuals.

Rather than seeing cities as objective sites, many postmodern writers stress the varied experiences of individuals in cities and the different points of view that people have of urban life and events. A symbol of the postmodern viewer of the city is the *flâneur* or stroller – someone who casually observes others, enjoys the experiences that others are having, but does not directly engage with others as part of their social groups.

Globalization and Its Impact on Cities

Although the countries of the world have been integrated into an economic system for at least four centuries, recent improvements in transportation and communication technology have intensified and hastened the pace of global integration. The decline of the colonial empires and the more recent disintegration of the communist economies have contributed to the unification of a single global market for goods, services, and labor. As mentioned above, economic globalization is one of the major developments that have affected cities in the past three decades.

The globalization of the economy has weakened or removed barriers to the flow of information, goods, money, and people across national boundaries. International free-trade agreements have replaced the tariffs and immigration controls that formerly kept national economies somewhat insulated from each other. Consider how globalization has changed the nature and location of manufacturing, for example. Driven by competition, companies looking for cheaper labor have increasingly moved production offshore to the developing nations of the third world. Modern transportation and communication technology have made it possible for companies to coordinate a manufacturing process that takes place in several locations in different countries. This "global assembly line" has driven manufacturing wages down and moved manufacturing jobs out of the industrialized nations.

Globalization has created a new corporate environment, one that requires the coordination of geographically dispersed planning and production processes. Paradoxically, as corporations and their subcontractors have dispersed geographically, the functions that control the process of production have centralized in large cities. These control functions include corporate headquarters, large banks and financial services, and other advanced corporate services (e.g., advertising, accounting, law firms) that the global companies require. A relatively small number of "global cities" in the industrial nations have become central to the global economy.

Globalization has also had a major impact on labor. In the industrialized nations, many experienced workers have been displaced from stable, well-paying manufacturing jobs (steel, for example) and forced to work in the service sector. At the same time, new manufacturing positions are being created in a low-wage, downgraded industrial sector (clothing, for example) in which workers of the industrialized nations compete with workers around the world. In the rapidly industrializing nations such as China, globalization has opened up new jobs for women who previously would not have been able to obtain paid employment. In these societies, industrialization is also leading to ever more rapid urbanization, as rural residents who can no longer support themselves on the land migrate to cities, putting pressure on housing and services.

Economic globalization also encourages immigration. As money, ideas, and goods are freer to move around the world, so are people. People in poor countries move off the land and into the cities in search of jobs and a better life. For the same reasons, people move from the cities of the less industrialized to the more industrialized nations within all regions of the world. For example, large numbers of immigrants from Mexico and the Philippines enter the United States, immigrants from India and Jamaica enter England, immigrants from Spain and the former Yugoslavia enter Germany, and those from Korea and China enter Japan. Some immigrants are educated professionals, and when they have language proficiency they can often secure professional employment. Others, however, find jobs in low-wage manufacturing, the informal sector (or underground economy), and ethnic-oriented services such as restaurants and grocery stores.

The Changing Urban Economy

Since 1975, the restructuring of the economy, in combination with intensified globalization, has had a profound effect on the types of jobs available in the United States, United Kingdom, and the other industrialized nations. As industrial jobs have decreased, employment has grown in industries such as computer technology, medical services, corporate services, hospitality, and tourism. These jobs tend to be either very high or very low paying. The current situation for employment is that highly-educated workers are finding their opportunities increasing, while workers with less than a college education are seeing opportunities for stable, well-paying employment decreasing.

As a result of these changes, income data show that social inequality is increasing. The middle class, which in the United States was growing until 1973, has been shrinking since then, and the proportion of the population that is either wealthy or poor has been increasing. One visible consequence is that the numbers of poor homeless people in cities has increased steadily, due to falling incomes, the disruption of social services, and increasing housing costs. Another consequence of economic restructuring is gentrification, or the influx of wealthier households moving into working-class neighborhoods. Gentrification has many causes, including an increase in the professional middle class working in the city, high prices for suburban housing, the availability of attractive older buildings in cities, and the growth in the number of childless households (both of young singles and empty-nesters) seeking alternatives to suburban housing.

As a response to changing urban economies, many cities have adopted economic development strategies to attract and retain employment. A typical mix of strategies for a city would include a combination of supporting new industries (e.g., tourism), strengthening existing industries (e.g., banking), and attracting mobile industries (e.g., high-tech manufacturing or "back office" work such as accounting). In addition, many cities have initiated urban redevelopment programs to modernize the physical plant of the city. Redevelopment schemes usually involve demolishing outmoded factories, housing, and transportation lines and replacing them with infrastructure suitable to the industries they hope to attract.

Public Policy Choices

It is clear that the trends of the past 50 years – suburbanization, globalization, and economic transformation – have had a major impact on cities. What have elected officials and other policymakers done to address the problems caused by these changes? As we saw earlier, one policy response has been to redevelop cities to facilitate the change from an industrial to a service economy. But as urban economies change, what is being done about the people who are not employable in the new industries of corporate services, tourism, and technology? As poverty becomes more concentrated in cities, what role should suburban communities play in assuring access to jobs and housing for all groups? This section will examine several policy choices relating to the increase in concentrated poverty among racial minorities, the increased separation of the rich and poor, and the relationships between cities and their suburbs.

Concentrated poverty

As suburbs have grown and businesses have moved out of the cities, some urban neighborhoods have been left with few or no economic resources. The hardest hit areas are inner-city neighborhoods that combine a high rate of poverty with large numbers of racial minority (particularly African American) residents. Widespread economic disruption and the migration of middle-class African American residents to better neighborhoods have combined to create areas of concentrated poverty in most large cities. Researchers have searched for the causes of concentrated poverty, investigating whether high unemployment rates in such areas are the result of a *mismatch* between the available jobs and the residents' skills. According to this line of reasoning, poorly-educated urban residents cannot qualify for the growing high-skill urban labor market, nor can they easily access the entry-level manufacturing and retail jobs that have moved to the suburbs. Another question about concentrated poverty is the extent to which residents of high-poverty neighborhoods constitute an *underclass* with a distinctive subculture. Although several authors have documented distinctive cultural traits in neighborhoods of concentrated poverty, they disagree on the extent to which these cultural traits are causes or consequences of being poor.

Several policies have been proposed to address the problem of concentrated poverty. One strategy is to give residents of high-poverty neighborhoods better economic and educational opportunities by assisting them to move to better neighborhoods. This is embodied in a program called Moving to Opportunity (MTO), which the US Department of Housing and Urban Development initiated in five cities beginning in 1994. This program uses rent vouchers or certificates to subsidize rents in privately-owned apartments as an alternative to public housing in poor neighborhoods. A contrasting strategy is *community development*, that is, infusing resources to improve housing, education, and economic development in inner-city neighborhoods. Community development strategies assume that urban residents, even in poor neighborhoods, have assets including their labor, income, and community organizations that can help them improve their environments. They also note that although many poor people choose to leave poor neighborhoods, the remaining people, buildings, and institutions constitute assets that cities cannot afford to abandon. Some combination of both strategies is probably necessary to address the problem of concentrated poverty.

Social class separation and urban–suburban relations

We have seen that the United States is experiencing increased polarization into distinct social classes: the rich and the poor are becoming more numerous as the middle class shrinks. In addition to this income polarization, people of different social classes are increasingly divided spatially into different residential communities. This separation is occurring not just within cities but more significantly within entire metropolitan areas, which are increasingly fragmented and geographically dispersed. Until the 1970s, city neighborhoods brought rich, poor, and middle-class residents into reasonable proximity with each other; but since then the trend has been toward class-homogeneous suburban towns and gated communities for the wealthiest households. As a result, children of today are less likely to have contact with children of other social classes at play or in school than children of the 1970s had.

Social problems caused by changes in the urban economy and increased class segregation are exacerbated by continuing racial and ethnic segregation. Racial residential segregation, many studies show, is due only in small part to economic differences among races. By far the most important cause is the host of barriers, legal and illegal, that continue to channel darker-skinned people into different residential neighborhoods than white people. African American households of all income levels face restricted housing choices which in turn limit the educational opportunities for their children.

The fragmentation of metropolitan areas into separate and unequal communities has raised many questions for social policymakers. To what extent should the consequences of social class and racial segregation be encouraged, discouraged, or ignored? Should cities and suburban communities collaborate with each other, and if so, how? Should we place limits on suburban growth to halt sprawl and minimize its environmental impacts? These are some of the policy questions the authors address in the final section of this volume.

Bibliographic Resources

The introduction above is based on the works cited below, which formed the foundation for the issues raised in this volume. This list is by no means exhaustive but provides a basis for reading the selections in this volume and a resource for further study.

I. Theoretical perspectives

The classic works of Human Ecology include: Park (1915; 1936); Park, Burgess, and McKenzie (1925); Wirth (1938); and Hoyt (1939).

Critiques of human ecology and the early development of political economy include: Harvey (1973; 1978); Gottdeiner and Feagin (1988); Gottdiener (1985); Castells (1977; 1979). See also the collections in Pickvance (1976); Harloe (1976); Pahl (1975); and Tabb and Sawers (1978) for examples of early political economy writings in Europe, the UK, and the US.

Major contributors to the literature on economic restructuring were: Aglietta (1976); Piore and Sabel (1984); Noyelle and Stanback (1984); Markusen (1987); Castells (1989); and Harvey (1989).

Gender was introduced into the urban studies literature through such writers as Hayden (1981); Saegert (1988); Massey (1994); Greed (1994). See also the collections by Garber and Turner (1994) and Baxandall and Ewen (2000).

The following thinkers have influenced the development of *the postmodern approach to urban form and life*: Bordieu (1977); Benjamin (1978); Soja and Scott (1996); Zukin (1991; 1995); and Dear (2000).

II.   Globalization and its impact on cities

The *overall view of the world-economy* was first presented by Wallerstein (1976); its implication for cities is discussed in Chase-Dunn (1989). Recent changes in globalization are explained by Smith and Feagin (1987); Castells (1996); and Scott (1988).

Sassen (1988) discusses implications of *globalization* for cities, including the downgrading of manufacturing. Portes, Castells, and Benton (1989) address the informal economy in global cities.

A number of good studies document various aspects of *immigration*, including Portes and Rumbaut (1996); Lamphere, Stepick, and Grenier (1993); Zhou (1992); and Hirschman, Kasinitz, and Dewind (1999).

III.   The changing urban economy

The *changing labor market and growing income inequality* are documented and explained by Harrison and Bluestone (1988); Reich (1991); and Mishel, Bernstein, and Schmitt (2000). A good resource on economic development is Mier (1993).

The *physical separation of high-income populations in gated communities* is the subject of Blakely and Snyder (1997). Gentrification is examined in Smith (1996); Smith and Williams (1986); and Zukin (1982).

IV.   Urban policy choices

On *concentrated poverty and the underclass debate*, see Wilson (1987; 1989); Kasarda (1984; 1989); and Katz (1993); also Anderson (1990) and Bourgeois (1995). For a discussion of mobility solutions to the problem of concentrated poverty see Rubinowitz and Rosenbaum (2000); Briggs (1997); and Goering et al. (2002). Squires and O'Connor (2001) and Oliver and Shapiro (1995) analyze the impact of race on resources across the income spectrum.

Political solutions to urban problems and urban–suburban cooperation are discussed in Clavel (1986); Rusk (1993); and Orfield (2002).

On *suburban growth* see Jackson (1985) and Garreau (1991). The case against increased suburbanization is made by Duany, Plater-Zyberk, and Speck (2001).

A good general overview of urban policy issues is US Department of Housing and Urban Development (2000).

References

Aglietta, Michel. 1976. *A Theory of Capitalist Regulation: The US Experience*. London: New Left Books.

Anderson, Elijah. 1990. *Streetwise: Race, Class and Change in an Urban Community*. Chicago: University of Chicago Press.

Baxandall, R. and E. Ewen. 2000. *Picture Windows: How the Suburbs Happened*. New York: Basic Books.

Benjamin, Walter. 1978. *One Way Street and Other Writings*, trans. E. Jephcott and K. Shorter. London: Verso.

Blakely, Edward and Mary Gail Snyder. 1997. *Fortress America: Gated Communities in the United States*. Washington, DC: The Brookings Institution.

Bourdieu, Pierre. 1977. *Outline of a Theory of Practice*. Cambridge: Cambridge University Press.

Bourgeois, Philippe. 1995. *In Search of Respect: Selling Crack in El Barrio*. New York: Cambridge University Press.

Briggs, Xavier de Sousa. 1997. "Moving Up Versus Moving Out: Neighborhood Effects in Housing Mobility Programs." *Housing Policy Debate* 8(1): 195–234.

Castells, Manuel. 1996. *The Rise of the Network Society*. Oxford: Blackwell.

——. 1989. *The Informal City*. Oxford: Blackwell.

——. 1979. *City, Class and Power*. New York: St. Martin's Press.

——. 1977. *The Urban Question*. Cambridge, MA: MIT Press.

Chase-Dunn, Christopher. 1989. *Global Formation: Structures of the World-Economy*. Malden, MA: Blackwell.

Clavel, Pierre. 1986. *The Progressive City*. New Brunswick, NJ: Rutgers University Press.

Dear, Michael. 2000. *The Postmodern Urban Condition*. Oxford: Blackwell.

Duany, Andres, Elizabeth Plata-Zyberk, and Jeff Speck. 2001. *Suburban Nation: The Rise of Sprawl and the Decline of the American Dream*. New York: North Point Press.

Garber, Judith and Robyne Turner, eds. 1994. *Gender in Urban Research*. Thousand Oaks, CA: Sage Publications.

Garreau, Joel. 1991. *Edge City*. New York: Doubleday.

Goering, John, Judith D. Feins, and Todd M. Richardson. 2002. "A Cross-Site Analysis of Initial Moving Opportunity Demonstration Results." *Journal of Housing Research* 13(1): 1–30.

Gottdiener, Mark. 1985. *The Social Production of Urban Space*. Austin: University of Texas Press.

Gottdiener, Mark and Joe Feagin. 1988. " The Paradigm Shift in Urban Sociology." *Urban Affairs Quarterly* 24(2): 163–87.

Greed, Clara. 1994. *Women and Planning: Creating Gendered Politics*. London: Routledge.

Harloe, Michael, ed. 1976. *Captive Cities*. London: John Wiley.

Harrison, Bennett and Barry Bluestone. 1988. *The Great U-Turn: Corporate Restructuring and the Polarizing of America*. New York: Basic Books.

Harvey, David. 1989. *The Urban Experience*. Baltimore: Johns Hopkins University Press.

——. 1978. "The Urban Process Under Capitalism: A Framework for Analysis." *International Journal of Urban and Regional Research* 2: 101–31.

——. 1973. *Social Justice and the City*. Baltimore: Johns Hopkins University Press.

Hayden, Dolores. 1981. *The Grand Domestic Revolution*. Cambridge, MA: MIT Press.

Hirschman, Charles, Philip Kasinitz, and Josh Dewind, eds. 1999. *The Handbook of International Migration: The American Experience*. New York: Russell Sage Foundation.

Hoyt, H. 1939. *The Structure and Growth of Residential Neighborhoods in American Cities*. Washington, DC: Federal Housing Administration.

Jackson, Kenneth. 1985. *Crabgrass Frontier*. New York: Oxford University Press.

Kasarda, John. 1984. "Entry-Level Jobs, Mobility, and Urban Minority Employment." *Urban Affairs Quarterly* 19(1): 21–40.

——. 1989. "Urban Industrial Transformation and the Underclass." *Annals of the American Academy of Political and Social Science* 501: 26–47.

Katz, M. B. 1993. *The Underclass Debate: Views from History*. Princeton: Princeton University Press.

Lamphere, Louise, Alex Stepick, and Guillermo Grenier, eds. 1993. *Newcomers in the Workplace: Immigrants and the Restructuring of the US Economy*. Philadelphia: Temple University Press.

Markusen, Ann. 1987. *Regions: The Economics and Politics of Territories*. Totowa, NJ: Rowman and Littlefield.

Massey, Doreen. 1994. *Space, Place and Gender*. Minneapolis: University of Minnesota Press.

Mier, Robert. 1993. *Social Justice and Local Economic Development Policy*. Newbury Park, CA: Sage.

Mishel, Lawrence, Jared Bernstein, and John Schmidt. 2000. *State of Working America, 2000*. Washington, DC: Economic Policy Institute.

Noyelle, Thierry and Thomas Stanback. 1984. *The Economic Transformation of American Cities*. Totowa, NJ: Rowman and Allenheld.

Oliver, Melvin and Thomas Shapiro. 1995. *Black Wealth/White Wealth: A New Perspective on Racial Inequality*. New York: Routledge.

Orfield, Myron. 2002. *American Metropolitics: The New Suburban Reality*. Washington, DC: Brookings Institution.

Pahl, Ray, ed. 1975. *Whose City?* Harmondsworth: Penguin Books.

Park, Robert E. 1936. "Human Ecology." *American Journal of Sociology* 42: 1–15.

——. 1915. "The City: Suggestions for the Investigation of Human Behavior in the City Environment." *American Journal of Sociology* 20: 577–612.

Park, Robert E., Ernest W. Burgess, and Roderick McKenzie, eds. 1925. *The City*. Chicago: University of Chicago Press.

Pickvance, Chris. 1976. *Urban Sociology: Critical Essays*. New York: St. Martin's Press.

Piore, Michael and Charles Sabel. 1984. *The Second Industrial Divide*. New York: Basic Books.

Portes, Alejandro, Manuel Castells, and L. Benton, eds. 1989. *The Informal Economy: Studies in Advanced and Less Developed Countries*. Baltimore: Johns Hopkins University Press.

Portes, Alejandro and Ruben Rumbaut. 1996. *Immigrant America: A Portrait*, 2nd ed. Berkeley: University of California Press.

Reich, Robert. 1991. *The Work of Nations*. New York: Alfred A. Knopf.

Rubinowitz, Leonard and James Rosenbaum. 2000. *Crossing the Class and Color Lines: From Public Housing to White Suburbia*. Chicago: University of Chicago Press.

Rusk, David. 1993. *Cities Without Suburbs*. Baltimore: Johns Hopkins University Press.

Saegert, Susan. 1988. "The Androgenous City: From Critique to Practice." In *Women, Housing and Community*, ed. Willem Van Vliet–. Aldershot: Avebury.

Sassen, Saskia. 1988. *The Mobility of Labor and Capital*. New York: Cambridge University Press.

Scott, Allen J. 1988. *Metropolis: From the Division of Labor to Urban Form*. Berkeley: University of California Press.

Smith, Michael P. and Joe Feagin. 1987. *The Capitalist City: Global Restructuring and Community Politics*. Oxford: Blackwell.

Smith, Neil. 1996. *The New American Frontier: Gentrification and the Revanchist City*. New York: Routledge.

Smith, Neil and P. Williams, eds. 1986. *Gentrification of the City*. London: Allen and Unwin.

Soja, Edward and Allen Scott, eds. 1996. *The City: Los Angeles and Urban Theory at the End of the Twentieth Century*. Berkeley: University of California Press.

Squires, Gregory and S. O'Connor. 2001. *Color and Money*. Albany: State University of New York Press.

Tabb, William and Larry Sawers, eds. 1984. *Marxism and the Metropolis*, 2nd ed. New York: Oxford University Press.

US Dept. of Housing and Urban Development. 2000. *State of the Cities, 2000*. Washington, DC: US Dept. of Housing and Urban Development.

Wallerstein, Immanuel. 1976. *The Modern World System*. New York: Academic Press.

Wilson, William J., ed. 1989. *The Ghetto Underclass*. Newbury Park, CA: Sage.

——. 1987. *The Truly Disadvantaged*. Chicago: University of Chicago Press.

Wirth, Louis. 1938. "Urbanism as a Way of Life." *American Journal of Sociology* 44: 1–24.

Zhou, Min. 1992. *Chinatown: The Socioeconomic Potential of an Urban Enclave*. Philadelphia: Temple University Press.

Zukin, Sharon. 1995. *The Cultures of Cities*. Oxford: Blackwell.

——. 1991. *Landscapes of Power: From Detroit to Disney World*. Berkeley: University of California Press.

——. 1982. *Loft Living: Culture and Capital in Urban Change*. Baltimore: Johns Hopkins University Press.

Part I

Recent Theoretical Perspectives on Cities and Society

1 The City as a Growth Machine: Toward a Political Economy of Place

Harvey Molotch

This groundbreaking article represents the early development of the political economy of cities. Using the metaphor of a "growth machine," Harvey Molotch explains why economics and politics shape the growth of cities. He points out that certain powerful groups benefit from urban growth and therefore act more or less in concert to promote growth. He argues that local politics largely revolve around creating the conditions for growth and distributing the resources derived from growth. The significance of Molotch's contribution to urban sociology is that, in contrast with the Chicago School theorists, he emphasizes groups' differences in power as they compete for space and other resources.

Molotch and John Logan later expanded this article into a book, *Urban Fortunes*, one of the best-developed statements of urban political economic theory.

Conventional definitions of "city," "urban place," or "metropolis" have led to conventional analyses of urban systems and urban-based social problems. Usually traceable to Wirth's classic and highly plausible formulation of "numbers, density and heterogeneity" (1938), there has been a continuing tendency, even in more recent formulations (e.g., Davis 1965), to conceive of place quite apart from a crucial dimension of social structure: power and social class hierarchy. Consequently, sociological research based on the traditional definitions of what an urban place is has had very little relevance to the actual, day-to-day activities of those at the top of local power structures whose priorities set the limits within which decisions affecting land use, the public budget, and urban social life come to be made. It has not been very apparent from the scholarship of urban social science that land, the basic stuff of place, is a market commodity providing wealth and power, and that

Molotch, Harvey, "The City as a Growth Machine: Toward a Political Economy of Place." *American Journal of Sociology*, 82 (1976): 309–18, 326–32. Copyright © 1976 by the University of Chicago Press.

some very important people consequently take a keen interest in it. Thus, although there are extensive literatures on community power as well as on how to define and conceptualize a city or urban place, there are few notions available to link the two issues coherently, focusing on the urban settlement as a political economy.

This paper aims toward filling this need. I speculate that the political and economic essence of virtually any given locality, in the present American context, is *growth*. I further argue that the desire for growth provides the key operative motivation toward consensus for members of politically mobilized local elites, however split they might be on other issues, and that a common interest in growth is the overriding commonality among important people in a given locale – at least insofar as they have any important local goals at all. Further, this growth imperative is the most important constraint upon available options for local initiative in social and economic reform. It is thus that I argue that the very essence of a locality is its operation as a growth machine.

The clearest indication of success at growth is a constantly rising urban-area population – a symptom of a pattern ordinarily comprising an initial expansion of basic industries followed by an expanded labor force, a rising scale of retail and wholesale commerce, more far-flung and increasingly intensive land development, higher population density, and increased levels of financial activity. Although throughout this paper I index growth by the variable population growth, it is this entire syndrome of associated events that is meant by the general term "growth." I argue that the means of achieving this growth, of setting off this chain of phenomena, constitute the central issue for those serious people who care about their locality and who have the resources to make their caring felt as a political force. The city is, for those who count, a growth machine.

The Human Ecology: Maps as Interest Mosaics

I have argued elsewhere (Molotch 1967, 1973) that any given parcel of land represents an interest and that any given locality is thus an aggregate of land-based interests. That is, each landowner (or person who otherwise has some interest in the prospective use of a given piece of land) has in mind a certain future for that parcel which is linked somehow with his or her own well-being. If there is a simple ownership, the relationship is straightforward: to the degree to which the land's profit potential is enhanced, one's own wealth is increased. In other cases, the relationship may be more subtle: one has interest in an adjacent parcel, and if a noxious use should appear, one's own parcel may be harmed. More subtle still is the emergence of concern for an aggregate of parcels: one sees that one's future is bound to the future of a larger area, that the future enjoyment of financial benefit flowing from a given parcel will derive from the general future of the proximate aggregate of parcels. When this occurs, there is that "we feeling" (McKenzie 1922) which bespeaks of community. We need to see each geographical map – whether of a small group of land parcels, a whole city, a region, or a nation – not merely as a demarcation of legal, political, or topographical features, but as a mosaic of competing land interests capable of strategic coalition and action.

Each unit of a community strives, at the expense of the others, to enhance the land-use potential of the parcels with which it is associated. Thus, for example, shopkeepers at both ends of a block may compete with one another to determine in front of which building the bus stop will be placed. Or, hotel owners on the north side of a city may compete with those on the south to get a convention center built nearby (see Banfield 1961). Likewise, area units fight over highway routes, airport locations, campus developments, defense contracts, traffic lights, one-way street designations, and park developments. The intensity of group consciousness and activity waxes and wanes as opportunities for and challenges to the collective good rise and fall; but when these coalitions are of sufficiently enduring quality, they constitute identifiable, ongoing communities. Each member of a community is simultaneously the member of a number of others; hence, communities exist in a nested fashion (e.g., neighborhood within city within region), with salience of community level varying both over time and circumstance. Because of this nested nature of communities, subunits which are competitive with one another at one level (e.g., in an interblock dispute over where the bus stop should go) will be in coalition at a higher level (e.g., in an intercity rivalry over where the new port should go). Obviously, the anticipation of potential coalition acts to constrain the intensity of conflict at more local loci of growth competition.

Hence, to the degree to which otherwise competing land-interest groups collude to achieve a common land-enhancement scheme, there is community – whether at the level of a residential block club, a neighborhood association, a city or metropolitan chamber of commerce, a state development agency, or a regional association. Such aggregates, whether constituted formally or informally, whether governmental political institutions or voluntary associations, typically operate in the following way: an attempt is made to use government to gain those resources which will enhance the growth potential of the area unit in question. Often, the governmental level where action is needed is at least one level higher than the community from which the activism springs. Thus, individual landowners aggregate to extract neighborhood gains from the city government; a cluster of cities may coalesce to have an effective impact on the state government, etc. Each locality, in striving to make these gains, is in competition with other localities because the degree of growth, at least at any given moment, is finite. The scarcity of developmental resources means that government becomes the arena in which land-use interest groups compete for public money and attempt to mold those decisions which will determine the land-use outcomes. Localities thus compete with one another to gain the *preconditions* of growth. Historically, US cities were created and sustained largely through this process, it continues to be the significant dynamic of contemporary local political economy and is critical to the allocation of public resources and the ordering of local issue agendas.

Government decisions are not the only kinds of social activities which affect local growth chances; decisions made by private corporations also have major impact. When a national corporation decides to locate a branch plant in a given locale, it sets the conditions for the surrounding land-use pattern. But even here, government decisions are involved: plant-location decisions are made with reference to such issues as labor costs, tax rates, and the costs of obtaining raw materials and transporting goods to markets. It is government decisions (at whatever level) that help determine the cost of access to markets and raw materials. This is especially so in the present era of raw material subsidies (e.g., the mineral depletion allowance) and reliance on government approved or subsidized air transport, highways, railways, pipelines, and port developments. Government decisions influence the cost of overhead expenses (e.g., pollution abatement requirements, employee safety standards), and government decisions affect the costs of labor through indirect manipulation of unemployment rates, through the use of police to constrain or enhance union organizing, and through the legislation and administration of welfare laws (see Piven and Cloward 1972).

Localities are generally mindful of these governmental powers and, in addition to creating the sorts of physical conditions which can best serve industrial growth, also attempt to maintain the kind of "business climate" that attracts industry: for example, favorable taxation, vocational training, law enforcement, and "good" labor relations. To promote growth, taxes should be "reasonable," the police force should be oriented toward protection of property, and overt social conflict should be minimized. Increased utility and government costs caused by new development should be borne by the public at large, rather than by those responsible for the "excess" demand on the urban infrastructure. Virtually any issue of a major business magazine is replete with ads from localities of all types (including whole countries) trumpeting their virtues in just these terms to prospective industrial settlers. In addition, a key role of elected and appointed officials becomes that of "ambassador" to industry, to communicate, usually with appropriate ceremony, these advantages to potential investors.

I aim to make the extreme statement that this organized effort to affect the outcome of growth distribution is the essence of local government as a dynamic political force. It is not the only function of government, but it is the key one and, ironically, the one most ignored. Growth is not, in the present analysis, merely one among a number of equally important concerns of political process (cf. Adrian and Williams 1963). Among contemporary social scientists, perhaps only Murray Edelman (1964) has provided appropriate conceptual preparation for viewing government in such terms. Edelman contrasts two kinds of politics. First there is the "symbolic" politics which comprises the "big issues" of public morality and the symbolic reforms featured in the headlines and editorials of the daily press. The other politics is the process through which goods and services actually come to be distributed in the society. Largely unseen, and relegated to negotiations within committees (when it occurs at all within a formal government body), this is the politics which determines who, *in material terms*, gets what, where, and how (Lasswell 1936). This is the kind of politics we must talk about at the local level: it is the politics of distribution, and land is the crucial (but not the only) variable in this system.

The people who participate with their energies, and particularly their fortunes, in local affairs are the sort of persons who – at least in vast disproportion to their representation in the population – have the most to gain or lose in land-use decisions. Prominent in terms of numbers have long been the local businessmen (see Walton 1970), particularly property owners and investors in locally oriented financial institutions (see, e.g., Spaulding 1951; Mumford 1961, p. 536), who *need* local government in their daily money-making routines. Also prominent are lawyers, syndicators, and realtors (see Bouma 1962) who need to put themselves in situations where they can be most useful to those with the land and property resources. Finally, there are those who, although not directly involved in land use, have their futures tied to growth of the metropolis as a whole. At least, when the local market becomes saturated one of the few possible avenues for business expansion is sometimes the expansion of the surrounding community itself (see Adrian and Williams 1963, p. 24).

This is the general outline of the coalition that actively generates the community "we feeling" (or perhaps more aptly, the "our feeling") that comes to be an influence in the politics of a given locality. It becomes manifest through a wide variety of techniques. Government funds support "boosterism" of various sorts: the Chamber of Commerce, locality-promotion ads in business journals and travel publications, city-sponsored parade floats, and stadia and other forms of support for professional sports teams carrying the locality name. The athletic teams in particular are an extraordinary mechanism for instilling a spirit of civic jingoism regarding the "progress" of the locality. A stadium filled with thousands (joined by thousands more at home before the TV) screaming for Cleveland or Baltimore (or whatever) is a scene difficult to fashion otherwise. This enthusiasm can be drawn upon, with a glossy claim of creating a "greater Cleveland," "greater Baltimore," etc., in order to gain general acceptance for local growth-oriented programs. Similarly, public school curricula, children's essay contests, soapbox derbies, spelling contests, beauty pageants, etc., help build an ideological base for local boosterism and the acceptance of growth. My conception of the territorial bond among humans differs from those cast in terms of primordial instincts: instead, I see this bond as socially organized and sustained, at least in part, by those who have a use for it (cf. Suttles 1972, pp. 111–39). I do not claim that there are no other sources of civic jingoism and growth enthusiasm in American communities, only that the growth-machine coalition mobilizes what is there, legitimizes and sustains it, and channels it as a political force into particular kinds of policy decisions.

The local institution which seems to take prime responsibility for the sustenance of these civic resources – the metropolitan newspaper – is also the most important example of a business which has its interest anchored in the aggregate growth of the locality. Increasingly, American cities are one-newspaper (metropolitan daily) towns (or one-newspaper-company towns), and the newspaper business seems to be one kind of enterprise for which expansion to other locales is especially difficult. The financial loss suffered by the *New York Times* in its futile effort to establish a California edition is an important case in point. A paper's financial status (and that of other media to a lesser extent) tends to be wed to the size of the locality. As the metropolis expands, a larger number of ad lines can be sold on the basis of the increasing circulation base. The local newspaper thus tends to occupy a rather unique position: like many other local businesses, it has an interest in growth, but unlike most, its critical interest is not in the specific geographical pattern of that growth. That is, the crucial matter to a newspaper is not whether the additional population comes to reside on the north side or south side, or whether the money is made through a new convention center or a new olive factory. The newspaper has no axe to grind, except the one axe which holds the community elite together: growth. It is for this reason that the newspaper tends to achieve a statesman-like attitude in the community and is deferred to as something other than a special interest by the special interests. Competing interests often regard the publisher or editor as a general community leader, as an ombudsman and arbiter of internal bickering and, at times, as an enlightened third party who can restrain the short-term profiteers in the interest of more stable, long-term, and properly planned growth. The paper becomes the reformist influence, the "voice of the community," restraining the competing subunits, especially the small-scale, arriviste "fast-buck artists" among them. The papers are variously successful in their continuous battle with the targeted special interests. The media attempt to attain these goals not only through the kind of coverage they develop and editorials they write but also through the kinds of candidates they support for local office. The present point is not that the papers control the politics of the city, but rather that one of the sources of their special influence is their commitment to growth per se, and growth is a goal around which all important groups can rally.

Thus it is that, although newspaper editorialists have typically been in the forefront expressing sentiment in favor of "the ecology," they tend nevertheless to support growth-inducing investments for their regions. The *New York Times* likes office towers and additional industrial installations in the city even more than it loves the environment. The *Los Angeles Times* editorializes against narrow-minded profiteering at the expense of the environment but has also favored the development of the supersonic transport because of the "jobs" it would lure to Southern California. The papers do tend to support "good planning principles" in some form because such good planning is a long-term force that makes for even more potential future growth. If the roads are not planned wide enough, their narrowness will eventually strangle the increasingly intense uses to which the land will be put. It just makes good sense to plan, and good planning for "sound growth" thus is the key "environmental policy" of the nation's local media and their statesmen allies. Such policies of "good planning" should not be confused with limited growth or conservation: they more typically represent the opposite sort of goal.

Often leaders of public or quasi-public agencies (e.g., universities, utilities) achieve a role similar to that of the newspaper publisher: they become growth "statesmen" rather than advocates for a certain type or intralocal distribution of growth. A university may require an increase in the local urban population pool to sustain its own expansion plans and, in addition, it may be induced to defer to others in the growth machine (bankers, newspapers) upon whom it depends for the favorable financial and public-opinion environment necessary for institutional enhancement. […]

Thus, because the city is a growth machine, it draws a special sort of person into its politics. These people – whether acting on their own or on behalf of the constituency which financed their rise to power – tend to be businessmen and, among businessmen, the more parochial sort. Typically, they come to politics not to save or destroy the environment, not to repress or liberate the blacks, not to eliminate civil liberties or enhance them. They may end up doing any or all of these things once they have achieved access to authority, perhaps as an inadvertent consequence of making decisions in other realms. But these types of symbolic positions are derived from the fact of having power – they are typically not the dynamics which bring people to power in the first place. Thus, people often become "involved" in government, especially in the local party structure and fund raising, for reasons of land business and related processes of resource distribution. Some are "statesmen" who think in terms of the growth of the whole community rather than that of a more narrow geographical delimitation. But they are there to wheel and deal to affect resource distribution through local government. As a result of their position, and in part to develop the symbolic issues which will enable them (in lieu of one of their opponents or colleagues) to maintain that position of power, they get interested in such things as welfare cheating, busing, street crime, and the price of meat. This interest in the symbolic issues (see Edelman 1964) is thus substantially an after-effect of a need for power for other purposes. This is not to say that such people don't "feel strongly" about these matters – they do sometimes. It is also the case that certain moral zealots and "concerned citizens" go into politics to right symbolic wrongs; but the money and other supports which make them viable as politicians is usually nonsymbolic money.

Those who come to the forefront of local government (and those to whom they are directly responsive), therefore, are not statistically representative of the local population as a whole, nor even representative of the social classes which produce them. The issues they introduce into public discourse are not representative either. As noted by Edelman, the distributive issues, the matters which bring people to power, are more or less deliberately dropped from public discourse (see Schattschneider 1960). The issues which are allowed to be discussed and the positions which the politicians take on them derive from the world views of those who come from certain sectors of the business and professional class and the need which they have to whip up public sentiment without allowing distributive issues to become part of public discussion. It follows that any political change which succeeded in replacing the land business as the key determinant of the local political dynamic would simultaneously weaken the power of one of the more reactionary political forces in the society, thereby affecting outcomes with respect to those other symbolic issues which manage to gain so much attention. Thus, should such a change occur, there would likely be more progressive positions taken on civil liberties, and less harassment of welfare recipients, social "deviants," and other defenseless victims. [...]

The Emerging Countercoalition

Although growth has been the dominant ideology in most localities in the United States, there has always been a subversive thread of resistance. Treated as romantic, or as somehow irrational (see White and White 1962), this minority long was ignored, even in the face of accumulating journalistic portrayals of the evils of bigness. But certainly it was an easy observation to make that increased size was related to high levels of pollution, traffic congestion, and other disadvantages. Similarly, it was easy enough to observe that tax rates in large places were not generally less than those in small places; although it received little attention, evidence that per capita government costs rise with population size was provided a generation ago (see Hawley 1951). But few took note, though the very rich, somehow sensing these facts to be the case, managed to reserve for themselves small, exclusive meccas of low density by tightly imposing population ceilings (e.g., Beverly Hills, Sands Point, West Palm Beach, Lake Forest).

In recent years, however, the base of the antigrowth movement has become much broader and in some localities has reached sufficient strength to achieve at least toeholds of political power. The most prominent cases seem to be certain university cities (Palo Alto, Santa Barbara, Boulder, Ann Arbor), all of which have sponsored impact studies documenting the costs of additional growth. Other localities which have imposed growth controls tend also to be places of high amenity value (e.g., Ramapo, NY; Petaluma, Calif.; Boca Raton, Fla.). The antigrowth sentiment has become an important part of the politics of a few large cities (e.g., San Diego) and has been the basis of important political careers at the state level (including the governorship) in Oregon, Colorado, and Vermont. Given the objective importance of the issue and the evidence on the general costs of growth, there is nothing to prevent antigrowth coalitions from similarly gaining power elsewhere – including those areas of the country which are generally considered to possess lower levels of amenity. Nor is there any reason, based on the facts of the matter, for these coalitions not to further broaden their base to include the great majority of the working class in the localities in which they appear.

But, like all political movements which attempt to rely upon volunteer labor to supplant political powers institutionalized through a system of vested economic interest, antigrowth movements are probably more likely to succeed in those places where volunteer reform movements have a realistic constituency – a leisured and sophisticated middle class with a tradition of broad-based activism, free from an entrenched machine. At least, this appears to be an accurate profile of those places in which the antigrowth coalitions have already matured.

Systematic studies of the social make up of the antigrowth activists are only now in progress (e.g., Fitts 1976), but it seems that the emerging countercoalition is rooted in the recent environmental movements and relies on a mixture of young activists (some are veterans of the peace and civil rights movements), middle-class professionals, and workers, all of whom see their own tax rates as well as life-styles in conflict with growth. Important in leadership roles are government employees and those who work for organizations not dependent on local expansion for profit, either directly or indirectly. In the Santa Barbara antigrowth movements, for example, much support is provided by professionals from research and electronics firms, as well as branch managers of small "high-technology" corporations. Cosmopolitan in outlook and pecuniary interest, they use the local community only as a setting for life and work, rather than as an exploitable resource. Related to this constituency are certain very wealthy people (particularly those whose wealth derives from the exploitation of nonlocal environments) who continue a tradition (with some modifications) of aristocratic conservation.

Should it occur, the changes which the death of the growth machine will bring seem clear enough with respect to land-use policy. Local governments will establish holding capacities for their regions and then legislate, directly or indirectly, to limit population to those levels. The direction of any future development will tend to be planned to minimize negative environmental impacts. The so-called natural process (see Burgess 1925; Hoyt 1939) of land development which has given American cities their present shape will end as the political and economic foundations of such processes are undermined. Perhaps most important, industrial and business land users and their representatives will lose, at least to some extent, the effectiveness of their threat to locate elsewhere should public policies endanger the profitability they desire. As the growth machine is destroyed in many places, increasingly it will be the business interests who will be forced to make do with local policies, rather than the local populations having to bow to business wishes. New options for taxation, creative land-use programs, and new forms of urban services may thus emerge as city government comes to resemble an agency which asks what it can do for its people rather than what it can do to attract more people. More specifically, a given industrial project will perhaps be evaluated in terms of its social utility – the usefulness of the product manufactured – either to the locality or to the society at large. Production, merely for the sake of local expansion, will be less likely to occur. Hence, there will be some pressure to increase the use value of the country's production apparatus and for external costs of production to be borne internally.

When growth ceases to be an issue, some of the investments made in the political system to influence and enhance growth will no longer make sense, thus changing the basis upon which people get involved in government. We can expect that the local business elites – led by land developers and other growth-coalition forces – will tend to withdraw from local politics. This vacuum may then be filled by a more representative and, likely, less reactionary activist constituency. It is noteworthy that where antigrowth forces have established beachheads of power, their programs and policies have tended to be more progressive than their predecessors' – on all issues, not just on growth. In Colorado, for example, the environmentalist who led the successful fight against the Winter Olympics also successfully sponsored abortion reform and other important progressive causes. The environmentally based Santa Barbara "Citizens Coalition" (with city government majority control) represents a fusion of the city's traditional left and counterculture with other environmental activists. The result of the no-growth influence in localities may thus be a tendency for an increasing progressiveness in local politics. To whatever degree local politics is the bedrock upon which the national political structure rests (and there is much debate here), there may follow reforms at the national level as well. Perhaps it will then become possible to utilize national institutions to effect other policies which both solidify the death of the growth machine at the local level and create national priorities consistent with the new opportunities for urban civic life. These are speculations based upon the questionable thesis that a reform-oriented, issue-based citizens' politics can be sustained over a long period. The historical record is not consistent with this thesis; it is only emerging political trends in the most affected localities and the general irrationality of the present urban system that suggest the alternative possibility is an authentic future.

References

Adrian, Charles R., and O. P. Williams. 1963. *Four Cities; A Study in Comparative Policy Making*. Philadelphia: University of Pennsylvania Press.

Banfield, Edward. 1961. *Political Influence*. New York: Macmillan.

Bouma, Donald. 1962. "Analysis of the Social Power Position of a Real Estate Board." *Social Problems* 10 (Fall): 121–32.

Burgess, Ernest W. 1925. *The Growth of the City: An Introduction to a Research Project*. Chicago: University of Chicago Press.

Davis, Kingsley. 1965. "The Urbanization of the Human Population." *Scientific American* 212 (September): 41–53.

Edelman, Murray. 1964. *The Symbolic Uses of Politics*. Urbana: University of Illinois Press.

Fitts, Amelia. 1976. "No-Growth as a Political Issue." Ph.D. dissertation, University of California, Los Angeles.

Hawley, Amos. 1951. "Metropolitan Population and Municipal Government Expenditures in Central Cities." *Journal of Social Issues* 7 (January): 100–8.

Hoyt, Homer. 1939. *The Structure and Growth of Residential Neighborhoods in American Cities*. Washington, DC: Federal Housing Administration.

Lasswell, Harold. 1936. *Politics: Who Gets What, When, How*. New York: McGraw-Hill.

McKenzie, R. D. 1922. "The Neighborhood: A Study of Local Life in the City of Columbus, Ohio – *Conclusion*." *American Journal of Sociology* 27 (May): 780–99.

Molotch, Harvey L. 1967. "Toward a More Human Ecology." *Land Economics* 43 (August): 336–41.

——. 1973. *Managed Integration: Dilemmas of Doing Good in the City*. Berkeley: University of California Press.

Mumford, Lewis. 1961. *The City in History*. New York: Harcourt Brace Jovanovich.

Piven, Francis Fox, and Richard Cloward. 1972. *Regulating the Poor*. New York: Random House.

Schattschneider, E. E. 1960. *The Semisovereign People*. New York: Holt, Rinehart & Winston.

Spaulding, Charles. 1951. "Occupational Affiliations of Councilmen in Small Cities." *Sociology and Social Research* 35 (3): 194–200.

Suttles, Gerald. 1972. *The Social Construction of Communities*. Chicago: University of Chicago Press.

Walton, John. 1970. "A Systematic Survey of Community Power Research." Pp. 443–64 in *The Structure of Community Power*, eds. Michael Aiken and Paul Mott. New York: Random House.

White, Morton, and Lucie White. 1962. *The Intellectual versus the City*. Cambridge, Mass.: Harvard and MIT Press.

Wirth, Louis. 1938. "Urbanism as a Way of Life." *American Journal of Sociology* 44 (July): 1–14.

2 Urban Restructuring: A Critical View

John R. Logan and Todd Swanstrom

This excerpt is from the introduction to the edited collection *Beyond the City Limits*. John Logan and Todd Swanstrom developed the volume as a response to the major economic upheavals of the 1970s and 1980s, especially the decline of manufacturing and the growth of a service economy that devastated many older industrial cities. The central question of the book is, "Are cities simply at the mercy of the changing economy, or can people shape the future of their cities?"

According to Logan and Swanstrom, both conservative and neo-Marxist theorists characterize cities as incapable of altering the forces of the global economy. Conservative analysts argue that economic restructuring will bring about positive change over time. Neo-Marxists argue that worldwide changes in the capitalist economy have caused a transition in the socio-economic regimes of the industrialized nations, from Fordism to flexible production. Both lines of reasoning portray global economic change as inevitable and therefore not subject to intervention on the local level. In sociological terms, they stress *structure* over *agency*.

By comparing case studies from England, France, Japan, and the United States, Logan and Swanstrom show that cities are affected by three factors: market forces, the sociopolitical context of the nation and region, and government policy (at both the national and local levels). These differences indicate that cities are not controlled solely by market forces but can be shaped by policymakers.

The failure of the centrally planned economies of China, Eastern Europe, and the Soviet Union has captured the world's attention. As market-oriented reforms have spread in those countries, accompanied by political changes, the reaction in the

Logan, John R. and Todd Swanstrom, "Urban Restructuring: A Critical View." From *Beyond the City Limits: Urban Policy and Economic Restructuring in Comparative Perspective*, eds. John R. Logan and Todd Swanstrom (Philadelphia: Temple University Press, 1990), pp. 3–21. Reprinted by permission of Temple University Press. © by Temple University Press. All rights reserved.

West has been one of smug self-congratulations. Imitation, after all, is the highest form of flattery. We knew all along that communist leaders could not indefinitely prop up inefficient industries or subsidize selected consumer goods without causing gross misallocations and inefficiencies. If they are not to fall even further behind the West technologically, communist nations must dismantle the bureaucratic hierarchies that are stifling their economies. The free market triumphs.

Our view is that this "triumph" is mostly a rhetorical and ideological device. No Western economy today operates under a "free market"; all experience the interventions of monopolistic producers, interlocked financial institutions, confederated labor unions, and the state. The real question is, what form should these interventions take? In the East, *market reform* is a synonym for raising prices, reducing some types of consumption, and accepting structural unemployment. It is also increasingly the precondition for foreign investment and financing through Western institutions. Seen in this light, the failure of communist central planning is as much a political as an economic event, and the "triumph of markets" is more a convenient rhetoric than empirical support for an economic principle.

This ideological interpretation of events in the communist world should be interesting to urban theorists because it parallels a case that is closer to home. Conservative policy elites and scholars have applied the same rhetoric of flexible markets to issues of urban development within Western nations. They argue that economies are being restructured, and that urban restructuring inevitably follows. Advances in transportation and communication technology have freed production and consumption from a dependence on the accessibility advantages of dense urban agglomerations. Correspondingly, cities have changed from centers of manufacturing to centers of advanced services, from metal benders to paper pushers. The increased mobility of capital further heightens the competition between cities for economic growth. Forced to adapt to the imperatives of economic restructuring, cities must participate in the market for mobile capital or face economic decline and fiscal crisis. Competition forces even nation-states to adapt (as also seen in the socialist bloc), cutting back on social welfare expenditures and thus leaving city governments even more sensitive to market forces.

The market, it is said, dictates policy. This is the message of political scientist Paul Peterson, whose book, *City Limits* (1981), legitimizes developmental (growth-oriented) policies over redistributive (social welfare) municipal policies. Peterson argues that cities are limited in their choices for two reasons. One is political: local politics is dominated by a mobilized elite primarily interested in growth. The second and more fundamental reason is that too great a concern for social welfare would doom a locality to stagnation and decline. In Peterson's view, concerns with welfare issues of urban growth are more realistically handled at the national level than by city governments. The market determines the local agenda.

Others, however, use similar logic to argue for a policy of benign neglect at the national level as well. Declining cities cannot be saved, they assert, because the market forces that have undermined them are unstoppable. Attempts to slow down urban decline or compensate cities for the costs of economic restructuring may be compassionate in the short run, but inevitably they slow down economic growth, harming everyone in the long run. "Federal efforts to revitalize urban areas through a national urban policy concerned principally with the health of specific places will inevitably conflict with efforts to revitalize the larger economy" (Hicks 1982, 3).

In *Beyond the City Limits* we challenge the notion that there is a market logic of capitalism to which urban policy at all levels must submit. We intend to make a contribution to the literature on economic restructuring as it applies to the futures of cities. All too often this literature has represented markets as natural forces, separable from public policies, and portrayed economic restructuring as a unified global process. We argue that markets are always embedded in particular social and political relations; economic restructuring is not a single, global process. Formerly, American capitalism was regarded as the mold from which all other capitalist systems, regardless of cultural or political background, would be cast. No longer. The stunning success of the Japanese model, with its corporatist organization clearly reflecting Japanese historical experience, destroys any unitary theory of capitalism. As Rick Hill (1990) observes, there is not one capitalism; there are many "species of capitalism." And so, we believe, are there many species of restructuring. Whatever the common trends, the decline of manufacturing and expansion of services affect Detroit differently from Aichi Prefecture (the Japanese auto-producing region) because these urban regions have different regimes of governance and labor relations, they are tied to different sorts of multinational firms, and they have different relations to national governments whose principal institutions are dissimilar.

The implication of our argument is that a great deal more discretion exists to shape economic and urban restructuring than is commonly believed. Many cities have more options to forge their own future development and to allocate costs and benefits among social groups than they have been willing to consider.

A central theme of our work, however, is that cities cannot be abstracted from their national context. The comparative method is most effective not when one city is compared with another but when a city in one national context is compared to a city in another national context. As Saskia Sassen (1990) notes, national policies have a powerful effect on urban restructuring. In particular, we argue, the limits of local policy depend to a large degree on relationships between local and national governments, which vary greatly among countries and which are themselves subject to bitter contest. The confrontation of "market forces" with urban policy in New York, for example, must be considered in juxtaposition with the case of London, or Paris, or Milan. And the local dynamics of policy formation lies within the national political economy that is the context for municipal action.

We believe that a careful application of the comparative method to the study of urbanization and urban policy around the Western world will force researchers to refine the theory of economic restructuring, and especially to revise its implications for urban policy. There has been a revival of interest in comparative urban political economy in the past few years (Smith and Feagin 1987; Peet 1987; Gurr and King 1987; Dogan and Kasarda 1988; Savitch 1988; Parkinson, Foley, and Judd 1989). As we noted above, the decline of American hegemony has increased interest in different, sometimes highly successful, production systems in other countries. Similarly, with regard to urban development, the expectation that the American pattern is the model that other nations will necessarily follow has been shattered. [...]

Urban Restructuring and the Economic Imperative

Theories of economic restructuring are relatively new, originating in the 1970s. We cannot fairly characterize the points of view of all contributors to this literature, but we can draw out some common themes. These theories rest on the notion that a fundamental crisis struck the world capitalist economy about 1973 (the date of the first OPEC oil cartel). Restructuring is the system's attempt to resolve the crisis. Part of that restructuring involves shifts in the geographical location of production, consumption, and residence that have profound implications for cities.

According to this view, city economies have reflected a global change from a goods-producing to a service-producing economy. While there has been relatively little shift in final product from goods to services, there has been a major shift in employment from goods production to service provision. Faster increases in labor productivity in the goods-producing sector have meant that progressively higher portions of total employment are in services.

Not only is manufacturing employment falling overall as a portion of total employment, but breakthroughs in transportation and communications have made industrial capital much more mobile. The result is intense competition for industry, with much routine manufacturing moving from developed to less developed regions, principally in search of lower wages. The globalization of production has rendered older, compact, industrial cities obsolete. In the United States, formerly prosperous industrial cities lost jobs to sprawled-out Sunbelt cities and to foreign countries (Bluestone and Harrison 1982). Over a 10-year period Western Europe lost 20 percent of its manufacturing jobs, principally to newly industrializing countries like Brazil, South Korea, and Taiwan (Peet 1987, 21). As the geography of industrial production changes, previously agricultural countries, such as some countries of the Pacific Rim, have become centers of manufacturing. In addition, certain areas in developed countries have become centers of high-tech manufacturing, such as Silicon Valley in California or along the M4 motorway from London to Bristol.

Far-reaching trends are also evident in the service sector. Besides the three basic sectors of the economy – primary (agriculture and mining), secondary (goods production), and tertiary (services) – Jean Gottman (1983) argues we need a fourth category, the "quaternary sector." Whereas traditional services are generally tied to the population they serve, the quaternary functions (closely associated with producer services) are freer to move about geographically. Routine, low-wage service employment tends to decentralize in search of low-cost sites of production. On the other hand, what Cohen (1979) called advanced corporate services tend to centralize in large cities (Manners 1974; Stanback et al. 1981; Daniels 1982; Noyelle 1986).

All these trends tend to reshape the interurban hierarchy. At the top sit so-called world cities, which become centers of international finance and headquarters of multinational corporations (Hymer 1971; Friedmann 1986; Beauregard 1989b). Other cities take on different functions within the changing international division of labor, from regional headquarters cities to centers of low-wage manufacturing. Within many cities, economic restructuring leads to increasing class polarization as the growth of high-wage jobs is accompanied by rapid expansion of low-wage jobs and the so-called informal sector, in which work remains undocumented and unprotected (Sassen 1988).

Economic restructuring is an elusive concept with multiple meanings. Nevertheless, it is possible to identify three core themes that are common to most, if not all, of the literature.

> 1. *Historical rupture:* First is the idea that the world economy is undergoing a radical break with the past.
>
> *Restructuring* denotes a transition from an old economic structure to a new one. Scholars such as Bluestone and Harrison (1982), Castells (1985), and Harvey (1989) identify a crisis in the old regime of industrial capital that peaked about 1973. Since then, according to the economic restructuring literature, the world economy has been going through a complex transition into a new postindustrial economic order. Part of the solution of the crisis of the old structure is a "territorial fix," a rearranging of production across space.
>
> 2. *Priority of economic forces:* By calling the process economic restructuring (not political or social restructuring), theorists stress that it originates in the economy, in the processes of private exchange and wealth generation. Implicitly, the term views economic relations as more basic or deterministic than other relations.
>
> 3. *Structure over agency:* Finally, the core term *structure*, contrasted with its theoretical antonym *agency*, suggests a process that is independent of human will. The movement from one structure to another is viewed as something that takes place according to an economic logic, essentially the logic of capitalist competition and factor cost reduction. This logic is, perforce, the same no matter where it takes place, no matter what the religion practiced or the language spoken by the capitalists and the workers.

While agreeing on how to describe the broad trends of economic restructuring, scholars on the left and right disagree on how to evaluate the effects of these trends. Market-oriented analysts focus on the benefits of economic restructuring:

job creation, urban revitalization, greater efficiency, and enhanced national competitiveness. Scholars on the left focus on its costs: unemployed blue-collar workers left behind by capital flight, the "missing middle" in the wage structure, displacement caused by gentrification, and the fiscal crises of local governments. Both sides generally agree, however, that the process of economic restructuring has a powerful logic and that efforts to resist it will be largely futile and may only hinder capital accumulation and growth.

In the hands of market theorists, economic restructuring has conservative implications for public policy. These are evident in the work of John Kasarda and John Hicks, both of whom influenced the report of the McGill Commission, *Urban America in the Eighties*, a seminal document in the evolution of American urban policy (President's Commission for a National Agenda 1980). These theorists view restructuring as the result of private economic forces; simultaneous deindustrialization and reindustrialization occur as capital migrates to more efficient sites for production. This process follows a logic of its own that transcends national boundaries; public policy does not play a determinative role (President's Commission 1980, 105; Kasarda 1980, 389; Hicks 1982, 5). Efforts to counteract this logic "are as unrealistic as they are nostalgic" (Kasarda 1988, 79). In the commission's words,

> The nation can no longer assume that cities will perform the full range of their traditional functions for the larger society. They are no longer the most desirable setting for living, working, or producing. They should be allowed to transform into more specialized service and consumption centers within larger urban economic systems. The Panel believes that this nation should reconcile itself to these redistribution patterns (p. 4).

Those who lobby for older cities are another "special interest" trying to get public handouts in opposition to the public interest in economic growth (McGill 1983, xiv). Urban policies should aid the process of economic restructuring. Efforts to help those who cannot take care of themselves may be needed. Redistributive policies, however, should be people-specific, not place-specific. Place-specific policies anchor people and production in places that the market has signaled are not efficient locations for production. People-specific redistributive policies, on the other hand, can facilitate labor mobility instead of hindering it. In short, social policy must adapt to the imperatives of economic restructuring. After all, "we must be able to produce wealth before we can redistribute it" (Hicks 1982, 575).

The neo-Marxist literature on economic restructuring rejects the conservative policy implications of market theorists. Instead of seeing the glass of economic restructuring as half full, scholars on the left tend to see it as half empty. If left to itself, the process of restructuring will leave many victims in its wake, exacerbating class inequalities. However, like market theory, neo-Marxist analysts do not stress the discretionary power of public policy but focus on the power of economic and technological change that manifests itself in a global process of restructuring. In a 1985 essay, for example, Manuel Castells stresses that "economic restructuring and technological change" are a "major underlying cause" of the changing spatial structure of American cities (p. 32). Specifically, he argues, new communication technologies will render most dense urban agglomerations anachronistic, while anointing a few places as centers of elite decision making, thus reinforcing the interurban hierarchy.

The global logic of economic restructuring can be seen most clearly in the theory of capitalist regulation and its reflections on the transition from a Fordist to a flexible regime of accumulation (Gramsci 1971; Aglietta 1976; Lipietz 1986). Again we stress that a brief treatment of this literature risks falling into caricature, but some main themes are clear. The concept of Fordism combines the extreme development of the technical division of labor, of Taylorization, with highly mechanized assembly-line production. The resulting massive gains in productivity required new forms of mass consumption to stave off crises of overproduction. The Fordist "regime of accumulation" required a corresponding "mode of regulation," or set of norms, laws, habits, and institutions that uphold the system of production. Under Fordism, the centerpiece of the mode of regulation was mass consumption, upheld by Keynesian economics, the welfare state, and other policies, such as those promoting suburbanization (Florida and Feldman 1988).

Scholars argue that a crisis of the Fordist regime of accumulation occurred in the 1970s; fundamentally, it was a crisis of profitability, with heightened international competition placing new pressures on the organization of production. The new regime of flexible accumulation is an attempt to resolve the crisis (Piore and Sabel 1984; Scott and Storper 1986; Harvey 1989). The new system requires less specialized and more flexible labor (usually accompanied by low rates of unionization), short production runs, and high-quality production for specialized market niches. The old Fordist cities with concentrations of industrial mass production give way to decentralized urban agglomerations with flexible specialization tied into networks of suppliers and consumers.

The new regime also brings into being a new mode of regulation, which addresses the crisis of profitability by heightening competition at all levels, depressing both private wages and the social wage. The Keynesian welfare state, which helped legitimate redistributive policies for declining urban areas, is dismantled in favor of a more decentralized entrepreneurial state deemphasizing social welfare and emphasizing developmental policies in public–private partnerships with business. The entire edifice of the mode of regulation based on mass consumption gives way to more differentiated and specialized consumption. Urban space becomes more differentiated as cities break down into playgrounds for the urban gentry and wastelands for the legions of low-paid service workers or denizens of the underground economy. Even broad cultural trends are determined by economic restructuring. "There is strong evidence that post-modernity is nothing more than the cultural clothing of flexible accumulation" (Harvey 1989, 274).

In sum, whether viewed through the lens of market theory or neo-Marxism, theories of economic (and urban) restructuring have argued that restructuring follows a global economic logic that carries other social and political institutions in its wake. Understood in these general terms, economic restructuring, we believe, is an abstraction that obscures the facts as much as it illuminates them. The economic restructuring literature imparts an unwarranted global uniformity to urban development. And it implies, for better or for worse, a paralysis of urban policy. [. . .]

From Global Logic to National Variation

We do not intend to ignore the effects of economic relations, especially systems of production, in shaping urban development. But as Edmond Preteceille (1990) argues, it is necessary to link the organization of work to broader social and political processes. The term *capital* is an abstraction that needs to be broken down, because different sectors of capital behave differently. By focusing on industry, Preteceille argues, the theorists of the transition from Fordist to flexible production have ignored major sectors of the economy that never adopted Fordist production methods, including large parts of the service sector (including finance capital), military production, public infrastructure, and housing. Even within industry, large sectors, including producer goods such as the tool and die industry, were never characterized by Fordist mass-production methods.

Clearly, the massive military buildup in the United States, which has had a profound effect on cities (Markusen 1987, 106–14; Warsh 1988), was not mandated by economic restructuring. In areas such as the military or public infrastructure, the role of the political system in establishing systems of production is evident. Even in private industrial production, as Richard Hill (1990) shows in his analysis of systems of production in Japan and the United States, government plays a decisive role. Toyotaism was created not through natural market forces, Hill argues, but through a close collaboration between the Toyota Motor Corporation, Toyota City, and Aichi Prefecture. The state of Michigan has attempted to copy the developmental policies of Japan. Hill's analysis makes it clear that production systems are not easily transported across national boundaries because of the complex institutional arrangements that must be built up over time to make them work.

The role of political institutions, especially the relationship between the central government and local governments, is a central theme of our analysis. In the past, theorists have argued that state structures must adapt to the imperatives of capital accumulation. In 1973, for example, James O'Connor argued that economic restructuring required the centralization of state power. In order to resolve the fiscal crisis of the state, power needed to be removed from local governments, which represented small business, into powerful regional planning bodies that would better represent the interests of monopoly capital. Today many argue just the opposite: that the restructuring of capital requires the decentralization of state power. Giving more policymaking authority to local governments can be seen as helping to privatize governmental functions, to cut social welfare spending (compared to national welfare entitlements), and to shift priorities toward business as local governments become locked in a cutthroat competition for the new mobile investment. We show, however, that economic restructuring does not mandate any particular organization of state power. The restructuring of state power, particularly the changing national–local relationships, has been quite varied.

The comparison between Britain and the United States demonstrates the variety of national–local relations, which in turn affects the variety of urban outcomes. Both countries have moved decisively to dismantle urban and regional planning policies and to substitute market-oriented policies. After World War II Britain developed an extensive regional policy designed to bolster industry in declining areas and restrain the growth of London. By the mid-1980s, British regional policy was "in ruins" (Hall 1985, 49). The much smaller US regional policies, which basically began in the 1960s, were also cut back severely in the 1980s. Urban policies directed toward declining inner cities were also cut during the Reagan years and what remained was oriented more toward aiding the private sector (Wolman 1986). While always small compared to American standards, British programs oriented toward inner cities [grew] under the Thatcher government, but cuts in central government support for local authorities meant that overall support for cities declined (Gurr and King 1987, 161). The convergence of policy in the two countries is enough that Dennis Judd and Michael Parkinson refer to "the Americanization of urban policy in Britain" (1989, 4).

These similarities in the market-oriented shift of urban policy in Britain and the United States, however, hide important political differences. In Britain, the central government has always focused more on investment and productivity, while local governments were more oriented toward social consumption. Traditionally, municipalities in Great Britain controlled a wide range of social welfare expenditures, including social services, higher education (the polytechnics), and a massive – by American standards – public housing sector. (By 1976, 30 percent of British households lived in public housing; in the United States the figure is less than 2 percent [Headey 1978].) In the United States, the division of labor was just the opposite: "If the federal government has earned the label 'warfare-welfare state,' local and state governments deserve the name 'productivity state'" (O'Connor 1973, 99). City governments in the United States have always been directly concerned with promoting growth, especially through infrastructural investments.

As Michael Parkinson (1990) argues, the Thatcher government saw municipalities as a threat to its goal of reducing state expenditures and promoting entrepreneurism. Many municipal governments were controlled by Labour and had pursued experiments in local socialism in the 1970s. As a result, the Thatcher government acted to remove decision-making power from local governments through such actions as abolishing regional authorities (including the Greater London Council), rate capping (limiting the local tax rate), selling off public housing, and privatizing municipal services. Control over urban economic development has been placed in the hands of development corporations that are free from local democratic control. In short, the shift to market-oriented urban policy in Britain has led to a radical centralization of power, enough that one scholarly study concluded that Britain now "stands within sight of a form of government which is more highly centralised than anything this side of East Germany" (Newton and Karran 1985, 129, quoted in Hambleton 1989, 369).

In the United States, by contrast, market-oriented urban policy has not led to a dramatic centralization of power. Under Reagan, federal grants to cities were cut but they were also deregulated, giving local governments more freedom of choice on how to spend the money. A case in point is the Community Development Block Grant: after deregulation, local governments shifted block-grant funds from the poor to economic development (Wong and Peterson 1986). Reagan, it seems, could rely on American cities' traditional preoccupation with growth to keep them in line. Indeed, most American cities are dominated by what Harvey Molotch first called "growth machines": coalitions centered around landowners whose goal is to maximize economic development, and therefore land rents, within the city (Molotch 1976; Logan and Molotch 1987). It is possible, however, to have alternative local policies in the United States in those cities where economic conditions are strong and where political alternatives to the growth machine coalesce. While calling the system of exactions "very imperfect," Molotch nevertheless documents the real choices made by some southern California municipalities, reflecting their values and political alignments, in implementing growth controls. In the British unitary state, on the other hand, experiments in local socialism have been frustrated by a powerful and hostile central government.

Historically, France has had one of the most centralized governments in the West. Here, more than in other countries, discretionary power over urban policy was placed in the hands of governmental technocrats, relatively autonomous of immediate political pressures. Under the Gaullists, France developed some of the most powerful regional planning policies in any capitalist country. A wide array of regulations and incentives were used to disperse both population and jobs away from Paris to "growth poles" in surrounding suburbs and other regions. The policies were successful in "dedensifying" Paris; without these controls, the low-rise skyline in Paris would have come more to resemble New York's (Savitch 1988). Opposition to the unchecked power of government technocrats, however, developed out of the participatory movements of the 1960s and 1970s. By 1977, Paris had its own elected mayor and a measure of autonomy. When the socialists came to power, as Edmond Preteceille describes, they enacted a series of decentralizing measures to promote a "new citizenship." Local governments were given more power over their budgets and were allowed to issue construction permits and make loans to businesses. As Preteceille argues, the results have been mixed.

Like in Britain, Italy, Spain, and the United States, an "economic mobilization of local governments" has occurred in France. No local politician in France can hope to stay in power without claiming, at least, to address the growing problem of unemployment. On the other hand, Preteceille points out, only about 2 percent of municipal expenditures are directly applied to economic development. Unlike the American case, he notes, "French municipalities have not, as a whole, entered a wild competition promising all sorts of deductions, abatements, helps and advantages to attract business." Primarily due to political traditions and the power of left-wing parties, decentralization has had a different result in France.

In summary, a review of state restructuring in Britain, France, and the United States reveals that economic restructuring did not dictate a uniform process of political restructuring. In the context of economic restructuring, state power centralized in Britain and decentralized in France and the United States. The organization of state power was a reflection of the conflicts between different classes and groups over state policy. Rather than a result of economic restructuring, state power was more a tool used by dominant political interests to advance their economic agenda. [. . .]

Image and Agenda in Urban Restructuring

How people view economic restructuring may be as important as the facts of economic restructuring themselves. Between the stimulus of economic restructuring and the response of urban policy lies the "image" that politically relevant actors have of economic change and what problems need to be addressed by public policies. As Bryan Jones and Frank Baumgartner show (1989) using survey data, in the United States the public's image of the primary problems facing the country has shifted between economic growth and social issues. Partly this is due to the underlying objective conditions of the country, but it is also due to changing public perceptions of similar facts. The prevailing growth rhetoric in recent times has defined the problems of the United States in terms of lagging economic expansion, not in terms of fairness or the distribution of wealth. This has the effect of narrowing the political agenda in ways favorable to conservative political interests.

In urban policy, the dominant image of economic change has, likewise, legitimated conservative policies in the present period. (While less sophisticated, the prevailing image closely resembles the abstract formulations of economic restructuring found in the academic literature discussed earlier.) The dominant metaphor is the image of mobile capital spanning the globe in search of the lowest-cost production sites. The implications are far-reaching: economic development is a matter of attracting more of this thing called capital, which is increasingly demanding of its potential suitors.

At the national level in Great Britain and the United States the capital-mobility model has dominated thinking about economic development. The goal of national policy under Thatcher and Reagan/Bush [was] to free up capital, reducing its social and financial obligations. At the local level, this [led] to what Clavel and Kleniewski (1990), following Markusen (1988), call bidding down (against other cities to attract manufacturing jobs) and bailing out (of manufacturing to attract mobile service employment).

At best, this image of how cities grow is incomplete; at worst it is grossly misleading. Of course some kinds of capital, such as routinized manufacturing, are highly mobile. But relying upon that type of capital can lead to what has in a Third World context been called "dependent development" (Evans 1979). In dependent development, capital investment is based on how the investment fits into the firm's international holdings rather than how it fits into the local economy. The local multiplier effects of the investment are minimal, and the firm exacts important concessions on labor control and financing or taxation. The jobs created are often low value-added, low-skilled, and low-wage. Such economic growth depends on maintaining a low wage structure, including a low social wage.

An alternative image of economic development would recognize that the most valuable forms of capital investment are deeply embedded in particular social and geographical contexts. This is an old-fashioned concept, but in this respect perhaps the insights of agglomeration theory have been jettisoned prematurely in an effort to keep up with economic restructuring. While the physical barriers to capital mobility have increasingly been overcome by technology, many sectors of capital remain dependent on what could be called a social ecology of skilled labor that ties them to particular geographical contexts. The concentration of white-collar decision-making functions in the central business districts of cities is a good case in point. Another example is the revival of mature industrial regions, like northern Italy and western Massachusetts, based on the flexible specialization of small machine shops using skilled labor (Doeringer, Terkla, and Topakian 1988). Such embedded industries are more attractive than hyper-mobile capital, because they will not move at the drop of a hat when asked to contribute to the commonwealth.

Basing their argument partly on the embeddedness of certain kinds of capital investment, Clavel and Kleniewski (1990) argue that "local governments have more room to maneuver than is commonly assumed." Cities with strong service economies, for example, recognizing that capital will not take flight when required to contribute to the commonweal, have enacted linkage policies designed to redistribute some of the benefits of growth. In both Britain and the United States there have been numerous attempts at the local level to go beyond such redistributive measures to actually shape economic restructuring before it occurs. Experiments in alternative local economic development have been based on an image of economic development that does not revolve around attracting mobile capital but focuses, instead, on nurturing community relations – between labor and capital, between networks of small businesses, between the political system and firms.

An alternative image of economic development, then, would shift from the masculine metaphor of cutthroat competition for mobile capital to a more feminine image of nurturing the strengths of the local context. The alternative image of economic development based on embeddedness shifts attention from cutting the costs of capital to upgrading the skills of labor and nurturing the context of self-generating economic development. Educational expenditures have the potential of transcending the supposedly ironclad tradeoff of equality and growth. Research has shown that local economies can buck national and international trends (Doeringer, Terkla, and Topakian, 1988). By upgrading skills, innovating new businesses, or finding specialized niches within flexible systems of production, it is possible for mature economies to nurture development with higher wages and broader benefits for the population. This requires, however, that we move beyond a simplistic concept of economic growth mesmerized by the mobility of capital. [...]

References

Aglietta, Michel. 1976. *A Theory of Capitalist Regulation: The US Experience*. London: New Left Books.

Beauregard, Robert A. 1989. *Atop the Urban Hierarchy*. Totowa, NJ: Rowman and Littlefield.

Bluestone, Barry, and Bennett Harrison. 1982. *The Deindustrialization of America*. New York: Basic Books.

Castells, Manuel. 1985. "High Technology, Economic Restructuring, and the Urban-Regional Process in the United States." In *High Technology, Space and Society*, ed. Manuel Castells. Beverly Hills, Calif.: Sage.

Clavel, Pierre and Nancy Kleniewski. 1990. "Space for Progressive Local Policy: Examples from the United States and United Kingdom. In *Beyond the City Limits*, eds. J. Logan and T. Swanstrom. Philadelphia: Temple University Press.

Cohen, Robert. 1979. "The Changing Transactions Economy and Its Spatial Implications." *Ekistics* 274: 7–15.

Daniels, Peter. 1982. *Service Industries: Growth and Location*. Cambridge: Oxford University Press.

Doeringer, Peter B., David G. Terkla, and Gregory C. Topakian. 1988. *Invisible Factors in Local Economic Development*. New York: Oxford University Press.

Dogan, Mattei, and John D. Kasarda. 1988. *The Metropolis Era*, vol. I. Beverly Hills, Calif.: Sage.

Evans, Peter. 1979. *Dependent Development: The Alliance of Multinational, State, and Local Capital in Brazil*. Princeton, NJ: Princeton University Press.

Florida, Richard L., and Marshall M. A. Feldman. 1988. "Housing in US Fordism." *International Journal of Urban and Regional Research* 12(2): 187–209.

Friedmann, John. 1986. "The World City Hypothesis." *Development and Change* 17(1): 69–83.

Gottman, Jean. 1983. *The Coming of the Transactional City*. College Park: University of Maryland, Institute for Urban Studies.

Gramsci, Antonio. 1971. *Selections from the Prison Notebooks*, ed. and trans. Q. Hoare and G. N. Smith. London: Lawrence and Wishart.

Gurr, Ted Robert, and Desmond S. King. 1987. *The State and the City*. Chicago: University of Chicago Press.

Hall, Peter. 1985. "Technology, Space, and Society in Contemporary Britian." In *High Technology, Space, and Society*, ed. Manuel Castells. Beverly Hills, Calif.: Sage.

Hambleton, Robin. 1989. "Urban Government under Thatcher and Reagan." *Urban Affairs Quarterly* 24(3): 359–88.

Harvey, David. 1989. *The Urban Experience*. Baltimore: Johns Hopkins University Press.

Headey, Bruce. 1978. *Housing Policy in the Developed Economy*. New York: St. Martin's.

Hicks, Donald A. 1982. "Urban and Economic Adjustment to the Post-Industrial Era." *Hearings Before the Joint Economic Committee, Congress of the United States, Ninety-Seventh Congress, Part 2*. Washington, DC: US Government Printing Office.

Hill, Richard. 1990. "Industrial Restructuring, State Intervention, and Uneven Development in the United States and Japan." In *Beyond the City Limits*, eds. J. Logan and T. Swanstrom. Philadelphia: Temple University Press.

Hymer, Stephen. 1971. "The Multinational Corporation and the Law of Uneven Development." In *Economics and the World Order*, ed. J. N. Bhagwati. London: Macmillan.

Jones, Bryan D., and Frank Baumgartner. 1989. "Image and Agenda in Urban Politics." Paper presented at A Tiger by the Tail Conference, Albany, New York, April 7–8, 1989.

Judd, Dennis R., and Michael Parkinson. 1989. "Urban Revitalization in America and the UK: The Politics of Uneven Development." In *Regenerating the Cities: The UK Crisis and the US Experience*, ed. Dennis R. Judd, Bernard Foley, and Michael Parkinson. Glenview, Ill.: Scott, Foresman and Company.

Kasarda, John D. 1980. "The Implications of Contemporary Redistribution Trends for National Urban Policy." *Social Science Quarterly* 61: 373–400.

——.1988. "Economic Restructuring and America's Urban Dilemma." In *The Metropolis Era*. vol. I, ed. Mattei Dogan and John D. Kasarda. Beverly Hills, Calif.: Sage.

Lipietz, Alain. 1986. "New Tendencies in the International Division of Labor: Regions of Accumulation and Modes of Regulation." In *Production, Work, Territory: The Geographical Anatomy of Industrial Capitalism*, ed. A. J. Scott and Michael Storper. Boston: Allen & Unwin.

Logan, John R., and Harvey Molotch. 1987. *Urban Fortunes: The Political Economy of Place*. Berkeley and Los Angeles: University of California Press.

McGill, William J. 1983. Foreword to *Transition to the 21st Century: Prospects and Policies for Economic and Urban-Regional Transformation*, ed. Donald A. Hicks and Norman J. Glickman. Greenwich, Conn.: JAI Press.

Manners, Gerald. 1974. "The Office in Metropolis: An Opportunity for Shaping Urban America." *Economic Geography* 50(2): 93–110.

Markusen, Ann. 1987. *Regions: The Economics and Politics of Territory*. Totowa, NJ: Rowman & Littlefield.

——.1988. "Planning for Industrial Decline: Lessons from Steel Communities." *Journal of Planning Education and Research* 7: 173–84.

Molotch, Harvey. 1976. "The City as a Growth Machine: Toward a Political Economy of Place." *American Journal of Sociology* 82: 309–32.

Newton, Kenneth, and T. J. Karran. 1985. *The Politics of Local Expenditure*. London: Macmillan.

Noyelle, Thierry J. 1986. "Advanced Services in the System of Cities." In *Local Economies in Transition*, ed. Edward M. Bergman. Durham, NC: Duke University Press.

O'Connor, James. 1973. *The Fiscal Crisis of the State*. New York: St. Martin's.

Parkinson, Michael. 1990. "Political Responses to Urban Restructuring: The British Experience under Thatcherism." In *Beyond the City Limits*, eds. J. Logan and T. Swanstrom. Philadelphia: Temple University Press.

Parkinson, Michael, Bernard Foley, and Dennis R. Judd. 1989. *Regenerating the Cities: The UK Crisis and the US Experience*. Glenview, Ill.: Scott, Foresman and Company.

Peet, Richard. 1987. *International Capitalism and Industrial Restructuring: A Critical Analysis*. Boston: Allen & Unwin.

Peterson, Paul E. 1981. *City Limits*. Chicago: University of Chicago Press.

Piore, Michael J., and Charles F. Sabel. 1984. *The Second Industrial Divide: Possibilities for Prosperity*. New York: Basic Books.

President's Commission for a National Agenda for the Eighties. 1980. *Urban America in the Eighties*. Washington, DC: US Government Printing Office.

Preteceille, Edmond. 1990. "Political Paradoxes of Urban Restructuring: Globalization of the Economy and Localization of Politics?" In *Beyond the City Limits*, eds. J. Logan and T. Swanstrom. Philadelphia: Temple University Press.

Sassen, Saskia. 1988. *The Mobility of Labor and Capital: A Study in International Investment and Capital Flow*. New York: Cambridge University Press.

——.1990. "Beyond the City Limits: A Commentary." In *Beyond the City Limits*, eds. J. Logan and T. Swanstrom. Philadelphia: Temple University Press.

Savitch, H. V. 1988. *Post-Industrial Cities: Politics and Planning in New York, Paris, and London*. Princeton, NJ: Princeton University Press.

Scott, A. J., and Michael Storper, eds. 1986. *Production, Work, Territory: The Geographical Anatomy of Industrial Capitalism*. Boston: Allen & Unwin.

Smith, Michael Peter, and Joe R. Feagin, eds. 1987. *The Capitalist City: Global Restructuring and Community Politics*. Oxford: Blackwell.

Stanback, Thomas M., et al. 1981. *Services: The New Economy*. Totowa, NJ: Allanheld, Osmun.

Warsh, David L. 1988. "War Stories: Defense Spending and the Growth of the Massachusetts Economy." In *The Massachusetts Miracle*, ed. David R. Lampe. Cambridge: MIT Press.

Wolman, Hal. 1986. "The Reagan Urban Policy and Its Impacts." *Urban Affairs Quarterly* 21(3): 311–35.

Wong, Kenneth K., and Paul E. Peterson. 1986. "Urban Response to Federal Program Flexibility: Politics of Community Development Block Grant." *Urban Affairs Quarterly* 21(3): 293–309.

3 Space and Status

Daphne Spain

Until the 1980s, urban sociologists virtually ignored the issue of gender and its impact on urban and community life. Daphne Spain contributed to urban theory by her study comparing women's and men's experiences in both pre-industrial and contemporary societies.

Spain examines the ways in which certain spaces are identified as "men's" or "women's" spaces – i.e., they are *gendered spaces*. She argues that spatial segregation between the sexes reinforces and exacerbates gender differences because it is often used to exclude women from the knowledge and experiences that give men status and power. In settings such as homes, schools, and places of worship, Spain documents widespread gender segregation. She concludes that women's status is derived not just from their roles in the family and in the economy but also from the systematic ways in which societies use space to reinforce male privilege.

Throughout history and across cultures, architectural and geographic spatial arrangements have reinforced status differences between women and men. The "little tactics of the habitat," viewed through the lenses of gender and status, are the subjects of this inquiry. Women and men are spatially segregated in ways that reduce women's access to knowledge and thereby reinforce women's lower status relative to men's. "Gendered spaces" separate women from knowledge used by men to produce and reproduce power and privilege.

Sociologists agree that, whether determined by the relationship to the means of production, as proposed by Marx, or by "social estimations of honor," as proposed by Weber, status is unequally distributed among members of society and that men as a group are universally accorded higher status than women as a group. Status distinctions among groups of people constitue the stratification (social ranking) system of a society. Women's status is thus a component of gender

Spain, Daphne, "Space and Status." From *Gendered Spaces* (Chapel Hill: University of North Carolina Press, 1992), pp. 3–7, 10–21, 25–6. Copyright © 1992 by the University of North Carolina Press. Used by permission of the publisher.

stratification, as is men's status. "Women's status" and "gender stratification" are used interchangeably throughout this [work] to designate women's status in relation to men's. "Gender" refers to the socially and culturally constructed distinctions that accompany biological differences associated with a person's sex. While biological differences are constant over time and across cultures (i.e., there are only two sexes), the social implications of gender differences vary historically and socially.

Women and men typically have different status in regard to control of property, control of labor, and political participation. A variety of explanations exists for the persistence of gender stratification. Most theories are based on biological, economic, psychological, or social interpretations (Chafetz 1990). Our understanding of the tenacity of gender inequalities, however, can be improved by considering the architectural and geographic spatial contexts within which they occur. Spatial arrangements between the sexes are socially created, and when they provide access to valued knowledge for men while reducing access to that knowledge for women, the organization of space may perpetuate status differences. The "daily-life environment" of gendered spaces thus acts to transmit inequality (Dear and Wolch 1989, 6). To quote geographer Doreen Massey, "It is not just that the spatial is socially constructed; the social is spatially constructed too" (Massey 1984a, 6).

The history of higher education in America provides an example of the spatial contexts with which gender relations are entwined. Colleges were closed to women until the late nineteenth century because physicians believed that school attendance endangered women's health and jeopardized their ability to bear children (Rothman and Rothman 1987). In 1837 Mary Lyon defended her creation of the first college for women, Mt. Holyoke, by citing its role in "the preparation of the Daughters of the Land to be good mothers" (Watson 1977, 134). Mt. Holyoke was built in rural Massachusetts to protect its students from the vices of big cities.

An initial status difference (the fact that few women were physicians and none sat on college admissions boards) translated into the exclusion of women from colleges. Spatial segregation, in turn, reduced women's ability to enter the prestigious medical profession to challenge prevailing assumptions about the suitability of educating women. The location of knowledge in a place inaccessible to women reinforced the existing gender stratification system that relegated women to the private sphere and men to the public sphere.

A few pioneering women gained access to higher education, initially through segregated women's colleges. They entered a different world from that of men's colleges such as Harvard, Amherst, and the University of Virginia, which consisted of separate buildings clustered together around common ground. Male students moved from chapel to classroom to their rooms; dormitories had several entrances; rooms were grouped around stairwells instead of on a single corridor; and faculty lived in separate dwellings or off the campus entirely. In contrast, the first women's colleges were single large buildings that housed and fed faculty and students in addition to providing space for classrooms, laboratories, chapel, and library under the same roof. Compared to the relative freedom of dispersed surroundings enjoyed by men, women were enclosed and secluded in a single structure that made constant supervision possible.

Women eventually entered coeducational institutions with men. Initially, though, they were relegated to segregated classrooms or to coordinate (i.e., "sister") colleges on separate campuses. Spatial barriers finally disappeared as coeducation became increasingly acceptable. As women attended the same schools and learned the same curricula as men, their public status began to improve – most notably with the right to vote granted by the Nineteenth Amendment in 1920.

Thus, both geographic distance and architectural design established boundaries between the knowledge available to women and that available to men. The existing stratification system depended on an ideology of women's delicate health to deny them access to college. These resultant spatial arrangements, in turn, made it difficult for women to challenge the status quo. Once spatial barriers were breached, however, the stratification system began to change.

The Social Construction of Space

Geographers have been the most vocal advocates of the integration of space into social theories. It is not sensible, they argue, to separate social and spatial processes: to "explain why something occurs is to explain why it occurs where it does" (Sack 1980, 70). Space is essential to social science; spatial relations exist only because social processes exist. The spatial and social aspects of a phenomenon are inseparable (Massey 1984, 3; Dear and Wolch 1989). [. . .]

My hypothesis is that initial status differences between women and men create certain types of gendered spaces and that institutionalized spatial segregation then reinforces prevailing male advantages. While it would be simplistic to argue that spatial segregation causes gender stratification, it would be equally simplistic to ignore the possibility that spatial segregation reinforces gender stratification and thus that modifying spatial arrangements, by definition, alters social processes.

Feminist geographers have been pioneers on the frontier of theories about space and gender. In an article titled "City and Home: Urban Housing and the Sexual Division of Space," McDowell (1983) argues that urban structure in capitalist societies reflects the construction of space into masculine centers of production and feminine suburbs of reproduction. The "home as haven" constituting a separate sphere for women, however, becomes less appropriate as more women enter the labor force.

According to feminist geographers, a thorough analysis of gender and space would recognize that definitions of femininity and masculinity are constructed in particular places – most notably the home, workplace, and community – and the reciprocity of these spheres of influence should be acknowledged in analyzing status differences between the sexes. Expectations of how men and women should behave in the home are negotiated not only there but also at work, at school, and at social events (Bowlby, Foord, and McDowell 1986). [. . .]

Architectural space also plays a role in maintaining status distinctions by gender. The spatial structure of buildings embodies knowledge of social relations, or the taken-for-granted rules that govern relations of individuals to each other and to society. Thus, dwellings reflect ideals and realities about relationships between women and men within the family and in society. The space outside the home becomes the arena in which social relations (i.e., status) are produced, while the space inside the home becomes that in which social relations are reproduced. Gender-status distinctions therefore are played out within the home as well as outside of it [. . .]

Spatial Institutions

Over the course of the life cycle, everyone experiences one or more of the institutions of family, education, and the labor force. If we are to understand the systemic nature of gender stratification, it is to the interplay of these institutions that we must look. Equally important are the spaces within which institutional activities occur. Families must be analyzed in the context of dwellings, education in the context of schools, and labor in the context of workplaces. These "spatial institutions" form barriers to women's acquisition of knowledge by assigning women and men to different gendered spaces. Masculine spaces (such as nineteenth-century American colleges) contain socially valued knowledge of theology, law, and medicine, while feminine spaces (such as the home) contain devalued knowledge of child care, cooking, and cleaning.

An institution, in sociological terms, refers to a patterned set of activities organized around the production of certain social outcomes. For example, the family is an institution because it is organized to reproduce future generations. Certain institutions are universal and evolve to fill requirements necessary to the maintenance of society. All societies must have the ability to biologically reproduce themselves, convey knowledge to members, produce goods and services, deal with the unknown, and preserve social order. Thus, some form of family, education, military, economy, religion, and system of legal justice exists in every society.

The activities that constitute institutions, of course, occur in specific places. Families live in homes, while education and religion are carried out in schools and churches. There is some overlap in institutions and the spaces they occupy. Educational and religious instruction, for example, may take place in the home, as does economic production in nonindustrial societies. Yet if one were to assign a primary spatial context to each major institution, the family would occupy the dwelling, education the school, economy the workplace, religion the church, and the legal system a courthouse. [My research] addresses the relationship between gender stratification and the spatial institutions of the family/dwelling, education/school, and labor force/workplace.

The family and segregated dwellings

Nonindustrial societies often separate women and men within the dwelling. In a typical Purum house, for example, domestic space is divided into right/left, male/female quarters, with higher value attributed to areas and objects associated with right/male and lower value associated with left/female (Sciama 1981, 91). Dwellings of the South American Jivaro Indians demonstrate a similar pattern, with the women's entrance at the left end of the rectangular hut and a men's entrance at the right end; women's beds and men's beds are arranged at their respective ends of the *jivaria* (Stirling 1938). The traditional courtyard pattern of the Nigerian Hausa (used by both Muslim and non-Muslim families) also differentiates men's from women's spaces (Moughtin 1985, 56). Traditional Muslim households are divided into the *anderun* at the back for the women and the *birun* at the front for men (Khatib-Chahidi 1981).

A variety of cultural, religious, and ideological reasons have been used throughout history to justify gender segregation. Muslims, for example, believe that women should not come into contact with men who are potential marriage partners. The system of purdah was developed to keep women secluded in the home in a space safe from unregulated sexual contact, yet it also served to restrict women's educational and economic opportunities. Muslim women therefore have lower status outside the home, compared with women in less sexually segregated societies (Mandelbaum 1988).

Nineteenth-century America and Great Britain had less overt forms of sexual spatial segregation than nonindustrial societies. They were still characterized, however, by gendered spaces. The ideal Victorian home contained a drawing room for ladies and smoking and billiard rooms for gentlemen; the "growlery" was the husband's retreat from domesticity. Contemporary American society has been characterized by reduced levels of gender segregation within the dwelling. An era of open floorplans was ushered in by Frank Lloyd Wright's "Usonian" home, and today many high-priced suburban houses are built with "great rooms" in which men, women, and children all share the same space during part of each day.

Education and segregated schools

In nonindustrial societies, ceremonial men's huts are the locus of formal education. The huts are places in which men teach boys the techniques of hunting, fishing, warfare, and religious rituals. Initiation rites accompanying passage through the age-set require the proper execution of a series of tasks set forth by the elders.

Since girls and women are not allowed to enter the hut, they are excluded from avenues of formal education (Hogbin 1970; Maybury-Lewis 1967). [...]

Schools are the loci of formal education in American society. Just as ceremonial men's huts are places in which boys learn to hunt and fight in nonindustrial societies, schools are the places in which, until relatively recently, occupational skills were conveyed only to boys. Excluding girls from schools – elementary through college – insured that, as a group, women would be less able than men to read, write, and cipher. Paths to public status therefore were limited. Elementary and high schools became sexually integrated as industrialization proceeded, but American colleges did not become coeducational until the late nineteenth century. Women did not begin to enter places of higher education in large numbers until the mid-twentieth century. Spatial segregation thereby reduced women's access to knowledge and likely had a greater negative association with women's status than the form of dwellings.

The labor force and the segregated workplace

The division of labor in nonindustrial societies is simultaneously spatial and gendered. Men and women tend to perform different tasks divided fairly consistently along gender role stereotypes: men hunt, and women cook and care for children (Murdock and Provost 1973). Since hunting typically occurs far from the dwelling, while cooking and child care occur close to it, spatial distinctions are an integral part of the gender division of labor.

Such spatial arrangements may also be related to gender stratification. Men's labor is more universally valued because men tend to distribute excess goods (from a successful hunt, for example) to families outside the immediate household, while women prepare food primarily within the family (Friedl 1975). To the extent that women do not accompany men to learn hunting skills, the reciprocity between spatial segregation and gender stratification is reinforced. The initial reason for women not learning to hunt – immobility due to responsibility for child care – becomes obscured as spatial segregation insures that few women acquire the ability to hunt.

Segregated workplaces also exist in industrialized societies. When American women began to enter the labor force in the nineteenth century, the relatively few jobs open to them were highly segregated by gender. Domestic service and teaching were acceptable female occupations, but factory and clerical work were controversial because they placed women in the same spaces as men. Women in typically male occupations, however, earned more and had higher status than women in typically female occupations (Aron 1987).

Today, when more than one-half of American women are in the labor force, they still work in a small number of occupations and in places separate from men (Baron and Bielby 1985). "Thus in modern workplaces there are not only men's and women's jobs but also men's and women's spaces" (Scott 1982, 176). In an era in which the majority of women's and men's daily lives are spent outside the dwelling, and to the extent that they do not share the same workplace, contact between the sexes is reduced. Since public status derives at least partially from occupational skills, many of which are learned on the job, workplace segregation contributes to women's lower status. Once again, access to knowledge and spatial relations mediate the status of women. [. . .]

Space, Knowledge, and Secrecy

Spatial segregation is one of the mechanisms by which a group with greater power can maintain its advantage over a group with less power. By controlling access to knowledge and resources through the control of space, the dominant group's ability to retain and reinforce its position is enhanced. Thus, spatial boundaries contribute to the unequal status of women. For women to become more knowledgeable, they must also change places.

Many types of knowledge exist, only some of which is highly valued. "Masculine" knowledge is almost universally more prestigious than "feminine" knowledge. Men's ability to hunt in nonindustrial societies is therefore more highly valued than women's ability to gather, although women's efforts actually provide more of the household's food (Friedl 1975). In advanced industrialized societies, math and science skills (at which men excel) are more highly valued than verbal and relationship skills (at which women excel).

Shared knowledge can bind the members of society together. Well-known origin myths, for example, create solidarity around a group identity. Knowledge can also separate the members of society, however. Every society restricts some types of knowledge to certain members. Successful hunting techniques are known only to a few men in nonindustrial societies, just as medical expertise is known only to an elite few in advanced industrial societies. Sometimes the distribution of knowledge is controlled through institutionalized gate-keeping organizations (such as a men's hut or the American Medical Association). Thus, every society possesses differently valued knowledge that theoretically is available to all members but in reality is not. [. . .]

The group with less-valued knowledge may contest the legitimacy of its unequal distribution. Nineteenth-century American feminists, for example, fought vigorously to open medical colleges to women. Many other examples exist of women (both white and black) organizing to open schools, achieve the vote, and join labor unions (Foner 1988; Kessler-Harris 1982). The long battles accompanying each of these efforts demonstrate how contentious acquiring access to knowledge can be. Those with valued knowledge are the most powerful, which buttresses their ability to define their knowledge as the most prestigious and to maintain control of it. Knowledge thus forms the basis for a stratification system. [. . .]

Spatial barriers become established and then institutionalized for reasons that have little to do (manifestly) with power, but which tend to maintain prevailing advantages. This is because space is a "morphic language," one of the means by which society is interpreted by its members (Hillier and Hanson 1984, 198). The reciprocity between space and status arises from the constant renegotiation and re-creation of the existing stratification system. Bourdieu (1977) proposes that the power of a dominant group lies in its ability to control constructions of reality that reinforce its own status so that subordinate groups accept the social order and their own place in it. The powerful cannot maintain their positions without the cooperation of the less powerful. If a given stratification system is to persist, then, both powerful and less-powerful groups must be engaged in its constant renegotiation and re-creation. Women in nonindustrial societies who observed taboos barring them from ceremonial men's huts and women in nineteenth-century America who accepted the medical opinion that they should not attend college were as engaged in upholding gendered power differentials as were men. From Moore's perspective, "the dominated are as involved in the use and maintenance of power as the dominant, because there are no available forms of discourse which do not appeal to the given categories, divisions and values which simultaneously produce and expose the relations of power" (Moore 1986, 194).

Thus, women and men together create spatial segregation and stratification systems. Both sexes subscribe to the spatial arrangements that reinforce differential access to knowledge, resources, and power: men because it serves their interests, and women because they may perceive no alternative. In fact, greater and lesser degrees of cooperation exist within stratification systems. Some women may believe in the legitimacy of their lower status due to strong ideological pressures or religious creeds. Other women may participate in a stratification system because they have little choice (e.g., if they have not received the training necessary for more prestigious status). Still other women struggle against the prevailing system, calling for the right to vote, equal pay for equal work, and reproductive freedom. Most status differences are reinforced by subtle forms of spatial segregation. Instead of being visibly manifest in spatial barriers, status hierarchies often are determined in secret. Secrets, in turn, are preserved often through spatial boundaries. [...]

Knowledge, secrecy, and women's status

Several examples of spatially segregated institutions in American history exist to illustrate how separating women from sources of knowledge influences women's status. The first is the college, in which very few women were enrolled until after World War II. When higher education first opened to women, it took the form of spatially segregated women's colleges. Women did not gain the training necessary for careers outside the home until the end of the nineteenth century, when professional programs became coeducational. Bitter controversy ensued over women's rights to share the same space and the same knowledge with men. The battle over coeducation in state universities began in 1862 and did not end for over a century. Such intense resistance to gender integration reflects the perceived costs to the powerful group of sharing space and knowledge with the less powerful.

The second "men's club" was the labor union. When the Knights of Labor (organized in 1869 as a secret society) opened its doors to women in the 1880s, about 10 percent of its membership was female. The proportion of women in unions declined after the Knights of Labor disbanded in 1886 (Kessler-Harris 1982, 86). Women constituted approximately 2 percent of union membership in 1900, although 18 percent of the labor force was female at that time (US Bureau of the Census 1975, 127). One reason for the decline in the proportion of female participation was that union meetings were often held in saloons that excluded women.

Labor unions served one of the same educational functions for blue-collar workers that colleges did for white-collar workers, as the following passage suggests: "Skilled trades had traditionally been a province of unionized craftsmen who jealously guarded access to training in their fields. Though women frequently taught each other, and occasionally managed to 'steal' a trade from a willing male relative, they were rarely admitted to the requisite apprenticeships. Where they managed to acquire skills and posed a threat to male workers, craft unions sometimes grudgingly helped women to form separate, affiliated unions" (Kessler-Harris 1982, 171). In both Great Britain and the United States, labor unions have actively discouraged women from gaining technical expertise crucial to success in blue-collar jobs (Bradley 1989; Cockburn 1983).

Predominantly male unions, like predominantly male colleges, retained control of information until their "secrets" were discovered by a few pioneering women. When that happened, separate organizations – *separate places* – were created in which women were segregated from men. Whether that contributed to a different curriculum, as it did in colleges, or in lack of access to apprenticeships, as it did in unions, the result was a lack of female access to masculine knowledge and status. Lack of status, in turn, reduced women's ability to sexually integrate places of knowledge.

Information control is thus a way to control prestige, power, and wealth. The role of secrecy in maintaining social control is suggested by the following passage: "Social divisiveness which is generated by conflicting interests creates the social conditions under which secrecy thrives. To the extent that secrecy denies social actors information which might reveal that they are exploited, or manipulated by others, to that extent then secrecy promotes order" (Tefft 1980, 67). As long as the medical profession was closed to women, for example, men like Dr. Edward Clarke could warn women that higher education would damage their health (Rosenberg 1982, 5). Only after numbers of women had risked becoming educated and continued to lead healthy lives was the ill-health myth abandoned. The period in which that assumption was being challenged was a period of turmoil in regard to gender stratification, however, Dr. Clarke's ideas existed side by side with the ideas of the first feminist convention at Seneca Falls and women's entry into the labor force. Once the "secrets" of higher education were released to women, their suspicions of the causes of their lower status were confirmed, threatening the social order that dictated private spheres for women and public spheres for men. [...]

Most explanations of gender stratification identify the family and/or the economy as the foundation from which status differences arise. No existing explanations, however, consistently incorporate the spatial context in which the activities constituting these institutions occur. Adding the spatial dimension of institutions helps form a new perspective on gender stratification by grounding abstract concepts in physical space. [...]

References

Aron, Cindy. 1987. *Ladies and Gentlemen of the Civil Service*. New York: Oxford University Press.

Baron, James N., and William T. Bielby. 1985. "Organizational Barriers to Gender Equality: Sex Segregation of Jobs and Opportunities." In *Gender and the Life Course*, ed. Alice Rossi. New York: Aldine.

Bourdieu, Pierre. 1977. *Outline of a Theory of Practice*. Cambridge: Cambridge University Press.

Bowlby, S. R., J. Foord, and L. McDowell. 1986. "The Place of Gender in Locality Studies." *Area* 18(4): 327–31.

Bradley, Harriet. 1989. *Men's Work, Women's Work*. Cambridge: Polity Press.

Chafetz, Janet. 1990. *Gender Equity*. Newbury Park, CA: Sage.

Cockburn, Cynthia. 1983. *Brothers: Male Dominance and Technological Change*. London: Pluto Press.

Dear, Michael and Jennifer Wolch. 1989. "How Territory Shapes Social Life." In *The Power of Geography*, eds. Jennifer Wolch and Michael Dear. Boston: Unwin Hyman.

Foner, Eric. 1988. *Reconstruction: America's Unfinished Revolution: 1863–1877*. New York: Harper and Row.

Friedl, Ernestine. 1975. *Women and Men: An Anthropologist's View*. New York: Holt, Rinehart, and Winston.

Hillier, Bill, and Julienne Hanson. 1984. *The Social Logic of Space*. New York: Cambridge University Press.

Hogbin, Ian. 1970. *The Island of Menstruating Men*. London: Chandler Publishing.

Kessler-Harris, Alice. 1982. *Out to Work: A History of Wage-Earning Women in the United States*. New York: Oxford University Press.

Khatib-Chahidi, Jane. 1981. "Sexual Prohibitions, Shared Space, and Fictive Marriages in Shi'ite Iran." In *Women and Space*, ed. Shirley Ardner. London: Croom Helm.

Mandelbaum, David. 1988. *Women's Seclusion and Men's Honor.* Tucson: University of Arizona Press.

Massey, Doreen. 1984. "Introduction: Geography Matters." In *Geography Matters!*, eds. Doreen Massey and John Allen. Cambridge: Cambridge University Press.

Maybury-Lewis, David. 1967. *Akwĕ-Shavante Society.* Oxford: Clarendon Press.

McDowell, Linda. 1983. "City and Home: Urban Housing and the Sexual Division of Space." In *Sexual Divisions: Patterns and Processes*, eds. Mary Evans and Clare Ungerson. London: Tavistock.

Moore, Henrietta. 1986. *Space, Text, and Gender.* Cambridge: Cambridge University Press.

Moughtin, J. C. 1985. *Hausa Architecture.* London: Ethnographica.

Murdock, George P., and Caterina Provost. 1973. "Factors in the Division of Labor by Sex: A Cross-Cultural Analysis." *Ethnology* 12 (April): 203–25.

Rosenberg, Rosalind. 1982. *Beyond Separate Spheres.* New Haven: Yale University Press.

Rothman, David, and Sheila Rothman (eds.). 1987. *The Dangers of Education: Sexism and the Origin of Women's Colleges.* New York: Garland Publishing.

Sack, Robert David. 1980. *Conceptions of Space in Social Thought.* Minneapolis: University of Minnesota Press.

Sciama, Lidia. 1981. "The Problem of Privacy in Mediterranean Anthropology." In *Women and Space*, ed. Shirley Ardener. London: Croom Helm.

Scott, John Wallach. 1982. "The Mechanization of Women's Work." *Scientific American* 247 (Sept.): 167–87.

Stirling, M. W. 1938. "Historical and Ethnographic Material on the Jivaro Indians." Smithsonian Institution Bureau of American Ethnology, Bulletin 117. Washington, DC: US Government Printing Office.

Tefft, Stanton K. 1980. "Secrecy, Disclosure, and Social Theory." In *Secrecy: A Cross-Cultural Perspective*, ed. Stanton Tefft. New York: Human Sciences Press.

US Bureau of the Census. 1975. *Historical Statistics of the United States, Colonial Times to 1970, Bicentennial Edition, Part 1.* Washington, DC: US Government Printing Office.

Watson, Joellen. 1977. "Higher Education for Women in the United States: A Historical Perspective." *Educational Studies* 8 (Summer): 133–46.

4 Los Angeles and the Chicago School: Invitation to a Debate

Michael Dear

If the city of Chicago was the model for the Chicago School of urban sociology, could the city of Los Angeles be the model for a new school of urban studies? This is exactly what Michael Dear proposes. In this article, he recounts the thinking of the pioneering Chicago School of the early twentieth century and contrasts it with the perspective of the emerging Los Angeles School. The chief source of the theoretical differences Dear describes is the difference in the nature of the two cities. Whereas he characterizes Chicago as a *modern* city organized around a single center, he sees Los Angeles as a *postmodern* city, (dis)organized around many suburban nuclei.

Introduction

The state of theory, now and from now on, isn't it California? And even Southern California?

– Jacques Derrida (quoted in Carrol, 1990, p. 63)

More than 75 years ago, the University of Chicago Press published a book of essays entitled *The City: Suggestions for Investigation of Human Behavior in the Urban Environment*. The book is still in print. Six of its 10 essays are by Robert E. Park, then Chair of the University's Sociology Department. There are also two essays by Ernest W. Burgess, and one each from Roderick D. McKenzie and Louis Wirth. In essence, the book announced the arrival of the "Chicago School" of urban sociology, defining an agenda for urban studies that persists to this day. Shrugging off challenges from competing visions, the School has maintained a remarkable longevity that is a tribute to its model's beguiling simplicity, to the tenacity of its adherents who subsequently constructed a formidable literature, and

Dear, Michael, "Los Angeles and the Chicago School: Invitation to a Debate." From *City & Community* 1(1) (2002): 5–6, 14–19, 21–5, 29–32. Reprinted by permission of the American Sociological Association.

to the fact that the model "worked" in its application to so many different cities over such a long period of time.

The present essay begins the task of defining an alternative agenda for urban studies, based on the precepts of what I shall refer to as the "Los Angeles School." Quite evidently, adherents of the Los Angeles School take many cues from the Los Angeles metropolitan region, or (more generally) from Southern California – a five-county region encompassing Los Angeles, Orange, Riverside, San Bernardino, and Ventura Counties. This exceptionally complex, fast-growing megalopolis is already home to more than 16 million people. It is likely soon to overtake New York as the nation's premier urban region. Yet, for most of its history, it has been regarded as an exception to the rules governing American urban development, an aberrant outlier on the continent's western edge.

All this is changing. During the past two decades, Southern California has attracted increasing attention from scholars, the media, and other social commentators. The region has become not the exception to but rather a prototype of our urban future. For many current observers, LA is simply confirming what contemporaries knew throughout its history: that the city posited a set of different rules for understanding urban growth. An alternative urban metric is now overdue, since as Joel Garreau (1991, p. 3) observed in his study of edge cities: "Every American city that is growing, is growing in the fashion of Los Angeles."

Just as the Chicago School emerged at a time when that city was reaching new national prominence, Los Angeles is now making its impression on the minds of urbanists across the world. Few argue that the city is unique, or necessarily a harbinger of the future, even though both view-points are at some level demonstrably true. However, at a very minimum, they all assert that Southern California is an unusual amalgam – a polycentric, polyglot, polycultural pastiche that is deeply involved in rewriting American urbanism. Moreover, their theoretical inquiries do not end with Southern California, but are also focused on more general questions concerning broader urban socio-spatial processes. The variety, volume, and pace of contemporary urban change almost *requires* the development of alternative analytical frameworks; one can no longer make an unchallenged appeal to a single model for the myriad global and local trends that surround us. These proliferating social logics insist upon multiple theoretical frameworks that overlap and coexist in their explanations of the burgeoning world order. The consequent epistemological difficulties are manifest in the problem of naming the present condition, witness the use of such terms as *post-modernity, hyper-modernity,* and *super-modernity.*

The particular conditions that have led now to the emergence of a Los Angeles School may be almost coincidental: (1) that an especially powerful intersection of empirical and theoretical research projects have come together in this particular place at this particular time; (2) that these trends are occurring in what has historically been the most understudied major city in the United States; (3) that these projects have attracted the attention of an assemblage of increasingly self-conscious scholars and practitioners; and (4) that the world is facing the prospect of a Pacific century, in which Southern California is likely to become a global capital. The vitality and potential of the Los Angeles School derive from the intersection of these events, and the promise they hold for a renaissance of urban theory. In this essay, I shall examine this potential, first through a history of the emergence of a "Los Angeles School," and a brief contrast with the precepts of the Chicago School. I turn next to empirical evidence of contemporary urban process in Southern California, using this evidence to sketch an orientation toward LA urbanism. Finally, I assess the promise of the putative Los Angeles School, inviting others to join the debate toward a revised urban theory. [...]

From Chicago to LA

The basic primer of the Chicago School was *The City.* Originally published in 1925, the book retains a tremendous vitality far beyond its interest as a historical document. I regard the book as emblematic of a modernist analytical paradigm that remained popular for most of the twentieth century. Its assumptions included:

- a "modernist" view of the city as a unified whole, i.e., a coherent regional system in which the center organizes its hinterland;
- an individual-centered understanding of the urban condition; urban process in *The City* is typically grounded in the individual subjectivities of urbanites, their personal choices ultimately explaining the overall urban condition, including spatial structure, crime, poverty, and racism; and
- a linear evolutionist paradigm, in which processes lead from tradition to modernity, from primitive to advanced, from community to society, and so on.

There may be other important assumptions of the Chicago School, as represented in *The City*, that are not listed here. Finding them and identifying what is right or wrong about them is one of the tasks at hand, rather than excoriating the book's contributors for not accurately foreseeing some distant future.

The most enduring of the Chicago School models was the zonal or *concentric ring theory*, an account of the evolution of differentiated urban social areas by E. W. Burgess (1925). Based on assumptions that included a uniform land surface, universal access to a single-centered city, free competition for space, and the notion that development would take place outward from a central core, Burgess concluded that the city would tend to form a series of concentric zones (figure 4.1). The main ecological metaphors invoked to describe this dynamic were invasion, succession, and segregation, by which populations gradually filtered outwards from the center as their status and level of assimilation progressed. The model was predicated on continuing high levels of immigration to the city.

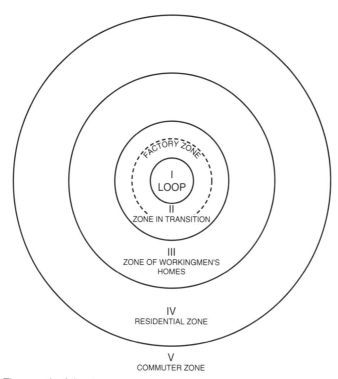

Figure 4.1 The growth of the city

At the core of Burgess's schema was the central business district (CBD), which was surrounded by a transitional zone, where older private houses were being converted to offices and light industry, or subdivided to form smaller dwelling units. This was the principal area to which new immigrants were attracted; and it included areas of "vice" and generally unstable or mobile social groups. The transitional zone was succeeded by a zone of working-men's homes, which included some of the city's oldest residential buildings inhabited by stable social groups. Beyond this, newer and larger dwellings were to be found, occupied by the middle classes. Finally, the commuter zone was separate from the continuous built-up area of the city, where much of the zone's population was employed. Burgess's model was a broad generalization, and not intended to be taken too literally. He anticipated, for instance, that his schema would apply only in the absence of "opposing factors" such as local topography (in the case of Chicago, Lake Michigan). He also anticipated considerable internal variation within the different zones.

Other urbanists subsequently noted the tendency for cities to grow in star-shaped rather than concentric form, along highways that radiate from a center with contrasting land uses in the interstices. This observation gave rise to a *sector theory* of urban structure, an idea advanced in the late 1930s by Homer Hoyt

(1933, 1939), who observed that once variations arose in land uses near the city center, they tended to persist as the city expanded. Distinctive sectors thus grew out from the CBD, often organized along major highways. Hoyt emphasized that "non-rational" factors could alter urban form, as when skillful promotion influenced the direction of speculative development. He also understood that the age of the buildings could still reflect a concentric ring structure, and that sectors may not be internally homogeneous at one point in time.

The complexities of real-world urbanism were further taken up in the *multiple nuclei theory* of C. D. Harris and E. Ullman (1945). They proposed that cities have a cellular structure in which land-uses develop around multiple growth-nuclei within the metropolis – a consequence of accessibility-induced variations in the land-rent surface and agglomeration (dis)economics. Harris and Ullman also allow that real-world urban structure is determined by broader social and economic forces, the influence of history, and international influences. But whatever the precise reasons for their origin, once nuclei have been established, general growth forces reinforce their pre-existing patterns.

Much of the urban research agenda of the twentieth century has been predicted on the precepts of the concentric zone, sector, and multiple-nuclei theories of urban structure. Their influences can be seen directly in factorial ecologies of intra-urban structure, land-rent models, studies of urban economies and diseconomies of scale, and designs for ideal cities and neighborhoods. The specific and persistent popularity of the Chicago concentric ring model is harder to explain, however, given the proliferation of evidence in support of alternative theories. The most likely reasons for its endurance (as I have mentioned) are related to its beguiling simplicity and the enormous volume of publications produced by adherents of the Chicago School (e.g., Abbott, 1999; and Fine, 1995). However, there was also an enormous, persuasive substance in the burgeoning school, summarized by Louis Wirth in his well-known article on "Urbanism as a Way of Life" (Wirth, 1938). In this, he argued for a sociology that emphasized the city as a distinctive mode of human life based in core questions of population size, density, and heterogeneity, and focused not only on the physical spaces of the city but also on the constellation of personalities that collectively amounted to social organization and control.

In the final chapter of *The City*, the same Louis Wirth (1925) had already provided a magisterial review of the field of urban sociology, entitled (with deceptive simplicity and astonishing self-effacement) "A Bibliography of the Urban Community." But what Wirth does in this chapter, in a remarkably prescient way, is to summarize the fundamental premises of the Chicago School and to isolate two fundamental features of the urban condition that was to rise to prominence at the beginning of the twenty-first century. Specifically, Wirth establishes that the city lies at the center of, and provides the organizational logic for, a complex regional hinterland based on trade. But he also notes that the development of "satellite cities" is characteristic of the "latest phases" of city growth and that the location of such satellites can exert a "determining influence" on the direction of growth (Wirth, 1925, p. 185). He further observes that modern communications have transformed the world into a "single mechanism," where the global and the local intersect decisively and continuously (Wirth, 1925, p. 186).

And there, in a sense, you have it. In a few short paragraphs, Wirth anticipates the pivotal moments that characterize Chicago-style urbanism, those primitives that eventually will separate it from an LA-style urbanism. He effectively foreshadowed the shift from what I term a "modernist" to a "postmodern" city, and, in so doing, the necessity of the transition from the Chicago to the Los Angeles School. *For it is no longer the center that organizes the urban hinterlands, but the hinterlands that determine what remains of the center.* The imperatives toward decentralization (including suburbanization) have become the principal dynamic in contemporary cities; and the twenty-first century's emerging world cities (including LA) are ground-zero loci in a communications-driven globalizing political economy. From a few, relatively humble first steps, we gaze out over the abyss – the yawning gap of an intellectual fault line separating Chicago from Los Angeles.

Contemporary Urbanisms in Southern California

I turn now to review the empirical evidence of recent urban developments in Southern California. In this task, I take my lead from what exists rather than what may be considered as a normative taxonomy of urban research. From this, I move quickly to a synthesis that is prefigurative of a proto-postmodern urbanism that serves as a basis for a distinctive LA school of urbanism.

Edge cities

Joel Garreau noted the central significance of Los Angeles in understanding contemporary metropolitan growth in the United States. He refers to LA as the "great-granddaddy" of edge cities, claiming there are 26 of them within a five-county area in Southern California (Garreau, 1991, p. 9). For Garreau, edge cities represent the crucible of America's urban future. The classic location for contemporary edge cities is at the intersection of an urban beltway and a hub-and-spoke lateral road. The central conditions that have propelled such development are the dominance of the automobile and the associated need for parking; the communications revolution; and the entry of women in large numbers into the labor market. One essential feature of the edge city is that politics is not yet established there. Into the political vacuum moves a "shadow government" – a privatized protogovernment that is essentially a plutocratic alternative to normal politics. Shadow governments can tax, legislate for, and police their communities, but they are rarely accountable, are responsive primarily to wealth (as opposed to numbers of voters), and subject to few constitutional constraints (Garreau, 1991, p. 187;

Wolch, 1990). Other studies of suburbanization in LA, most notably by Hise (1997) and Waldie (1996), provide a basis for comparing past practices of community planning in Southern California.

Privatopia

Privatopia, perhaps the quintessential edge city residential form, is a private housing development based in common-interest developments (CIDs) and administered by homeowner associations. There were fewer than 500 such associations in 1964; by 1992, there were 150,000 associations privately governing approximately 32 million Americans. In 1990, the 11.6 million CID units constituted over 11 percent of the nation's housing stock (McKenzie, 1994, p. 11). McKenzie (1994, p. 184) warns that far from being a benign or inconsequential trend, CIDs already define a new norm for the mass production of housing in the United States. Equally importantly, their organizations are now allied through something called the Community Associations Institute, "whose purposes include the standardizing and professionalizing of CID governance." He notes how this "secession of the successful" has altered concepts of citizenship, in which "one's duties consist of satisfying one's obligations to private property" (McKenzie, 1994, p. 196). In her futuristic novel of LA wars between walled-community dwellers and those beyond the walls, Octavia Butler (1993) envisioned a dystopian privatopian future. It includes a balkanized nation of defended neighborhoods at odds with one another, where entire communities are wiped out for a handful of fresh lemons or a few cups of potable water; where torture and murder of one's enemies is common; and where company-town slavery is attractive to those who are fortunate enough to sell their services to the hyper-defended enclaves of the very rich. (See also Blakely and Snyder, 1997.)

Cultures of heteropolis

One of the most prominent sociocultural tendencies in contemporary Southern California is the rise of minority populations (e.g., Ong et al., 1994; Myers, 2001; Roseman et al., 1996; Waldinger and Bozogmehr, 1996). Provoked to comprehend the causes and implications of the 1992 civil disturbances in Los Angeles, Charles Jencks zeroes in on the city's diversity as the key to LA's emergent urbanism: "Los Angeles is a combination of enclaves with high identity, and multienclaves with mixed identity, and, taken as a whole, it is perhaps the most heterogenenous city in the world" (Jencks, 1993, p. 32). The vigor and imagination underlying the consequent cultural dynamics is everywhere evident in the region, from the diversity of ethnic adaptations (Park, 1996), through the concentration of cultural producers in the region (Molotch, 1996), to the hybrid complexities of emerging cultural forms (Boyd, 1996, 1997). The consequent built environment is characterized by transience, energy, and unplanned vulgarity, in which Hollywood is never far away. Jencks (1993, p. 75) views this improvisational quality as a hopeful sign: "The main point of hetero-architecture is to accept the different voices that create a city, suppress none of them, and make from their interaction some kind of greater dialogue." This is especially important in a city where *minoritization*, "the typical postmodern phenomenon where most of the population forms the 'other'," is the order of the day, and where most city dwellers feel distanced from the power structure (Jencks, 1993, p. 84). Despite Jencks's optimism, other analysts have observed that the same Southern California heteropolis has to contend with more than its share of socio-economic polarization, racism, inequality, homelessness, and social unrest (Anderson, 1996; Baldassare, 1994; Bobo et al., 2000; Bullard et al., 1994; Gooding-Williams, 1993; Rocco, 1996). Yet these characteristics are part of a sociocultural dynamic that is also provoking the search for innovative solutions in labor and community organizing (Keil, 1998; Kenny, 2001; Pulido, 1996), as well as in inter-ethnic relations (Abelmann and Lie, 1995; Martínez, 1992), and spiritual life (Miller, 2001).

City as theme park

California in general, and Los Angeles in particular, have often been promoted as places where the American (suburban) Dream is most easily realized. Its oft-noted qualities of optimism and tolerance coupled with a balmy climate have given rise to an architecture and society fostered by a spirit of experimentation, risk-taking, and hope. Many writers have used the "theme park" metaphor to describe the emergence of such variegated cityscapes. For instance, Michael Sorkin (1992), described theme parks as places of simulation without end, characterized by aspatiality plus technological and physical surveillance and control. The phone and modem have rendered the street irrelevant, and the new city threatens an "unimagined sameness" characterized by the loosening of ties to any specific space, rising levels of surveillance, manipulation, and segregation, and the city as a theme park. Of this last, Disneyland is the archetype, described by Sorkin (1992, p. 227) as a place of "Taylorized fun," the "Holy See of Creative Geography." What is missing in this new cybernetic suburbia is not a particular building or place, but the spaces between, i.e., the connections that make sense of forms. What is missing, then, is connectivity and community. *In extremis*, California dreamscapes become simulacra. Ed Soja (1992) identified Orange County as a massive simulation of what a city should be. He describes Orange County as: "a structural fake, and enormous advertisement, yet functionally the finest multipurpose facility of its kind in the country." Calling this assemblage "exopolis," or the city without, Soja (1992, p. 120) asserts that in this "politically-numbed" society, conventional politics is dysfunctional. Orange County has become a "scamscape," notable principally as home of massive mail fraud operations, savings and loan failures, and county government bankruptcy.

Fortified city

The downside of the Southern Californian dream has, of course, been the subject of countless dystopian visions in histories, movies, and novels. In one powerful account, Mike Davis (1992a) noted how Southern Californians' obsession with security has transformed the region into a fortress. This shift is accurately manifested in the physical form of the city, which is divided into fortified cells of affluence and places of terror where police battle the criminalized poor. These urban phenomena, according to Davis (1992a, p. 155), have placed Los Angeles "on the hard edge of postmodernity." The dynamics of fortification involve the omnipresent application of high-tech policing methods to protect the security of gated residential developments and panopticon malls. It extends to space policing, including a proposed satellite observation capacity that would create an invisible Haussmannization of Los Angeles. In the consequent carceral city, the working poor and destitute are spatially sequestered on the mean streets, and excluded from the affluent forbidden cities through security by design. [...]

Fordist versus post-Fordist regimes of accumulation and regulation

Many observers agree that one of the most important underlying shifts in the contemporary political economy is from a Fordist to a post-Fordist industrial organization. In a series of important books, Allen Scott (1988a, 1988b, 1993, 2000) has portrayed the burgeoning urbanism of Southern California as a consequence of this deep-seated structural change in the capitalist political economy. Scott's basic argument is that there have been two major phases of urbanization in the United States. The first related to an era of Fordist mass production, during which the paradigmatic cities of industrial capitalism (Detroit, Chicago, Pittsburgh, etc.) coalesced around industries that were themselves based on ideas of mass production. The second phase is associated with the decline of the Fordist era and the rise of a post-Fordist "flexible production" (what some refer to as "flexible accumulation"). This is a form of industrial activity based on small-size, small-batch units of (typically sub-contracted) production that are nevertheless integrated into clusters of economic activity. Such clusters have been observed in two manifestations: labor-intensive craft forms (in Los Angeles, typically garments and jewelry); and high technology (especially the defense and aerospace industries). According to Scott, these so-called "technopoles" until recently constituted the principal geographical loci of contemporary (sub)urbanization in Southern California. An equally important facet of post-Fordism is the significant informal sector that mirrors the gloss of the high-tech sectors (Hondagneu-Sotelo, 2001). Post-Fordist regimes of accumulation are associated with analogous regimes of regulation, or social control. Perhaps the most prominent manifestation of changes in the regime of regulation has been the retreat from the welfare state (Wolch, 1990). The rise of neoconservatism and the privatization ethos have coincided with a period of economic recession and retrenchment that has led many to the brink of poverty just at the time when the social welfare "safety net" is being withdrawn. In Los Angeles, as in many other cities, an acute socio-economic polarization has resulted. In 1984, the city was dubbed the "homeless capital" of the United States because of its concentration of homeless people (Wolch and Dear, 1993).

Globalization

Needless to say, any consideration of the changing nature of industrial production sooner or later must encompass the globalization question. In his reference to the global context of LA's localisms, Mike Davis (1992b) claims that if LA is in any sense paradigmatic, it is because the city condenses the intended and unintended spatial consequences of a global post-Fordism. He insists that there is no simple master-logic of restructuring, focusing instead on two key localized macro-processes: the overaccumulation in Southern California of bank and real-estate capital principally from the East Asian trade surplus of the 1980s; and the reflux of low-wage manufacturing and labor-intensive service industries following upon immigration from Mexico and Central America. For instance, Davis (1992b, p. 26) noted how the City of Los Angeles used tax dollars gleaned from international capital investments to subsidize its downtown (Bunker Hill) urban renewal, a process he refers to as "municipalized land speculation." Through such connections, what happens today in Asia and Central America will tomorrow have an effect in Los Angeles. This global/local dialectic has already become an important (if somewhat imprecise) leitmotif of contemporary urban theory, most especially via notions of "world cities" and global "city-regions" (Scott, 1998, 2001).

Politics of nature

The natural environment of Southern California has been under constant assault since the first colonial settlements. Human habitation on a metropolitan scale has only been possible through a widespread manipulation of nature, especially the control of water resources in the American West (e.g., DeBuys and Myers, 1999; Gottlieb and FitzSimmons, 1991; Reisner, 1993). On the one hand, Southern Californians tend to hold a grudging respect for nature, living as they do adjacent to one of the earth's major geological hazards, and in a desert environment that is prone to flood, landslide, and fire (Darlington, 1996; McPhee, 1989). On the other hand, its inhabitants have been energetically, ceaselessly, and often carelessly unrolling the carpet of urbanization over the natural landscape for more than a century. This uninhibited occupation has engendered its own range of environmental problems, most notoriously air pollution, but also issues related to habitat loss and encounters between humans and other animals. The force of nature in Southern California has spawned a literature that attempts to incorporate environmental issues into the urban problematic (Pincetl, 1999). The politics of environmental regulation have long been studied in many places. However, the particular combination of circumstances in Southern California has stimulated an especially political view of nature, focusing both on its emasculation through human intervention (Davis, 1996), and on its potential for political mobilization by grass-roots movements (Keil, 1998; Pulido, 1996). It was also a foundation for Jennifer Wolch's alternative vision of the relationship between humans and non-humans (Wolch and Emel, 1998).

Los Angeles as Postmodern Urbanism

If all these observers of the Southern California scene could talk with each other, how might they synthesize their visions? At the risk of misrepresenting their work, I can suggest a synthesis that outlines a "proto-postmodern" urban process (figure 4.2). It is driven by a global restructuring that is permeated and balkanized by a series of interdictory networks; whose populations are socially and culturally heterogeneous, but politically and economically polarized; whose residents are educated and persuaded to the consumption of dreamscapes even as the poorest are consigned to carceral cities; whose built environment, reflective of these processes, consists of edge cities, privatopias, and the like; and whose natural environment is being erased to the point of unlivability while at the same time providing a focus for political action.

While there could be widespread agreement about the terms of this diagnostic (figure 4.2), based on these "texts" of contemporary urban landscapes, I want to go further toward a revised theory of urbanism. In what follows, I am not summarizing any kind of consensus about what the Los Angeles School suggests; instead, I will present my own construction of what such a theory might look like. In the space available, only a sketch of this alternative will be provided. Interested readers can turn for fuller presentations to Dear (2000, 2001) and Dear and Flusty (1998). I also want to emphasize that one does not have to agree with everything in the following formulation to be persuaded of the challenge it presents to prevailing wisdom.

Let me begin by noting some of the principal assumptions that distinguish a distinctive LA-based urban theory. As I will show, the shift toward a Los Angeles School may be regarded as a move away from modernist perspectives on the city (à la Chicago School) to a postmodern view of urban process. We are all by now aware that the tenets of modernist thought have been undermined and discredited; in their place, a multiplicity of new ways of knowing has been substituted.

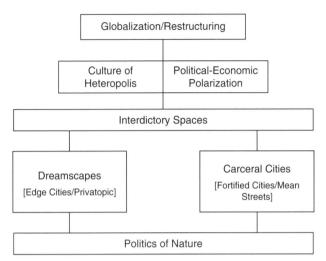

Figure 4.2 A "proto-postmodern" urban process

Analogously, in postmodern cities, the logics of previous urbanisms have evaporated; and, in the absence a single new imperative, multiple (ir)rationalities clamor to fill the vacuum. The Los Angeles School is distinguishable from the Chicago precepts (as noted above) by the following counter-propositions:

- Traditional concepts of urban form imagine the city organized around a central core; in a revised theory, the urban peripheries are organizing what remains of the center.
- A global, corporate-dominated connectivity is balancing, even offsetting, individual-centered agency in urban processes.
- A linear evolutionist urban paradigm has been usurped by a non-linear, chaotic process that includes pathological forms such as transnational criminal organizations, common-interest developments (CIDs), and life-threatening environmental degradation (e.g., global warming).

In empirical terms, these assumptions find expression in the following urban dynamics:

1. *World City*: The emergence of a relatively few centers of command and control in a globalizing economy;
2. *Dual City*: An increasing social polarization, i.e., the increasing gap between rich and poor; between nations; between the powerful and the powerless; between different ethnic, racial, and religious groupings; and between genders;
3. *Hybrid City*: The ubiquity of fragmentation both in material and cognitive life, including the collapse of conventional communities, and the rise of new cultural categories and spaces, including, especially, cultural hybrids; and

4. *Cybercity*: The challenges of the information age, especially the seemingly ubiquitous capacity for connectivity to supplant the constraints of place.

"Keno capitalism" is the synoptic term that Steven Flusty and I have adopted to describe the spatial manifestations that are consequent upon the (postmodern) urban condition implied by these assumptions (figure 4.3). Urbanization is occurring on a quasi-random field of opportunities, in which each space is (in principle) equally available through its connection with the information superhighway (Dear and Flusty, 1998). Capital touches down as if by chance on a parcel of land, ignoring the opportunities on intervening lots, thus sparking the development process. The relationship between development of one parcel and non-development of another is a disjointed, seemingly unrelated affair. While not truly a random process, it is evident that the traditional, center-driven agglomeration economies that have guided urban development in the past no longer generally apply. Conventional city form, Chicago-style, is sacrificed in favor of a non-contiguous collage of parcelized, consumption-oriented landscapes devoid of conventional centers yet wired into electronic propinquity and nominally unified by the mythologies of the

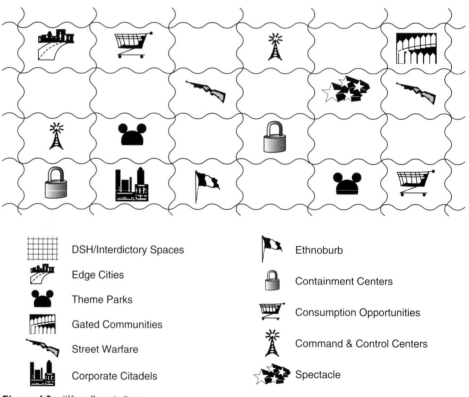

Figure 4.3   "Keno" capitalism

(dis)information superhighway. Los Angeles may be a mature form of this post-modern metropolis; Las Vegas comes to mind as a youthful example (cf. Dear, 2000, ch. 10). The consequent urban aggregate is characterized by acute fragmen-tation and specialization – a partitioned gaming board subject to perverse laws and peculiarly discrete, disjointed urban outcomes. Given the pervasive presence of crime, corruption, and violence in the global city (not to mention geopolitical transitions, as nation-states give way to micro-nationalisms and transnational criminal organizations), the city as gaming board seems an especially appro-priate twenty-first-century successor to the concentrically ringed city of the early twentieth.

I am insisting on the "postmodern" as a vehicle for examining LA urbanism for a number of reasons, most especially to encourage different ways of seeing the urban process. I have long understood postmodernism as a concept that embraces three principal referents:

- A series of *distinctive cultural and stylistic practices* that are in and of themselves intrinsically interesting;
- The totality of such practices, viewed as a *cultural ensemble characteristic of the contemporary epoch of capitalism* (often referred to as postmodernity); and
- A set of *philosophical and methodological discourses antagonistic to the precepts of Enlightenment thought*, most particularly the hegemony of any single intellec-tual persuasion.

Implicit in each of these approaches is the notion of a "radical break," that is, a discontinuity between past and present political, socio-cultural, and economic trends. My working hypothesis is that there is sufficient evidence to support the notion that we are witnessing a radical break in each of these three categories. The localization (sometimes literally the concretization) of these multiple effects is creating the emerging time-space fabric of a postmodern society. This is not to suggest that existing (modernist) rationalities have been obliterated from the urban landscape or from our mind-sets; on the contrary, they persist as palimpsests of earlier logics and continue to influence the emerging spaces of postmodernity. For instance, they are presently serving to consolidate the power of existing place-based centers of communication technologies, even as such technologies are sup-posed to free development from the constraints of place. However, newer urban places, such as LA, are being created by different intentionalities, just as older places such as Chicago are being overlain by the altered intentionalities of post-modernity. Neither am I suggesting that earlier theoretical logics have been (or should be) entirely usurped. For instance, in his revision of the Chicago School, Abbott (1999, p. 204) claims that the "variables paradigm" of quantitative soci-ology has been exhausted, and that the "cornerstone of the Chicago vision was location" – points of departure that I regard as totally consistent with the time–space obsessions of the LA school of postmodern urbanism. Another example of overlap between modern and postmodern in current urban sociology is Smith's evocation of a transnational urbanism (Smith, 2001).

In these postmodern times, the gesture to a Los Angeles School might appear to be a deeply contradictory intellectual strategy. A "school" has semantic overtones of codification and hegemony; it has structure and authority. Modernists and post-modernists alike might shudder at the irony implied by these associations. And yet, ultimately, I am comfortable in proclaiming the existence of an LA school of urbanism for two reasons. First, the Los Angeles School exists as a body of litera-ture, as this essay attests. It exhibits an evolution through history, beginning with analysis of Los Angeles as an aberrant curiosity distinct from other forms of urbanism. The tone of that history has shifted gradually to the point that the city is now commonly represented as indicative of a new form of urbanism supplanting the older forms against which Los Angeles was once judged deviant. Second, the Los Angeles School exists as a discursive strategy demarcating a space both for the exploration of new realities and for resistance to old hegemonies. It is proving to be far more successful than its detractors at explaining the form and function of the urban. [...]

References

Abbott, A. 1999. *Department and Discipline: Chicago Sociology at One Hundred*. Chicago, IL: University of Chicago Press.

Abelmann, N. and Lie, J. 1995. *Blue Dreams: Korean Americans and the Los Angeles Riots*. Cambridge, MA: Harvard University Press.

Anderson, S. 1996. "A City Called Heaven: Black Enchantment and Despair in Los Angeles" in A. J. Scott and E. Soja (eds.), *The City: Los Angeles & Urban Theory at the End of the Twentieth Century*. Los Angeles, CA: University of California Press.

Baldassare, M. ed., 1994. *The Los Angeles Riots*. Boulder, CO: Westview Press.

Banham, R. 1971. *Los Angeles: The Architecture of Four Ecologies*. Harmondsworth, Eng-land: Penguin Books.

Blakely, E. and Snyder, M. 1997. *Fortress America: Gated and Walled Communities in the United States*. Washington, DC: Brookings Institution.

Bobo, L. D., Oliver, M. L., Johnson Jr. J. H., and Valenzuela, A., eds. 2000. *Prismatic Metropolis: Inequality in Los Angeles*. New York: Russell Sage Foundation.

Boyd, T. 1996. "A Small Introduction to the 'G' Funk Era: Gangsta Rap and Black Masculin-ity in Contemporary Los Angeles," in M. Dear, H. E. Schockman, and G. Hise, eds., *Rethinking Los Angeles*. Thousand Oaks, CA: Sage Publications.

Boyd, T. 1997. *Am I Black Enough for You? Popular Culture from the 'Hood and Beyond*. Bloomington, IN: Indiana University Press.

Bullard, R. D., Grigsby, J. E., and Lee, C. 1994. *Residential Apartheid*. Los Angeles, CA: UCLA Center for Afro-American Studies.

Burgess, E. W. 1925. "The Growth of the City," in R. E. Park, E. W. Burgess, and R. McKenzie, *The City: Suggestions of Investigation of Human Behavior in the Urban Environment*, pp. 47–62. Chicago, IL: University of Chicago Press.

Butler, O. L. 1993. *Parable of the Sower*. New York. Four Walls Eight Windows.

Darlington, D. 1996. *The Mojave: Portrait of the Definitive American Desert*. New York: Henry Holt and Company.

Davis, M. 1992a. "Fortress Los Angeles: The Militarization of Urban Space" in M. Sorkin (ed.), *Variations on a Theme Park*. New York: Noonday Press.

Davis, M. 1992b. "*Chinatown* Revisited? The 'Internationalization' of Downtown Los Angeles," in Reid, D. (ed.), *Sex, God and Death in L.A.* New York: Pantheon Books.

Davis, M. 1996. "How Eden Lost Its Garden: A Political History of the Los Angeles Landscape," in A. J. Scott and E. Soja (eds.), *The City: Los Angeles & Urban Theory at the End of the Twentieth Century*. Los Angeles, CA: University of California Press.

Dear, M. 2000. *The Postmodern Urban Condition*. Oxford: Blackwell Publishers.

Dear, M. (ed.) 2001. *From Chicago to LA: Making Sense of Urban Theory*. Thousand Oaks, CA: Sage Publications.

Dear, M. and Flusty, S. 1998. "Postmodern Urbanism," *Annals, Association of American Geographers*, 88(1), 50–72.

Dear, M. and Flusty, S. (eds.) 2002. *The Spaces of Postmodernity: A Reader in Human Geography*. Oxford: Blackwell Publishers.

DeBuys, W. and Myers, J. 1999. *Salt Dreams: Land and Water in Low-Down California*. Albuquerque, NM: University of New Mexico Press.

Fine, G. A. (ed.). 1995. *A Second Chicago School?: The Development of a Postwar American Sociology*. Chicago, IL: University of Chicago Press.

Fishman, R. 1987. *Bourgeois Utopias: The Rise and Fall of Suburbia*. New York: Basic Books, Inc.

Garreau, J. 1991. *Edge City: Life on the New Frontier*. New York: Anchor Books.

Gooding-Williams, R. (ed.) 1993. *Reading Rodney King, Reading Urban Uprising*. New York: Routledge.

Gottlieb, R. and FitzSimmons, M. 1991. *Thirst for Growth: Water Agencies and Hidden Government in California*. Tucson, AZ: University of Arizona Press.

Harris, C. D. and Ullman, E. L. 1945. "The Nature of Cities," *Annals of the American Academy of Political and Social Science*, 242, 7–17.

Hise, G. 1997. *Magnetic Los Angeles: Planning the Twentieth-Century Metropolis*. Baltimore, MD: Johns Hopkins University Press.

Hondagneu-Sotelo, P. 2001. *Domestica: Immigrant Workers Cleaning and Caring in the Shadows of Affluence*. Berkeley, CA: University of California Press.

Hoyt H. 1933. *One Hundred Years of Land Values in Chicago*. Chicago, IL: University of Chicago Press.

Hoyt, H. 1939. *The Structure and Growth of Residential Neighborhoods in American Cities*. Washington, DC: US Federal Housing Administration.

Jencks, C. 1993. *Heteropolis: Los Angeles, the Riots and the Strange Beauty of Hetero-Architecture*. New York: St. Martin's Press.

Keil, R. 1998. *Los Angeles*. New York: Wiley.

Kenny, M. R. 2001. *Mapping Gay LA*. Philadelphia, PA: Temple University Press.

Martínez, R. 1992. *The Other Side: Notes from the New L.A., Mexico City, and Beyond.* New York: Vintage Books.

McKenzie, E. 1994. *Privatopia: Homeowner Associations and the Rise of Residential Private Government.* New Haven, CT: Yale University Press.

McPhee, J. 1989. *The Control of Nature.* New York: The Noonday Press.

Miller, D. 2001. "Religion in Los Angeles: Patterns of Spiritual Practice in a Postmodern City," in M. Dear (ed.), *From Chicago to LA: Making Sense of Urban Theory.* Thousand Oaks, CA: Sage Publications.

Molotch, H. 1996. "L.A. as Design Product: How Art Works in a Regional Economy," in A. J. Scott and E. Soja (eds.), *The City: Los Angeles & Urban Theory at the End of the Twentieth Century.* Los Angeles, CA: University of California Press.

Myers, D. 2001. "Demographic Dynamism in Los Angeles, Chicago, New York, and Washington, DC," in M. Dear (ed.), *From Chicago to LA: Making Sense of Urban Theory.* Thousand Oaks, CA: Sage Publications.

Ong, P., Bonacich, E., and Cheng, L. (eds.) 1994. *The New Asian Immigration in Los Angeles and Global Restructuring.* Philadelphia, PA: Temple University Press.

Park, E. 1996. "Our L. A.? Korean Americans in Los Angeles After the Civil Unrest," in M. Dear, H. E. Schockman, and G. Hise (eds.), *Rethinking Los Angeles.* Thousand Oaks, CA: Sage Publications.

Pincetl, S. 1999. *Transforming California: A Political History of Land Use and Development.* Baltimore, MD: Johns Hopkins University Press.

Pulido, L. 1996. "Multiracial Organizing Among Environmental Justice Activists in Los Angeles," in M. Dear, H. E. Schockman, and G. Hise (eds.), *Rethinking Los Angeles.* Thousand Oaks, CA: Sage Publications.

Reisner, M. 1993. *Cadillac Desert: The American West and its Disappearing Water.* New York: Penguin Books.

Rocco, R. 1996. "Latino Los Angeles: Reframing Boundaries/Borders," in A. J. Scott and E. Soja (eds.), *The City: Los Angeles & Urban Theory at the End of the Twentieth Century.* Los Angeles, CA: University of California Press.

Roseman, C., Laux, H. D., and Thieme, G. (eds.) 1996. *EthniCity.* Lanham, MD: Rowman and Littlefield.

Scott, A. J. 1988a. *New Industrial Spaces: Flexible Production Organization and Regional Development in North America and Western Europe.* London: Pion.

Scott, A. J. 1988b. *Metropolis: From the Division of Labor to Urban Form.* Berkeley, CA: University of California Press.

Scott, A. J. 1993. *Technopolis: High-Technology Industry and Regional Development in Southern California.* Berkeley, CA: University of California Press.

Scott, A. J. 1998. *Regions and the World Economy: The Coming Shape of Global Production, Competition, and Political Order.* Oxford: Oxford University Press.

Scott, A. J. 2000. *The Cultural Economy of Cities.* London: Sage Publications.

Scott, A. J. (ed.) 2001. *Global City-Regions: Trends, Theory, Policy.* Oxford: Oxford University Press.

Smith, M. P. 2001. *Transnational Urbanism: Locating Globalization.* Oxford: Blackwell Publishers.

Soja, E. 1992. "Inside Exopolis: Scenes from Orange County," in M. Sorkin (ed.), *Variations on a Theme Park.* New York: Noonday Press.

Sorkin, M. (ed.) 1992. *Variations on a Theme Park: The New American City and the End of Public Space*. New York: Hill and Wang.

Waldie, D. J. 1996. *Holy Land: A Suburban Memoir*. New York: W. W. Norton & Company.

Waldinger, R. and Bozorgmehr, M. (eds.) 1996. *Ethnic Los Angeles*. New York: Russell Sage Foundation.

Wirth, L. 1925. "A Bibliography of the Urban Community" in R. E. Park, E. W. Burgess, and R. McKenzie, *The City: Suggestions of Investigation of Human Behavior in the Urban Environment*. Chicago, IL: University of Chicago Press.

Wirth, L. 1938. "Urbanism as a Way of Life," *American Journal of Sociology*, XLIV(1), 1–24.

Wolch, J. 1990. *The Shadow State: Government and Voluntary Sector in Transition*. New York: Foundation Center.

Wolch, J. and Dear, M., 1993. *Malign Neglect: Homelessness in an American City*. San Francisco, CA: Jossey-Bass.

Wolch, J. and Emel, J. (eds.) 1998. *Animal Geographies*. London: Verso.

5 Modernity, Post-modernity and Urban Culture

Mike Savage and Alan Warde

In this reading, Mike Savage and Alan Warde explore several claims about the increasingly postmodern nature of the city. The term "postmodern" has been used in architecture to describe a shift away from the functional International Style of steel, glass, and concrete boxes toward buildings that are stylistically eclectic, more elaborate, and distinctive. "Postmodern" has also been used in city planning to describe the emergence of new urban spaces such as shopping malls and waterfront mixed-use developments. A third meaning of "postmodern" is the view that cities have changed from production sites to consumption sites. These uses all imply that large-scale economic changes have transformed urban form and city life in a radical departure from the past.

In their analysis, Savage and Warde reject the claim that cities have undergone a major transition to postmodernity, and argue that recent urban forms reflect more continuity with the past than disjuncture with it. They conclude that cities are shaped not by economic forces and structures but by the cultural meanings people attach to space.

The post-modernity debate, the question of whether we now live in post-modern times, became, during the 1980s, the most central field for contemporary theoretical development. It raised profound questions about self-identity and social scientific knowledge, social progress and political programmes, throwing into doubt many entrenched personal, intellectual, social and political commitments. The debate has reverberated through many disciplines, philosophy, literature, aesthetics and media studies, and it has been widely taken up in urban sociology.

The term 'post-modernism' is an extremely flexible one. For some writers its use is primarily epistemological, a critique of the rationalist assumptions underlying the 'enlightenment project'. In Lyotard's (1979) influential discussion,

Savage, Mike and Alan Warde, "Modernity, Post-modernity and Urban Culture." From *Urban Sociology, Capitalism, and Modernity* (London: Macmillan, 1993), pp. 138–46. © 1993 by Mike Savage and Alan Warde.

post-modernists criticise the modernist use of 'meta-narratives' in which to ground claims about truth and justice. Lyotard claimed that the problem about meta-narratives is that they ignore the contextual nature of knowledge, the fact that all statements gain their meaning only in specific contexts and 'language games', and if abstracted from these and grounded by general principles they become totalitarian (see Connor, 1989). We do not find claims about post-modern epistemologies convincing, and we are more concerned to evaluate the idea of an emerging 'condition of post-modernity'. This is more of an ontological claim about the way that the social world is changing in the contemporary period, and is linked to debates about the rise of post-industrialism (Lash, 1990; Smart, 1992), 'disorganised capitalism', (Lash and Urry, 1987), flexible accumulation (Harvey, 1989) and the like. Among the shared key-themes of many accounts of the post-modern condition are included a new radical scepticism about the role of scientific knowledge; a new concern with aesthetics rather than morality; enhanced reflexivity on the part of individuals about their identity and the grounds for their conduct; a magnified importance for mass media in the framing of everyday life; an intensification of consumerism, the demise of socialist politics and its replacement by the local and personal politics of new social movements.

As this brief discussion of post-modernity indicates, there is major confusion and disagreement about both the way that the condition of post-modernity can best be defined and its implications for understanding urban cultural differentiation. One perspective, derived from architecture, argues that the development of post-modern architecture allows a much greater attention to urban difference and specificity. Architecture was one of the first areas where the term post-modern was applied (Jencks, 1984). Post-modern architecture claims to be a rejection of the uniformity of modernist practice, which was held responsible for the creation of a bland uniform style of building characterised by high-rise flats, shopping centres, and standardised plans. Modernist architecture was also blamed for the creation of styles of building insensitive to context (most notable in the 'international style' of Gropius and Mies van der Rohe) and hence seemed to perpetuate uniformity of urban cultures as all city centres came to be dominated by similar high-rise glass and concrete buildings.

In one of the most notable accounts, *Learning from Las Vegas*, Venturi, Scott Brown and Izenour argued that architects had to learn from local vernacular traditions, and abandon the pretensions of the uniform modernist style. Post-modern architecture claimed to celebrate multivalence (many meanings), over univalence (one meaning), and to promote a fresh aesthetic borrowing from different architectural styles from various historical periods. Between 1970 and 1990 many city centres have seen massive building and redevelopment projects, many of which are deliberately grand and lavish, announcing their own uniqueness and presence. One of the first of these was the AT&T building in New York, a skyscraper designed like a Chippendale chair, so that its roofline was of curious, non-functional appearance.

Post-modern architecture celebrated local variety and reasserted the importance of urban differentiation. There are however grounds for scepticism. Post-modernist architects consciously reacted against modernist uniformity and functionality. However, it is doubtful that modernist architecture can really be seen purely in these terms. Although Le Corbusier's claim that 'buildings are machines for living in' has become notorious, many modernist projects of urban grandeur and specificity had similar objectives to the post-modernists. It thus seems that Jencks's post-modernist attack on Mies van der Rohe's architecture is not because of its supposed functionality or univalence, but because it was an architecture of 'confusion' in which Mies upset architectural convention, by building a boiler-house like a cathedral, for instance (see Jencks, 1984, p. 16).

This point bears out Connor's (1989) observation that in reality as opposed to rhetoric, post-modernist architecture cannot be radically distinguished from its modernist forbears. Just as modernist architecture claimed to be new and 'modern', so post-modern architecture gains its following from being a departure from orthodoxy, and hence 'state of the art'. Clearly there are some changes in architectural style which might usefully be labelled post-modern – for instance, its concern to re-evaluate past styles and traditions, and to develop a greater aesthetic and playful sense. However, not all contemporary architecture is post-modern. 'High-Tech' architecture, itself a mutated form of modernism – such as expressed in the Lloyds building in London – does not easily fit the label of post-modernism. Much building continues to be in a more modernist style. It might hence be argued that alongside the much-heralded post-modern architecture of corporate office blocks and prestigious developments the 1980s saw the rise of a bland architecture of uniformity and functionality – the architecture of the warehouse, retail and factory unit and the shopping mall.

It is precisely these sorts of rather bland, functional buildings, that have been scrutinised by other commentators on post-modernism. David Harvey, for instance, while arguing that there is a distinct post-modern architectural style also pays attention to the creation of 'new urban spaces'. Harvey argues that the condition of post-modernity can best be seen as related to 'time–space compression' in contemporary capitalism. For Harvey, the most important development brought about under conditions of flexible accumulation is the growing ease of spatial mobility of people and artefacts. In this situation the condition of post-modernity is largely concerned with the development of a new 'placeless' urban environment.

Harvey's argument is elaborated by his analysis of 'new urban spaces'. These are the characteristic sites of urban development in the 1980s and 1990s – the out-of-town hypermarket, the shopping mall, and the motorway network have gained new prominence in urban living, appearing to herald a new 'placeless' city. Once inside a shopping mall, or on a motorway interchange, one could be almost anywhere in the world; links to other parts of the urban fabric seem tangential and haphazard.

Shopping malls are particularly interesting examples. Most widespread in North America where they have largely eclipsed central shopping venues, but also found throughout Europe, they offer a self-contained, roofed and enclosed environment in which shoppers move off the city streets and enter an environment geared exclusively to the selling of products. In some malls, such as one of the world's largest at West Edmonton in Canada (Shields, 1989), references to other countries and cities are made inside the mall itself, so that the visitor is wrenched even further away from the culture of the specific city in which it is located, into a new, imaginary realm.

Shopping malls are only one instance of emerging interchangeable urban spaces divorced from local context. Similar architectural styles – based on the manipulation of concrete and glass – are used in most cities. Many British and North American cities sport 'waterfront' developments, in which leisure facilities and middle-class housing – sometimes in the form of warehouse conversions, sometimes newly built – intermingle. Where high streets continue to flourish, each contains branches of the same major retailers. Private housing estates on the outskirts of large conurbations seem indistinguishable from one another, as do motorway systems.

These new urban spaces have been seen as distinctive, not simply in terms of their architecture, but also in terms of the cultural values they embody. Perhaps the most important of these are concerned with the redefinition of social boundaries such as the distinction between inside and outside. Fredric Jameson (1984, 1991) claims that post-modern architecture has a number of distinct features: 'the strange new feeling of an absence of inside and outside, the bewilderment and loss of spatial orientation in Portman's hotels, the messiness of an environment in which things and people no longer find their place (Jameson, 1991, pp. 117–18). In his study of the Frank Gehry House in Santa Monica, California, Jameson shows how parts of the house are glassed over and so open to the outside gaze, whilst the house itself has an older and newer part, each in very different styles, so undermining the integrity of the interior.

Shields makes a similar point, that 'post-modern spatialisation' means that:

> boundaries may be becoming more than lines defining the enclosed from the unenclosed, the ordered from the unordered, the known from the unknown. Boundaries have marked the limit where absence becomes presence. But such boundaries appear to be dissolving. They appear less as impermeable barricades and more as thresholds, limen across which communication takes place and where things of different categories – local and distant, native and foreign, and so on, interact. (Shields, 1992, p. 195)

This new form of urban space has led Fredric Jameson to call for fresh forms of 'cognitive mapping', in order to restore critical sense to our understanding of the modern urban environment. Yet the extent to which there has been such a dramatic change in the nature of urban boundaries is questionable. For although some areas may have lost a clear boundary between the inside and outside, others have gained it. The increasing fitting of security doors in blocks of flats has meant that the staircase and lobby, a previous example of a realm between the inside and outside, has been reduced in importance. Furthermore the idea that there ever has been a clearly defined public realm in stark opposition to a private realm is itself problematic, as Habermas's idea that the public realm was defined by the bourgeoisie, or feminist observations about the male-defined nature of this terrain indicate.

Many examples of new built forms in which boundaries are blurred are in fact high-status developments, built for wealthy individuals or corporate clients. Perhaps behind these new forms is the tendency for ostentatious display of wealth, partly in order for it to function as cultural capital. This is the line of argument taken by Mike Davis (1985) who sees post-modernism as the architectural product of a *laissez-faire* political regime. In this context Shields's argument that 'presence and proximity is no longer an indicator of inside status, of citizenship, of cultural membership' (Shields, 1992, p. 195) seems erroneous. There is very little evidence that social segregation is in decline, and the rise of gentrification appears to mark the rezoning of cities to accommodate specific groups defined both by gender and class – gentrified areas do not have a social mix except in the very early stages when older residents have not been entirely displaced.

The fact that some boundaries are being redrawn is not in doubt. What is doubtful is whether the changes taking place in the present day are any different in scale from those which have occurred constantly throughout the history of the modern city. Benjamin himself saw the precursors of today's shopping malls – the Paris Arcades – as an allegory for the modern city, the shopping mall can simply be seen as the development of this. Equally, Benjamin recognised that the experience of being lost in vast and complex urban space characterised our perception of the modern city. Paris, for Benjamin, 'was a maze not only of paths but also of tunnels. I cannot think of the underworld of the Metro and the north–south line opening their hundreds of shafts all over the city without recalling my endless *flâneries*' (Benjamin, 1978, p. 299, see also Frisby, 1985). In this line of thought the shopping mall is simply the last in a long line of tunnels, which need to be reconnected, by the wanderer, back into the urban landscape. If the shopping mall appears new and placeless today, this is because it has not yet been integrated back into its surrounding urban fabric, either by wear and tear, by feats of imagination, or by reputation. Urban-dwellers of the nineteenth-century regarded innovations such as the subway as heralding a new, placeless realm. Today these have been moulded into their contextual environments. We should therefore be cautious about assuming that the shopping mall has revolutionised urban culture.

Sharon Zukin (1992) attempts another way of formulating the idea of the post-modern city. She has identified two important types of post-modern spaces: gentrified areas and the new fantasy theme-parks such as Disneyland. She claims that these new developments mark a major break from older urban structures. In traditional and modern cities landscape – the city spaces of the culturally and politically dominant – stands opposed to the vernacular – the spaces of the dispossessed and powerless. Zorbaugh's (1983) contrast between the Gold Goast and the slum is perhaps the perfect example. In the post-modern city, Zukin argues the distinction between landscape and vernacular breaks down. Gentrification implies the revaluation of formerly run-down areas of the city – the vernacular becomes part of the landscape.

More generally, Zukin depicts the post-modern city as increasingly commodified and as the site of consumption. This relates to a broader conception of the post-modern city developed by Harvey and others, which sees it as primarily the site for a new consumerism, in contrast to the modernist city – such as Chicago – which was primarily defined by its role in industrial production. The idea that post-modernism can be seen as the culture of consumerism has been developed by Fredric Jameson (1984) and echoed by Harvey (1989), Featherstone (1987) and many others. One way of developing this argument in relation to urban development is to relate it to the expansion of tourism. Tourism also has a long history, but it has grown markedly in recent years, and places are increasingly forced to sell themselves in order to attract trade (Urry, 1990). Promoters of tourism use urban symbols to attract visitors. A celebrated example of the successful use of urban imagery is the case of Glasgow in Scotland, which launched a campaign in the mid-1980s to improve its image. The campaign, 'Glasgow's Miles Better', involved using an easily reproducible logo and the use of *art-nouveau* decorative styles on buildings, pictures and letterheads which could be associated with the Glasgow architect, Charles Rennie Mackintosh (who was ironically largely ignored by Glasgow patrons during his lifetime). This symbolic strategy succeeded in boosting tourist numbers from 700,000 to 3 million in less than a decade (Wishart, 1991). Many other European cities have pursued equivalent strategies (Bianchini, 1991).

The problem, however, with characterising the post-modern city in terms of consumption is that the modern city could equally plausibly be defined in the same way. Benjamin argued precisely this when, in his reflections on the Paris Arcades, he perceived the commodity as the clue to the lost dream-worlds of the inhabitants of the modern city. Berman likewise maintained that the experience of modernity suffused the shopping streets of the Nevsky Prospect. Similarly, whilst tourism has expanded massively in scope, it seems in many ways simply to represent the extension of the *flâneur*'s role which Benjamin again saw as symptomatic of modernity (see Urry, 1990). As Buck-Morss (1989, p. 344) writes, 'the Utopian moment of *flânerie* was fleeting. But if the *flâneur* disappeared as a specific figure, the perceptive attitude that he embodied saturates modern existence, specifically the society of mass consumption'.[1] Hence, it appears that the post-modern can be seen only as a quantitative rather than a qualitative shift within modernity.

Finally, notwithstanding the major interest in new forms of urban development, whether high-prestige office-blocks, shopping malls, warehouse conversions or whatever, many older parts of the urban fabric remain – and decay. Benjamin laid particular stress on the importance of these sites of dereliction and his lead has been taken up by a number of cultural critics who search for meaning amongst the rubbish. The foremost of these is Patrick Wright (1991), who has shown how it is possible to read contemporary social change through the scrutiny of our urban ruins. One example is the way that a now-forgotten 'Town Guide Cabinet' listing municipal services, now largely closed down, can be used to indicate the decline of state welfare.

In general, then, we are sceptical about claims about the post-modern city. This is not to say that there are not important urban changes taking place, but rather we believe that labelling them post-modern is unhelpful, since it implies that they represent new developments, rather than being the contemporary manifestation of the contradictory nature of modernity. Our position is therefore closer to that developed by Giddens who argues for the persistence of modernity. Within the voluminous literature on modernity, his theoretical work has had considerable appeal in urban studies, his conceptual framework having often been applied by social geographers and social historians. The city plays an important role in Giddens's thought and specifically in his conception of modernity. In *A Contemporary Critique of Historical Materialism* Giddens used an analysis of the changing role of the city to understand everyday life. He observed that 'life is not experienced as "structures", but as the *durée* of day-to-day existence . . . the continuity of daily life is not a "directly motivated" phenomenon, but assured in the routinisation of practices' (ibid, p. 150). He then argued that tradition loses its capacity to routinise practices for three reasons: the commodification of labour; the 'transformation of the "time–space paths" of the day' (ibid, p. 153); and the commodification of urban land which results in 'created space', the manufactured environments of the modern world. In such societies, the routinisation of day-to-day practice is no longer bound by tradition and is therefore not strongly normatively embedded: 'the moral bindingness of traditionally established practices is replaced by one geared extensively to habit against a background of economic constraint' (ibid, p. 154). The modern condition of personal anxiety and insecurity emerges from a deficit of legitimacy which appears as normative uncertainty. This condition emanates from the normative disembedding of the routine practices rather than from control over labour, reification or material aspects of commodification. For Giddens, cities are not fundamentally the products of capitalist economic forces, but rather those of a search for meaning.

In Giddens' most recent work (1990, 1991), these themes recur as central to his understanding of modernity. The existential and social problems of the age are concerned with developing sufficient trust in others to allay the fears inspired by the ever-present risks of life in an uncertain world. Thus he explores the dynamics of personal intimate relationships and addresses the risks posed by nuclear war and ecological catastrophe. He argues, nevertheless, that the present is better grasped as high modernity rather than as post-modernity. There is no abrupt transformation. The tribulations of the 1990s represent perhaps an intensification of the paradox of modernity but no qualitative break.

The approaches to urban meaning considered here offer stimulating insights into the old question of urban culture. Rather than seeking some universal cultural characteristics of all cities, they propose that meanings vary from group to group and that there are plural interpretations of the symbols and images visible in cities. They suggest that cities and neighbourhoods are appreciated for their unique and distinctive, rather than their common, features. Nevertheless meanings have to be constructed and sustained, for they remain open to challenge. The radical doubt characteristic of modernity induces perpetual re-evaluation of the truthfulness and efficacy of collective perceptions of space. Under such conditions Benjamin's formulation of the way that personal experience and dominant meanings grate upon one another provides an axis for the appreciation of the role of the symbolic in urban social conflict.

Observing the diversity and plurality of images of place reminds us that imagery is created and can be manipulated. Many actors, from estate agents to local authorities, have vested interests in presenting places in their most favourable light. Increasingly, local authorities try to present their own area as appealing, sometimes to tourists, sometimes to affluent households. If people generally can be persuaded to think a neighbourhood 'good', an old town 'historic', or a downtown 'exciting', then a place may attract residents who can pay higher local taxes, new commercial opportunities may arise and additional jobs may be generated. A reputation for distinctiveness and quality is beneficial. The economic strategies of the local state represent the reassertion of the dull compulsion of economic life even in the sphere of memory and the imaginary. Indeed, in the urban manifestations of the consumer-culture may be discerned the coincidence of the relentless impulse of capital accumulation and many of the dreams and aspirations of personal life. [. . .]

Notes

1   *Flâneur*: a term associated with Baudelaire and Benjamin: the man of the crowd, the strolling and loitering inhabitant of the modern city.

References

Benjamin, W. 1978. *One Way Street and Other Writings*. London: Verso.
Bianchini, F. 1991. 'Cultural Policy and Urban Development: The Experience of West European Cities', a paper delivered to Eighth Urban Change and Conflict Conference, Lancaster University.

Buck-Morss, S. 1989. *The Dialects of Seeing: Walter Benjamin and the Arcades Project*. Cambridge, Mass.: MIT Press.

Connor, S. 1989. *Postmodernist Culture*. Oxford: Blackwell.

Davis, M. 1985. 'Urban Renaissance and the Spirit of Postmodernism', *New Left Review* 151, 106–14.

Featherstone, M. 1987. 'Lifestyle and Consumer Culture', in *Theory, Culture and Society* 4, 1, 55–70.

Frisby, D. 1985. *Fragments of Modernity: Theories of Modernity in the Work of Simmel, Kracauer and Benjamin*. Cambridge: Polity.

Giddens, A. 1981. *A Contemporary Critique of Historical Materialism*. Berkeley: University of California Press.

Giddens, A. 1990. *The Consequences of Modernity*. Cambridge: Polity.

Giddens, A. 1991. *Modernity and Self Identity*. Cambridge: Polity.

Harvey, D. 1989. *The Condition of Postmodernity*. Oxford: Blackwell.

Jameson, F. 1984. 'Postmodernism, or the Cultural Logic of Late Capitalism', *New Left Review* 146, 53–92.

Jameson, F. 1991. *Postmodernism, or, the Cultural Logic of Late Capitalism*. London: Verso.

Jencks, C. 1984. *The Language of Postmodern Architecture*. London: Academy.

Lash, S. 1990. *A Sociology of Postmodernism*. London: Routledge.

Lash, S. and Urry, J. 1987. *The End of Organized Capitalism*. Cambridge, Mass.: Polity.

Lyotard, J.-F. 1979. *The Postmodern Condition*. Manchester: Manchester University Press.

Shields, R. 1989. 'Social Spatialisation and the Built Environment: The Case of the West Edmonton Mall', *Society and Space* 7, 2, 147–64.

Shields, R. 1992. 'A Truant Proximity: Presence and Absence in the Space of Modernity', *Environment and Planning D: Society and Space* 10, 2, 181–98.

Smart, B. 1992. *Modern Conditions, Postmodern Controversies*. London: Routledge.

Urry, J. 1990. *The Tourist Gaze*. London: Sage.

Venturi, R. Scott Brown, D. and Izenour, S. 1977. *Learning from Las Vegas*. Cambridge, Mass.: MIT.

Wishart, R. 1991. 'Fashioning the Future: Glasgow', in M. Fisher and U. Owen (eds.), *Whose Cities?* Harmondsworth: Penguin, 43–52.

Wright, P. 1991. *A Journey Through the Ruins*. London: Paladin.

Zorbaugh, H. W. 1983. *The Gold Coast and the Slum*. Chicago: University of Chicago Press.

Zukin, S. 1992. 'Postmodern Urban Landscapes: Mapping Culture and Power', in S. Lash and J. Friedman (eds.), *Modernity and Identity*. Oxford: Blackwell, 221–47.

Part II

Globalization and Its Impact on Cities

6 Overview of Global Cities

Saskia Sassen

> Saskia Sassen's work focused the attention of sociologists on the process of economic globalization and its consequences for cities. Her book, *The Global City*, was a groundbreaking study of the impact of economic globalization on three cities: New York, London, and Tokyo.
>
> Sassen shows that, despite their historical and cultural differences, the three cities are changing in parallel ways because they perform similar functions in the world economy. Those functions include control and coordination of global production processes, control of financial markets, and sites for the production of corporate services. Sassen points out the many social changes that have occurred in these three cities, including increases in immigration and growing polarization between the rich and the poor.

For centuries, the world economy has shaped the life of cities. Beginning in the 1960s, the organization of economic activity entered a period of pronounced transformation. The changes were expressed in the altered structure of the world economy, and also assumed forms specific to particular places. Certain of these changes are by now familiar: the dismantling of once-powerful industrial centers in the United States, the United Kingdom, and more recently in Japan; the accelerated industrialization of several Third World countries; the rapid internationalization of the financial industry into a worldwide network of transactions. Each of these changes altered the relation of cities to the international economy.

In the decades after World War II, there was an international regime based on United States dominance in the world economy and the rules for global trade contained in the 1945 Bretton Woods agreement. By the early 1970s, the conditions supporting that regime were disintegrating. The breakdown created a void into which stepped, perhaps in a last burst of national dominance, the large US transnational industrial firms and banks. In this period of transition, the

Sassen, Saskia, "Overview of Global Cities." From *The Global City: New York, London, Tokyo* (New Brunswick, NJ: Rutgers University Press, 1991), pp. 3–12. © Princeton University Press. Reprinted by permission of Princeton University Press.

management of the international economic order was to an inordinate extent run from the headquarters of these firms. By the early 1980s, however, the large US transnational banks faced the massive Third World debt crisis, and US industrial firms experienced sharp market share losses from foreign competition. Yet the international economy did not simply break into fragments. The geography and composition of the global economy changed so as to produce a complex duality: a spatially dispersed, yet globally integrated organization of economic activity.

The point of departure for the present study is that the combination of spatial dispersal and global integration has created a new strategic role for major cities. Beyond their long history as centers for international trade and banking, these cities now function in four new ways: first, as highly concentrated command points in the organization of the world economy; second, as key locations for finance and for specialized service firms, which have replaced manufacturing as the leading economic sectors; third, as sites of production, including the production of innovations, in these leading industries; and fourth, as markets for the products and innovations produced. These changes in the functioning of cities have had a massive impact upon both international economic activity and urban form: Cities concentrate control over vast resources, while finance and specialized service industries have restructured the urban social and economic order. Thus a new type of city has appeared. It is the global city. Leading examples now are New York, London, and Tokyo.

As I shall show, these three cities have undergone massive and *parallel* changes in their economic base, spatial organization, and social structure. But this parallel development is a puzzle. How could cities with as diverse a history, culture, politics, and economy as New York, London, and Tokyo experience similar transformations concentrated in so brief a period of time? Not examined at length in my study, but important to its theoretical framework, is how transformations in cities ranging from Paris to Frankfurt to Hong Kong and São Paulo have responded to the same dynamic. To understand the puzzle of parallel change in diverse cities requires not simply a point-by-point comparison of New York, London, and Tokyo, but a situating of these cities in a set of global processes. In order to understand why major cities with different histories and cultures have undergone parallel economic and social changes, we need to examine transformations in the world economy. Yet the term *global city* may be reductive and misleading if it suggests that cities are mere outcomes of a global economic machine. They are specific places whose spaces, internal dynamics, and social structure matter; indeed, we may be able to understand the global order only by analyzing why key structures of the world economy are *necessarily* situated in cities.

How does the position of these cities in the world economy today differ from that which they have historically held as centers of banking and trade? When Max Weber analyzed the medieval cities woven together in the Hanseatic League, he conceived their trade as the exchange of surplus production; it was his view that a medieval city could withdraw from external trade and continue to support itself, albeit on a reduced scale. The modern molecule of global cities is nothing like the trade among self-sufficient places in the Hanseatic League, as Weber understood it. [My] first thesis is that the territorial dispersal of current economic activity creates a need for expanded central control and management. In other words, while in principle the territorial decentralization of economic activity in recent years could have been accompanied by a corresponding decentralization in ownership and hence in the appropriation of profits, there has been little movement in that direction. Though large firms have increased their subcontracting to smaller firms, and many national firms in the newly industrializing countries have grown rapidly, this form of growth is ultimately part of a chain. Even industrial homeworkers in remote rural areas are now part of that chain. The transnational corporations continue to control much of the end product and to reap the profits associated with selling in the world market. The internationalization and expansion of the financial industry has brought growth to a large number of smaller financial markets, a growth which has fed the expansion of the global industry. But top-level control and management of the industry has become concentrated in a few leading financial centers, notably New York, London, and Tokyo. These account for a disproportionate share of all financial transactions and one that has grown rapidly since the early 1980s. The fundamental dynamic posited here is that the more globalized the economy becomes, the higher the agglomeration of central functions in a relatively few sites, that is, the global cities.

The extremely high densities evident in the business districts of these cities are one spatial expression of this logic. The widely accepted notion that density and agglomeration will become obsolete because global telecommunications advances allow for maximum population and resource dispersal is poorly conceived. It is, I argue, precisely because of the territorial dispersal facilitated by telecommunication that agglomeration of certain centralizing activities has sharply increased. This is not a mere continuation of old patterns of agglomeration; there is a new logic for concentration. In Weberian terms, there is a new system of "coordination," one which focuses on the development of specific geographic control sites in the international economic order.

[My] second major theme concerns the impact of this type of economic growth on the economic order within these cities. It is necessary to go beyond the Weberian notion of coordination and Bell's (1973) notion of the postindustrial society to understand this new urban order. Bell, like Weber, assumes that the further society evolves from nineteenth-century industrial capitalism, the more the apex of the social order is involved in pure managerial process, with the content of what is to be managed becoming of secondary importance. Global cities are, however, not only nodal points for the coordination of processes (Friedmann 1986); they are also particular sites of production. They are sites for (1) the production of specialized services needed by complex organizations for running a spatially dispersed network of factories, offices, and service outlets; and (2) the production of financial innovations and the making of markets, both central to the internationalization and expansion of the financial industry. To understand the structure of a global city, we have to understand it as a place where certain kinds of work can get done, which is to say that we have to get beyond the dichotomy between manufacturing and services. The "things" a global city makes are services and financial goods.

It is true that high-level business services, from accounting to economic consulting, are not usually analyzed as a production process. Such services are usually seen as a type of output derived from high-level technical knowledge. I challenge this view. Moreover, using new scholarship on producer services, I shall examine the extent to which a key trait of global cities is that they are the most *advanced* production sites for creating these services. [. . .]

[My] third major theme concerns the consequences of these developments for the national urban system in each of these countries and for the relationship of the global city to its nation-state. While a few major cities are the sites of production for the new global control capability, a large number of other major cities have lost their role as leading export centers for industrial manufacturing, as a result of the decentralization of this form of production. Cities such as Detroit, Liverpool, Manchester, and now increasingly Nagoya and Osaka have been affected by the decentralization of their key industries at the domestic and international levels. According to the first hypothesis presented above, this same process has contributed to the growth of service industries that produce the specialized inputs to run global production processes and global markets for inputs and outputs. These industries – international legal and accounting services, management consulting, financial services – are heavily concentrated in cities such as New York, London, and Tokyo. We need to know how this growth alters the relations between the global cities and what were once the leading industrial centers in their nations. Does globalization bring about a triangulation so that New York, for example, now plays a role in the fortunes of Detroit that it did not play when that city was home to one of the leading industries, auto manufacturing? Or, in the case of Japan, we need to ask, for example, if there is a connection between the increasing shift of production out of Toyota City (Nagoya) to offshore locations (Thailand, South Korea, and the United States) and the development for the first time of a new headquarters for Toyota in Tokyo.

Similarly, there is a question about the relation between such major cities as Chicago, Osaka, and Manchester, once leading industrial centers in the world, and global markets generally. Both Chicago and Osaka were and continue to be important financial centers on the basis of their manufacturing industries. We would want to know if they have lost ground, relatively, in these functions as a result of their decline in the global industrial market, or instead have undergone parallel transformation toward strengthening of service functions. Chicago, for example, was at the heart of a massive agroindustrial complex, a vast regional economy. How has the decline of that regional economic system affected Chicago?

In all these questions, it is a matter of understanding what growth embedded in the international system of producer services and finance has entailed for different levels in the national urban hierarchy. The broader trends – decentralization of plants, offices, and service outlets, along with the expansion of central functions as a consequence of the need to manage such decentralized organization of firms – may well have created conditions contributing to the growth of regional subcenters, minor versions of what New York, London, and Tokyo do on a global and national scale. The extent to which the developments posited for New York, London, and Tokyo are also replicated, perhaps in less accentuated form, in smaller cities, at lower levels of the urban hierarchy, is an open, but important, question.

The new international forms of economic activity raise a problem about the relationship between nation-states and global cities. The relation between city and nation is the political dimension of the economic changes I explore. I posit the possibility of a systemic discontinuity between what used to be thought of as national growth and the forms of growth evident in global cities in the 1980s. These cities constitute a system rather than merely competing with each other. What contributes to growth in the network of global cities may well not contribute to growth in nations. For instance, is there a systemic relation between, on the one hand, the growth in global cities and, on the other hand, the deficits of national governments and the decline of major industrial centers in each of these countries?

[My] fourth and final theme concerns the impact of these new forms of and conditions for growth on the social order of the global city. There is a vast body of literature on the impact of a dynamic, high-growth manufacturing sector in the highly developed countries, which shows that it raised wages, reduced inequality, and contributed to the formation of a middle class. Much less is known about the sociology of a service economy. Daniel Bell's (1973) *The Coming of Post-Industrial Society* posits that such an economy will result in growth in the number of highly educated workers and a more rational relation of workers to issues of social equity. One could argue that any city representing a post-industrial economy would surely be like the leading sectors of New York, London, and increasingly Tokyo.

I examine to what extent the new structure of economic activity has brought about changes in the organization of work, reflected in a shift in the job supply and polarization in the income distribution and occupational distribution of workers. Major growth industries show a greater incidence of jobs at the high- and low-paying ends of the scale than do the older industries now in decline. Almost half the jobs in the producer services are lower-income jobs, and half are in the two highest earnings classes. In contrast, a large share of manufacturing workers were in the middle-earnings jobs during the postwar period of high growth in these industries in the United States and United Kingdom.

Two other developments in global cities have also contributed to economic polarization. One is the vast supply of low-wage jobs required by high-income gentrification in both its residential and commercial settings. The increase in the numbers of expensive restaurants, luxury housing, luxury hotels, gourmet shops, boutiques, French hand laundries, and special cleaners that ornament the new urban landscape illustrates this trend. Furthermore, there is a continuing need for low-wage industrial services, even in such sectors as finance and specialized services. A second development that has reached significant proportions is what I call the downgrading of the manufacturing sector, a process in which the share of unionized shops declines and wages deteriorate while sweatshops and industrial homework proliferate. This process includes the downgrading of jobs within existing industries and the job supply patterns of some of the new industries, notably electronics assembly. It is worth noting that the growth of a downgraded manufacturing sector has been strongest in cities such as New York and London.

The expansion of low-wage jobs as a function of *growth* trends implies a reorganization of the capital–labor relation. To see this, it is important to distinguish the characteristics of jobs from their sectoral location, since highly dynamic, technologically advanced growth sectors may well contain low-wage dead-end jobs. Furthermore, the distinction between sectoral characteristics and sectoral growth patterns is crucial: Backward sectors, such as downgraded manufacturing or low-wage service occupations, can be part of major growth trends in a highly developed economy. It is often assumed that backward sectors express decline trends. Similarly, there is a tendency to assume that advanced sectors, such as finance, have mostly good, white-collar jobs. In fact, they contain a good number of low-paying jobs, from cleaner to stock clerk.

[There are several] reasons why producer services and finance have grown so rapidly since the 1970s and why they are so highly concentrated in cities such as New York, London, and Tokyo. The familiar explanation is that the decade of the 1980s was but a part of a larger economic trend, the shift to services. And the simple explanation of their high concentration in major cities is that this is because of the need for face-to-face communication in the services community. While correct, these cliches are incomplete.

 We need to understand first how modern technology has not ended nineteenth-century forms of work; rather, technology has shifted a number of activities that were once part of manufacturing into the domain of services. The transfer of skills from workers to machines once epitomized by the assembly line has a present-day version in the transfer of a variety of activities from the shop floor into computers, with their attendant technical and professional personnel. Also, functional specialization within early factories finds a contemporary counterpart in today's pronounced fragmentation of the work process spatially and organizationally. This has been called the "global assembly line," the production and assembly of goods from factories and depots throughout the world, wherever labor costs and economies of scale make an international division of labor cost-effective. It is, however, this very "global assembly line" that creates the need for increased centralization and complexity of management, control, and planning. The development of the modern corporation and its massive participation in world markets and foreign countries has made planning, internal administration, product development, and research increasingly important and complex. Diversification of product lines, mergers, and transnationalization of economic activities all require highly specialized skills in top-level management (Chandler 1977). These have also "increased the dependence of the corporation on producer services, which in turn has fostered growth and development of higher levels of expertise among producer service firms" (Stanback and Noyelle 1982: 15). What were once support resources for major corporations have become crucial inputs in corporate decisionmaking. A firm with a multiplicity of geographically dispersed manufacturing plants contributes to the development of new types of planning in production and distribution surrounding the firm.

The growth of international banks and the more recent diversification of the financial industry have also expanded the demand for highly specialized service inputs. In the 1960s and 1970s, there was considerable geographic dispersal in the banking industry, with many regional centers and offshore locations mostly involved in fairly traditional banking. The diversification and internationalization of finance over the last decade resulted in a strong trend toward concentrating the "management" of the global industry and the production of financial innovations in a more limited number of major locations. This dynamic is not unlike that of multisite manufacturing or service firms.

Major trends toward the development of multisite manufacturing, service, and banking have created an expanded demand for a wide range of specialized service activities to manage and control global networks of factories, service outlets, and branch offices. While to some extent these activities can be carried out in-house, a large share of them cannot. High levels of specialization, the possibility of externalizing the production of some of these services, and the growing demand by large and small firms and by governments are all conditions that have both resulted from and made possible the development of a market for freestanding service firms that produce components for what I refer to as global control capability.

The growth of advanced services for firms, here referred to as producer services, along with their particular characteristics of production, helps to explain the centralization of management and servicing functions that has fueled the economic boom of the early and mid-1980s in New York, London, and Tokyo. The face-to-face explanation needs to be refined in several ways. Advanced services are mostly producer services; unlike other types of services, they are not dependent on proximity to the consumers served. Rather, such specialized firms benefit from and need to locate close to other firms who produce key inputs or whose proximity makes possible joint production of certain service offerings. The accounting firm can service its clients at a distance but the nature of its service depends on proximity to other specialists, from lawyers to programmers. Major corporate transactions today typically require simultaneous participation of several specialized firms providing legal, accounting, financial, public relations, management consulting, and other such services. Moreover, concentration arises out of the needs and expectations of the high-income workers employed in these firms. They are attracted to the amenities and lifestyles that large urban centers can offer and are likely to live in central areas rather than in suburbs. [...]

References

Bell, Daniel. 1973. *The Coming of Post-Industrial Society: A Venture in Social Forecasting.* New York: Basic Books.

Chandler, Alfred. 1977. *The Visible Hand: The Manager in American Business.* Cambridge, Mass.: Harvard University Press.

Friedmann, J. 1986. "The World City Hypothesis." *Development and Change* 17(1): 69–83.

Stanback, Thomas M., Jr., and Thierry J. Noyelle. 1982. *Cities in Transition: Changing Job Structures in Atlanta, Denver, Buffalo, Phoenix, Columbus (Ohio), Nashville, Charlotte.* Totowa, NJ: Allanheld, Osmun.

7 The Urban–Rural Interface and Migration

Alan Gilbert and Josef Gugler

Although most of the readings in this volume focus on the cities of the industrialized nations, the globalization of the economy has also had a huge impact on third world nations. One of the most persistent trends is massive and continuing migration of people from the countryside to the cities, usually to a single large city. Urban-bound migrants, often confined to squatter settlements, face poverty, homelessness, illness, and unemployment. Yet their numbers continue to grow.

In this reading, Alan Gilbert and Josef Gugler explain why, if there are few jobs or services for newcomers to the cities, people continue to migrate. Their answer is that, although the prospect for work may be uncertain in the cities, the prospects in the countryside are even worse. The global economy has made small-scale agriculture impractical, thus forcing rural people off the land and increasing the gap in living standards between the city and countryside. These circumstances will contribute to the growth of very large cities in developing nations for the foreseeable future.

Until the nineteenth century, many rural populations had little connection with urban centres. They lived in quite self-centred societies. They operated subsistence economies maintaining only limited external contacts. [T]he expansion of the capitalist system, however, under way for half a millennium and accelerated by the Industrial Revolution, incorporated ever more outlying regions into the emerging world economy (Wallerstein, 1974, 1980, 1989; Chase-Dunn, 1989). Existing cities were integrated into the new system, their functions transformed. New cities were established to exercise political control and to channel resources to the metropolitan centres. And rural populations all over the world have been drawn into the urban nexus.

Gilbert, Alan and Josef Gugler, "The Urban–Rural Interface and Migration." From *Cities, Poverty, and Development* (Oxford: Oxford University Press, 1992), pp. 62–4, 66–73. Copyright © Oxford University Press.

The process of incorporation into the world system has spread across the entire globe. The self-centred society that had only limited contact with the outside world has virtually disappeared. Rural populations have become subject to political control exerted from urban centres. Coerced to provide labour, conscripted into the army, and subjected to taxation, they became part of colonial or national polities – even while they remained by and large disenfranchised.

Along with political incorporation has come economic incorporation. Rural populations began to produce for urban markets. Or they went to work on plantations, in mines, or indeed in the cities. Whether they sell their products on the market or their own labour, they are part of a far-reaching economic system, a system which is beyond their control. They experience the vagaries of the world economic system: their earnings from a crop are depressed by a sudden drop in its price on the world market, they lose their jobs during a recession. At the same time, their culture is transformed as they are indoctrinated by foreign missionaries, taught in schools according to curricula mandated by urban élites, and exposed to radio programmes, films, and most recently television series, produced in distant cities, some of them half-way across the globe.

For many peoples the incorporation into the world capitalist system was traumatic. American Indians were forced into the *encomienda*. Africans were enslaved and shipped to the Americas. Indians and Chinese were sent around the globe as indentured labour. Colonial governments conscripted labour. Eventually, the imposition of taxes provided a more subtle means of coercion: unless they grew cash crops or sold some of their cattle, people were forced to earn wages to pay their taxes.

Nearly everywhere incorporation created new desires in the rural areas that only money could satisfy. The high degree of self-sufficiency of traditional farmers thus was ever more compromised as they became dependent on goods and services in the market. Today rural populations need cash to settle taxes, purchase manufactured goods, and pay school fees. Some continue to farm their own lands. Many no longer own their land; they have become proletarians: some are tenant farmers or share-croppers at the mercy of landowners, others have become wage-earners on plantations, in mines, or in the cities.

Some rural populations were exploited to such an extent that their living conditions declined. Elsewhere, specific groups experienced pauperization. For most rural dwellers, however, living conditions improved; in terms of better health and longer life the change was usually dramatic. However, these same improvements accelerated population growth, and population pressure on the available land became severe in many areas.

Incorporation into the world system brought considerable differentiation to what had frequently been quite egalitarian societies. Certainly, many had known severe inequalities in the past. Captured enemies were held as slaves, entire people were subjugated and forced to provide goods and services for their masters. Still, a measure of equality founded on general access to land was the more common pattern. In any case, as these societies became part of larger societies, new

elements of differentiation came to the fore. The first to be converted by
aries and to attend their schools had a head start in employment as
government officials, or commercial clerks. The first to accumulate a little
in employment, or from the sale of their crops, established themselves as tra
transporters. And the first to become agents for the colonial government (...e
independent state expanded their control over land or derived the benefits that
flow from wielding patronage. Rural populations thus came to experience relative
deprivation. As incorporation proceeded, they recognized their own poverty: they
saw a few in their midst rise to levels of affluence undreamt of in the past, and
they came face to face with the life-style of outsiders – missionaries, traders,
government officials, foreign experts, and tourists.

With the perception of a better life enjoyed by a few came an awareness of the
means towards such an end. Throughout the world today few are the rural
dwellers who have not sold and bought in markets or shops, who have not seen
what a school certificate can do for the future of a child, who have not listened to
a firsthand account of work in the city. Some improve their condition while
staying where they were born, or moving to other rural areas as farmers, traders,
or artisans. But rural prospects appear dim to many, the urban scene more promising. [...]

Why People Move

According to the substantial body of research on rural–urban migration which has
accumulated over the last three decades the evidence is overwhelming: most people
move for economic reasons. When people are asked why they moved, they usually
cite the better prospects in the urban economy as their chief reason. Also, migration streams between regions have been shown to correspond to income differentials between those regions. And over time, as economic conditions at alternative
destinations change, migration streams alternate accordingly.

Material considerations are of prime importance to most people. Certainly, poor
people who ignore their material circumstances are rapidly threatened in their very
survival. Migration entails costs, economic and frequently psychological, as well as
risks. Those migrants who are not motivated by the prospect of material rewards
are a minority. The 'bright lights' theory of rural–urban migration has enjoyed a
certain vogue, but the simple fact is that most new arrivals do not have the means
to spend much time in bars, dance halls, or movie theatres. Indeed, many people,
when the rural environment where they have grown up offers a similar standard of
living and equivalent prospects for their children, prefer to stay rather than move
to the city. As Hemalata Dandekar (1986: 216–20) reports:

> I asked [a textile worker] if he didn't prefer to live in Bombay. Wouldn't he miss the
> excitement if he went back to live in Sugao, I wondered. 'What kind of question is that?'

he said. 'There is no question about it. Of course I would live at home if I could make enough money there.' Waving his arm to encompass the dirty pavement and the roaring pedestrian and vehicular traffic outside the door of the Sugao *talim* (exercise place) where we were sitting, he said, 'There's no excitement here, the air smells of the mills, the food is bad, and there is nowhere to go for a walk that isn't as crowded as this.' He was right. It did smell of the mills. We were in the heart of the textile area of the city, and the nearest beaches, which are literally the lungs for congested Bombay, would be packed with the city's population strolling shoulder to shoulder. 'In Sugao,' he continued, 'at least the fields are open and the breeze from the hills is fresh, the *bhakari* made in one's own home tastes so much sweeter than what the *khanawal bai* (the woman who prepares meals for pay) throws on your plate here.' Bombay, the queen of India's cities, with its thriving commerce, cosmopolitan and heterogenous population, more open society, and huge entertainment industry, has little to offer one in his economic class. Working long days in the textile mill, he earns barely enough to maintain himself in the city and his family in the village in a very modest lifestyle. He has little surplus income with which to splurge on the city's luxuries and allurements.

The sight of severe and widespread poverty in Third World cities easily leads to the assumption that migrants do not know what to expect, that illusions about the prospects lying ahead bring them to an urban environment in which they find themselves trapped. This happens occasionally. Grindal's (1973) account of a group of northern Ghanaian immigrants in Accra suggests that they had been misled by returning migrants who described the South as a land of great wealth, where the buildings are many storeys high, where the people ride in cars or on bicycles, where the 'social life' abounds, and where one can earn money for things such as bicycles, clothing, and finery. Such myths were perpetuated by returning migrants who wished to build up their image and their exploits. They underplayed the problems they had encountered in the cities of the South. For successor migrants whose expectations had thus been raised, the first contact with southern urban life was an unexpected and often shattering experience. Their pride forced many to remain in the South in order to spare themselves the humiliation of coming home in poverty.

Studies not limited to a small ethnic group tell a different story. Caldwell (1969: 122) surveyed predominantly migrant areas in the four principal cities of Ghana. Nearly two-thirds of the migrants said that life in the town approximated what they thought it would be. Among those whose experiences did not match their expectations, almost half had been overly apprehensive about urban conditions. Only about one in six migrants had been disappointed. The unexpected disappointments of the town divided almost evenly into less economic opportunity than anticipated and greater problems. Studies throughout the Third World similarly report, time and again, that most migrants consider that they have improved their condition. They are satisfied with their move.

The relative success of most migration is due in large part to the fact that it is embedded in social relations. Migrating is not a solitary affair. The days when elders disapproved of young men 'running' away and left them no alternative but to abscond at night (Banton, 1957: 48–59; Rouch, 1956; Skinner, 1965: 67) are long past. Going to town became the thing to do. Patterns of migration were established. The urban experience took on positive connotations. Thus, in the 1950s, young men in many parts of the Sudanic belt were expected to spend one or several spells of seasonal migration in Ghana (Rouch, 1956). Cultural norms exalted the challenge to the young to prove themselves, the experience to be gained. Such norms can become so generally established that individuals are swept along even when they do not share the economic rationale for going to the city.

Today, rural communities virtually everywhere accept the outmigration of young adults. Communities have developed migration strategies. Their strategies are informed by the experience of migrants who have kept in touch, who return to the village on visits or to stay, and by villagers who have visited kin and friends in the city. These strategies are modified over time as experience dictates. Potential migrants are thus presented with quite well-defined options.

The decision to migrate in turn is rarely an individual one, rather it is usually a family decision. Much rural–urban migration of individuals is part of a family strategy to ensure the viability of the rural household (van Velsen, 1960; Arizpe, 1981). Parry (1979: 44–5) characterizes the situation in a region in northernmost India in these terms:

> Kangra . . . is a district with a high population density and insufficient land to meet even the barest subsistence requirements of its people. A large proportion of the adult men are forced to look for work outside, but because even the smallest holdings offer a degree of security and even the most factious kin groups will preserve their own from total destitution, few abandon their villages altogether. These social and demographic conditions allow the city access to a vast pool of cheap labour; while – to a significant degree – the urban economy supplies the material base for the perpetuation of the rural social structure . . . Provided that it is understood that the local community only maintains itself as a community to the extent that it retains its peasant basis, we might characterize the Kangra economy as a remittance economy backed up by subsistence agriculture.

The family character of the migration decision is obvious where young women are sent out to supplement the family income from their urban wages – Trager (1988) gives an account of such a strategy from the Philippines; Kate Young (1982) traces the 'expulsion' of young daughters from rural Oaxaca, Mexico, to the requirements of their parental households. The migration decision appears as more of an individual decision where migrants are family heads who take family decisions largely on their own.

Finally, migrants typically receive considerable assistance in the move, in adapting to the urban environment, in securing a foothold in the urban economy. In a sample of blue- and white-collar workers who had moved to Bombay, over three-quarters had one or more relatives living in the city. More than half gave this as an important factor for choosing Bombay over another city. Nine out of ten reported that they had been assisted by relatives or friends on their arrival: about two-thirds received free accommodation and food, and two-thirds of the blue-collar workers and over one-third of the white-collar workers acknowledged help in finding a job (Gore, 1971: 48–52, 62–7). Similar accounts abound. Indeed, in some cases potential migrants wait in their village until their urban contacts signal a job opportunity.

Kin groups can mobilize greater resources than nuclear families. Frequently a wide range of relatives can be drawn on to help pay for an education for the future migrant, provide a home for children who are sent to town to go to school, offer the newly arrived migrant shelter and food for a while, take care of parents and assist wife and children who stay behind. The extended family thus acts as an agent of urbanization (Flanagan, 1977; Eames, 1967).

The push from rural areas and the pull of urban areas are often distinguished in discussions of migration. Indicating push or pull stresses a particular motive in the decision to migrate. Refugees, for example, may be said to be pushed out of their rural homes. During the civil strife that followed the Partition of India in 1947, about 16 million people fled across the newly established boundaries. Most of those uprooted from rural areas sought a new beginning in cities. War, the man-made calamity, frequently makes rural areas insecure so that peasants pack up and leave for the relative security of cities. During the many years of the blood-bath in Indo-China, peasants sought shelter in the cities. Many others were relocated by force. In Indonesia, the independence struggle, as well as regional rebellions following independence, led to a mass exodus from the affected rural areas. Civil wars in Malaysia, the Sudan, Zaïre, Ethiopia, Chad, Angola, and Mozambique made peasants abandon their ancestral lands. In Colombia *la violencia*, the violent conflict in the countryside which lasted for over a decade, was a major force in rural–urban migration.

Elsewhere droughts, earthquakes, cyclones, volcanoes, or floods have brought not only immediate physical danger, but threatened hunger and disease as well. Such disasters thus frequently force rural dwellers to abandon their homes and seek relief in urban areas. They are commonly referred to as 'natural', but they are man-made to the extent that political action, or inaction, increases the severity of their impact. Thus the famines of the 1970s and 1980s in sub-Saharan Africa were not simply the outcome of an act of nature. They must be traced first and foremost to government policies. Policies that did little to develop rural areas, leaving much of the peasantry in a precarious condition, resourceless to deal with a natural calamity. The peasantry was disadvantaged in general, and few specific efforts were made to render marginal lands less prone to drought, for example by supporting well construction or reafforestation. Indeed, many rural areas lack the roads to carry relief supplies: the hungry have no alternative but to move to urban areas or camps. Urban decision-makers' disregard for the rural masses was exposed when some governments, refusing to acknowledge famine conditions, delayed relief operations. There is also the culpability of rich countries: in an age of highly productive agriculture in major parts of the world, and efficient global transport, there is no justification for hunger anywhere.

When men instigate wars, when they are unable to control the elements, or unwilling to help fellow men in their struggle with nature, entire populations become refugees. There are also less noticeable refugees, individuals who, having fallen foul of the rural community, or the locally powerful, seek refuge in the city.

The push from rural areas is dramatized in the case of refugees. Even in such extreme cases, however, it can be seen that a comparison is at stake: the refugees move to more secure settings. The decision to migrate involves choosing among locations. This is also true where the pull looms large. To take the archetypal case, joining the Gold Rush implied a perception of more limited opportunities at home.

Discussions of rural–urban migration, and of changes over time, tend to focus on the urban labour market. The rural areas, however, are experiencing major transformations that have profound effects on migration. First of all, population pressure on land increases as the rural population continues to grow in most Third World countries: natural population growth in the rural areas exceeds outmigration in all but some already highly urbanized countries. Second, access to land is transformed: communal land tenure breaks down, land becomes concentrated in the hands of the rural wealthy and absentee landlords, even while elsewhere land is redistributed under land reform programmes. Third, agricultural labour is made redundant in some countries through a shift to either extensive farming such as cattle ranching or to capital-intensive farming such as the introduction of tractors. Fourth, as rural areas become more fully incorporated into national and international markets, they become increasingly subject to the price dictates of markets, some of them free, many government-regulated.

Migrating to Join the Unemployed?

Rural–urban migration continues unabated throughout the Third World. 'Why do so many come', the question usually goes, 'when urban unemployment is widespread and underemployment common?' To which a peasant might respond with the counter-question: 'Why do so few go, when the rural–urban gap is so unmistakable?' Two interpretations explain migratory behaviour under these circumstances. Both establish that the decision to migrate is a rational response to economic conditions. Variations in the structure of urban labour markets account for the difference between the two interpretations.

In Tropical Africa, analysis focused on migrants coming in search of jobs that offered wages and working conditions regulated by legislation and/or collective bargaining. They would spend several months trying to secure such a job but, if unsuccessful, eventually return to the village. Thus in Kampala, Uganda, Hutton (1973: 61–2) found a clearly established pattern in the middle 1960s. Of the unemployed men she interviewed, three-quarters intended to leave if they could not find work, typically within less than six months. More than three-quarters of these intended to return to their rural home. Going home, however, was only a temporary measure: only 11 per cent of the unemployed surveyed said that they would stay there.

In the 1950s and 1960s much urban unemployment in tropical Africa conformed to this pattern. With independence, urban wages rose substantially in many countries – the advent of independence raised expectations that governments had to meet at least to some extent. Rural–urban migration surged, the labour shortages that had plagued colonial governments vanished, and urban unemployment appeared. Much labour migration had been short-term, and new immigrants faced little competition from entrenched urban workers and their descendants. Moreover, independence was frequently accompanied by a significant rise in urban employment. The system of recruiting unskilled labour approximated a random process. Since minimum wages were high, relative to rural incomes, even an extended job search was a promising strategy. Joining the urban unemployed, rural–urban migrants tried their luck at the urban job lottery. [. . .]

In retrospect it is clear that the urban job lottery pattern occurred in exceptional circumstances. More commonly, labour turnover is low, job creation slow, and recruitment anything but random. A more widely applicable interpretation of rural–urban migration has to focus on the fact that urban labour markets, like many markets, are fragmented in a variety of ways, i.e. different categories of people enjoy differential access to earning opportunities. [A]ccess is usually largely a function of three criteria: education and training, patronage, and gender. Differential access in turn shapes the composition of the migrant stream. The role of formal education as a prerequisite for access to the more privileged strata motivates parents in rural areas and small towns to relocate with their children or to send their children away to better or more prestigious schools. For those who have climbed the educational ladder, the most attractive career opportunities are in the city. Others, while not so fortunate, have the right connections and come with reasonable assurance that the assistance of their kinsman, fellow villager, or patron will get them a job. Women, finally, are disadvantaged in the urban labour markets of the Third World, as everywhere else, but their migratory response varies across major Third World regions. [. . .]

References

Arizpe, L. 1981. 'Relay migration and the survival of the peasant household.' In *Why People Move: Comparative Perspectives on the Dynamics of Internal Migration*, ed. J. Balán. Paris: Unesco Press.

Banton, M. 1957. *West African City: A Study of Tribal Life in Freetown*. Oxford: Oxford University Press.

Caldwell, J. C. 1969. *African Rural–Urban Migration: The Movement to Ghana's Towns*. New York: Columbia University Press.

Chase-Dunn, C. 1989. *Global Formation: Structures of the World-Economy*. Oxford: Blackwell.

Dandekar, H. C. 1986. *Men to Bombay, Women at Home: Urban Influence on Sugao Village, Deccan Maharashtra, India, 1942–1982*. Michigan Papers on South and Southeast Asia, Center for South and Southeast Asian Studies, University of Michigan.

Eames, E. 1967. 'Urban migration and the joint family in a North Indian village.' *Journal of Developing Areas* 1: 163–78.

Flanagan, W. G. 1977. 'The extended family as an agent in urbanization: a survey of men and women working in Dar es Salaam, Tanzania.' Ph.D. dissertation, University of Connecticut.

Gore, M. S. 1971. *Immigrants and Neighborhoods: Two Aspects of Life in a Metropolitan City*. Bombay: Tata Institute of Social Sciences.

Grindal, B. T. 1973. 'Islamic Affiliations with urban adaptations: the Sisala migrant in Accra, Ghana.' *Africa* 43: 333–46.

Hutton, C. 1973. *Reluctant Farmers? A Study of Unemployment and Planned Rural Development in Uganda*. East African Publishing.

Parry, J. P. 1979. *Caste and Kinship in Kangra*. New York: Routledge & Kegan Paul.

Rouch, J. 1956. 'Migrations au Ghana (Gold Coast): enquête 1953–1955.' *Journal de la société des africanistes* 26: 33–196.

Skinner, R. 1965. 'Self-help, community organization and politics: Villa El Salvador, Lima.' In *Self-Help Housing: A Critique*, ed. P. Ward. London: Mansell, 209–29.

Trager, L. 1988. *The City Connection: Migration and Family Interdependence in the Philippines*. Ann Arbor: University of Michigan Press.

Velsen, J. van. 1960. 'Labor migration as a positive factor in the continuity of Tonga tribal society.' *Economic Development and Cultural Change* 8: 265–78.

Wallerstein, I. 1974. *The Modern World-System: Capitalist Agriculture and the Origins of the European World Economy in the Sixteenth Century*. New York: Academic Press.

Wallerstein, I. 1980. *The Modern World-System*, vol. 2: *Mercantilism and the Consolidation of the European World-Economy, 1600–1750*. New York: Academic Press.

Wallerstein, I. 1989. *The Modern-World System*, vol. 3: *The Second Era of the Great Expansion of the Capitalist World-Economy, 1730–1840*. New York: Academic Press.

Young, K. 1982. 'The creation of a relative surplus population: a case study from Mexico.' In *Women and Development: The Sexual Division of Labor in Rural Societies*, ed. L. Benería. New York: Praeger Special Studies.

8 Community, Ethnicity, and Urban Sociology

Jan Lin

> Ethnic neighborhoods have long been a feature of cities. In this reading, Jan Lin provides an overview of how sociologists have thought about ethnic neighborhoods: the reasons they exist, the functions they serve for their inhabitants, and the reasons for their persistence or disappearance.
>
> Although Chinatowns are a longstanding feature of cities in North America, they have recently been transformed by changes in the global economy. Immigrants to New York's Chinatown today enter a community polarized between wealthy entrepreneurs and near-destitute illegal immigrants working in the informal sector (nonregular employment such as peddling and working "off the books"). Immigrants can find abundant work opportunities within their ethnic enclaves, in industries dominated by fellow-Chinese employers. It is unclear, however, whether this employment provides opportunities for eventual upward mobility outside of the enclave.

The place, function, and future of immigrant communities and ethnic institutions in the American city have historically been of interest to academics, planners, public officials, and citizens alike. Traditional assumptions regarding the mode and direction of immigrant incorporation into American society, however, have shifted in tune with the changing political economy of American cities. The early view, derived from the human ecology school of urban sociology propagated in the early twentieth century at the University of Chicago, conceived of immigrant enclaves as impermanent "natural areas," flowering in the low-rent "zone-in-transition" ringing the central business district, which would disappear with the assimilation and upward mobility of later generations into the American middle classes (Park and Burgess 1925; Zorbaugh 1926: 223; Thomas and Znaniecki 1958). Rose Hum Lee, one of the first Chinese American sociologists to apply human ecological concepts to the comparative study of a number of Chinatowns, noted their demographic decline and physical deterioration in the post-war period, and predicted their eventual "withering away" through the combined effects of the restrictive immigration laws, intergenerational occupational mobility of the immigrants, and cultural assimilation through time (1949).

Anti-ethnic assumptions were implicit among the founders of human ecology theory. Robert E. Park suggested that the "keener, the more energetic, and the more ambitious" immigrants would quickly move out of their "ghettos and immigrant colonies" into secondary settlement areas in outer zones of the city, or into more cosmopolitan areas where they would associate with members of several different immigrant and racial groups (1926: 9). In separate writings on the "race relations cycle," he conceived of new immigrant groups as moving through stages of contact, conflict, and accommodation prior to their ensuing assimilation into American society (Matthews 1977). Ethnic affiliation was seen to retard Americanization, and immigrant communities were seen to harbor syndicate crime, vice, and a host of other social problems. Chicago school sociologist Walter C. Reckless wrote:

> The relationship of Chinatown to the commercialized vice areas of American cities is too well known to need elaboration. It is only fair to say, however, that the assumption of the usual parasitic activities by the Chinese in the Western World is probably to be explained by their natural segregation at the center of cities, as well as by their uncertain economic and social status. (1971: 246)

Paul Siu, another early Chinese American sociologist, who held a less critical but similarly pathological perspective on ethnic institutions, observed that Chinese laundry and restaurant workers labored in a "social isolation" and residential self-segregation that impeded their successful assimilation into American society (1952).

Louis Wirth, who later codified the thesis of "anti-urbanism" through his seminal essay "Urbanism as a Way of Life" (1938), began a shift from the anti-ethnic bias through his positive depiction of the Jewish "ghetto" of Chicago as a neighborhood of close primary ties and rich cultural life (1927). The Wirthian perspective conceived of the immigrant colony as a functioning vestige of traditional society in the face of the alienating encroachments of the dense, heterogeneously populated metropolis. The affirmative conception of the ethnic community continued with two landmark studies of Italian American communities, both in Boston. William Foote Whyte's *Street Corner Society* (1943) portrayed the efforts of his locally bound "corner boy" informant, "Doc," to gain a streetwise livelihood in marked contrast to the middle-class aspirations of "college boys" who were departing their North End neighborhood. Examining the West End neighborhood in the late 1950s before its wholesale demolition, Herbert Gans found that the close-knit "peer group society" granted its denizens a sense of identity, custom, attachment to place, and social order. His portrayal of this neighborhood in *The Urban Villagers* (1962) countered the popular sentiment that ethnic neighborhoods were socially disorganized slums whose denizens were arguably provincial but firmly anti-assimilationist and had a resilient pride in locality and ethnicity.

Gerald Suttles followed with *The Social Order of the Slum* (1968), which found that though Black, Italian, Mexican, and Puerto Rican youth gangs usually experienced tense relationships in periodic conflicts over territory in the "Addams area" (a pseudonym for his study area), a unified sense of "provincial morality" took over when there was a perceived threat from the outside. From a comparative perspective, Albert Hunter and Suttles (1972) later suggested that the strongest sense of "community" exists in the case of the "defended neighborhood," when residents come to recognize a common interest in responding to intrusions from beyond. This cohesion was strongly apparent in street-corner gangs, vigilante-like citizens' groups, and restrictive covenants. From this standpoint, "community" was not something backward, an atavistic remnant of traditional "folk society," but a socially constructed phenomenon that arose from the interaction of individuals across a defined territory in response to redevelopmental incursions or urban change.

New conceptual work on urban communities was also produced with the emergence of the community action movement in the 1950s and 1960s. A voice of urban populism came with Jane Jacobs, the notorious critic of urban renewal, who led home owners in Manhattan's West Village neighborhood in successfully opposing a redevelopment plan engineered by Mayor Robert Wagner in the late 1950s (Zukin 1989: 114–15). Another classic case of the defended community during this era involved citizen opposition to the Yerba Buena urban renewal project in the "South of Market" neighborhood of San Francisco (Hartman 1974). Ira Katznelson (1981) examined the convergences between racial/ethnic demographic succession and the political "assault" of neighborhood action movements on the established "trenches" of territorially based patronage politics in upper Manhattan in the early 1970s. Ranging historically and geographically across a variety of European, Latin American, and American case studies, Manuel Castells (1983) has drawn our attention to the growth of community-based "urban social movements" as a cross-national phenomenon. More recently, Janet Abu-Lughod and her research team (1994) delivered a complex, nuanced account of local resistance to redevelopmental gentrification in Manhattan's East Village.

Running parallel with these community action movements were the civil rights movement and the urban disturbances of the 1950s and 1960s, which by the early 1970s had fomented a new racial/ethnic consciousness and concern regarding inequality and intergroup relations in urban America. Liberal authors Nathan Glazer and Daniel Patrick Moynihan (1963) urged us to look "beyond the melting pot" model of US society. The death knell of assimilation discourse was increasingly rung by an artillery of new conceptual paradigms that privileged cultural pluralism and ethnic persistence. The conceptual rethinking extended to conservative sociologists such as Michael Novak (1971), who noted a new group awareness among white ethnic Americans in describing the "rise of the unmeltable ethnics." Observing that the occupational and residential concentration of immigrant groups accompanies rather than impedes social change, William Yancey et al. (1976) suggested that ethnicity should be reconceptualized as an "emergent" phenomenon. Rather than being a status or attachment that was biological, primordial, or ancestral, ethnicity could now be viewed as something that was the situational product of evolving intergroup relations in a changing US society.

Ethnic Enclaves

Associated with the new models of ethnic persistence is the ethnic enclave economies perspective, which highlights the economic dynamism displayed in contemporary urban ethnic enclaves such as Miami's Cuban enclave and the Chinese enclaves of San Francisco and New York City. These ethnic enclave economies are seen to proffer socioeconomic opportunity for the latest immigrants to American cities in a fashion different from the low-wage, dead-end employment in the secondary labor market experienced by African Americans. Utilizing a complex "returns on human capital" statistical methodology, proponents of this approach conceptualize immigrant occupational niches as urban subeconomies that grant labor-market rewards and upward socioeconomic mobility over time (Wilson and Portes 1980; Wilson and Martin 1982; Portes and Manning 1986; Sanders and Nee 1987; Zhou and Logan 1989). There has been some debate among these writers, however, regarding positive versus negative functions of the enclave economy, specifically over the question of different rewards conferred on employees versus employers. Another concern is whether the enclave is defined by place of work, place of residence, or industry sector. Furthermore, examining New York's Chinatown, Min Zhou and John Logan found evidence of significant gender differences in enclave labor market outcomes. Positive returns on human capital for men as opposed to absent or negative returns for women led these investigators to ponder "to what degree the positive functions of the enclave for men are derived from the subordinate position of women" (1989: 818).

In summary, the ethnic enclave may be conceived as having a double-edged character that rewards bosses mainly at the expense of workers, who labor in jobs that are mostly dead-end in terms of future occupational mobility. The entrepreneurial accomplishments of the immigrant small-business sector, in other words, are based to a great extent on the exploitation of their co-ethnic workforce, who labor long hours for low wages in poor working conditions, with little employment security. As Jimy Sanders and Victor Nee have noted,

> The "embeddedness" of economic activity in networks of ethnic relations can trap immigrant workers in patron–client relationships that bind them, in exchange for

assistance at an early stage, to low-wage jobs. A detailed analysis of the actual pattern of exchange between bosses and workers within immigrant enclaves is needed before generalizations can be made about ethnic solidarity's effect on the socioeconomic mobility of immigrant workers. (1987: 765)

On the other hand, we may recognize that immigrant bosses also work hard, provide opportunities for immigrants with limited English-speaking ability, give them on-the-job training, and may overlook undocumented immigration status. Additionally, through the multiplier effect, enclave earnings are recirculated through purchases in co-ethnic businesses and through forward, backward, and consumption linkages, and accumulated earnings are eventually reinvested in residential and commercial real estate. Thus, although there may be short-run disparities in the economic benefits conferred on enclave participants, the aggregate economic effect is positive. The local economy in ethnic enclaves is generally robust, and the built environment is in constant use or in a process of upgrading; this situation is in contrast to the capital-scarce, deteriorated urban terrain of the "barrio" or "ghetto."

This focus on ethnic enclave economies differs from the earlier assimilationist studies in identifying positive rather than negative outcomes from ethnicity and ethnic solidarity. Rather than predicting the eventual dissolution of ethnic communities, the enclave thesis suggests their persistence. Alejandro Portes and Robert Manning (1986) point out also that ethnic enclaves have a historical dimension, using the examples of the Jewish enclave of Manhattan's Lower East Side and the Japanese of the West Coast.

Globalization and Polarized Cities

Clear demographic and geopolitical shifts prompted these conceptual reassessments of ethnicity and immigrant communities in the United States. The Hart-Cellar Immigration Act of 1965, in the spirit of the civil rights era, finally lifted decades-long immigration restrictions. Immigration to the United States after 1965 began to acquire a more nonwhite, Asian and Latin American/Caribbean character as the American economy similarly became differentially integrated into the changing global economy, forming trade and investment links with these developing world regions. In this broader context of globalization, the issue of immigrant acculturation into a prospective American melting pot was becoming less the question than that of their political and economic incorporation into a restructuring post-industrial American society. Emerging perspectives in urban political economy contextualized the transformation of American cities within this backdrop of globalization (Feagin and Smith 1987).

The globalization thesis distinguishes the post-World War II era as a new phase of capitalist production, management, and finance in the world economy.

Beginning in the 1960s, analysts of industrial relations and the international economy began to call attention to an increasingly transnational strategy in the
marketing as well as production activities of corporations based in the advanced
capitalist nations. Fiscal uncertainty, two oil shocks, simultaneous inflation and
recession (stagflation), and structural unemployment and domestic economic
"crisis" in capitalist core nations such as the United States in the 1970s were
increasingly attributed to global restructuring (Harvey 1989; O'Connor 1984).
From this standpoint, the growth of immigrant sweatshops and new immigrant
communities filled the vacuum in the United States left by economic "deindustrialization" because of the "capital flight" of American "runaway shops" to third-
world locations (Bluestone and Harrison 1982; Glickman 1987).

As articulated by Frobel et al. (1980), a "new international division of labor"
(NIDL) has emerged in the world economy since the 1960s, which involves the
strategy of firms in advanced capitalist "core" nations shifting production facilities
to lesser developed "periphery" nations to take advantage of cross-national differentials in wage rates and labor bargaining power. In many cases, governments of
the less developed nations encouraged the direct investment of transnational corporations in specifically designated free-trade zones or export processing zones
close to airports or harbors. Among the inducements offered were basic infrastructure, a ready low-wage labor supply, tax reductions, and lifting of quota restrictions and tariffs on the import of intermediate inputs and the export of finished
products. The NIDL was also facilitated by technological advances in global transport (especially shipping containerization) and communications (satellites, computers, and, more recently, fiber optics and facsimile machines).

In the 1970s, however, came growing shop-floor militancy, labor organizing,
and rising wage levels in the less developed countries. The declining power of
organized labor in the advanced industrial core and a new movement of immigrants from peripheral to core states also helped mediate an increasing switching
of production from offshore locations back to onshore. Electronic assembly factories staffed particularly by Asian, Latino, and Caribbean immigrant women
appeared in Silicon Valley, Southern California, New York City, and other immigration gateway locations. Garment sweatshops and other unregulated labor-
intensive economic activities appeared in the same sites. The phenomenon was
variously depicted as one of "reperipheralization at the core" (Sassen-Koob 1982),
"bringing the Third World home" (Smith 1988: 214), and growth of "downgraded
manufacturing" in postindustrial cities (Sassen 1988). Comparisons were made
with trends in European cities (Portes et al. 1989). The original expositors of the
NIDL thesis were compelled to acknowledge that transnational capitalism was
now practicing a kind of "shifting cultivation" of production facilities in both the
core and periphery (Kreye, Heinrichs, and Frobel 1986).

Associated with the concept of a global system of production sites is the notion
that the headquarters of international banks and corporations have become linked
through a hierarchical system of *world cities*. The term *world cities* was initially

promulgated by Peter Hall (1966) in reference to the seven most influential metro-politan areas in the advanced capitalist world. Robert Cohen (1981), John Fried-mann and Goetz Wolff (1982), and Warwick Armstrong and T. G. McGee (1985) subsequently associated the concept with global economic change and the notion of an urban hierarchy spanning both developed and less developed nations. Saskia Sassen (1988) finally linked "global cities" with patterns of labor and capital mobility. As codified by Sassen (1988), the global city concept rests on the notion that the emergent "producer services" sectors of advanced global capitalism are becoming structurally concentrated in certain nodal "command centers," such as New York, Los Angeles, London, and Tokyo. Sassen also suggests that growth in producer services creates low-wage work through demand for a range of personal services, domestic household services, customized construction and repair work, and building security services in offices and high-income gentrified neighborhoods. Thus postindustrial global cities require not only a corps of highly skilled and educated managers and administrators but also a phalanx of low-skilled and low-paid clerical staff, who are often recent immigrants.

These forms of high-income employment spur residential gentrification in the urban core. High-income gentrification, furthermore, creates a demand for high-priced specialized products usually manufactured via labor-intensive methods and sold through small boutiques, rather than for the standardized, mass-marketed items that historically have been produced by capital-intensive technology and marketed through department stores. Examples are custom-designed apparel, foot-wear, jewelry, fur, furniture, and electronics products. A highly publicized illustra-tion of these linkages is the garment industry, in which high-fashion designers, such as Liz Claiborne and Norma Kamali, have contracted assembly work to low-paying, unregulated immigrant sweatshops (Sassen-Koob 1987).

As advanced and less developed economies have become more closely inte-grated, the globalization perspective suggests growing structural similarities among constituent cities in the contemporary capitalist world system. Concepts traditionally derived from studies of third-world cities have increasingly been ap-plied to the advanced capitalist milieu. The emergence of unregulated economic activities and a marginalized underclass in postindustrial first-world cities such as New York, Los Angeles, London, and Paris has invited comparison with the *infor-mal sector* of third-world metropolises such as Jakarta, Lima, Manila, and Mexico City, where rural-to-urban migrants have historically generated their own employ-ment opportunities and resided in self-built squatter housing (Abu-Lughod and Hay 1979; Sassen 1988; Portes et al. 1989). The dualist paradigm classically employed in the third-world urbanization literature identifies the existence of a vast locally oriented, petty capitalist *lower circuit* of informal-sector activities operating in marked separation from an *upper circuit* of transnational sector oper-ations oriented toward the global economy (Santos 1979; Friedmann and Wolff 1982; Armstrong and McGee 1985). This economic bifurcation leads to a process of uneven development and aggravates social inequality in urban residential life.

In New York City, the recent growth of Latino, Caribbean, and Asian residential enclaves has been accompanied by the appearance of unregulated and exploitative forms of sweatshop production of apparel and footwear and other light manufacturing activities. At the same time, there has been a pronounced growth of employment in high-wage advanced corporate and managerial services in the midst of a long-term decline in medium-wage skilled manufacturing employment. Transnational interests have dramatically increased their presence. The result has been a cleavage in the New York City class structure that is reflected through polarization in housing markets, race and ethnic relations, political coalitions, and the spatial configuration of the broader metropolitan region (Mollenkopf and Castells 1991).

Where migrants to the favelas, barrios, and kampongs of the developing world have largely relied on self-built squatter housing, new immigrants to New York City have settled into existing, mostly deteriorated low-rent housing stock in the urban core (Manhattan) and the inner ring of outer boroughs. To some extent, it is a story of immigrant succession; they have used housing filtered down from upwardly mobile white ethnic populations, who have dispersed into better housing in the outer ring of suburbs on the metropolitan periphery. Accelerating gentrification and redevelopment in the core and some inner-ring neighborhoods, however, cast doubt over the continued viability of the residential filtration model. Similarly, economic transition to postindustrialism clouds opportunities for occupational upward mobility for the newest immigrants to New York City.

I employ the dual city concept in examining the process of urban development under economic change in a nodal metropolis of the new world economy through the microcosm of the central-city enclave of Chinatown. Rather than unity or extreme heterogeneity, there is a pronounced polarity in the Chinatown enclave economy. Socioeconomic differentiation is further articulated through the built environment in the form of spatial differentiation. A telling illustration of these contrasts in New York's Chinatown is the sight of sidewalk peddlers plying their wares and produce from tables or canvas sheets on Canal Street in front of the guarded glass offices of transnational banks such as the Bank of East Asia and the Hong Kong and Shanghai Banking Corporation (which is the twenty-fifth largest bank in the world). New York's Chinatown presents an interesting case where both processes of the informal sector and the advanced transnational sector can be observed in direct juxtaposition within the microcontext of the community.

[...]

References

Abu-Lughod, Janet. 1994. *From Urban Village to East Village: The Battle for New York's Lower East Side*. Oxford: Blackwell.

Abu-Lughod, Janet and Richard Hay, Jr. 1979. *Third World Urbanization*. New York: Methuen.

Armstrong, Warwick, and T. G. McGee. 1985. *Theatres of Accumulation*. New York: Methuen and Company.

Bluestone, Barry, and Bennett Harrison. 1982. *The Deindustrialization of America*. New York: Basic Books.

Castells, Manuel. 1983. *The City and the Grassroots*. Berkeley: University of California Press.

Cohen, Robert. 1981. "The New International Division of Labor, Multinational Corporations and Urban Hierarchy." In *Urbanization and Urban Planning in Capitalist Society*, eds. Michael Dear and Allen Scott. New York: Methuen, 287–315.

Feagin, Joe R. and Michael Peter Smith. 1987. "Cities and the New International Division of Labor: An Overview." In *The Capitalist City*, eds. Michael Peter Smith and Joe R. Feagin. New York: Blackwell, 3–34.

Friedmann, John and Goetz Wolfe. 1982. "World City Formation: An Agenda for Research and Action." *International Journal of Urban and Regional Research* 6(3) (Sept.): 309–44.

Frobel, Folker, Jurgen Henrichs, and Otto Kreye. 1980. *The New International Division of Labor*. London: Cambridge University Press.

Gans, Herbert. 1962. *The Urban Villagers*. New York: The Free Press.

Glazer, Nathan and Daniel Patrick Moynihan. 1963. *Beyond the Melting Pot*. Cambridge, MA: MIT Press.

Glickman, Norman. 1987. "Cities and the International Division of Labor." In *The Capitalist City*, eds. Michael Peter Smith and Joe R. Feagin. Malden, MA: Blackwell, 66–86.

Hall, Peter. 1966. *The World Cities*. New York: McGraw-Hill.

Hartman, Chester. 1974. *Yerba Buena: Land Grab and Community Resistance in San Francisco*. San Francisco: Glide Publications.

Harvey, David. 1989. *The Condition of Postmodernity*. Malden, MA: Blackwell.

Hunter, Albert, J. and Gerald D. Suttles. 1972. "The Expanding Community of Limited Liability." In *The Social Construction of Communities*, ed. Gerald D. Suttles. Chicago: University of Chicago Press.

Katznelson, Ira. 1981. *City Trenches*. New York: Pantheon.

Kreye, Otto, Jürgen Henrichs, and Folker Frobel. 1986. "Export Processing Zones in Developing Countries: Results of a New Survey." Working Paper No. 43. Geneva: International Labor Organization Multinational Enterprises Programme.

Lee, Rose Hum. 1949. "The Decline of Chinatowns in the United States." *American Journal of Sociology* 54(5) (March): 422–32.

Matthews, Fred. 1977. *The Quest for an American Sociology: Robert E. Park and the Chicago School*. Montreal: McGill-Queen's University Press.

Mollenkopf, John H. and Manuel Castells. 1991. *Dual City: Restructuring New York*. New York: Russell Sage Foundation.

Novak, Michael. 1971. *The Rise of the Unmeltable Ethnics*. New York: Macmillan.

O'Connor, James. 1984. *Accumulation Crisis*. Malden, MA: Blackwell.

Park, Robert E. 1926. "The Urban Community as a Spatial Pattern and a Moral Order." In *The Urban Community*, ed. Earnest W. Burgess. Chicago: University of Chicago Press, 3–18.

Park, Robert E. and Earnest W. Burgess. 1925. *The City*. Chicago: University of Chicago Press.

Portes, Alejandro, et al. 1989. *The Informal Economy*. Baltimore: John Hopkins University Press.

Portes, Alejandro, and Robert D. Manning. 1986. "The Immigrant Enclave: Theory and Empirical Examples." In *Competitive Ethnic Relations*, eds. Susan Olzak and Joane Nagel. New York: Academic Press, 47–68.

Reckless, W. C. 1971. "The Distribution of Vice in the City." In *The Social Fabric of the Metropolis: Contributions of the Chicago School of Urban Sociology*, ed. J. Short, Jr. Chicago: University of Chicago Press.

Sanders, Jimy M. and Victor Nee. 1987. "Limits of Ethnic Solidarity in the Ethnic Enclave." *American Sociological Review* 52(6) (Dec.): 745–67.

Santos, Milton. 1979. *The Shared Space: The Two Circuits of the Urban Economy in Underdeveloped Countries*. London: Methuen.

Sassen, Saskia. 1988. *The Mobility of Labor and Capital*. Cambridge: Cambridge University Press.

Sassen-Koob, Saskia. 1982. "Recomposition and Reperipherazation at the Core." *Contemporary Marxism* 5 (summer): 88–100.

Sassen-Koob, Saskia. 1987. "Growth and Informalization at the Core: A Preliminary Report on New York City." In *The Capitalist City*, eds. Michael P. Smith and Joe R. Feagin. New York: Blackwell, 138–54.

Siu, Paul C. P. 1952. "The Sojourner." *American Journal of Sociology* 58(1) (July): 34–44.

Smith, Michael Peter. 1988. "Global Capital Restructuring and Local Political Crises in US Cities." In *Global Restructuring and Territorial Development*, eds. Jeffrey Henderson and Manuel Castells. New York: Sage.

Thomas, William I. and Florian Znaniecki. 1958. *The Polish Peasant in Europe and America*. New York: Dover.

Whyte, William Foote. 1943. *Street Corner Society*. Chicago: University of Chicago Press.

Wilson, Kenneth L. and W. Allen Martin. 1982. "Ethnic Enclaves: A Comparison of the Cuban and Black Economies in Miami." *American Journal of Sociology* 88(1): 135–60.

Wilson, Kenneth L. and Alejandro Portes. 1980. "Immigrant Enclaves: An Analysis of the Labor Market Experiences of Cubans in Miami." *American Journal of Sociology* 86(2) (Sept.): 295–319.

Wirth, Louis. 1927. *The Ghetto*. Chicago: University of Chicago Press.

Wirth, Louis. 1938. "Urbanism as a Way of Life." *American Journal of Sociology* 4: 1–24.

Yancey, William L., Eugene P. Ericksen, and Richard N. Juliani. 1976. "Emergent Ethnicity: A Review and Reformation." *American Sociological Review* 41(3) (June): 391–402.

Zhou, Min and John R. Logan. 1989. "Returns on Human Capital in Ethnic Enclaves: New York City's Chinatown." *American Sociological Review* 54 (Oct.): 809–20.

Zorbaugh, Harvey W. 1926. "The Natural Areas of the City." In *The Urban Community*, ed. Earnest W. Burgess. Chicago: University of Chicago Press, 219–29.

Zukin, Sharon. 1980. "A Decade of the New Urban Sociology." *Theory and Society* 9: 539–74.

Zukin, Sharon. 1989. *Loft Living: Culture and Capital in Urban Change*. Foreword and Postscript by David Harvey. New Brunswick, NJ: Rutgers University Press.

9 The New Urban Reality

Roger Waldinger

Recent immigrants to the United States and other industrialized nations have faced a restructured economy, the decline of unionized manufacturing, and the erosion of wages. Yet they find jobs, and their success draws other immigrants. Roger Waldinger's work explores the economic and social condition of immigrants to New York City and compares their experience with that of the city's African American residents. Waldinger explains that New York's labor market has incorporated repeated waves of immigrants who take entry-level jobs and eventually move upward, leaving jobs for other newcomers to fill. Because of recruitment through personal connections, workers of a single ethnicity can quickly dominate an occupation or industry, developing an ethnic niche in the city's labor market.

According to Waldinger, immigrants and African American workers have developed different ethnic niches in the labor market. New immigrants have tended to cluster in the industries abandoned by old immigrant groups, such as clothing manufacturing, convenience stores, restaurants, and domestic service. African Americans have developed a niche in public-sector employment, such as civil service jobs and teaching, a more limited group of jobs and one that requires substantial education and skills.

Waldinger challenges two common assumptions of how the urban economy affects low-skill workers: the "polarization" or "dual city" hypothesis that the restructured economy provides jobs for both high- and low-skill workers and the "dislocation" or "mismatch" hypothesis that says that there are few or no jobs for uneducated minority workers in the new urban economy. He argues that by studying how people actually get jobs, we see that neither explanation works for all groups. Instead, different minority groups can have different labor market experiences based on how they and others construct their place in the labor queue.

Waldinger, Roger, "The New Urban Reality." From *Still the Promised City? African-Americans and New Immigrants in Postindustrial New York* (Cambridge, MA: Harvard University Press, 1996), pp. 1–7, 21–6, 27–32. Copyright © 1996 by the President and Fellows of Harvard College. Reprinted by permission of the publisher.

New York's brush with fiscal insolvency in the mid-1970s signaled the end for the old industrial cities of the United States. Its revival in the 1980s heralded the emergence of the nation's largest cities as world service centers. The smokestack cities of the industrial heartland unfortunately have no replacement for their run-of-the-mill production activities, steadily eroding under the twin impact of computerization and foreign competition. But in the largest urban agglomerations – Chicago, Los Angeles, Philadelphia, and, especially, New York – the advent of a postindustrial economy has triggered a new phase of growth. The key activities of the new economy – information processing, the coordination of large organizations, and the management of volatile financial markets – are overwhelmingly urban-based. And their dynamism has yanked these largest cities out of the economic torpor into which they had sunk.

The new urban vitality notwithstanding, cities remain deeply troubled – perhaps more so than before. The paradox of urban plenty is that comparatively few of the city's residents have been able to enjoy the fruits of growth. The number of poor people living in central cities has not fallen but risen, and dramatically so. Instead of arresting social dislocation, the economic turnaround has exacerbated the urban social problems identified thirty years ago. Though right and left differ on social policy responses, both camps agree that a sizable segment of the poor has been lopped off into an "urban underclass" – persistently poor and with no connection to legitimate ways of making a living.[1]

Demography is the subtext to the contemporary tale of urban woe. "Back to the city" has been the catchword of the new urban professionals – today's huddled masses, piled up in neighborhoods in and around the downtown business centers. But the influx of this much maligned gentry never matched the attention it received in the press. The tide of people flowing cityward remains what it has been for the past forty years: America's big cities attract mainly nonwhites. First came blacks, displaced from the technological backwaters of the agrarian South. Then came a wave of immigrants from the labor-surplus areas of the developing world: today's urban newcomers are arriving in numbers that rival the great migrations of a century ago.[2]

Thus the city of services is also a "majority minority" city. But how does this population base fit into the urban economy of today?

The received academic wisdom maintains that there is no fit at all. The industrial city grew because it possessed labor, and what it demanded of its labor was willing hands and strong muscles – not diplomas or technical expertise. But in the city of information processing and the transaction of high-level business deals, these qualities count no more. The equation between the city's economic function and its population base has no place for the unlettered, no matter how willing. The decline of the industrial city has left minorities high and dry.[3]

But a dissenting interpretation, now sufficiently repeated to have become a conventional wisdom, tells a different tale. Modern urban development simultaneously generates high-level professional and managerial jobs and a proliferation of low-skilled, low-income "service" jobs. The polarized metropolis leaves minorities far from useless; instead, they serve as the new drawers of water and hewers of wood. In this version, it is not the poor who depend on the rich for their benefi-cence or for jobs and income to trickle down. Rather, the rich need the poor – to provide low-cost services, to maintain the city's underbelly, and to prop up what remains of the depressed manufacturing sector.[4]

I argue that both stories – however intuitively appealing they may be separately or together – have it wrong. Neither metaphor, of polarization or of dislocation, captures the impact of the post-industrial urban transformation. At root, both depict faceless, impersonal structures inexorably performing their actions on an inert urban mass. Not subjected to analysis, the structures are instead taken for granted, abstracted from any historical context, and divorced from the specific interests and forces that might have given them shape. Conflict and politics do not enter into these accounts of the making of the postindustrial economic world. Passing over dominant groups and their interests, these rival stories treat the new polyglot working and middle classes as an undifferentiated mass, helplessly playing out the scripts written for them by history.

But no *deus ex machina* determines which people get jobs, how they do so, and whether they then move ahead. The mechanisms of matching and mobility are social arrangements, shaped by the historical contexts in which they have grown up and subject to change – not simply as a result of pressures from the impersonal forces of the world economy, but in response to the actions of contending parties in specific societies and places. This book places the people and groups that have made, maintained, and changed the structures of today's postindustrial urban economy at the very center of the discussion.

My interpretation of the new urban reality will be developed in a single, sus-tained argument in the pages that follow. In briefest compass, the argument reads like this: The story of ethnics in America's cities is a collective search for mobility, in which the succession of one migrant wave after another alternatively stabilizes and disrupts the labor queue. In a market economy, employers allocate jobs to the most desirable workers they can recruit; but each market economy bears the im-print of the social structure in which it is embedded. In a race-conscious society like the United States, employers rank entire groups of people in terms of their ethnic and racial characteristics. All things being equal, members of the core cul-tural group stand at the top, followed by others.

The instability of America's capitalist economy subjects the labor queue's ordering to change. Growth pulls the topmost group up the totem pole; lower-ranking groups then seize the chance to move up the pecking order; in their wake, they leave behind vacancies at the bottom, which employers fill by recruiting workers from outside the economy – namely, migrants. The structure of the labor queue goes unchallenged as long as these newest arrivals are content to work in the bottom-level jobs for which they were initially recruited. But the economic orientations of the newcomers inevitably change, and when they do, complementarity is likely to be replaced by competition – which fans continuing ethnic strife over access to good jobs.

Competition between newcomers and insiders takes the form of conflict over the ethnic niche. Although migrants start at the bottom, they enter the economy under the auspices of friends or kin, which means that they begin with connections. Networks funnel the newcomers into specialized economic activities: as new-comers flow into the workplaces where earlier settlers have already gotten estab-lished, ethnic concentrations, or niches, gradually develop. The path up from the bottom involves finding a good niche and dominating it – which means that good jobs are reserved for insiders, leaving the next wave of outsiders excluded. Thus, the search by an earlier migrant group for labor market shelters eventuates in barriers that the next round of arrivals must confront.

Of course, economic life in America's cities is not all conflict. In some cases, the queue process simply pulls insider groups up the totem pole, leading them to abandon niches that a new group of outsiders can take over. In other instances, conditions in the niche undergo relative deterioration, in which case the barriers to outsiders get relaxed. These conditions ensure that ethnics in the labor market are sometimes noncompeting, segmented groups. But the scarcity of good jobs relative to the surplus of job seekers guarantees that competition never disappears.

Thus, the structures that African-Americans and new immigrants confront result from America's serial incorporation of outsider groups and from those groups' attempts to create protective economic shelters. The continuous recourse to migra-tion as a source of low-level labor, so characteristic of the United States, has made ethnicity the crucial and enduring mechanism that sorts groups of categorically different workers into an identifiably distinct set of jobs. For this reason, the ethnic division of labor stands as the central division of labor in the cities of twentieth-century America; the fates of new immigrants and African-Americans are bound up in its making and remaking.

New York City is the prism through which I develop this argument in full. As America's first postindustrial place, New York is a critical case for any explanation of urban change and its impact. I mean "first" in the sense of arriving at postin-dustrialism before its urban rivals and in the sense of having moved further toward the advanced service economy than any other principal urban center. New York also exemplifies the new melting pot – heated to full boil. New York is not only a minority majority city. It is also the Mecca for the newest immigrants, just as it has been throughout the history of the United States. Nowhere else does one find quite so complex an ethnic mosaic. Consequently, no other city provides as good a platform for studying how ethnic group resources and strategies interact with structural changes to shape ethnic group fates.

[My research] recounts the transformation of New York's ethnic division of labor since midcentury, a story I tell in two parts. One details how the very instability of the labor queue and the ethnic division of labor it engenders create opportunities for outsiders and newcomers. The second shows how these pieces of the pie have been divided up.

The conventional wisdom attributes urban disaster to the loss of white city residents. In fact, the outflow of white New Yorkers is what has given newcomers their chance. During economic downturns, whites fled the city faster than the rate of decline. And when the economy reheated, the outward seepage of whites slowed down but never stopped.

Over the years, the disproportionately declining white presence produced a ladder effect, creating empty spaces for newcomers up and down – though mainly down – the economic totem pole. Reflecting the influence of *prior* migration histories, the impact of white population decline rippled through New York's diversified economic complex in an uneven way. With the exception of those in construction and a few other skilled trades, New York's white ethnic proletariat disappeared after 1970, though a myriad of blue-collar jobs remained. Consequently, ethnic succession generated opportunities both in declining industries, where the rate of white outflows often outpaced the rate of job erosion, and in growth industries, where whites poured out of bottom-level positions even as demand for low-skilled workers increased. New York's small-business sector experienced the same round of musical chairs: newcomers moved in as white ethnics abandoned petty retailing, garment contracting, and other less remunerative business lines. A similar sequence of events occurred in many parts of the public sector, especially after 1975, when whites left municipal service for better opportunities elsewhere.

Since succession provides the backdrop for the economic stories of new immigrant and African-American New Yorkers, the central question concerns who got which jobs and why. In the 1970s and 1980s, black New Yorkers built up and consolidated the niche they had earlier established in government work. Public sector employment offered numerous advantages, including easier access to jobs and an employer that provided better, more equitable treatment. But convergence on government employment had the corollary effect of heightening the skill thresholds of the chief black economic base. To be sure, connections helped in gaining access to municipal jobs; and my case studies show that black civil servants networked as much as anyone else. However, civil service positions held promise only to those members of the community with the skills, experience, and credentials that government required – qualities not shared by the many African-American New Yorkers who have found themselves at economic risk.

Of course, work in the bowels of New York's economy could have been a possibility. Yet the data and the case studies demonstrate a steady erosion of African-Americans' *share* of the large number of remaining, low-skilled jobs – even as the *number* of low-level jobs held by minorities, native and immigrant, steadily grew. The African-American concentrations of old, from the most menial occupations in domestic service to later clusters like garment or hotel work, largely faded away. And African-Americans simultaneously failed to make headway in those low-skilled sectors where competition with whites had previously kept them locked out.

The immigrants, by contrast, responded to ethnic succession in ways that expanded their economic base. Initially, the match between their aspirations and broader labor market dynamics created openings that the newcomers could fill. On the one hand, the immigrants' social origins predisposed them to embrace jobs that native New Yorkers would no longer accept; meager as they appeared to New Yorkers, the paychecks in the city's garment, restaurant, or retail sectors looked good in comparison to the going rate in Santo Domingo, Hong Kong, or Kingston. On the other hand, the city's factory sector was suffering a hemorrhage of older, native workers that outpaced the leakage of jobs, leading employers to take on new hands.

The initial portals into New York's economy channeled the newcomers into bottom-level jobs. The links between the workplace and the immigrant community helped convert these positions into platforms for upward movement. Immigrants were simply tied to others who would help them, right from the start. The connections among newcomers and settlers provided an informal structure to immigrant economic life; that structure, in turn, furnished explicit and implicit signposts of economic information and mechanisms of support that helped ethnics acquire skills and move ahead through business and other means.

In the end, new immigrant and African-American New Yorkers shaped their own fates by creating distinctive ethnic economic niches. But history had much to do with where each group could find a place. Looking over their shoulders toward conditions in the societies from which they have just departed, migrants move into industrial economies at the very bottom, taking up the jobs that natives will no longer do. While today's immigrants follow this traditional pattern, African-Americans, by contrast, are the migrants of a generation ago. The earlier pattern of rejections and successes shapes their searches of today, foreclosing options that immigrants, with their very different experiences and orientations, will pursue. Unlike the immigrants, African-Americans aspire to the rewards and positions enjoyed by whites. But the niches that African-Americans have carved out require skills that the least-educated members of that community simply don't have; African-Americans networks no longer provide connections to these more accessible jobs; and relative to the newcomers, employers find unskilled African-Americans to be much less satisfactory recruits. As for better-skilled African-Americans, they often compete with whites on unequal terrain, since past and present discrimination in housing and schools makes African-American workers less well prepared than whites. In this way, the mismatch between the aspirations of the *partly* disadvantaged and the requirements of the jobs to which they aspire provides the spark for persistent economic racial conflict between blacks and whites.

By contrast, immigrants have moved into noncompeting positions, taking over jobs that whites have deserted in their move up the occupational pecking order. Once the immigrants gain a lock on low-level jobs, ethnic connections funnel a steady stream of newcomers, excluding black New Yorkers who are not members of the same ethnic club.

Thus, the advent of a majority minority economy marks the emergence of a new division of labor, in which the various groups of new New Yorkers play distinct economic roles. Niche creation by African-Americans and immigrants has evolved into a mutually exclusive carving up of the pie: in carving out a place in the ethnic division of labor, the two groups effectively open or foreclose opportunities for each other. As in the past, control over good jobs and desired resources is subject to contest. Thus, the various components of New York's polyglot working and middle classes follow the example of their predecessors, continuing in, and reinvigorating, the pattern of interethnic economic competition that long characterized the city's white ethnic groups. [. . .]

The Making of the Immigrant Niche

We can think about the making of an immigrant niche as a two-stage process. First comes a phase of specialization in which placements are affected by skill, linguistic factors, or predispositions. Historians have argued that in the early to mid-nineteenth century migrants had far greater opportunities to transfer a skill directly into urban American economies than at any time since.[5] And yet premigration skills still affect the match between newcomers and employers. Greeks from the province of Kastoria, where a traditional apprenticeship in fur making is common, tend to enter the fur industry; Israelis move into diamonds, a traditional Jewish business centered in New York, Tel Aviv, and Brussels; Indians from Gujarat, previously traders, become small store owners; and West Indians, many of whom have had exposure to mechanical crafts in oil fields, sugar refineries, or shipyards, find work in construction.

Language facility may similarly be a barrier to, or a facilitator of, specialization. English-language ability has steered immigrants from the anglophone Caribbean into health care, where the importance of interpersonal communication has been an impediment to immigrants that are not native speakers. By contrast, Koreans arrive with professional degrees, but, because they are poor English speakers and lack appropriate credentials or licenses, turn to retailing.

Groups may also be predisposed toward certain types of work; the fact that migrants are people in a stage of transition has an especially important influence on the types of jobs they pick up. Not yet certain whether they will settle down for good or return home, still evaluating conditions in terms of lower-quality employment back home, immigrants are likely to be favorably disposed toward low-level, low-status jobs. And that favorable evaluation extends even to jobs in declining industries where the prospects for long-term employment are poor.

Whatever the precise mix of factors that determine the initial placements, occupational closure quickly sets in; this process represents the second stage. Networks of information and support are bounded by ethnic ties. Newcomers move and settle down under the auspices of friends, kin, and "friends of friends." When looking for work the new arrivals may prefer an environment in which at least some faces are familiar; they may feel uncomfortable with, or be ineligible for, the institutionalized means of labor market support; and they are likely to find that personal contacts prove the most efficient way of finding a place to work. Thus, later arrivals pile up in those fields where the first settlers established an early beachhead.

More important, the predilections of immigrants match the preferences of employers, who try to reproduce the characteristics of the workers they already have. Recruiting among the relatives and friends of incumbents is the cheapest way of finding help; it greatly increases the quantity and quality of information about the relevant characteristics of a prospective recruit; and since it brings new workers into an environment where they are surrounded by people who know them, network hiring provides an additional mechanism for maintaining control. Over time, hiring opportunities can become detached from the open market, being rationed instead to insiders' referrals as part of a quid pro quo between incumbents and employers.[6]

From Immigrant to Ethnic Niche

What happens after the initial immigrant niche is put in place? The answer depends, in part, on the nature of the niche itself. If the niche provides rewarding employment or mechanisms for expanding a group's economic base, specializations are likely to persist. Niches often vary by industry, with different industries holding out distinctive pathways for getting ahead. In a small-business industry, like retailing or construction, one succeeds by starting out on one's own. By contrast, where large organizations prevail, one moves up by getting more schooling, picking up a certification, acquiring seniority, or some combination of the three. Whatever the particulars of the employment context, acquiring industry-relevant contacts, information, and know-how can take place on the job in an almost costless way. By the same token, moving beyond the ethnic niche imposes considerable costs.

The structure of rewards among economic specializations varies, as does the potential for niche expansion. As already noted, time often changes the match between a group and its original niche. Immigrants, looking back at the conditions they left behind, are willing to start out at the bottom of the pecking ladder; their children, however, want a good deal more, looking askance at those very same jobs. The advent of the second generation, therefore, is a momentous event, though not so much, as some social scientists have suggested, because the second generation accepts the cultural patterns of natives. Far more important are the aspirations of the second generation, which in contrast to their parents' now extend to the economic goals and standards of natives. Moreover, job predispositions are rarely abstract preferences; rather, they are informed by understandings about the probability that movement down one economic branch or the other will lead to failure or success. If group A experienced discrimination in industry B, and has reason to think that some level of discrimination there will persist, job seekers from group A have good reason to look for work in other fields. This same assessment of opportunities and constraints might create a preference for those types of work where exclusionary barriers exercise the least effect.

Thus, members of the second generation may move on to different jobs. Do they shift as a group? Or do they scatter, moving outward as they filter upward from the ethnic niche, as the conventional thinking suggests? The argument for the latter view rests on its assumptions about why the first generation concentrated in the first place. To the extent that concentration is explained by lack of skills and education, and seen as a source of disadvantage, then rising levels of education and growing similarity with the core cultural group imply that upward mobility goes hand in hand with dispersion out of the immigrant niche.

Skill deficiencies are only one of the factors in my account of the first-generation niche, however. I place much greater weight on the role of ethnic networks and their impact on the actions of both workers and employers. Consequently, my view suggests a different scenario, in which the continuing importance of ethnic networks shapes a group's employment distribution into the second, and later, generations. Just as with the first generation, the second generation's search for advancement takes on a *collective* form. Starting out from an immigrant niche, the second generation is already embedded in a cluster of interlocking organizations, networks, and activities. Not only do these commonalities shape aspirations, they also create the organizational framework for the rapid diffusion of information and innovations. Thus, the social organization of the second generation serves as a mechanism for channeling people into the labor market; once a favorable niche develops, informal recruitment patterns can quickly funnel in new hires.

The Advantages of the Ethnic Niche

The process of niche formation turns ethnic disadvantage to good account, enabling social outsiders to compensate for the background deficits of their groups and the discrimination they encounter. The networks that span ethnic communities constitute a source of "social capital," providing social structures that facilitate action, in this case, the search for jobs and the acquisition of skills and other resources needed to move up the economic ladder.[7] Networks among ethnic incumbents and job seekers allow for rapid transmission of information about openings from workplaces to the communities. And the networks provide better information within workplaces, reducing the risks associated with initial hiring.

Once in place, ethnic hiring networks are self-reproducing, since each new employee recruits others from his or her own group.

While the development of an ethnic niche provides a group with privileged access to jobs, one classic example – that of small business – suggests that it can do far more. Ethnic businesses emerge as a consequence of the formation of ethnic communities, with their sheltered markets and networks of mutual support. Individual firms may die off at an appalling rate, but business activity offers a route to expansion into higher profit and more dynamic lines. Retailers evolve into wholesalers; construction firms learn how to develop real estate; garment contractors gain the capital, expertise, and contacts to design and merchandise their own clothing. As the ethnic niche expands and diversifies, the opportunities for related ethnic suppliers and customers also grow.

With an expanding business sector comes both a mechanism for the effective transmission of skill and a catalyst for the entrepreneurial drive. From the standpoint of ethnic workers, the opportunity to acquire managerial skills through a stint of employment in immigrant firms both compensates for low pay and provides a motivation to learn a variety of different jobs. Employers who hire co-ethnics gain a reliable work force with an interest in skill acquisition – attributes that diminish the total labor bill and make for greater flexibility. Thus, a growing ethnic economy creates a virtuous circle: business success gives rise to a distinctive motivational structure, breeding a community-wide orientation toward small business and encouraging the acquisition of skills within a stable, commonly accepted framework.[8]

Sociologist Suzanne Model coined the concept of "hierarchically organized niches" to denote ethnic economic concentrations in which employees not only work among their co-ethnics but are hired and overseen by co-ethnic owners and managers.[9] These characteristics usually define the ethnic economy; they can also be found in the public sector. Along with small business, the civil service forms the other classic ethnic niche, even though it is governed by seemingly opposite principles. Moving into civil service has been an ethnic mobility strategy for over one hundred years, and not just because ethnic networks increase a group's access to jobs. Once in place, groups of ethnic workers repeatedly engage in bargaining games that shelter them from competition and exclude opportunities for promotion from all but insiders. Thus, the public sector comes under group pressures that make it a protected, self-regulating enclave. And that trait increases its attraction for stigmatized groups that fare poorly in the private market.

Job Competition

I have depicted niche formation as the unintended result of activities of which people are only partly aware. But once the niche is in place, different dynamics occur. The higher the level of concentration in the niche, the more frequent and more intense the interaction among group members. These interactions make them feel that they belong to a group. If the niche is one of the salient traits that group members share, it also helps define who they are. As a result, members pay greater attention to the boundaries of the niche and the characteristics of those who can and cannot cross those boundaries. As the niche strengthens group identity, it sharpens the distinction between insiders and outsiders.[10]

Once established, the niche also takes on properties that make it difficult for outsiders to get in the door. A variety of factors incline ethnics toward working with others of their own kind whenever they can. Fearful that outsiders might undercut wages, workers prefer to train co-ethnic neophytes whom they trust; anxious about the reliability and performance of job applicants who walk in off the street, employers prefer to hire the friends and relatives of their key workers; concerned that a vendor might not deliver on time, or that a customer might delay in paying the bill, business owners look for known entities with track records of successful dealings with others. In effect, membership in an ethnic community serves as an index of trust in an economic transaction, telling co-ethnic actors that one can rely on another. The web of contacts within a community works in the same direction; the history of prior exchanges with members of an ethnic network provides a baseline against which future behavior can be assessed. Since relations among co-ethnics are likely to be many-sided rather than specialized, community effects go beyond their informational value, engendering both codes of conduct and the mechanisms for sanctioning those who violate norms.

The trust extended from one member of a community to another, though both efficient and efficacious, is not available to everyone. Outsiders lack the traits, histories, and relational ties conducive to collaboration or trust; on these grounds alone, rational considerations lead insiders toward economic exchanges with their own.

Since employers and employees in the niche tend to arrive at agreement over hiring practices and promotional rules, past practices operate with a similar, exclusionary effect. To be sure, the parties often fight with one another over the content of the rules. But the quarrels rarely get out of hand: in hierarchically organized niches, such as the civil service, managers and workers often come from the same group and identify with one another. In other cases, where higher management and the rank and file have little in common, the line managers who make key personnel decisions generally share the views, and often the origins, of the important workers with whom they interact. [. . .]

There is more to job competition than the human or social capital of insider and outsider groups. Groups' resource-bearing capacities in the political realm often count for a great deal: shifts in the relative balance of *political* power between incumbents and outsiders can lead to policy changes that alter recruitment practices, opening up defended, previously closed ethnic niches. While political pressure can make a difference, the range of exposure to political forces varies with the characteristics of labor market arrangements. Government's instruments will be most effective in those segments of the economy where hiring and recruitment practices are most institutionalized, and thus most susceptible to internal and external monitoring. By contrast, political intervention will carry much less weight in small-firm sectors, which mainly rely on informal recruitment mechanisms.

Discrimination

This account of job competition provides an explanation of the activation, persistence, and possible decline of discrimination; because it stands at variance with established economic and sociological views, a comparison with the alternative, better-known accounts deserves attention. In economics, the most powerful statement explains the behavior of discriminators as a manifestation of their "tastes": thus, whites have a distaste for working with blacks.[11] The economists' assumptions about whites' preferences have been subject to criticism on several grounds – don't whites really want to maintain social distance? aren't they principally concerned with preserving status differences relative to blacks? But the most damaging criticism is simply that by assuming distinctive preferences, the economists beg the question at hand, namely, what causes whites' peculiar tastes?[12] As the ethnic order becomes more complex, the import of this failure becomes increasingly grave, since whites seem to have a much stronger distaste for blacks than they do for the various foreign-born groups who are just as visibly identifiable.

But let us assume that whites do indeed have such a strong distaste for working alongside blacks; what difference would it make? White employers with a "taste for discrimination" would pay a premium to hire mainly white crews, deducting the costs of the psychic discomforts they must endure from the wages of any blacks they engage. Like any other preference, the taste for discrimination is not equally shared by all white employers; those employers who experience less psychic pain from proximity to blacks should be happy to hire an entirely black crew at bargain rates. In a competitive market, the lowest-cost, nondiscriminating producer would inevitably compel the discriminators to either swallow their distastes and hire more blacks or else go out of business.

By definition, the economic model thus predicts declining discrimination. The problem, of course, is that persistent discrimination is what requires explanation. Moreover, the economists' approach focuses almost entirely on wages, whereas occupational segregation and access to employment lie at the heart of black-white disparities.

Sociologists, by contrast, are wont to explain discrimination as the reaction of "high-priced" labor to competition from "lower-priced" competitors, as can be seen in William J. Wilson's highly influential book *The Declining Significance of Race*.[13] In this account, black migrants entered the north as low-price labor: willing to work at rates below those acceptable to whites, blacks were used by employers in their efforts to "undercut the white labor force by hiring cheaper labor." These attempts fanned whites' antagonism toward blacks and efforts at either excluding African-Americans outright or else confining them to low-level jobs. As the American state expanded its role in regulating industrial and race relations from the New Deal on, the potential for wage competition between blacks and whites steadily diminished. With whites no longer having to fear displacement from low-priced blacks, they lost their motivation to discriminate.

The conventional economic approach predicts declining discrimination without, however, accounting for what activates discrimination in the first place. The conventional sociological framework goes one step better in addressing the question of motivation but, likewise, forecasts discrimination's decline. Unlike the economists' approach, the job-competition perspective provides an answer to the question of motivation; unlike the sociologists' approach, it also tells us why discrimination might persist.

The economists are certainly right in thinking that discrimination is in part a matter of tastes; as I contended above, however, those tastes are not exogenous but rather a consequence of the development of an ethnic niche. Moreover, the motivation to maintain boundaries around the niche does not just emanate from an abstract desire to be with others of one's own kind (or even to maintain social distance from some stigmatized other); rather, it derives from the process of serial migrant labor market incorporation, which in turn spurs the cycle of complementary and competitive relationships between old-timer and newcomer groups.

The instability of capitalist economies leads to a recurrent recourse to outsider groups, who enter the queue at the bottom, where they work in complementarity to higher-ranked insiders. But the initial situation of complementarity lasts only as long as the economic orientations of the two groups diverge; once the aspirations and orientations of the two groups converge, job competition ensues. Under these circumstances, a combination of economic and noneconomic factors impel insider groups to prevent outsiders from gaining access to the niche. The influx of a stigmatized other threatens the overall standing of the group's niche – itself often recently won. More important, incumbents in a good niche have a scarce commodity to protect. Even in the best of times, good jobs attract a surplus of applicants, which tells us that there are never enough truly desirable positions. The exclusion of outsiders keeps competition in check, serving the needs of incumbents while also preserving a resource for future cohorts of insiders not yet admitted to the niche. Finally, competition activates cultural and ideological sources of group affinity and exclusiveness, since incumbents' sense of group identity is embedded in stable networks and patterns of hiring, recruitment, and mobility.

Black–White Antagonism

Thus, discrimination can be seen as the consequence of job competition, with the niche taking the form of a kind of group property. Though perhaps Balkanized, the labor market is not yet the Balkans, with each group pitted against the next. On the contrary, as one black skilled-trades worker pointed out to me: "When the white workers are in the room, it's fuckin' guinea this, stinking kike that, polack this. When I come into the room, they're all white."

This statement pungently crystallizes the intellectual puzzle of why so much more antagonism characterizes the encounters between whites and blacks than those among the plethora of culturally distinctive, visibly identifiable groups that joust with one another over economically desirable slots.

The answer to that puzzle, I suggest, has several parts. First, race is a particularly convenient marker, with slightly more subtle ethnic criteria providing more difficult, and therefore more costly, means around which to organize exclusion. Second, in the American context race is far more than a marker: it is a characteristic suffused with meaning, adding an extraeconomic dimension to the entry of blacks into a dominant white niche. Third, conflict has been crucial to blacks' efforts to move into dominant white niches, and far more so than has been true for other outsider groups.

The persistence and intensity of black–white conflict reflects, in part, the mismatch between black economic ambitions and the thresholds needed to enter the jobs to which blacks aspire. Whereas African-American migrants accepted jobs that whites would no longer do, the migrants' children and grandchildren have sought positions in niches which whites have not left. In this quest, African-Americans resemble other outsider groups who began as migrants at the bottom. But earlier groups of outsiders like Italians or Jews, as well as contemporary counterparts like Chinese, Koreans, and even Jamaicans or Dominicans, have had access to resources – education, skills, capital, and most important, assistance from their co-ethnics – that have helped them find alternate routes into defended niches and improve their bargaining position with incumbent groups. Lacking these resources, African-Americans have been more likely than other outsider groups to pursue a directly competitive strategy for entering a niche. That strategy, in turn, has heightened the defensive orientations of whites, intensifying their concern with boundary maintenance and markers, and breeding a cycle of escalating conflict.

Slicing the Pie

Thus far, I have tried to explain why ethnic groups develop economic specializations and how those specializations evolve. But the problem is still more complex, because I need to provide an account of how the same opportunity – the vacancies created by the diminishing presence of whites – has had such different effects on immigrants and on African-Americans.

The answer lies in the framework developed above. A group's *prior* place in the ethnic division of labor exercises a crucial influence on its chances of benefiting from the opportunities that arise from succession. To inherit the positions abandoned by departing whites, one needs a recruitment network already in place. Since hiring works with a built-in bias toward incumbents, recruitment into an industry can become a self-feeding process; consequently, replacement processes will work to the advantages of those groups that most easily and quickly produce new recruits.

Timing also influences the outcome. When ethnic succession stirred up New York's ethnic division of labor, history had put African-Americans and new immigrants in different places. At the high tide of black migration to New York, whites were still solidly entrenched in the city's working class; even low-level, traditionally immigrant industries retained whites within their effective labor supply; in more skilled, manual jobs, whites maintained virtually complete control. In contrast to the circumstances under which the post-1965 immigrants entered the economy, African-Americans encountered a situation in which white ethnic incumbents held on to all but the bottom-most positions; the strength of these network-based tendencies toward social closure narrowed the scope of black employment and shaped their pattern of job concentration.

By the time compositional changes in the 1970s and 1980s produced widespread vacancies, African-Americans had developed alternative feeding points into the economy. These black niches were shaped by previous experience. Sectors that provided more and better opportunities gained a heavier flow of recruits. Where, by contrast, discrimination continued to prevail, the potential supply of African-American workers dwindled. Although the transitional nature of the migration experience had conditioned earlier cohorts of black workers to accept jobs in the traditional immigrant industries, the children and grand-children of the southern migrants had taken on aspirations that precluded this type of work. Consequently, employers turned to immigrants to fill the vacancies created by the massive outflow of whites. Once a small cluster of "seedbed" immigrants implanted itself, networks among newcomers and settlers quickly directed new arrivals into the appropriate places in the job market. Given employers' preference for hiring through networks – and the ability of employees to pressure their bosses to do so – information about job openings rarely penetrated outside the groups that concentrated in a particular trade. As the newcomers built up their niches, they limited entry to members of the club. Thus, history became crucial in understanding who got which pieces of New York's pie and why.

Notes

1 William J. Wilson, *The Truly Disadvantaged: The Inner City, the Underclass, and Public Policy* (Chicago: University of Chicago Press, 1987); Christopher Jencks and Paul Peterson, eds., *The Urban Underclass* (Washington, DC: Brookings Institution, 1991).

2 Sharon Zukin, "Gentrification," *Annual Review of Sociology*, 13 (1987): 129–47; William Frey and Alden Speare, *Regional and Metropolitan Growth and Decline in the United States* (New York: Russell Sage Foundation, 1988).

3 George Sternlieb and James Hughes, "The Uncertain Future of the Central City," *Urban Affairs Quarterly*, 18, no. 4 (1983): 455–72; John Kasarda, "Jobs, Mismatches, and Emerging Urban Mismatches," in M. G. H. Geary and L. Lynn, eds., *Urban Change and Poverty* (Washington, DC: National Academy Press, 1988), pp. 148–98.

4 Saskia Sassen, *The Mobility of Capital and Labor* (New York: Cambridge University Press, 1988) and *The Global City: New York, London, Tokyo* (Princeton: Princeton University Press, 1992); Bennett Harrison and Barry Bluestone, *The Great U-Turn* (New York: Basic Books, 1988).

5 John Bodnar, *The Transplanted: A History of Immigrants in Urban America* (Bloomington: University of Indiana Press, 1985).

6 Thomas Bailey and I developed this argument in our article "Primary, Secondary, Enclave Labor Markets: A Training Systems Approach," *American Sociological Review*, 56, no. 4 (August 1991): 432–45; for additional empirical examples, see Bailey's book *Immigrant and Native Workers: Contrasts and Competition* (Boulder, Colo.: Westview Press, 1987) and my *Through the Eye of the Needle: Immigrants and Enterprise in New York's Garment Trades* (New York: New York University Press, 1986), chap. 6.

7 On the concept of social capital, see James Coleman, "Social Capital in the Creation of Human Capital," *American Journal of Sociology*, 94, supplement (1988): S95–120; Alejandro Portes and Julia Sensenbrenner, "Embeddedness and Immigration: Notes on the Social Determination of Embeddedness," *American Journal of Sociology*, 98, no. 6 (1993): 1320–51; and Portes's edited volume *The Economic Sociology of Immigration: Essays in Networks, Ethnicity, and Entrepreneurship* (New York: Russell Sage Foundation, 1994).

8 On ethnic economies, their characteristics, and their consequences, see Roger Waldinger, Howard Aldrich, Robin Ward, and associates, *Ethnic Entrepreneurs* (Newbury Park, Calif.: Sage Publications, 1990), and Howard Aldrich and Roger Waldinger, "Ethnicity and Entrepreneurship," *Annual Review of Sociology*, 16 (1990): 111–35. The role of ethnic economies figures prominently in the work of Alejandro Portes, whose research on the Cuban "immigrant ethnic enclave" in Miami has been enormously influential, though quite controversial. See his books, *Latin Journey* (Berkeley: University of California Press, 1985; coauthored with Robert Bach) and *City on the Edge: The Transformation of Miami* (Berkeley: University of California Press, 1993; coauthored with Alex Stepick).

9 Suzanne Model, "The Ethnic Niche and the Structure of Opportunity: Immigrants and Minorities in New York City." In Michael Katz, ed., *The "Underclass" Debate*. Princeton, NJ: Princeton University Press, 1993, p. 168.

10 See Nathan Glazer and Daniel Moynihan, *Beyond the Melting Pot* (Cambridge, Mass.: MIT Press, 1963). William Yancey, Eugene Erickson, and Richard Juliani, "Emergent Ethnicity: A Critique and Review," *American Sociological Review*, 41 (1976), and Michael Hechter, "Group Formation and the Cultural Division of Labor," *American Journal of Sociology*, 84 (1978): 293–318.

11 The fundamental work remains Gary Becker's pioneering book *The Economics of Discrimination* (Chicago: University of Chicago Press, 1957); for a more recent review of the economic literature, see Glen Cain, "The Economic Analysis of Labor Market

Discrimination: A Survey," in Orley Ashenfelter and Richard Layard, eds., *Handbook of Labor Economics*, vol. 1, (Amsterdam: North-Holland, 1986), chap. 13.

12   Ray Marshall, "The Economics of Discrimination: A Survey," *Journal of Economic Literature*, 12, no. 3 (1974): 849–71.

13   William J. Wilson, *The Declining Significance of Race* (Chicago: University of Chicago Press, 1978). Wilson's argument here draws on the "split labor market theory" developed by Edna Bonacich in her articles "A Theory of Ethnic Antagonism: The Split Labor Market," *American Sociological Review*, 37 (1972), and "Advanced Capitalism and Black/White Relations in the United States: A Split Labor Market Analysis," *American Sociological Review*, 41 (1976): 34–51.

10 The Return of the Sweatshop

Edna Bonacich and Richard P. Appelbaum

In this chapter, Edna Bonacich and Richard Appelbaum describe the reemergence of sweatshops, sites in which poorly paid, often immigrant, workers in the United States produce or assemble clothing for major companies. They argue that global competition in the clothing industry, the decline of unionization, and the shift to flexible production have set the stage for rapid growth in this low-wage sector.

Bonacich and Appelbaum explain why Los Angeles has become the largest center for women's clothing manufacturing in the United States. A combination of the city's association with fashion, its large population of immigrants, and its antiunion tradition have allowed this exploitative form of employment to flourish.

Where does the money from the sale of a $100 dress actually go? The wholesale cost of a $100 dress made in the United States is about $50; half of the $100 sales price goes to the retailer. Of the $50 wholesale cost, 45 percent, or $22.50, is spent by the manufacturer on the fabric. Twenty-five percent, or $12.50, is profit and overhead for the manufacturer. The remaining 30 percent, or $15, goes to the contractor, and covers both the cost of direct labor and the contractor's other expenses, and profit. Only 6 percent, $6, goes to the person who actually sewed the garment. Furthermore, this individual was more than likely to have been paid by the number of sewing operations performed than by the hour and to have received no benefits of any kind. (See figure 10.1.)

Sweatshops have indeed returned to the United States. A phenomenon of the apparel industry considered long past is back, not as a minor aberration, but as a prominent way of doing business. Every once in a while, an especially dramatic story hits the news: an Orange Country family is found sewing in their home,

Bonacich, Edna and Richard P. Appelbaum, "The Return of the Sweatshop." From *Behind the Label: Inequality in the Los Angeles Apparel Industry* (Berkeley: University of California Press, 2000), pp. 1–14, 16–23, 25, notes. © 2000 by the Regents of the University of California. Permission granted by the Regents of the University of California and the University of California Press.

Retailer, $50

Manufacturer, $35
($22.50 for fabric)

Contractor, $15
(Workers, $6)

Figure 10.1   The distribution of the proceeds of a $100 dress.
Source: Elizabeth Weiner and Dean Foust, "Why Made-in-America Is Back in Style," *Business Week*, Nov. 1988, pp. 116–18. Data from Kurt Salmon Associates, Inc.

where a 7-year-old child works next to his mother. Thai workers in El Monte are found in an apartment complex, held against their will under conditions of semi-enslavement while earning subminimum wages. Kathie Lee Gifford, celebrity endorser of a Wal-Mart label, discovers that her line is being produced in sweatshops both offshore and in the United States and cries in shame on national television. The United States Department of Labor develops a program to make apparel manufacturers take responsibility for sweatshop violations. The President of the United States establishes the Apparel Industry Partnership to see if a solution can be found to the growth of sweatshops here and abroad. The nation is becoming aware that the scourge of sweatshops has returned.

Sweatshops first emerged in the United States apparel industry in the last decades of the nineteenth century with the development of the mass production of garments in New York City. Immigrant workers, mainly young women, slaved for long hours over their sewing machines in cramped and unsanitary factories, for very low wages. Workers eventually rebelled. In 1909 a major strike by shirtwaist factory workers, sometimes called the uprising of the 20,000, was the first mass strike by women workers in the United States. (Shirtwaists, a style of women's blouse, were the first mass-produced fashion items.) It was followed by strikes in other sectors of the industry. In 1911 the infamous Triangle Shirtwaist factory fire in New York resulted in the deaths of 146 young garment workers, and provoked public outrage.[1] Organized, militant, and supported by an aroused public, the workers founded the garment unions and demanded contracts that would protect them against sweatshop production. New Deal legislation reinforced basic standards of labor for workers and protected their right to join or form independent unions. A combination of government protection and strong apparel unions helped to relegate garment sweatshops to the margins of the industry until the 1970s, when they began to reappear.

What exactly is a "sweatshop"? A sweatshop is usually defined as a factory or a homework operation that engages in multiple violations of the law, typically the non-payment of minimum or overtime wages and various violations of health and safety regulations. According to this definition, many of the garment factories in Los Angeles are sweatshops. In a sample survey conducted by the United States Department of Labor in January 1998, 61 percent of the garment firms in Los Angeles were found to be violating wage and hour regulations. Workers were underpaid by an estimated $73 million dollars per year. Health and safety violations were not examined in that study, but in a survey completed in 1997, 96 percent of the firms were found to be in violation, 54 percent with deficiencies that could lead to serious injuries or death.

An emphasis merely on violations of the law fails to capture the full extent of what has been happening. In recent years the garment industry has been moving its production offshore to countries where workers earn much lower wages than are paid in the United States. In offshore production, some manufacturers may follow local laws, but the legal standard is so low that the workers, often including young teenagers, live in poverty, although they are working full time. The same problem arises in the United States. Even if a factory follows the letter of the law in every detail, workers may suffer abuse, job insecurity, and poverty. In 1990, according to the United States census, the average garment worker in Los Angeles made only $7,200, less than three-quarters of the poverty-level income for a family of three in that year. Thus we wish to broaden the definition of sweatshops to include factories that fail to pay a "living wage," meaning a wage that enables a family to support itself at a socially defined, decent standard of living.[2] We include in the concept of a living wage the idea that people should be able to afford decent housing, given the local housing market, and that a family should be covered by health insurance. If wages fail to cover these minima, and if families with working members still fall below the official poverty line, they are, we claim, working in sweatshops.

Why are sweatshops returning to the apparel industry a number of decades after they had more or less disappeared? Why have their numbers grown so rapidly, especially in the last two decades of the twentieth century? And why has Los Angeles, in particular, become a center of garment sweatshops?

Global, Flexible Capitalism

The reemergence of apparel industry sweatshops is part of a much broader phenomenon, namely, the restructuring of global capitalism – a phenomenon we refer to as the new global capitalism. Starting in the 1970s, and accelerating rapidly especially in the 1980s and 1990s, the restructuring included a series of complex changes: a decline in the welfare state in most of the developed industrial countries; a growth in multinational corporations and an increase in global production; entry into manufacturing for export by many countries, among them some of the poorest in the world; a rise in world trade and intensification of competition; deindustrialization in the developed countries; a decrease in job security and an increase in part-time work; a rise in immigration from poorer countries to the richer ones; and renewed pressure on what remains of the welfare state.[3]

These changes are all interconnected, and it is difficult to establish a first cause. Combined, they are associated with an effort by capitalists, supported by national governments, to increase profits and push back the effects of egalitarian movements that emerged in the 1960s and 1970s and that achieved some redistributive policies. The new global capitalism is characterized by an effort to let the free market operate with a minimum of government interference. At the same time, nations are themselves promoting the hegemony of the free market and imposing it as a standard for the entire world.

Among policies that foster the free market are the elimination of trade barriers and the encouragement of international free trade, as exemplified by the North American Free Trade Agreement (NAFTA) and the World Trade Organization (WTO); the insistence by strong states on the rights of their corporations to invest abroad with a minimum of local regulation; and pressure by state-backed, world financial institutions on developing countries that they restructure their political economies so as to foster free markets. Internal policies associated with the disestablishment of the welfare state have included deregulation, the privatization of state functions, and the minimization of state interference in business practices. In the United States, for example, affirmative action, welfare, and other efforts to increase equality through state intervention have come under attack.

The new global capitalism is often touted for its so-called flexibility. The decades of the 1980s and 1990s have been described as post-Fordist; i.e., we have moved beyond huge, mass-production plants making standardized products on the assembly line to a system in which smaller batches of specialized goods are made for an increasingly diverse consumer market. New systems of production, including contracting out the manufacture of specialized goods and services, and the ability to source goods and services wherever they can most efficiently be provided, enhance this flexibility. It is sometimes argued that the new, flexible production allows for more participation by the workers, by enabling them to develop several skills and encouraging them to use their initiative. Instead of repeating the same boring task, as did the workers on the Fordist assembly line, workers in the new factories may engage in more interesting, well-rounded activities. Critics have pointed out that, while some workers may benefit from the new, flexible production arrangements, others face increased job insecurity, more part-time and temporary work, a greater likelihood of working for subcontractors, and less opportunity for unionization. Flexibility for the employer may lead to the expansion of the contingent labor force, which must shift around to find short-term jobs as they arise.

One of the starkest areas of social change in the post-welfare state period has been the attack on organized labor. In the United States, for example, during the postwar period of the late 1940s and continuing until the 1960s, an accommodation was reached between industries and trade unions, whereby both sides accepted that the unions would help to eliminate industrial warfare under a "social contract." The tacit agreement was simple: In exchange for union-demanded wages and benefits, workers would cede control over industrial production to management. The cost of this arrangement would be paid for in the marketplace, through higher prices for goods, rather than in narrower profit margins. This arrangement particularly benefited workers in large, oligopolistic industries, where unions were strong and profits were substantial. The entire economy was seen to benefit from this arrangement because the workers would have enough expendable income to buy the products, thereby stimulating production, creating more jobs, and generating a spiraling prosperity. Even though unions were never popular with business, the major industries, including the apparel industry, came to accept them and accept the fact that they made an important contribution to the well-being of the economy at large.

This view of organized labor has collapsed. Business leaders in the United States now see unions as having pushed the price of American labor too high, thereby limiting the competitiveness of firms that maintain a workforce in this country. Firms in certain industries have increasingly moved offshore to seek out low-wage labor in less developed countries. Business owners and managers also see unions as irrelevant to the new flexible systems of production. Unions grew strong in response to the Fordist production regimes, but with more decentralized systems of production, they are viewed as rigid and impractical. Besides, argue the owners and managers, more engaged and multiskilled workers no longer need union protection, as they share in a commitment to the firm's goals. Unions interfere with a company's flexibility and therefore hurt everyone, including the firm's employees.

Organized labor has been weakened by various federal policies, among them, President Ronald Reagan's dismissal of the air traffic controllers, the appointment of antiunion members to the National Labor Relations Board, the acceptance of the right of firms to hire permanent replacements for strikers, the passage of NAFTA without adequate protections for workers in any of the three countries involved, and the encouragement of offshore contracting by special tariff provisions. The development of flexible production, with its contracting out and dispersion of production around the globe, has also served to undermine unions because it is much more difficult to organize workers in a decentralized system. As a result, the proportion of the workforce that is unionized has dropped, not only in the United States, but also in other industrial countries: in the United States from a high of 37 percent in 1946 to less than 15 percent of the total workforce in 1995, and only 11 percent of the private sector workforce.[4] These figures are much lower than for the rest of the industrial world.

Another significant aspect of the new global economy has been the rise of immigration from the less developed to the industrialized countries. Local economies have been disrupted by the arrival of multinational corporations, and many people see no alternative but to seek a means of survival elsewhere. The involvement of the more developed countries in the economies and governments of the Third World is not a new phenomenon, and it has long been associated with emigration. The countervailing movements of capital and labor in opposite directions have often been noted.

What is new about the recent phase of global capitalism is the accelerated proletarianization of much of the world's remaining peasantry. Young women, in particular, have been drawn into the labor force to become the main workers in plants that engage in manufacturing for export. In many ways they are the ideal workforce, as they frequently lack the experience and alternatives that would enable them to demand higher wages and better treatment. The poor working conditions are exacerbated by political regimes, often supported by the United States, that have restricted the workers' ability to organize and demand change.

The increased exploitation of workers in the Third World has a mirror image in the movement of immigrant workers to the more developed countries. Immigrants come not only because of economic dislocations that arise, in part, from the presence of foreign capital in their homelands, but also because of political struggles that have ensued in connection with the Cold War and its aftermath. A paradox of the new global capitalism is that, although the right of capital to move freely is touted by the supporters of the free market, no such right is afforded labor. Immigration is restricted by state policies. One consequence has been the creation of so-called illegal workers, who are stripped of many basic legal rights. Immigrant workers, especially the undocumented, are more easily exploited than are native workers.

In sum, there has been a shift in the balance of power between capital and labor. Although the working class, including women and people of color, made important gains during the three postwar decades (from the late 1940s through the early 1970s), a backlash began developing in the 1970s and achieved full momentum by the 1980s. This backlash corresponds closely to the "great U-turn" in the United

States and other capitalist economies, as a broadly shared postwar rise in living standards came to a halt.[5] Conservative governments in the United States and Europe have implemented policies that favor capital and the free market over labor and other disadvantaged groups. Even political parties that have traditionally supported the working class, such as the Democrats in the United States and the Labour Party in Britain, have shifted to the right.

The reappearance of sweatshops is a feature of the new global, flexible capitalism. The original sweatshops disappeared with the growth of unions and the development of the welfare state. Today, with both of those institutions weakened, markets have been able to drive down wages and reduce working conditions to substandard levels in many labor-intensive industries, such as electronics, toys, shoes, and sports equipment. Indeed, almost every manufacturing industry and some services are pressed to reduce labor costs by minimizing job stability, by contracting out, by using more contingent (part-time and temporary) workers, by reducing benefits, and by attacking unions. But the apparel industry is leading the way.

The Apparel Industry as a Paradigm

The very word *sweatshop* has its roots in the apparel industry. It is ironic that the apparel industry should be a leader in any trend since, as an old industry, it has remained backward in many areas. Significant advances have been made in certain aspects of production, notably computer-assisted design, computer-assisted grading and marking, and computerized cutting, and there have been innovations in sewing machine technology and in the organization of work flow, but the core production process, namely the sewing of garments, is still low-tech. The primary unit of production continues to be a worker, usually a woman, sitting (or standing) at a sewing machine and sewing together pieces of limp cloth.

Garment production is labor intensive, and, unlike many other industries, it does not require much capital to get into the sewing business. Consequently, sewing factories proliferate and the industry is exceedingly competitive – probably more competitive than most. In some ways the apparel industry is the epitome of free market capitalism because the barriers to entry are so low. Less-developed countries take up apparel production as their first manufacturing industry in their efforts to industrialize. In the shift to global production and manufacturing for export, apparel has been in the vanguard. Clothing firms in the United States began to move production offshore to Asia as early as the late 1950s. Today apparel manufacturers in a number of developed countries are opening production facilities and employing workers in almost every country of the world. The result in the United States has been a rise in imports (see figure 10.2), which started to grow in the 1960s and 1970s and grew at an explosive rate in the 1980s. In 1962 apparel imports totaled $301 million. They had tripled by the end of the decade, to $1.1 billion; increased another fivefold by 1980, to $5.5 billion; and nearly

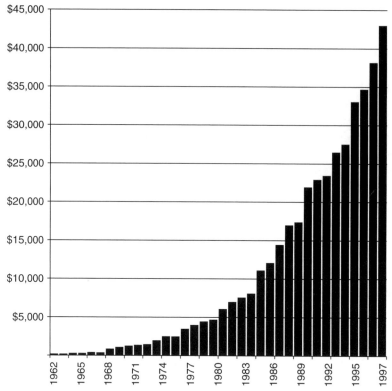

Figure 10.2 Apparel imports to the United States, 1962–1997 ($000,000)
Source: American Apparel Manufacturers Association, *Focus 1998*, p. 31; United States Office of Textiles and Apparel (OTEXA), Major Shipper's Report by Category, 9/1999 data.

another fourfold by 1990, to $21.9 billion. By 1997, apparel imports totaled $42 billion; they are projected to exceed $50 billion in 1999. According to estimates by the American Apparel Manufacturers Association, imports accounted for 60 percent of the $101 billion wholesale apparel market.[6] Needless to say, this has greatly increased the level of competition within the industry, creating a pressure to lower wages in the United States garment industry to meet the low wages paid overseas. Global production is certainly expanding in other industries, but apparel is the most globalized industry of all.

The United States is the largest consumer market for apparel in the world. One measure for comparing consumption that does not depend on relative prices is the average per-capita fiber consumption. In 1989–90 (the latest available figures), the average annual world consumption was 17.9 pounds per person. For the United States it was 57.3 pounds. Japan came second with 48.9 pounds per capita. Latin America consumed only 12.8 pounds per capita and Africa, 2.9. A primary target for exporting countries, the United States is by far the leading importer of apparel in the world.[7]

The return of sweatshops in the United States apparel industry can be partly, but not entirely, attributed to the dramatic rise in offshore production, and the concomitant increase in cheap imports. Much of the industry is driven by fashion, and sales of fashionable garments are highly volatile. The production of apparel is generally a risky business, which discourages heavy capital investment and limits the availability of capital for firms that want to expand or upgrade. The riskiness is augmented by time. Fashion can change quickly. Apparel manufacturers want to be sure that any demand is fully met, but must be wary of overproducing garments that may fall out of fashion. The industry needs to be especially sensitive to changes in consumer taste, to respond quickly to these shifts, and to cease production of dying trends in a timely manner.

Needless to say, the industry tries to mold the fickle consumers' tastes as much as possible, by heavy advertising, by producing fashion shows and magazines, and by publicizing the opinions of pundits who predict and help to determine the trends. Indeed, the industry has considerable internal variation in terms of susceptibility to the fashion dynamic. Some garments, considered to be basics, change only slowly. Basics include most underwear and sleepwear, T-shirts, sweatshirts and sweatpants, denim jeans, and men's shirts and pants. The areas of greatest fashion volatility include women's dresses, skirts and tops, women's bathing suits, and the broader area known as women's sportswear (casual clothing). Note that all the traditional basics also can include fashion lines. The Gap made a fortune by turning the basic T-shirt into a personal fashion statement. And denim jeans, when associated with the names of particular designers, have experienced the hot flash of fashion success.

Offshore production usually requires longer waiting times, thereby increasing the risk in making time-sensitive garments. Basics can be planned months in advance without much risk that the garments will go out of fashion. In the United States apparel industry, the production of basics has moved steadily offshore, and highly fashionable apparel is more likely to be made domestically. The distinction is likely to lessen with time as communication and transportation times decrease and as arrangements are made to produce garments in regions closer to their destination market. NAFTA, for example, has led to an enormous growth in Mexico's capacity to produce garments for the United States apparel industry. Because it is much closer to the United States than Asia is, some production has been shifted from Asia to Mexico; and it is possible that the production of more fashion-sensitive garments will also be shifted there. Their proximity also accounts for shifts to the Caribbean and Central America.

The fashion-sensitive sector of the industry is much more concentrated in women's wear than in men's wear, although this may be changing a little. Women in the United States spend twice as much on clothing as do men. The general difference between women's and men's wear has led to a segregation between the two sectors of the industry. For example, the major industry newspaper is called *Women's Wear Daily*. The two major sectors eventually produced two unions: the

International Ladies' Garment Workers' Union (ILGWU), which organized workers in the women's sector, and the Amalgamated Clothing and Textile Workers Union (ACTWU), which organized workers in the textile industry and the men's wear sector. The two unions merged in 1995 into UNITE, the Union of Needletrades, Industrial and Textile Employees, probably less because of a convergence between the two types of garment production than because of the loss of membership that each was suffering.

The differences have also led to a divergence in production systems. Men's wear has generally been produced in larger, mass-production factories, women's wear in smaller, contracted-out production units. Typically, in the production of women's clothing, apparel manufacturers (companies known by the brand names) design and engineer the garments, buy the textiles, and wholesale the completed clothing. The actual production of the garment, the cutting, sewing, laundering, and finishing, is usually done by independent contractors. Most garment contractors are sewing contractors, and they typically receive cut goods that their employees sew. Most garment workers are employed in small, contracting factories, sewing garments for manufacturers, who typically employ several contractors. Contracting out extends at the margins to industrial homework, with a single woman sitting at her home sewing machine, making clothing for a firm that employs her.

The contracting out of apparel production can be seen as an instance of flexible production. It allows apparel manufacturers to deal with fluctuations in fashion and seasons by hiring contractors when they need them and letting them go when they do not. In this respect the apparel industry is at the cutting edge of the new global economy: It has used contracting out for decades and has developed this flexible production system to a fine art. Moreover, the contracting system has been extended to global production. Manufacturers not only employ local contractors, but also often conduct their offshore production through contracting rather than through the ownership of subsidiaries. The lack of fixed assets enables them to move production wherever they can get the best deal in terms of labor cost, taxes and tariffs, environmental regulation, or any other factor that influences the quality and cost of their products.

The virtue of the contracting system for the manufacturers is that they do not need to invest a cent in the factories that actually sew their clothes. Manufacturers engage in arm's-length transactions with their contractors, enabling them to avoid any long-term commitment to a particular contractor or location. The formal commitment lasts only as long as the particular job order. In practice, manufacturers may develop longer-term relationships with a core group of dependable contractors, attempting to ensure that they receive steady work. Nevertheless, the absence of firm ties provides maximum flexibility for manufacturers and the elimination of costly inefficiencies associated with having dependent subsidiaries. Contracting out enables manufacturers to hire only the labor they actually need.

The picture is not quite so rosy from the other side. Contractors, who in the United States and other advanced industrial countries, are often immigrants, must scramble to maintain steady work. And rather than employ a stable workforce, they pass the problems created by flexible production on to their workers. In the United States most garment workers are employed on a piece-work basis, so that they are paid only for the work they actually do. If the work is slow, they do not get paid. In offshore production, workers are more likely to receive an hourly wage rather than piece rate, but they are required to produce an arduous daily quota. Their hours and quotas, like those of piece-rate workers, are determined by the shifting demands of their manufacturers; at the height of the season or if they are producing a hot fashion item, they are required to work long hours. During a lull, they are laid off and go unpaid.

It is out of such a system of contracting out that the sweatshop is born. What provides wonderful flexibility for the manufacturer provides unstable work, impoverishment, and often abusive conditions for the workers. The idea that smaller factories, making specialized goods for an everchanging market, means that workers are better trained and have more responsibility has not worked out for most garment workers. Instead, they continue to engage in Fordist-style, highly repetitive, boring tasks conducted at high speeds. But because they no longer work in large, centralized production facilities, it is much more difficult for them to join or form unions. In addition, the mobility of the industry makes the task of unionizing formidable because manufacturers can easily shift production away from contractors that show any signs of labor unrest. In sum, flexible production, at least in the apparel industry, has created a much more effective engine for exploiting workers than existed before the new era of global capitalism.

Another feature of the apparel industry that probably portends developments in other industries is the rapidly growing power of retailers in the new global economy, another consequence of the emphasis on increased flexibility. No longer selling to a mass market, retailers now expect to supply consumers with the variety that they want when they want it. Rather than carrying large quantities of inventory in standardized products, the retailers want to be able to order and reorder popular items on short notice. They cherry-pick from designers' and manufacturers' lines, order only the items that they want, and expect them to be delivered rapidly.

The power of retailers in the apparel industry is partly a product of the highly competitive character of the industry, which often gives them the upper hand in dealing with manufacturers. Retailers have also gained power by engaging in their own direct offshore sourcing. Recently, their power has been consolidated by a series of mergers; by 1996 the four largest retailers in the United States accounted for two-thirds of the total value of national apparel retail sales. Consolidation has increased the ability to demand more from manufacturers in terms of price and speed, demands that reverberate all the way down the system to the workers, who bear the brunt of lower wages and faster production.

The idea of fashion and of constantly changing products for specialized markets is spreading far beyond apparel to many other industries. However, the very word "fashion" is deeply associated with the garment industry. It can be seen as the first industry that developed the notion of constantly changing styles. And as we have seen, its highly flexible production system is the most advanced of any industry. [...]

The rise in apparel imports has inevitably led to a decline in jobs in the United States garment industry. Peak employment was reached in the early 1970s; since then, employment has more or less steadily decreased. In 1970 the industry employed 1,364,000 people. By 1980 the number had fallen to 1,264,000. In 1990 it was 1,036,000, and in 1997, 813,000. Between 1978 and 1998, in almost every state except California, employment in apparel declined. New York, New Jersey, Pennsylvania, and Massachusetts lost over half their apparel jobs.[8] In California, and mostly in Los Angeles, over 50,000 apparel jobs have been added since 1978.

Garment Production in Los Angeles

To the surprise of many people, Los Angeles is the manufacturing center of the nation, with 663,400 manufacturing jobs in 1997. Los Angeles has 5,900 more manufacturing jobs than the second city, Chicago, and over 200,000 more than Detroit, a distant third.[9] Equally surprising is the fact that the apparel industry is the largest manufacturing employer in Los Angeles County, with 122,500 employees enumerated by the Employment Development Department in April 1998. Thus, almost one out of five manufacturing employees in Los Angeles works in the apparel industry.

Los Angeles has felt the effects of global restructuring. Many high-paying union jobs in the automobile, tire, and aerospace industries have fled the region, while low-wage manufacturing jobs have multiplied. Among these low-wage industries, apparel "has been the lowest paying sector."[10] Nonetheless, Los Angeles is now the apparel manufacturing center of the United States. [...] More people are employed in the apparel industry in Los Angeles County than anywhere else in the nation, more than in New York, and far more than in any other center. (See figure 10.3)

Why has Los Angeles become such an important center of garment production? First, the city is a center of design and fashion. The entertainment industry is, through its movies, television, and music, but the most visible manifestation of the city's creation of style. Southern California represents a way of life that is idealized and emulated around the globe. The names Hollywood, California, Disneyland, and even Los Angeles itself conjure up images of fantasy, fun in the sun, the freedom of the western frontier, informality, rebellion, and the end of formal tradition. It is not surprising that Los Angeles attracts people from many different cultures. Los Angeles sells itself along with its products, and its products benefit from all the connotations of the place. The apparel industry finds a natural haven

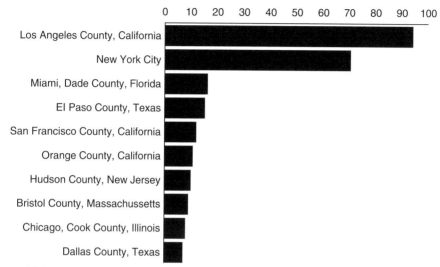

Figure 10.3   United States counties with highest levels of employment in the apparel sector ((SIC 23), 1994 (000 employees)
Source: Goetz Wolff, "The Apparel Cluster: A Regional Growth Industry" (pamphlet prepared for the California College Fashion Symposium, Los Angeles, April 1997). Data from United States Dept. of Commerce, *County Business Patterns*, 1994. © Goetz Wolff.

in Los Angeles in part because of the city's strong connections with fashion and style. The city produces style not only through the entertainment industry but also on its streets: The place creates fashion.

The apparel made in Los Angeles is overwhelmingly women's wear. In 1997 Goetz Wolff, using data from 1994 County Business Patterns, examined the various components of the local apparel industry to compare Los Angeles with the rest of the country. While 25 percent of the United States industry, excluding Los Angeles, was devoted to women's outerwear, 65 percent of the Los Angeles industry was so concentrated. Los Angeles accounts for about 10 percent of all apparel produced in the United States, but almost 25 percent of the women's outerwear.[11] Even in men's wear, Los Angeles tends to specialize in the fashion end, making hip-hop wear, or beach wear, or other garments for which the styles keep changing.

The fact that Los Angeles is also a major center for immigration, especially from Asia, Mexico, and Central America, combines with the industry's focus on fashion to create a location where the most "advanced" forms of flexible production are found. Los Angeles's apparel industry has spawned thousands of contractors who can produce small lots rapidly. In other words, the city's industry is primed for the production of fashion at cheap prices. Immigrants play a vital role in two aspects of the industry. They provide the workforce and the entrepreneurship to run the contracting shops. Many of the immigrant workers are undocumented, which means that they often lack the political wherewithal to resist exploitation. Meanwhile, anti-immigrant movements in California have made immigrants increasingly vulnerable and exacerbated their political disadvantage.

Los Angeles has a long antiunion tradition and has been a harbor for entrepreneurial activity that does not need to worry about union organizing. Many industries are less unionized in Los Angeles than they are in most other major cities in the country, including, importantly, New York and San Francisco. This adds to the attractiveness of Los Angeles as a center of flexible production. Without having to worry about a unionized work force, manufacturers and retailers can arrange production to their own maximal advantage, shifting all the risk to the contractors, and ultimately to the workers. Los Angeles can indeed be described as the "sweatshop capital of the United States."

The Race to the Bottom

The United States is growing more and more unequal, with increasing polarization along race and class lines. In Los Angeles the forces that are shaping inequality in the United States are more sharply focused. The city is characterized by immense wealth, on the one hand, and extreme poverty on the other. A study by a committee of the California legislature found that, between 1989 and 1996, the number of very rich Angelinos, including those with annual incomes over $25 million, doubled, from 165 to 376 individuals, and that, from 1994 to 1996, the numbers of the very poor, those with annual incomes of less that $20,000, grew by 13.5 percent from 2.5 million to 2.9 million people. The authors conclude that there has been a hollowing out of the middle class and that the individuals and families hardest hit by the recession of the early 1990s have been slowest to benefit from the recovery, while the wealthy have benefited strongly.[12] Multimillionaires and even billionaires build mansions in the mountains and canyons and in rich communities such as Beverly Hills and Bel Air, while unemployment soars in the African-American community, and immigrant workers do almost all of the physical labor to eke out a bare survival for themselves and their children. The developments came to a dramatic climax in the so-called riots of April 1992, when all the bitterness of growing inequality in a land of plenty burst out in violent fury.

The apparel industry shows these same extremes. It is an industry in which some people, such as retailers and manufacturers, managers and professionals, bankers and real estate owners, are able to acquire immense wealth. Others, most notably garment workers, are among the poorest, lowest-paid workers in the city. The industry is not only polarized along class lines, it also has a clear racial and ethnic structure and hierarchy. The wealthy at the top are almost all of European extraction. At the bottom, the workers are mainly Latino immigrants, especially from Mexico and Central America, and a minority are Asian immigrants. In the middle are the entrepreneurs who run the contracting shops that employ the workers, and who are mainly immigrants from Asia (and, to a lesser extent, from Mexico and Central America). [. . .]

The Los Angeles apparel industry participates in this kind of perverted logic. On the one hand, the industry's leaders are embarrassed by the proliferation of sweatshops. They hate the image of being a sweatshop industry. Obviously it creates unfavorable public relations, as well as various governmental efforts to regulate the industry. It also runs counter to the socially liberal self-image held by many of the leaders themselves, who contribute large amounts of money to worthy causes, oppose racism, and often vote for Democratic Party candidates. Moreover, the growth of sweatshops can provoke movements by consumers, religious leaders, and others that call the industry's practices into question, threatening sales and profits. On the other hand, industry leaders fight with all their might to keep the cost of labor down. They fought against the rise in the minimum wage. They objected when the city of Los Angeles passed a living wage ordinance because, even though it did not affect them directly, they saw it as the first crack in the door toward rising wages.[13] They cheered when the state Industrial Wage Commission eliminated daily overtime rates payable after eight hours in favor of weekly overtime rates payable only after 40 hours, which, of course, means that garment workers who work long days will be paid less. And they are ferociously antiunion, willing to spend millions of dollars fighting unionism rather than raising wages. [. . .]

Garment manufacturers may, as individuals, have an interest in undercutting their competition by lowering their prices and their costs, but they also have a contradictory, collective interest in maintaining their consumer market. The polarization of the population into rich and poor, a polarization that extends beyond the United States to the rest of the world, creates a stratified market. As poor people only can afford cheap clothing, discounters flourish, and the middle level of the market is threatened. The growth of discounters, which attracts not only impoverished buyers but also some of the middle-class consumers, creates a new level of pressure on wages: the lower the final price of the garment, the cheaper its cost of production must be. Wages and consumer prices spiral down together at the lower end. [. . .]

In many ways southern California resembles the old South, where African Americans were also a disenfranchised population. In the South, the major marker for disempowerment was race. In Los Angeles, it is a combination of race and immigration status. Immigration status alone marks off a segment of the population as unprotected by the basic laws of the land, but the effect is exacerbated by race because, of all undocumented immigrants, Latinos carry a special burden as the target of anti-immigrant movements. The racism of the system in southern California is more subtle than that in the South because it is hidden under a layer of legalese. In southern California, the combination of race and immigrant status is used to create a workforce without rights. Employers are the major beneficiaries of undocumented immigration from Mexico and Central America. They have under their control a highly exploitable workforce. They can pay illegally low wages and get away with it. The gross imbalance of power leads to a kind of corruption that very few are able to withstand.

Notes

1   Leon Stein, *The Triangle Fire* (New York: Carroll and Graf, 1962).
2   The Los Angeles City Council passed a living wage ordinance in early 1997: Holders of municipal contracts and firms receiving substantial financial aid from the city must pay their employees at least $7.25 an hour, plus health insurance, or $8.50 an hour without specified benefits. At the time, the state and federal minimum wage was $4.25 an hour. See Jean Merl, "Defiant Mayor Vetoes 'Living Wage' Ordinance," *Los Angeles Times*, 28 March 1997, sec. B, p. 3. The concept of a living wage has emerged in Los Angeles and other cities, where it has become clear that a minimum-wage job without benefits puts a family well below the official poverty level. Those who must labor under such conditions are the working poor.
3   A large and growing literature treats these developments: for example, David Harvey, *The Condition of Postmodernity* (Cambridge: Blackwell, 1989); Ankie Hoogvelt, *Globalization and the Postcolonial World: The New Political Economy of Development* (Baltimore: Johns Hopkins University Press, 1997); Kim Moody, *Workers in a Lean World* (New York: Verso, 1997); and Beth A. Rubin, *Shifts in the Social Contract: Understanding Change in American Society* (Thousand Oaks, Calif.: Pine Forge Press, 1996).
4   Kate Bronfenbrenner, Sheldon Friedman, Richard W. Hurd, Rudolph A. Oswald, and Ronald L. Seeber, eds., *Organizing to Win: New Research on Union Strategies* (Ithaca, NY: ILR Press, 1997), 2–3.
5   Bennett Harrison and Barry Bluestone, *The Great U-Turn: Corporate Restructuring and the Polarizing of America* (New York: Basic Books, 1990).
6   American Apparel Manufacturers Association, *Focus: An Economic Profile of the Apparel Industry* (Arlington, Va.: AAMA, 1998), 4. The apparel retail market in the United States reached $180 billion in 1997.
7   Kitty Dickerson, *Textiles and Apparel in the Global Economy*, 2d ed. (New York: Macmillan, 1995), 202–6, 225–6.
8   American Apparel Manufacturers Association, *Focus 1998* (Arlington, Va.), p. 10. In New York City there has recently been a slight rise in apparel employment. The city's apparel and textile manufacturing employment peaked in the mid-1970s at 250,000, but had dropped to 82,500 by 1996. In 1997 it rose to 84,000. "Rebirth of New York's Apparel Industry," *Apparel Industry Magazine*, March 1998, p. 12.
9   Daniel Taub, "LA Beats Out Chicago as No. 1 Manufacturing Center," *Los Angeles Business Journal*, 9 March 1998, p. 5. See also Louis Uchitelle, "The New Faces of US Manufacturing: California's Vision of the Future: Thriving, But with Fewer High-Wage Jobs," *New York Times*, 3 July 1994, sec. 3, p. 1; Jack Kyser, *Manufacturing in Los Angeles* (Los Angeles, Calif.: Economic Development Corp., 1997).

10 Taub, "LA Beats Out Chicago," p. 5.

11 Goetz Wolff, "The Apparel Cluster: A Regional Growth Industry," pamphlet prepared for the California Community College Fashion Symposium, CaliforniaMart, Los Angeles, April 1997.

12 California Legislature, Assembly Select Committee on the California Middle Class, *The Distribution of Income in California and Los Angeles: A Look at Recent Current Population Survey and State Taxpayer Data* (Sacramento, 1998). The chairman of the committee is Assemblyman Wally Knox.

13 Kristin Young, "The Living Wage Debate," *California Apparel News*, 31 January–6 February 1997, 6–7. Both the California Fashion Association, an organization of the major manufacturers, and the Downtown Property Owners Association, the major garment district real estate owners, opposed the ordinance.

Part III

The Changing Urban Economy

11 Understanding Homelessness: From Global to Local

Jennifer Wolch and Michael Dear

One of the consequences of economic restructuring is the increasing polarization between the rich and the poor in cities. Urbanites see upscale shops and restaurants opening every week along with increasing numbers of homeless people on the sidewalks and in the parks. Jennifer Wolch and Michael Dear explain the rise of homelessness in the 1980s and 1990s as due to three factors: decreases in wages, reductions in the social safety net, and changes in the housing market. The combined impact of these three factors leaves growing numbers of people on the brink of homelessness. Wolch and Dear describe how some individuals manage to avoid becoming homeless or are able to regain housing while others become permanently homeless.

Homelessness is a growth industry.
> – *Maxene Johnson, Director, Weingart Center, Los Angeles*

Few places in the United States remain untouched by homelessness. The shocking scale of the problem has provoked an explosion of popular and professional concern. Much effort has been directed toward explaining the genesis of the crisis, and a large number of contributing (sometimes contradictory) factors have been identified. Our objective is to devise a parsimonious yet comprehensive theory of homelessness, which will also serve as a framework for the remainder of our analysis. We emphasize three principal dynamics that create homelessness (figure 11.1): the structural forces that have caused widespread economic marginalization, along with the consequent increase in the demand for public assistance and the lack of a governmental response to that demand; the structural forces that have led to a dearth of available and affordable housing; and the personal circumstances that propel certain people (and not others) into homelessness.

Wolch, Jennifer and Michael Dear, "Understanding Homelessness: From Global to Local." From *Malign Neglect: Homelessness in an American City* (San Francisco: Jossey-Bass, 1993), pp. 1–14, 20–2, 24–43. Reprinted by permission of the authors.

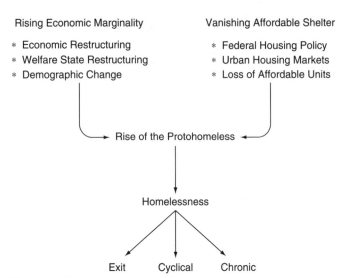

Figure 11.1   Dynamics of homelessness

The Rise of Economic Marginality

Reduced to its essentials, homelessness is an expression and extension of poverty in the United States. Simply stated, personal income has declined to such an extent that people can no longer afford to purchase or rent a home. In practice, of course, things are manifestly much more complicated. For instance: Why are there so many homeless people at this present moment? How can we account for such a broad range of victims? Why do some people get caught in a protracted, ongoing cycle of homelessness? And whatever happened to the social "safety net" that was supposed to protect people from the extremes of poverty and deprivation? Let us begin to answer these questions by focusing on economic restructuring, the restructuring of the welfare state, and demographic change in order to explain the rise of economic marginality in the population at large.

Economic restructuring: from Fordism to post-Fordism

At the core of US socioeconomic trends during the 1970s and 1980s was a massive restructuring of the international and domestic economies (Noyelle and Stanback, 1984). This restructuring process has involved fundamental alterations in patterns of international finance and trade, shifts in the mix of industrial outputs, and changes in the organization and geographic location of production systems. Its effect has been to create a transition from *Fordism* (traditional assembly-line, mass-production industry) to a qualitatively different mode of economic organization called *post-Fordism*.

Fordism as a system of industrial production emerged in the early years of the twentieth century and rose to dominance during and after World War II. Fordist production was associated initially with strong unions, well-paid employment with benefits for blue-collar workers, clear career ladders, and relatively stable union/ management relations predicated on continued growth in markets. Typical Fordist manufacturing industries included steel, automobiles, chemicals, and other capital-intensive heavy manufacturing sectors able to achieve economies of scale and produce large volumes of relatively standardized, low-cost output. Many industries never adopted a Fordist approach to production because they were too labor-intensive, prone to demand fluctuations, and faced with highly competitive markets (for example, furniture and garment manufacturing). Yet the Fordist manufacturing operation came to symbolize US industrial prowess during the post-war Pax Americana.

The 1970s witnessed the relative decline of Fordism as a system of industrial production. Jolts to the world economy included: the 1971 Bretton Woods agreements (which led to abandonment of the gold standard) and the 1973 decision to abandon fixed exchange rates, both of which dramatically altered the global monetary system and the relative advantages of alternate production locations, and the oil shock induced by OPEC in 1973–4 (and in 1978), which led to rapid inflation and created enormous trade deficits. The result was a major recession in the mid 1970s, without attenuation in inflation, leading to a dizzying wage/price spiral – in short, stagflation. These dynamics sparked the flight of US manufacturing to cheap-labor locations in the Third World. The "four dragons" (Hong Kong, Singapore, Korea, and Taiwan) emerged as newly industrialized countries; together with Japan and Germany, they threatened the economic hegemony of the United States. These (and other) countries continued to gain as a direct result of US monetary policy in the 1980s. A buildup in defense spending was financed by increased deficit spending, and monetary policy kept the dollar strong to attract capital; consequently, US exports became more expensive and foreign imports cheaper, hurting domestic production even further.

The stateside result was deindustrialization and slowing rates of wage growth. The declining fortunes of the traditional manufacturing sector involved wave after wave of plant closures. Over ten million jobs were lost nationally because of closures or decreased product demand between 1979 and 1985 (Research Group on the Los Angeles Economy, 1989). In addition, because of slow growth in industrial productivity, wage rates were kept down. Real hourly earnings, which had increased nationally by 90 percent between 1950 and 1969, grew by only 14 percent between 1969 and 1988 (Research Group on the Los Angeles Economy, 1989).

At the same time, reindustrialization created a total of 12 million new jobs between 1980 and 1988. As described by Rothschild (1988b), these jobs were in four main categories: "services to wealth" – that is, producer services such as finance, real estate and insurance, and business and professional services (2 million jobs); "the semi-private welfare industry," including health, education, and social services (3.1 million jobs); "poverty jobs," typically in the retail trade and consumer-service sectors and paying minimum wage (3 million jobs); and jobs for people who "handle and move material things" (2.3 million). According to Rothschild (1988a, p. 33), "The most successful single occupation of the recent boom – increasing five times as fast as all employment – was that of 'light truck driver.'" These employment shifts reflected the growing role of the United States in global financial operations and international trade; in medical, scientific, and engineering technology; and in military arms production, fueled largely by Department of Defense spending. They were also a response to increasing domestic reliance on personal consumer and professional services. The net result was a steady expansion of the service sector and high-technology manufacturing, as traditional manufacturing sectors declined. During the 1980s, for the first time in US industrial history, the service sector superseded manufacturing as the largest single division of the US economy.

The shift to post-Fordism involved new, flexible ways of doing business and organizing industrial operations, sometimes referred to as "disorganized capitalism." The shift was not simply a matter of job loss in one sector and gain of equivalent wages and working conditions in another. Many manufacturing firms attempted to reduce market uncertainty by switching to just-in-time inventory management or by subcontracting out many of their production processes; subcontracting transfers the risks of economic turbulence to small, competitive operations. Others adopted new technologies that allowed flexible specialization – the ability to make rapid shifts in product design in response to market trends and consumer preferences. Firms in both manufacturing and services reorganized their employment practices, hiring part-time workers to avoid paying fringe benefits and taxes, categorizing jobs as temporary to forestall claims on seniority, and eliminating in-house professionals (such as accountants) in favor of consultants to reduce fixed overheads. (This use of consultants is one of the main reasons for the explosion of business and professional services.)

Changes in the labor supply, rooted in demographic change (for example, more young workers and immigrants), facilitated many aspects of post-Fordist economic restructuring. But they were also powerfully linked to fundamental changes in the role of women in society. Women were being drawn into the wage labor force more readily than before (at lower wages than their male counterparts), irrespective of economic necessity. Targeted workers included, for instance, immigrant women with "nimble fingers" for electronics assembly work and suburban housewives for insurance or banking back offices. But the entry of women – especially married women – into wage labor also altered the domestic division of labor. With men generally unwilling to share the increasing burdens borne by their working wives, women were forced into a "second shift" and obliged to purchase services they had previously performed unpaid at home. Thus, the processes of household reproduction were increasingly commercialized, as people turned, for example, to prepared foods and child-care services in order to allow both spouses to work outside the home. In turn, this demand fueled the growth of jobs in retail trade, personal services, and social welfare – jobs typically filled by low-wage women themselves. The emerging reliance on female workers increased rates of long-term joblessness in other sectors – for example, among traditional blue-collar workers (especially African-American males) and less-educated, low-skilled workers, such as older men. Then, to complete the spiral, rising male unemployment forced more females into the labor force to maintain household income or to slow the pace of downward mobility.

The overall effects of post-Fordist economic restructuring have been rising unemployment and underemployment, a boom in low-wage/low-skill jobs, the highest rates of poverty since the early 1960s, and a dramatic increase in income inequality. [...]

As poverty deepened because of unemployment and low wages, the emergent service economy still managed to create unprecedented numbers of high-wage jobs (in business and professional services, high technology, aerospace). The overall outcome was a "great U-turn" in the country's income distribution. Between 1950 and 1970, the disparity between the wealthy and the less wealthy had been narrowing, but this pattern was reversed in the 1970s, when income disparities began to grow modestly. They became significant during the 1980s. By the end of the decade, the richest 1 percent received as much after-tax income as the bottom 40 percent combined (Greenstein and Barancik, 1990, pp. 1, 9). [...]

Restructuring the welfare state

All advanced industrial nations are welfare states, in that they do not permit natural or social contingencies to imperil the lives of their citizenry. The term *welfare state* implies the existence of an expressed policy or programmatic commitment to social welfare, the appropriation of funds to support social programs, and the creation of a designated apparatus/bureaucracy to administer such programs. The origins of the modern US welfare state can be traced to the New Deal. Prior to that, social assistance had been largely the prerogative of private industry and philanthropy. After 1929, publicly provided assistance predominated, but it was not until after World War II that the greatest growth in welfare expenditures occurred. This growth was fueled by changing perceptions of the scope and purpose of welfare and was achieved through an expansion of entitlements that provided increasing numbers of the middle class with the benefits of a welfare society. By 1980, programs aimed at low-income families constituted only one-fifth of federal welfare spending.

The deinstitutionalization movement, which began in the 1960s, serves as an emblematic tale for the welfare-state restructuring that was to dominate the 1980s. Deinstitutionalization in the United States received the federal seal of approval in 1963 with the passage of the Community Mental Health Centers Act. This legislation cleared the way for moving psychiatric patients out of state and local mental hospitals and (according to the plan) into community-based service settings. Many factors lay behind this transition, including a concern with the civil rights of those incarcerated in asylums, the rise of new treatment philosophies emphasizing community care, the discovery of new psychotropic drugs capable of controlling the extremes of behavior, and (very important) the willingnes of the federal government to fund not only community mental-health facilities but also income transfers that allowed ex-psychiatric patients to pay rent and live inde- pendently. Fiscal conservatives saw this as an opportunity to scale back rapidly growing expenditures on state hospitals without a commitment to fund alternative local services. Consequently, state- and county-funded asylums were speedily shut down in many parts of the nation. California, under the guidance of Governors Pat Brown and Ronald Reagan, led the nation in deinstitutionalization. Nation- wide, the 1950s asylum population of over half a million dwindled to just over 100,000 within two decades. Inspired by the example of the mentally disabled, others jumped on the bandwagon. Deinstitutionalization became fashionable for the mentally retarded, the physically disabled, the dependent elderly, and proba- tioners and parolees.

The deinstitutionalization movement sprang from honorable intentions. Unfortu- nately, a woefully inadequate sum was subsequently allocated by federal, state, and local governments to construct and staff the promised community-based services so critical to supporting the mentally disabled in the community. Ultimately, the service consumers themselves largely bore the costs of an essentially enormous retrench- ment in spending on mental health and other services. On discharge, many deinstitu- tionalized people drifted to inner-city neighborhoods, where cheap accommodations were available and where health and welfare services for the poor tended to be concentrated. Here they lived in poverty with unstable housing arrangements (such as rooming houses and single room occupancy, or SRO, hotels). When welfare retrenchment began in earnest in the 1980s, already-inadequate services were cut, and affordable housing opportunities grew scarce. Many mentally disabled people were unable to cope; they became among the first to join the ranks of the "new homeless" (Lamb, 1984; Dear and Wolch, 1987; Torrey, 1988). [...]

The Reagan administration, which came to power at the start of the worst recession since the Great Depression, dedicated itself to promoting economic growth via a redistribution of resources to the private sector and "getting govern- ment off the backs of the people." In practice, the federal administration presided over the biggest defense buildup in US history, shifting resources toward defense and away from social spending, and creating a "warfare state" from the ashes of the welfare state. The administration adopted three mechanisms in its avowed desire to "roll back" the welfare state: reduced eligibility; a shifting of responsi- bilities to state and local government (the "new federalism"); and privatization. [...]

The one program that is probably most clearly identified with welfare for the poor in the United States is Aid to Families with Dependent Children (AFDC), even though this program accounted for less than 2 percent of federal welfare spending in 1985. As a consequence of retrenchment in the benefits program enacted in the 1981 Omnibus Budget Reconciliation Act (especially the revised eligibility standards), more than half the working families who were on AFDC prior to 1981 were removed from the rolls. The percentage of poor receiving AFDC declined from 54.5 percent to 41.9 percent between 1979 and 1983 (Interagency Council on the Homeless, 1991, pp. 19–20). The number of poor people receiving Supplemental Security Income (SSI) and Medicaid also declined. In addition, the value of AFDC payments dropped significantly. The median value of AFDC payments fell, in constant 1989 dollars, from $606 to $449 between 1979 and 1983 (a 25 percent decrease), largely because of diminished state contributions (many states canceled cost-of-living adjustments). By 1990, the median AFDC monthly benefit was $364 for a family of three, less than half the poverty level (Children's Defense Fund, 1991, p. 14). [. . .]

The ideological core of the restructuring of the welfare state is the theory of privatization. According to Starr (1989, p. 42), privatization is about a "fundamental reordering of the claims in society." It is based on arguments about the desirability and competence of public provision, traditional conservative values of individual and familial responsibility, and a backlash against feminist claims for an expansion of women's roles beyond the home. Privatization was promulgated via three strategies. One was *dismantling*, the reduction of welfare services through cutbacks in spending, program elimination, and limitations on eligibility. Dismantling has increased responsibilities in the private sphere, as the demand for services has been shifted onto new and existing voluntary and commercial agencies, and onto households (especially female headed), which have had to take up the burden of caring for elderly, young, and disabled family members. Another strategy was the *internal transformation* of the welfare state, that is, the decentralization of responsibilities and resources from higher to lower tiers of the governmental hierarchy. Such shifts were often accompanied by a reorganization of agencies and programs to enhance efficiency and productivity – a reorganization usually based on a competitive model of service provision. The result has been increased contracting out and purchase of services. A third strategy was *externalization*, shifting the provision of services from within the state to external, nongovernmental organizations via transfer of assets and responsibilities for services to the private sector. [. . .]

Vanishing Affordable Housing

As the number of economically marginal people grew, the number of dwelling units for low- and moderate-income people was shrinking dramatically. After decades of improvement in housing conditions following World War II, why did the availability of affordable shelter shift so abruptly? This complex issue involved federal policies and the intricacies of urban housing markets, which together created an accelerating loss of low-cost housing units across the country.

Federal housing policy

Housing policy at the level of the federal government has, for many decades, been directed principally toward stimulating the construction of new housing for ownership. Individual homeowners benefit from this policy mainly through income tax deductions on mortgage interest and property taxes. In 1977, such deductions cost $10 billion in forgone revenues. During that same year, the federal government spent $28 billion on direct housing help for low-income families – a second important component in its housing strategy. By 1988, however, income tax deductions by homeowners cost the government $52 billion, while $12 billion was allocated to assist low-income households (Children's Defense Fund, 1991, p. 18).

The factor most commonly implicated in the homelessness crisis has been the federal government's retreat from affordable housing. Federal authorizations for housing plunged by three-quarters between the late 1970s and the late 1980s. Within the housing budget, authorizations for rental vouchers (Section 8), which was the largest category of subsidy, fell 82 percent from 1981 to 1988. Public-housing funds and loans to the elderly and handicapped (Section 2020) were cut by 85 percent. Homeownership subsidies (Section 235) were essentially eliminated. The number of federally subsidized housing units (both new and rehabilitated) fell from an average of 266,000 per year in 1980 to 78,000 per year in 1985. The proportion of subsidized units thus fell from about 20 percent to 6 percent of overall housing production (Sternlieb and Listokin, 1987, p. 29).

[By 1987] more than 1 million households were on waiting lists for subsidized housing; others were unable to join waiting lists that public-housing authorities had closed. In 1986, less than a quarter of all households with incomes under $10,000 received any public subsidy for housing (Apgar and Brown, 1988).

The mix of housing subsidies also shifted as the ideology of privatization pervaded the housing sector. The early years of federal housing assistance were characterized by reliance on public housing – housing units built by local housing authorities and their developers. But community support for public housing was severely eroded as such assistance increasingly became targeted to families in poverty and large-scale projects became "instant ghettos." Instead, vouchers became popular. Between 1980 and 1988, the proportion of the federal housing budget allocated for new public-housing units fell dramatically, while the allocation for tenant subsidies grew. [...]

As public housing waned, voucher programs grew – along with their own set of problems that limit the utility of the programs to low-income households. The

Section 8 voucher program was established in 1983 by the Reagan administration and soon dominated the housing-assistance budget. Conservatives favored vouchers on the grounds that they eliminated the need for public-housing construction, channeled funds directly into the private sector, and gave consumers greater choice in housing. But in practice the Section 8 voucher program has been plagued with problems. Discrimination against households with vouchers is extremely common. In addition, many Section 8 households are unable to locate units that meet program specifications and their own needs. [. . .]

Urban housing markets

Economic and demographic changes fundamentally altered the structure of urban land and housing markets, stimulating both gentrification and downtown redevelopment. While poverty was growing for many, the number of affluent households in which one or more people were employed in relatively high-wage occupations was also increasing. The affluence of this group led to new claims on urban territory. In the bidding wars that ensued over key properties and neighborhoods, low-income households had neither the economic nor the political power to turn back the wealthy households seeking to brave the "urban frontier" (Smith, 1986). Although dubbed by the media a "back-to-the-city" movement, or "urban renaissance," gentrification in central cities was driven less by changing life-styles than by basic shifts in the economy and in urban land markets. Let us examine these trends in detail.

Historically, affluent households settled at the urban fringe, but in the 1970s and 1980s they began to take over selected central-city neighborhoods from less well-off groups. A variety of specific forces created this shift. First, slow-growth movements and persistent exclusionary zoning limited the scale of development at the urban fringe and increased prices for suburban land and houses. For younger middle- and upper-middle-income people, the prospect of buying into the suburbs declined, so they began to look elsewhere.

Second, the rise of producer services in "revitalized" downtowns meant that land dedicated to low-income residential and industrial uses was converted to commercial and service-sector uses, often stimulated by public-sector urban renewal. Redevelopment agencies, largely stymied since inception because of the lack of developer interest in downtown parcels, were finally able to entice developers to build convention centers, sports stadiums, and, above all, high-rise office towers. Such efforts intensified the recentralization of key service industries and created heightened incentives for the gentrification of central-city neighborhoods.

Third, as a result of these historical developments, properties in many central-city neighborhoods were ripe for revalorization. These properties had an advantage because of their location, but actual rents and prices remained low because of the properties' undesirable structural condition. This situation created a gap between actual and potential rents. During the 1970s and 1980s, rent gaps became sufficiently large that such inner-area properties could be redeveloped profitably.

And they were. Conversions and demolitions spread like wildfire in many cities. Housing in the lowest-rent tiers was removed at rates far out of proportion to their share of the overall housing market. Low-cost housing units were replaced either by nonresidential units or by larger, more expensive residential units. The rate of rental rehabilitation rose sharply without protection for existing tenants, especially in the North-east and West. In 1982, HUD estimated that between 1.7 and 2.4 million low-income people were being displaced annually (Huttman, 1990); and 40 percent of this displacement was due to increasing rents, as opposed to demolitions and similar factors (Gilderbloom and Appelbaum, 1988). The gentrifiers tended to be young, white professionals living in one- or two-person households, earning middle to upper-middle incomes, and originating from the same city. Those who were displaced from gentrifying neighborhoods were socially heterogenous but were usually blue-collar or low-status white-collar workers, lower- and lower-middle income households, the elderly, and minorities. Displaced people faced an increasingly competitive housing market and the poorer among them invariably faced higher housing costs in their new locations. [. . .]

Local efforts to create affordable housing ran into barriers. Community opposition continued to frustrate attempts to build low-cost housing and "special-needs" housing (apartments for the physically handicapped, group homes for the deinstitutionalized). Many factors gave rise to the spread of "not-in-my-back-yard" (NIMBY) sentiments during the seventies and eighties. These decades witnessed the outpouring of former psychiatric-hospital patients onto the streets, the rise of homelessness, and the emergence of a lethal new disease whose sufferers and carriers were invisible until death was imminent. The mentally ill, the homeless, and the AIDS/HIV-positive populations met an increasingly introverted community, seemingly concerned more with individual rights than with community obligations. This was the "me decade," when members of proliferating no-growth and slow-growth movements attempted to exclude any kind of undesirable element from their neighborhoods. [. . .]

Shrinking low-cost housing

The cumulative effects of these public- and private-sector dynamics were devastating. Between 1973 and 1983, 4.5 million units were removed (demolished or converted to nonresidential use) from the nation's housing stock, half of which had been occupied by low-income households (National Housing Task Force, 1988). During the same period, about 1 million low-cost units were lost (either removed from the stock or no longer affordable because of rent inflation) (Apgar and Brown, 1988). In contrast, the number of up-market units increased by 4.5 million between 1974 and 1983 (Apgar and Brown, 1988).

The very lowest rungs of the housing ladder – single-room-occupancy (SRO) hotel units – were decimated. Their loss was a direct cause of homelessness and was related to the disappearance of skid row areas. Between 1970 and 1982, about one million SRO hotel units were lost nationally. Ironically, some of the SRO units were converted to homeless shelters and Section 8 units. [...]

Other types of small, low-end units were lost in large numbers, creating hardship for low-income populations. For example, the number of board-and-care beds for the mentally disabled shrank in many cities. A great deal of residential abandonment occurred, especially during the seventies, and much of that stock has yet to return to the market. Increasing numbers of units were torched, as arson for profit spread.

Housing Affordability and the Rise of the Protohomeless

The term *housing affordability* refers to the relationship between household income and the cost of available housing. During the 1970s and 1980s, household incomes declined drastically, and the need for low-cost housing intensified just at the time when the number of low-cost housing units was shrinking rapidly. The result was a crisis of housing affordability – an overwhelming rise in the proportion of household income that was perforce dedicated to rent.

Very few people escaped the significant rise in US housing costs. For instance, median rents grew twice as fast as median incomes during the 1970s and 1980s. Despite an overall increase in vacancy rates, rents were at their highest levels in two decades by 1987, growing 16 percent nationally (1981–7) and even more steeply in some regions. Cost increases also extended to the owner-occupied sector. The real cost of owning a home grew faster than the rise in median incomes during the 1970s and 1980s. Homeownership rates fell. Among young households, ownership rates dropped from 44 percent in 1979 to 36 percent in 1987 (National Housing Task Force, 1988). Among the poor, ownership rates plummeted by a third between 1974 and 1987. Fewer and fewer renter households could consider buying (only 15 percent of young renters could qualify for a median-price home by 1986).

The brunt of the affordability crisis was, needless to say, borne by the poor. Rent burdens (rent-to-income ratios) increased steadily. Average rent burdens rose from 23 percent in 1973 to 51 percent in 1986 (Interagency Council on the Homeless, 1991). Some types of households suffered disproportionately from the affordability crisis. For example, young, single-parent (mostly female-headed) households saw their real income fall by 34 percent between 1974 and 1987, and their rent burden climb from 35 percent to 58 percent. African-Americans and Hispanics were also hit hard. During the 1970s and early 1980s, their incomes rose more slowly than rents: by 1983 over 40 percent of African-American and Hispanic renters had rent burdens over 35 percent; more than a quarter faced burdens of over 50 percent (Gilderbloom and Appelbaum, 1988).

By 1987, 27 million households, or 78 million people, were "shelter poor" – that is, they had to spend so much on housing that other basic needs were unmet (Stone, 1990). The shelter poor thus constituted fully one-third of the entire US population. [...]

The spread of economic marginality combined with a decrease in affordable housing inevitably produced a growing pool of people who could scarcely afford the increased costs of shelter. These were the households at risk of homelessness, those whom we refer to as the *protohomeless*.

From Protohomelessness to Homelessness

Only a fraction of those who are protohomeless actually end up becoming homeless. What causes this subset, and not all others, to slip into homelessness? Part of the difficulty in answering this question lies in the problem of defining homelessness. Early definitions emphasized the absence of a place to sleep and receive mail, as well as a dimension of "social disaffiliation." More conceptually satisfying definitions posited a continuum between homed and homeless, with those living in temporary, insecure, or physically substandard dwelling units falling somewhere between the two extremes. The "hidden homeless" – namely, those precariously housed with family or friends or living in insecure units (units subject to demolition, for example) – were often included in the category of homeless, even though for all practical purposes they could not be enumerated.

Numerical estimates of homelessness tended to be based on simple definitions that could be readily operationalized. These typically relied on counts of the number of residents served by shelter operators plus "guesstimates" of the population beyond such services. Many counts of wildly varying scope and quality produced hotly debated estimates. These estimates ranged from 350,000 to 3 million homeless in the United States (US Department of Housing and Urban Development, 1984; Hombs and Snyder, 1982). More sophisticated approaches have produced middle-range estimates, such as the Urban Institute's census of 446,000 to 600,000 homeless people over the course of one week in March 1987 (Burt and Cohen, 1989) and the Congressional Budget Office's estimate of 700,000 people homeless on a single day in 1991 (Interagency Council for the Homeless, 1991). [...]

Despite controversy over baseline figures, service providers overwhelmingly report dramatic increases in the demand for emergency food and shelter. For example, in 1980 the largest soup kitchen in Washington, DC, reported serving fewer than one hundred meals per day, but it was serving more than ten times that number in 1990 (Dennis, 1991). And the number of adults and children housed in emergency shelters rose from 98,000 in 1983 to 275,000 in 1988 – a 180 percent increase in just five years (US Department of Housing and Urban Development, 1989).

Many studies have isolated a series of "adverse events" as the immediate precursors of personal homelessness. For most people, an eviction or a similar everyday event in the housing market is only a temporary setback. For the protohomeless, however, a single adverse event may be sufficient to propel them into homelessness. The five most commonly cited precursors of homelessness are eviction, job loss, release from an institution (mental hospital or jail) with nowhere to go, loss of welfare support, and personal crises (such as divorce/separation or domestic violence).

In a national survey of metropolitan-area homelessness (Burt and Cohen, 1990), respondents were asked about why they had left their last dwelling unit. Twenty percent had financial difficulties; 13 percent had been evicted; 13 percent had not been getting along with others in the unit; 9 percent had been asked to leave; 5 percent had to leave a condemned building; and the remainder listed a variety of reasons including being released from jail, migrating in order to look for work, entering a drug- or alcohol-treatment program, or family breakup. [...]

Care must be taken not to overemphasize the role of adverse events, even though they frequently act as the immediate precursor to homelessness. The image of a person falling from the last rung of the housing ladder into homelessness because of a single setback is both oversimple and misleading. The event that precipitates homelessness is best understood as the climax of an extended period of cumulative difficulties in that person's life. In what follows, we turn our attention to these personal circumstances in order to understand how certain people become homeless, why some remain so, and why others are able to escape the streets.

Becoming homeless

The pathways to homelessness are startlingly diverse, calling into question stereotypical notions of how people come to be homeless and what their experience is likely to be. Detailed ethnographic studies have concluded that there is no single pathway but only "recurrent themes" in how people enter homelessness. Most appear to make a series of transitions from being stably and securely homed, through stages of diminished residential security and stability, and finally to an insecure life on the streets.

People may proceed through these phases with varying speeds, ranging from a precipitous descent to a gradual, longer-term drift into homelessness. Many homeless people live with family or friends prior to their first experience of homelessness and from there move to a shelter or the street. In Burt and Cohen's national sample (1990), 68 percent of respondents reported sharing accommodations with family or friends prior to becoming homeless. Another recurrent theme is a direct move from a place of one's own to a shelter or the streets, suggesting a more rapid descent into homelessness. About one-fifth of the homeless people interviewed in a survey of Skid Row, Los Angeles, said that their usual sleeping place during the prior year had been their own apartment or home (Koegel, Burnam, and Farr, 1990). The same study found that more than one-quarter of respondents had usually slept in a motel or hotel. [...]

Further complications are common. Some homeless families have never established their own households; they made the transition to parenthood while living with their parents and subsequently were never able to afford independent living quarters. A study of homeless families assigned to public-housing units in New York City found that many had been living doubled up with kin and had never been primary tenants (Shinn and others, 1990). There is also the question of residential mobility among the homeless. Most homeless people are not frequent movers, but some portion of the population has made large numbers of moves. The frequency of moves is indicative of a downward cycle of increasing residential instability.

The probability of a drift, a gradual slide, or a precipitous descent into homelessness is linked to personal factors beyond economic status and housing availability. This is a vital point because the vast majority of persistently poor and precariously housed people do not become homeless. Instead, they end up being subsidized by their families and friends through the provision of cash, free or low-cost shelter (through doubling-up in the same housing unit), food, and other essentials. Such informal assistance allows many individuals and families to stabilize their situation and eventually to reestablish personal autonomy. Those most at risk in this situation tend to have limited resources to contribute to the household, to be difficult to live with (through, for example, substance abuse), or to be unable to tolerate the stress of crowded living conditions. Such individuals tend to wear out their welcome swiftly and are asked by their hosts to leave, even if it means consigning them to a shelter or the streets. [...]

Prior research has focused on how the personal characteristics of the homeless differ from those of the homed poor. Certain subgroups of the poverty population run particularly high risks of becoming homeless. These subgroups include: those persons burdened with personal vulnerabilities such as mental disability, posttraumatic stress syndrome associated with war service or victimization (especially domestic violence), chemical dependency, or health problems; those lacking sufficient social supports to tide them over potentially protracted periods of crisis (for example, people raised in foster homes, but also unattached people generally); and those least able to obtain jobs that pay enough to purchase housing (single women with young children, unskilled workers, women in general, and people of color) or to qualify for welfare support (single able-bodied persons, particularly men). The net result tends to be a homeless population that is disproportionately young, male, disabled, and people of color. However, the number of homeless women (with and without children) has also risen rapidly as a consequence of the declining real value of welfare payments and the vulnerability of women to dependence on men as wage earners and lease or mortgage holders. And the prevalence of veterans among homeless people has also been widely reported.

One personal vulnerability that significantly increases the risk of homelessness is substance abuse. As many as 50 percent of the currently homeless have significant problems with alcohol, drugs, or both. Alcohol-abuse prevalence rates among the homeless range from 20 to 50 percent (Schutt and Garrett, 1992a); and drug-abuse prevalence rates range from 10 to 15 percent (McCarty, Argeriou, Heubner, and Lubran, 1991). Other estimates place the number of street-based homeless who are serious drug users as high as 25 percent (Mulkern and Spence, 1984).

Excessive alcohol consumption has a long history among the homeless. The incidence of alcohol abuse and alcoholism is best understood as part of a distinct culture as well as an individual pathology because alcohol has traditionally provided an important context for social interaction among the "old" homeless (for example, see Cohen and Sokolovsky, 1989, on the "bottle gangs" of New York's Bowery). Even so, the youngest of the "new" homeless are no less vulnerable to alcohol. Moreover, as rates of drug abuse nationwide increased dramatically during the 1980s, drug-addiction problems among the homeless rose rapidly. The crisis deepened during the latter half of the decade because of the crack-cocaine epidemic (Burt, 1992, p. 114). [...]

Increased drug abuse has heightened the risk of health problems among the homeless. Among crack users, for instance, effects can commonly be seen in the form of cardiovascular and neurologic damage. In recent years, the most ominous threats have been associated with HIV, AIDS, and associated complications.

Many protohomeless face problems linked to both chemical dependency and mental disability. Dual diagnoses (chronic alcohol abuse or drug abuse plus mental disability) and even triple diagnoses (alcohol abuse, drug abuse, and mental disability) have become increasingly common. [...] Schutt and Garrett (1992b) suggest that the distinction between single diagnosis and multiple diagnoses may reflect an important distinction between "old" and "new" homelessness.

Despite the high prevalence of substance abuse among the homeless, its role as a risk factor directly contributing to homelessness remains ambiguous. For those suffering from alcoholism, social disaffiliation may be particularly rapid and severe. According to Burt (1992), alcohol-related problems contribute to homelessness because they have deleterious effects on earning capacity, accelerate downward social mobility, cause disruptive behavior, and hasten the onset of cognitive impairments. Heavy drinking typically precedes the loss of a dwelling. Yet it is also clear that the stresses experienced while homeless exacerbate alcohol consumption, which may be one part of an adaptive strategy among the homeless. With respect to drugs, the role of chemical dependency as a causal factor in homelessness is difficult to specify because it is simply one factor in a whole panoply of disadvantages.

Coming inside: exits from homelessness

Just as the risks of becoming homeless are not distributed evenly across the proto-homeless, the chances of making an exit from the streets and reentering the homed community are unequal across the homeless population. Conventional wisdom has been that the longer one is homeless, the slimmer are the prospects for a stable, secure exit. In many ways, this hypothesis makes sense. A downward spiral of declining appearance, health, and emotional well-being in association with lengthy periods on the street may make exit increasingly unlikely. Employability declines, material and psychological resources run out, and energies become devoted to making it one day at a time. Often unable to help themselves, refused aid, or given inappropriate assistance, homeless people face mounting difficulties.

But there are reasons to suspect that the link between duration of homelessness and exit probabilities is not as strong as initially believed. After a relatively short time (say, a few months) the status of a homeless person may stabilize, at either a low or relatively high level of functioning; at the bottom of the downward spiral may be social isolation, complete or partial dependence on formal helping services, and disaffiliation from the mainstream. Alternately, a homeless person may become adjusted to life on the outside, enjoying steady access to food, friends, supplementary income from casual labor, and occasional nights inside. Levels of functioning can vary enormously between these two states, so that the relationship between exit and length-of-time homeless tends to become muddied. In a Minneapolis study, similar proportions of homeless people made exits regardless of the number of times they had been homeless before or the duration of their homeless episodes (Sosin, Paliavin, and Westerfelt, 1990). Thus factors other than time influence who comes inside from the streets and who does not.

The most important determinant of exit potential is the extent of access to coping resources – the extensive set of material, financial, logistical, and emotional resources that allow homeless people to obtain income, shelter, food, and clothing; to maintain their health; and to protect or rebuild their self-esteem and personal identity as valued members of society. The amount of coping resources varies significantly from place to place. Job opportunities, welfare benefits, and other community and social services are distributed unevenly across towns, cities, and regions. The intense concentration of casual employment and cheap accommodations was largely responsible for the emergence of skid row zones earlier in this century. Today, the concentration of welfare services, soup kitchens, shelters, and SRO hotels remains the prime reason that homeless people cluster in certain areas. [...]

Several coping resources are of special significance, including a homeless person's experience in shelters, levels of welfare support, and personal strength. Living conditions in temporary and emergency shelters are often so bad that many homeless avoid the shelters. Some are centers of crime, including substance abuse and personal violence. Residence in a shelter can seriously depress the morale of the newly homeless. Some shelters systematically exclude certain groups through eligibility requirements (refusing admission to women or the mentally disabled, for example), while others have intrusive or degrading intake procedures and restrictive residence rules. [. . .]

The personal qualities of the homeless person also determine how effectively that person utilizes coping resources and hence shapes his or her exit chances. Personal strength and emotional resilience are easily eroded when money is scarce, cleanliness is an impossible goal, sleep a luxury, nutritious food scarce, and health care nonexistent. Specific vulnerabilities such as addiction, mental disability, exoffender status, or simply being female can make coping difficult. Life on the streets involves muggings and constant harassment from other street people or the police. Many homeless report that their principal daytime activity is "moving or walking" for self-protection.

No clear pattern enables us to predict who among the homeless will achieve a stable, secure exit. If the pathways into homelessness are varied in both time and number of transition states, so too are pathways off the streets. Initial studies of homelessness contrasted short- and long-term patterns of homelessness (a matter of months versus more than a year), but researchers soon recognized that many people were cyclically homeless, moving into and out of homelessness over extended periods of time. In order to capture the complexity of the pathways to exit from homelessness, we define three different states.

First, in short-term homelessness an individual is homeless for a brief period (from a few days to six months) before making an exit to a stable and secure residential situation. This category includes temporary homelessness, such as might be experienced by a runaway teenager who is reunited with his or her family after a week or so, as well as by those who need somewhat more time to organize their exit.

Second, chronic, or long-term, homelessness occurs when being on the outside becomes a predominant, even permanent, characteristic of a person's life-style and personal identity. This condition will, however, typically be punctuated by relatively brief periods of being on the inside.

Third, in cyclical or episodic homelessness, people make repeated moves across the boundary between homed and homeless. They are unable to secure a stable housing situation and thus are periodically obliged to return to the streets. Ultimately, a cyclically homeless individual makes a permanent exit, thus distinguishing this category from chronic homelessness.

It is difficult to determine the relative size of these groups without longitudinal studies spanning considerable periods and without broader knowledge of the diversity of homeless experiences. However, the proportion of short-term homeless may not be as large as often assumed; many newly homeless people who leave the streets soon become homeless again because of their inability to obtain stable housing.

A Predictable Crisis

Our narrative about homelessness begins with the rise of poverty in the United States. Deindustrialization and reindustrialization were associated with truly unprecedented shifts in national industry and employment patterns which resulted in a service economy. The net effects of this restructuring have been an upsurge in unemployment and underemployment and a decline in real incomes. During this same period, the safety net of the welfare state was shredded and recast. Hundreds of thousands of people were deinstitutionalized, to be joined on the streets by the never-institutionalized. At roughly the same time, an epidemic of drug abuse hit the country. In the rush to dismantle social welfare, governments canceled programs, reduced caseloads, and promoted privatization. The number of needy people on the welfare rolls was reduced by government fiat; and those who received assistance discovered that the real value of their benefits was significantly eroded. Demographic changes also contributed to the accelerated pace of impoverishment among certain sectors of the population. More women entered the labor force, and their relatively meager wages were instrumental in causing the feminization of poverty. The number of single-person households skyrocketed, intensifying the competition for small, low-cost housing units among people of limited means.

Next, our story shifts to the catastrophic loss of affordable housing units across the nation. During the 1980s, the federal government relinquished its traditional role in providing housing for the poor. The construction of public housing essentially stopped. A voucher system was introduced that did little to increase the amount of housing available to the poor. At the same time, gentrification and other publicly and privately sponsored redevelopment schemes provoked the wholesale demolition of much inner-city low-cost housing (especially SRO hotels). In addition, residents in many cities actively resisted attempts to build low-cost housing for the poor and special-needs groups in their communities. Rising poverty and the acute scarcity of low-cost accommodations conspired to create a crisis of housing affordability. Housing costs consumed more and more of the typical household budget. Many people were obliged to skimp on necessities in order to maintain a roof over their heads. These shelter-poor individuals constituted the bulk of those at risk of homelessness, the protohomeless.

The stage was thus set for the final chapter: the creation of a class of "new homeless." Household budgets among the protohomeless were so tight that even the slightest setback was sufficient to tip them over the edge into homelessness. Those people suffering from drug or alcohol addiction were at even greater risk. For some, the descent into homelessness was precipitous. But for most, homelessness was the result of a gradual drift through a series of transitional states: surrendering one's own home, moving in with family or friends, living awhile in a cheap hotel or shelter, and finally being out on the streets. The differential risks of becoming homeless and the speed of descent depend largely on the extent of personal and kinship-related resources available to the individual, as well as on drug or alcohol abuse.

The prospects facing the newly homeless on the outside are dismal: short-term homelessness if they are fortunate or, much worse, being caught in a web of episodic or chronic homelessness. Either way, exit from homelessness is rarely a clear-cut event. Individuals again pass through several transition states before finally being inside again. Progress depends critically on access to the coping resources available in each community. Because the quality of such resources varies, the fate of the homeless person is intimately tied to place.

References

Apgar, W. and L. Brown. 1988. *State of the Nation's Housing*. Cambridge, Mass.: Joint Center for Housing Studies.

Burt, M. R. 1992. *Over the Edge: The Growth of Homeless in the 1980s*. New York and Washington, DC: Russell Sage Foundation and Urban Institute Press.

Burt, M. R. and B. E. Cohen. 1989. *America's Homeless: Numbers, Characteristics, and Programs That Serve Them*. Washington, DC: Urban Institute Press.

Burt, M. R. and B. E. Cohen. 1990. "A Sociodemographic Profile of the Service-Using Homeless: Findings from a National Survey." In *Homelessness in the United States*, vol. 2: *Data and Issues*, ed. J. Momeni. New York: Praeger.

Children's Defense Fund. 1991. *Homeless Families: Failed Policies and Young Victims*. Washington, DC: Children's Defense Fund.

Cohen, C. I. and J. Sokolovsky. 1989. *Old Men of the Bowery: Strategies for Survival Among the Homeless*. New York: Guilford Press.

Dear, M. and J. Wolch. 1987. *Landscapes of Despair: From Deinstitutionalization to Homelessness*. Princeton, NJ: Princeton University Press.

Dennis, M. L. 1991. "Changing the Conventional Rules: Surveying Homeless People in Unconventional Locations." In *Proceedings of the Fannie Mae Annual Housing Conference*. Washington, DC: Fannie Mae.

Gilderbloom, J. I. and R. P. Appelbaum. 1988. *Rethinking Rental Housing*. Philadelphia: Temple University Press.

Greenstein, R. and S. Barancik. 1990. *Drifting Apart: New Findings on Growing Income Disparities Between the Rich, the Poor and the Middle Class*. Washington, DC: Center on Budget and Policy Priorities.

Hombs, M. E. and M. Snyder. 1982. *Homeless in America: A Forced March to Nowhere*. Washington, DC: Community for Creative Non-Violence.

Huttman, E. D. 1990. "Homeless as a Long-Term Housing Problem in America." In *Homeless in the United States*, vol. 2: *Data and Issues*, ed. J. Momeni. New York: Praeger.

Interagency Council on the Homeless. 1991. *Annual Report*. Washington, DC: Interagency Council on the Homeless.

Koegel, P. M., A. Burnam, and R. K. Farr. 1990. "The Prevalence of Specific Psychiatric Disorders Among Homeless Individuals in the Inner City of Los Angeles." *Archives of General Psychiatry* 45: 1085–92.

Lamb, R. 1984. *The Homeless Mentally Ill.* Washington, DC: American Psychiatric Association.

McCarty, D., M. Argeriou, R. Heubner, and B. Lubran. 1991. "Alcoholism, Drug Abuse, and the Homeless." *American Psychologist* 46(11): 1139–48.

Mulkern, V. and R. Spence. 1984. *Illicit Drug Use Among Homeless Persons: A Review of the Literature.* Boston: Human Research Institute.

National Housing Task Force. 1988. *A Decent Place to Live.* Washington, DC: National Housing Task Force.

Noyelle, T. J. and T. M. Stanback. 1984. *The Economic Transformation of America.* Totowa, NJ: Rowman and Allanheld.

Research Group on the Los Angeles Economy. 1989. *The Widening Divide: Income Inequality and Poverty in Los Angeles.* Los Angeles: University of California.

Rothschild, E. 1988. "The Reagan Economic Legacy." *New York Review of Books*, July 21: 33–41.

Rothschild, E. 1988. "The Real Reagan Economy." *New York Review of Books*, June 30: 47–53.

Schutt, R. K. and G. R. Garrett. 1992. "The Homeless Alcoholic: Past and Present." In *Homelessness: A National Perspective*, eds. M. J. Robertson and M. Greenblatt. New York: Plenum.

Schutt, R. K. and G. R. Garrett. 1992. *Responding to the Homeless: Policy and Practice.* New York: Plenum.

Shinn, M., et al. 1990. "Alternative Models for Sheltering Homeless Families." *Journal of Social Issues* 46: 175–90.

Smith, N. 1986. "Gentrification, the Frontier and the Restructuring of Urban Space." In *Gentrification of the City*, eds. N. Smith and P. Williams. London: Allen & Unwin.

Sosin, M., I. Paliavin, and H. Westerfelt. 1990. "Toward a Longitudinal Analysis of Homelessness." *Journal of Social Issues* 46: 157–74.

Starr, P. 1989. "The Meaning of Privatization." In *Privatization and the Welfare State*, eds. S. B. Kammerman and A. J. Kahn. Princeton, NJ: Princeton University Press.

Sternlieb, G. and D. Listokin. 1987. "A Review of National Housing Policy." In *Housing America's Poor*, ed. P. D. Salins. Chapel Hill and London: University of North Carolina Press.

Stone, M. 1990. *One Third of a Nation.* Washington, DC: Economic Policy Institute.

Torrey, E. F. 1988. *Nowhere to Go.* New York: Harper Collins.

US Department of Housing and Urban Development. 1984. "A Report to the Secretary on the Homeless and Emergency Shelters," *HUD Report on Homelessness.* Joint hearing before the Subcommittee on Housing and Community Development of the Committee on Banking, Finance, and Urban Affairs, and the Subcommittee on Manpower and Housing of the Committee on Government Operations, Banking Committee Serial 98–91. US Congress, House, 98th Cong., 2nd sess.

US Department of Housing and Urban Development. 1989. *A Report on the 1988 National Survey of Shelters for the Homeless.* Washington, DC: Division of Policy Studies, Office of Policy Development and Research.

12 Economic Restructuring and Redevelopment

Susan S. Fainstein

Redevelopment, or the destruction of old infrastructure to prepare for new uses, has been a common response to economic restructuring. As manufacturing has increasingly moved to suburbs or offshore, many cities of the industrialized nations have been left with obsolete buildings, transportation technology, and communication methods. At the same time, the development of new industries has created the demand for new spaces, with amenities such as parking lots, air conditioning, and internet connections. Decisions to re-develop old spaces for new uses can be made by private developers, local governments, or joint public–private partnerships.

In this reading, Susan Fainstein examines the role of private real estate developers in London and New York from 1978 to 2000. She investigates the causes behind the ups and downs of the real estate cycle, as the demand for various kinds of space changed over the period. She analyzes the relative importance of the private sector (the developers) and the public sector (regulation and incentives by local governments). She argues that in both London and New York, despite the cities' political and structural differences, local governments attempted to boost their sagging economies by helping create real-estate boom markets.

Our image of a city consists not only of people but also of buildings – the homes, offices, and factories in which residents and workers live and produce. This built environment forms contours which structure social relations, causing commonalities of gender, sexual orientation, race, ethnicity, and class to assume spatial identities. Social groups, in turn, imprint themselves physically on the urban structure through the formation of communities, competition for territory, and segregation – in other words, through clustering, the erection of boundaries, and establishing

Fainstein, Susan S., "Economic Restructuring and Redevelopment." From *The City Builders: Property, Politics, and Planning in London and New York*, 2nd edn (Lawrence, KS: University Press of Kansas, 2001), pp. 1–8, 16–26. Copyright © 1994, 2001 by the University of Kansas Press.

distance. Urban physical form also constrains and stimulates economic activity. The built environment etches the division in time and distance between home and work and generates the milieu in which productive enterprises relate to each other. As a source of wealth through the real-estate industry, a cost of doing business, and an asset and expense for households, physical structures are a critical element in the urban economy.

The distinction between the use of real estate for human activity and its market role is often summarized as the difference between use and exchange values (Logan and Molotch, 1987). Frequent tension between the two functions has provoked the community resistance to redevelopment and highway programs and the endemic antagonism between neighborhood groups and development agencies which have marked urban politics in the United States and the United Kingdom in recent years. The immense stakes involved have meant that decisions of real estate developers and the outcomes of struggles over the uses of urban land have become crucial elements in forming the future character of the urban economy.

For policy-makers, encouragement of real estate development seems to offer a way of dealing with otherwise intractable economic and social problems. Governments have promoted physical change with the expectations that better-looking cities are also better cities, that excluding poor people from central locations will eliminate the causes of "blight" rather than moving it elsewhere, and that property development equals economic development. The quandary for local political officials is that they must depend on the private sector to finance most economic expansion, and they have only very limited tools for attracting expansion to their jurisdictions. Their heavy reliance on the property sector partly results from their greater ability to influence it than other industries. How much government programs for urban redevelopment actually do stimulate business is, however, an open issue.

This inquiry is intended both to respond to theoretical questions concerning the building of cities and also to address important policy issues for community groups and local governments. Within the academic literature, the economic and political forces that shape real estate development and its social consequences are the subject of considerable debate. Does real estate development simply respond to speculative gambles by individuals out to make fast profits or is it an answer to genuine social needs? Does the type of development that characterized the 1980s in New York and London inevitably generate "two cities" – one for the rich and one for the poor? Do the subsidies that governments direct toward the property sector represent a sellout by politicians and planners to capitalists or a method by which the public can, with a small investment, gain employment and public amenities as externalities of development schemes? Progrowth coalitions, consisting of business groups and public officials, have expressed confidence in the efficacy of public–private partnerships as engines of economic expansion. Neighborhood groups have frequently, although not always, opposed large-scale redevelopment because they have feared its environmental effects and its tendency to displace low-income residents and small businesses. Other critics, tracing back to the economist, Henry George, have asserted that the profits from development are created by the whole community and are illegitimately appropriated by property owners. Generally leftist scholars have supported the pessimistic view on the causes and results of development, while conservatives have celebrated its entrepreneurial base and transforming consequences. [...]

Physical Development and the Contest over Urban Space

Since the mid-1970s American and British local governments in their policies toward property development have aimed more at stimulating economically productive activities than at enhancing the quality of life for residents. To achieve their objectives they have promoted the construction of commercial space over housing and public facilities. Even though many of the new skyscrapers, festive malls, and downtown atriums produced by commercial developers have arguably created more attractive cities, the provision of amenities has been only a secondary purpose of redevelopment efforts.

Economic development strategies have typically involved subsidies and regulatory relief to development firms, as well as to businesses that could be expected to engage in long-term productive activity. Indeed, in both London and New York, stimulation of commercial property development was the most important growth strategy used by government in the 1980s. Yet only for a short time in the middle of the decade did business expansion appear hampered by a shortage of office space. Public incentives for construction were not a response to a bottleneck that was stifling investment. Instead, the authorities in London and New York hoped that, by loosening regulations and offering subsidies, they would cause developers to offer higher quality, cheaper space. They intended that the lowered costs would draw leading businesses to these dense central areas. Evidently policy-makers believed that an increase in the supply of competitively priced, first-class space would create its own demand. [...]

Two reports from the 1980s, *London: World City* and *New York Ascendant*, written at the behest of governments in London and New York, embody the strategic considerations that guided policy-makers.[1] The documents are typical of a number of such efforts in Britain and the United States, which attempted to chart a course that would capitalize on service-sector advantages in the face of a continuing decline of manufacturing. Like most of these plans they were intended as guides to action and were not officially adopted as legally binding policies. Nevertheless, they represent a reasonable summary of the attitudes of public officials and private-sector leaders toward the likely prospects for economic growth.

The writers of the reports perceive the principal advantages of London and New York to be their world city status. They defend the governmental policies of the eighties and justify what they regard as the only practical course for attaining economic prosperity within their high-cost environments. In explaining their emphasis on a few industries, they point out that, despite out-migration of manufacturing and wholesaling enterprises, these two financial capitals have increased their prominence as centers for investment markets, banking, and business services. In their discussion of growth strategies, they call for heightened targeting of these core service businesses by lowering their operating costs. The London report stresses reducing business costs through improving telecommunications and transport and expanding the central business district. As well as identifying these ways in which government can assist the private sector, the report of the New York Commission endorses offering loans and tax subsidies to attract business to less expensive locations within the city.

Analyses of the development industry

Although government agencies play an important role in affecting the physical environment, the main progenitor of changes in physical form within London and New York is the private real estate development industry. Examination of real-estate investment decisions reveals the ways in which urban redevelopment is channelled at the same time by broad political and economic imperatives and by the industry's own specific *modus operandi*. An analysis of its operations shows how economic and social forces create its opportunities and hazards and, in turn, how its strategies etch themselves into the set of possibilities that exist for economic and social interaction.

To a greater extent than I initially anticipated when starting this research, I found that not just economic and political pressures but personality and gender factors affect the development industry. Development continues to be a highly entrepreneurial industry, and particular enterprises strongly reflect the aspirations of the men who run them. Although women now constitute a significant proportion of real estate brokers, men continue almost totally to dominate the major development firms. As I have studied the large projects that have changed the faces of London and New York, I have been struck by the extent to which they have been driven by individual male egos that find self-expression in building tall buildings and imprinting their personae on the landscape.

Despite its key economic role and political influence, the development industry has only recently become the focus of serious political-economic analysis. For almost a decade David Harvey was virtually alone in examining real estate development from a broad theoretical perspective.[2] More recently, especially in the United Kingdom, social scientists have begun to subject the property industry to extensive empirical and theoretical investigation.[3] American interest in this subject has also picked up, and several works examining the history, dynamics, and impacts of real estate investment have recently appeared.[4] The bulk of scholarship, however, remains within the domain of academic programs that train real-estate practitioners. As would be expected in such a context, the emphasis is on how to do it rather than causes and social impacts. [. . .]

Urban redevelopment has received far more scholarly attention than the real-estate sector alone. Studies of redevelopment, however, have largely focused on governmental rather than private decision-making. Although they have investigated the influence of private developers on public policy, they have taken the motives and responses of property investors as givens rather than inquiring into their sources. [My research] attempts to address that omission, while taking as its starting point the scenario which the redevelopment literature has fairly consistently chronicled and which is recounted below. For in most British cities during the Thatcher period and most American cities throughout the history of urban redevelopment, there is a typical story of urban redevelopment.[5]

The Typical Redevelopment Scenario

The story goes as follows: In the past 30 years almost all the major metropolitan areas of the advanced capitalist world have been affected by changes in the national and international economic system such that they have either attracted a surge of capital and well-to-do people or suffered from disinvestment and population withdrawal. In both advancing and declining cities, growth has been a contested issue, and groups have mobilized to affect population and capital flows, either to limit or attract development. Within the United States business groups, usually in concert with political leaders, have promoted growth and tried to impose their objectives within the context of elite coalitions, of which Pittsburgh's Allegheny Conference is the prototype. Urban movements, driven by equity, preservationist, and environmental concerns, have opposed subsidized downtown redevelopment and unregulated profit-driven expansion. They have also, although less frequently, promoted alternative plans for neighborhood redevelopment. The outcomes of these contests have varied. Regardless, however, of whether the result has been growth or decline, greater or less equity, deal making on a project-by-project basis rather than comprehensive planning has been the main vehicle for determining the uses of space.

Overall, business interests have dominated the negotiations among government, community, and the private sector on the content of redevelopment. They have been supported by elite and middle-class consumers seeking downtown "improvements" and attractive, centrally located housing. Neighborhood and lower-income groups have received some gains in some places from redevelopment. Generally, however, the urban poor, ethnic communities, and small businesses have suffered increased economic and locational marginalization as a consequence. Central business district (CBD) expansion has increased property values in areas of low-income occupancy, forcing out residents, raising their living expenses, and breaking up communities. The emphasis on office-based employment within most large redevelopment schemes has reinforced the decline of manufacturing jobs and contributed to the employment difficulties of unskilled workers. While businesses have received direct subsidies, taxpayers at large have borne the costs and received benefits only as they have trickled down.

US/UK redevelopment experiences

British and American experiences differed before the 1980s and, at the beginning of the new century, are diverging again. Until Margaret Thatcher's election in 1979, redevelopment in Britain conformed less closely to the logic of private capital than in the US. The intimate relationship between local elected officials and real-estate interests that is a hallmark of US local government, wherein developers are the largest contributors to municipal political campaigns, did not (and still does not) exist in Britain. British local authorities restricted private development and built millions of units of council (i.e. public) housing, whereas "slum clearance" was a major component of the American urban renewal program, resulting in the demolition but not the replacement of tens of thousands of units of poor people's housing. Furthermore, land taken for highway building produced an even greater loss of units.

In Britain, social housing (i.e. publicly owned or subsidized housing at below-market rents) was placed throughout metropolitan areas, minimizing gross ethnic and income segregation. American public housing, while much more limited in scope, was available only to the poorest residents and was usually located in low-income areas. Urban renewal efforts, often derisively labelled "Negro removal" programs by their opponents, targeted ghetto areas that were near to business centers or to more affluent residential districts. Their intent was either to extend the more prosperous area or to cordon it off from the threat of lower-class invasion. Their effect was to displace nonwhite residents into more isolated, homogeneously minority territories.

As in the United States, British local authorities raised revenues through taxation on business and residential property ("rates"). Unlike their American equivalents, however, British local governments that could not meet the service demands on them through internal sources received a compensating central government grant. They therefore did not need to attract business and high-income residents to maintain themselves, and could afford to be more attuned to the negative environmental and social impacts of growth.

During the periods when the Labour Party controlled the British central government, it enacted measures to limit the gain that private developers could achieve through enhanced property values resulting from attaining planning permission on a piece of land. Under the Community Land Act of 1975, adopted during the third postwar Labour government, local authorities were granted the power to acquire land needed for development at a price below market value. Developers would then lease the land from the local authority at market rents. The difference in value would constitute a development tax on landowners of about 70 percent. The purpose was to ensure that the community as a whole would recoup most of the development value of land. Local authorities largely failed to implement the scheme, and the Conservatives dismantled it; nevertheless, while in existence it acted as a deterrent to speculative increases in land prices (see Balchin et al., 1988).

Despite these differences, the British and American cases during the 20 years preceding the 1979 ascendance of Conservative government in the UK did not wholly diverge. Under the American urban renewal program, public authorities had tried to attract developers by putting roads, sewers, and amenities into land that municipalities had acquired for redevelopment. Similar efforts began early in London's outer boroughs. Thus, for example, in Croydon, where 6.5 million square feet of office space was constructed in the 1960s, the council made a major effort to reduce the costs of development through providing basic infrastructure (see Saunders, 1979).

As in the US, a major surge of speculative commercial construction occurred in the UK in the early 1970s. The British expansion began when the Conservative central government increased credit as a means to stimulate the economy. While its action was not specifically directed at the property sector, it set off an intense building boom (Ambrose, 1986). Despite the government's commitment to decentralizing population and economic activity out of London, much of the new construction arose in the core, and the Cities of London and Westminster, which made up the commercial center of the metropolis, increasingly took on the look of Manhattan (Pickvance, 1981). Parallel to the experience in a number of US cities, office growth in the center of London led to gentrification of adjacent areas, while government subsidies to owner occupancy hastened the transformation of private rental into owner-occupied units (Hamnett and Randolph, 1988). Despite many greater controls on development in Britain, its 1970s boom ended like its American counterpart in a wave of defaults and bankruptcies.

In the latter part of the 1970s, as had been the case in the US for a much longer time, commercial redevelopment became a specific tool of British urban policy. Thus the Labour government, in its growing economic desperation, encouraged commercial expansion into low-income areas next to the City of London (i.e. the financial district) well before the Thatcher regime took office and contrary to its avowed commitment to preserving working-class jobs and expanding the supply of affordable housing (Forman, 1989).

During the 1980s development policies in the UK and US converged.[6] The British Urban Development Corporations (UDCs), modelled after similar American ventures, insulated development projects from public input. Governed by independent boards and reporting only to the central government, they acted as the planning authorities for redevelopment areas. The consequence was the removal of decision-making powers from the local councils. The UDCs were oriented toward stimulating the private market rather than comprehensive planning. In another case of transatlantic cross-fertilization, the majority of American states, although not the federal government, adopted the British innovation of the enterprise zone. Put in place early in the Thatcher regime, enterprise zones are designated geographic areas where firms are rewarded for investments with a variety of tax incentives, regulatory relief, and access to financing.

In general, the dominant objective in both countries was to use public powers to assist the private sector with a minimum of regulatory intervention. Earlier emphases in redevelopment programs on the provision of housing, public amenities, and targeted benefits to low-income people were downplayed, as aggregate economic growth – measured by the amount of private investment "leveraged" – became the criterion of program success.

The sponsors of the regeneration programs of the eighties claimed that they had achieved a remarkable reversal in the trajectory of inner-city decline. Numerous studies, however, have characterized this growth as extremely uneven in its impacts, primarily benefiting highly skilled professionals and managers and offering very little for workers displaced from manufacturing industries except low-paid service-sector jobs. Moreover, as economic restructuring and contraction of social benefits produced a broadening income gap, growing social inequality expressed itself spatially in the increasing residential segregation of rich and poor, black and white. Rapid development also produced undesirable environmental effects. While the gleaming new projects upgraded the seedy appearance of many old core areas and brought middle-class consumers back to previously abandoned centers, their bulk and density often overwhelmed their surroundings, stifled diversity, and, in the crowded centers of London and New York, overloaded transportation and pedestrian facilities.[7]

The economic downturn of the early nineties eased pressures on inner-city land and for a while stemmed the negative environmental impacts of the extravagant ventures of the previous years. It also caused at least a temporary halt to gentrification, but it did not produce a turnaround in either the widening gap between rich and poor or the governmental pursuit of private investment through subsidies to real-estate developers. By the year 2000, economic recession was a dim memory, and demand for space surged once again, producing transformative influences on urban form, inflating real-estate prices, and sparking intense competition for well-located space. [. . .]

Can local officials produce growth with equity?

In the study of urban redevelopment the recognition that localities are embedded within a global economic system whose overall contours do not respond to local initiatives has caused a debate over the efficacy of local action. Urban redevelopment efforts have taken place within the larger framework of the hypermobility of capital and intensified national and international economic competition. These factors have seemingly inexorably caused the decline of manufacturing and the flight of employment from older cities. Within this context social scientists have questioned whether, regardless of who controls the local regime, local actors can affect their economies and carry out redistributional policies.

The feverish attempts by governments around the world to attract business challenge the view of economic determinists that market forces will by themselves allocate economic functions to their optimum locations. Interestingly, this belief in the power of the market is held not just by conservative economists but also by progressive critics of government subsidies to business. Both argue that businesses do not choose a location because governmental incentives are available but rather because of factors like the price of labor or the presence of clients, which immediately affect production costs or marketing effectiveness. Accordingly, businesses do not choose a location because of governmentally proffered concessions but simply take advantage of them to enhance their profits at the expense of taxpayers.

Paul Peterson, in his influential book, *City Limits* (1981), considers that local governments can affect the economic situation of their jurisdictions even though they cannot directly improve the welfare of their poorer citizens. He explicitly repudiates the possibility of redistributive actions by local governments, contending that they must pursue growth and cannot enact redistributional policies without sacrificing their competitive positions. For Peterson, if municipal officials attempt to assist poor people, thereby scaring away businesses through increasing their tax burden, they will have nothing to redistribute.

In response, Sanders and Stone (1987) maintain that political conflict determines who wins and who loses from the redevelopment process; while they do not explicitly stipulate an alternative path to redevelopment, they imply that it can be achieved through community-based rather than downtown expansion. In other words, local politics matters in determining both the geographic targets of redevelopment programs and who benefits from them. According to this school of thought, urban policy-makers do not have to submit to the logic of capitalism; if they do so, it is because of political pressure rather than economic necessity (Logan and Swanstrom, 1990).

Is the issue resolvable?

There are several ways to address the issue of local autonomy. Differences between American and European cities and variations among cities that had similar economic bases 30 years ago imply that political factors influence the capability of cities to fit into new economic niches. Within the United States, where local governments have a much greater say over levels of welfare spending than in the United Kingdom, economically comparable cities spend different amounts of money on poor people, indicating that the extent to which cities engage in redistribution is not simply determined by competition among localities. At the same time, the downward pressure on social welfare expenses that has characterized all of the advanced capitalist countries since the mid-1970s points to serious restrictions on local deviationism.

Definitive conclusions based on observation are, however, impossible: for every example of local activity resulting in regeneration or redistribution, there is a counterexample of seemingly insurmountable external forces. My own position is that incentives to investors do make a difference and that growth can be combined with greater equity than has typically been the outcome of redevelopment programs. But perhaps the farthest one can go in addressing the issue is to identify areas of indeterminacy that can be seized locally within the overall capitalist economic structure – that is, to identify courses of action that can produce lesser or greater growth, more or less progressive social policies, without expecting either an inevitable economic trajectory resulting from market position or socialism in one city deriving from effective political action. The research and policy problem then becomes to recognize those decisional points, rather than to inquire whether cities matter in general. The subject of investigation therefore switches to the strategies followed by local actors, the factors influencing their choices, and how and under what circumstances these strategies affect what happens. My intention is to raise these issues within London and New York in relation to the striking transformations that have occurred in their built environments in the last 25 years.

London and New York

Why study London and New York? In the first place, London and New York – with Tokyo – are the preeminent global cities, performing a vital function of command and control within the contemporary world system.[8] The contributions of property developers to the situations of global cities have so far been little explored, apart from investigations of the financial industry. Development firms, however, differ from purely financial institutions in their physicality and greater volatility. Their connection to globalization and overall economic stability, as well as their symbiotic relationship to the financial institutions that dominate the economies of global cities, require further inquiry.

Second, London and New York are ideal sites for the exploration of property-led redevelopment because the impact of the real estate industry within them during the 1980s was so uniquely large. Both cities were the locations of several mammoth projects as well as a range of lesser enterprises. Moreover, real-estate activity in the two cities generated some of the greatest fortunes made during that period of rampant money-making and became symbolic of the spirit of the era.

The reversal of economic decline in London and New York in the 1980s was based in considerable part on a property boom. The erection of such flashy projects as Trump Tower in Manhattan and Broadgate in London symbolized the creation of new wealth and seemingly testified to growing general prosperity. And indeed the flurry of new construction coincided with a major expansion in employment, income, and tax revenues. On both sides of the Atlantic, policies promoting physical redevelopment through public–private partnerships were heralded as the key to economic success.

The real estate crash of the nineties, accompanied by sharp economic contraction, however, called this model into question. Not only did empty office buildings and apartment houses act as a direct drag on economic activity, but the heavy commitment made by major financial institutions to the real estate industry threatened the soundness of major banks. The real-estate slump affected cities throughout the United States and the United Kingdom, but was particularly significant in New York and London, where the world's major developers were located, and where financial institutions both financed and consumed large amounts of space. Once the recession ended, however, the availability of cheap, vacant space facilitated the surprisingly quick business expansion at the century's end and bolstered the competitive position of the two cities. [. . .]

Local Conditions and National Contexts

London and New York also make a particularly useful comparison because their striking similarities simplify efforts at understanding the influence of national differences. The economic histories of the two metropolises have proceeded so synchronously as to highlight the roots of social and policy dissimilarities in politics and culture. Both cities developed as great ports; both act as centers of international trade – and the requirements for financing that trade caused them both to become the locations of the world's most important financial markets. Each has been the financial capital of the dominant global economic power, and each faces increased competition from other world centers. Although the United Kingdom's international economic position has declined, London has retained its place as a financial capital. In both cities manufacturing employment diminished by about three-quarters between the 1960s and the end of the century, while office employment increased (although far more dramatically in New York). Growth in employment stimulated an expansion of office space, including major government-sponsored development schemes, and pressure on conveniently located housing. The two cities each have inner-city concentrations of poverty and are surrounded by affluent suburban rings. In both, manufacturing jobs have moved out of easy access for the inner-city poor.

The two cities, however, have strikingly different political institutions. New York is governed by a mayor and council; governmental departments report to the mayor's office. London is divided into 33 localities, each headed by a council larger than the one that governs all of New York. The borough councils are organized in a fashion similar to Parliament, with the leader of the majority party acting as the head of an executive committee, each of whose members has responsibility for a particular governmental function. New York's government has considerable autonomy from higher levels of government, although its charter and its revenue-raising measures must be approved by the government of the state of New York. London's local authorities are strictly subordinate to the central government, which can overrule any local action, and there is no regional authority comparable to an American state government to which they are responsible. Although Londoners elected their first mayor in 2000, the powers of this office are quite limited compared with those of the mayor of New York. [...]

The systems of local government in the United Kingdom and the United States became less alike during the 1980s, when the Thatcher government eliminated general-purpose metropolitan authorities in Britain's largest conurbations. One could argue that the result simply reproduced the American situation, in which regions consist of numerous uncoordinated municipalities. Nowhere in the United States, however, do agglomerations exist on the scale and density of London's core area without an overarching general-purpose government. In addition, the move by the central government to exert ever-greater fiscal and policy control over local government restricted home rule to an extent unimaginable in the United States. Before the demise of the Greater London Council (GLC), which had jurisdiction over all of London within the surrounding Green Belt for purposes of planning, environmental controls, and transportation, London's government had considerable leeway. The GLC was able to pursue a course strikingly at variance with national policy – for example, by sharply reducing public-transit fares and by engaging in economic planning. Afterwards, however, the possibility of significant deviation became totally blocked.

The advent of a new national Labour government in 1997, and its decision to institute an elected mayor and council for London, represented a reversal of the trend toward greater centralization. It remains to be seen, however, what actual power these new entities will possess. [...]

Nationally, there are quite dissimilar policy frameworks, although these differences have lessened considerably during the 1980s as Conservative governments in the United Kingdom dramatically reduced the state's role in planning and social welfare. Throughout most of the twentieth century the British state took a much stronger role than the US government in promoting and regulating development. It constructed new towns, built council housing, and prohibited private investment in improvements on land unless they received specific planning permission. In the US the government engaged in very little direct construction activity, preferring to offer incentives to the private sector; although it did build public housing, the total amount produced was minuscule compared to what was achieved in the UK. The US government also did much less than the British to provide public social-service and recreational facilities. [...]

The British party system also continues to diverge from the American one in being far more programmatic. Great Britain now has a three-party system [...]; and at the city level there is not the single-party dominance that characterizes most big American municipalities and has shaped New York politics during the postwar years. The elimination of the metropolitan level of government meant that no one party had control throughout London; rather, party control varied among the 33 borough councils. [. . .]

Despite these important differences, London and New York increasingly share some political and social characteristics. Government agencies in each city have actively pursued private investment and have met strong opposition from neighborhood and preservationist forces. Borough councils in London and community boards in New York are comparable forums in which planning issues are first debated. In both cities ethnic divisions exacerbate conflict over turf. During the last two decades of the century each operated in a national context of conservative, market-oriented ideological ascendancy but had strong internal political forces demanding continued state intervention within a significant tradition of state-sponsored social-service and housing provision. Indeed New York has been the most "European" of American cities in the historic activism of its government.

The two cities have also both experienced important changes in the relations between men and women, which have expressed themselves in economic transformation, new family structures, and changed consciousness. These in turn have both affected and been affected by the uses of space, as women have sought access to work, better housing, and assistance in their parenting roles. The increased participation of women in the labor force and the strains they have felt as a consequence of the "double burden" of home and work have expanded their need for convenient job locations, better transportation systems, and day care. Their heightened political activism has intensified the community rebellion against systems of housing, land use, and transportation that do not take their needs into account.

During the 1980s and for much of the 1990s, the governing regimes of the two cities followed similar redevelopment strategies with similar results. Restructuring of the urban environment took place under comparable economic pressures and in the name of similar conservative ideologies. Economic factors did not determine these ideologies; the power of ideological formulations, however, reinforced the restructuring process within the cities' economic and spatial systems. The increasing integration of the world economy heightened the importance of these two global cities, as the worldwide investment opportunities of their dominant financial industries increased. At the same time globalization threatened their status through the challenge of increased competition from other aspirants for their economic niche. [. . .]

Notes

1   London Planning Advisory Committee (1991); Commission on the Year 2000 (1987). The London Planning Advisory Committee (LPAC) is composed of members of the 33

borough councils and gives advice to the London Office of the UK Department of the Environment. The Commission on the Year 2000 was a specially appointed group of notables brought together by Mayor Edward I. Koch.

2   See Harvey (1973); see also Lamarche (1976); Massey and Catalano (1978). An important contribution to the discussion in the early 1980s was contained in a number of the pieces in Dear and Scott (1981), especially those by Shoukry Roweis and Allen Scott, Chris Pickvance, and Martin Boddy.

3   See especially Balchin et al. (1988); Healey and Barrett (1990); Ball et al. (1985); Hamnett and Randolph (1988), Simmie (1994).

4   See Downs (1985); Feagin and Parker (1990); Frieden and Sagalyn (1990); Weiss (1989); Logan (1992).

5   Exceptions are the "progressive" cities, where political leadership elected by leftist or anti-developer constituencies has sought to channel development away from typical trickle-down programs oriented toward central business districts into neighborhood endeavors and to extract large public benefits from for-profit developers. See Clavel (1986) for a study of five such progressive cities; Krumholz and Forester (1990) for an examination of the Cleveland experience; Squires et al. (1987) on Chicago under Mayor Harold Washington; Lawless (1990) on the changing tactics of Labour authorities in Sheffield; Goss (1988), who chronicles the experience of the London Labour borough of Southwark; and Brindley et al. (1996), who examine "popular planning" within a London borough and "public-investment planning" in Glasgow. Of the various progressive cities described in the literature, only a minority have managed to maintain a consistent posture over the course of several elected administrations.

6   A number of studies are explicitly comparative and reach something of a consensus concerning the similarities in the impact of global economic restructuring on UK and US cities and on the direction of urban policy in the two countries. See Parkinson and Judd (1988); Barnekov, Boyle, and Rich (1989); Savitch (1988); King (1990); Sassen (1991); S. Fainstein et al. (1992); Zukin (1992).

7   Among the many studies that reach the conclusions summarized in this paragraph see Parkinson and Judd (1988), Squires (1989), and Logan and Swanstrom (1990) on growth strategies and their economic and social impacts; see Ambrose (1986), Sennett (1990), and Sorkin (1992) on impacts on diversity and the environment.

8   See Friedmann and Wolff (1982) and Friedmann (1986) for presentation of the "global city hypothesis." For research on global cities see Savitch (1988); King (1990); Sassen (1991; 1994); Fujita (1991); Mollenkopf and Castells (1991); S. Fainstein et al. (1992); Sudjic (1992).

References

Ambrose, Peter. 1986. *Whatever Happened to Planning?* London: Methuen.
Balchin, Paul N., Jeffrey L. Kieve, and Gregory H. Bull. 1988. *Urban Land Economics and Public Policy*, 4th ed. London: Macmillan.
Ball, Michael, V. Bentivegna, M. Edwards, and M. Folin. 1985. *Land Rent, Housing and Urban Planning*. London: Croom Helm.

Barnekov, Timothy, Robin Boyle, and Daniel Rich. 1989. *Privatism and Urban Policy in Britain and the United States*. New York: Oxford University Press.

Brindley, Tim, Yvonne Rydin, and Gerry Stoker. 1996. *Remaking Planning*, 2nd ed. London: Routledge.

Clavel, Pierre. 1986. *The Progressive City*. New Brunswick, NJ: Rutgers University Press.

Commission on the Year 2000. 1987. *New York Ascendant*. New York: Commission on the Year 2000.

Dear, Michael and Allen J. Scott. 1981. *Urbanization and Urban Planning in Capitalist Society*. London: Methuen.

Downs, Anthony. 1985. *The Revolution in Real Estate Finance*. Washington, DC: Brookings Institution.

Fainstein, Susan S. et al. 1992. "The Second New York Fiscal Crisis." *International Journal of Urban and Regional Research* 16 (March): 129–38.

Feagin, Joe R. and Robert Parker. 1990. *Rebuilding American Cities: The Urban Real Estate Game*, 2nd ed. Englewood Cliffs, NJ: Prentice-Hall.

Forman, Charlie. 1989. *Spitalfields: A Battle for Land*. London: Hilary Shipman.

Frieden, Bernard J. and Lynne B. Sagalyn. 1990. *Downtown, Inc*. Cambridge, MA: MIT Press.

Friedmann, John. 1986. "The World City Hypothesis." *Development and Change* 17: 69–83.

Friedmann, John and Gortz Wolff. 1982. "World City Formation: An Agenda for Research and Action." *International Journal of Urban and Regional Research* 6(3): 69–83.

Fujita, Kuniko. 1991. "A World City and Flexible Specialization: Restructuring of the Tokyo Metropolis." *International Journal of Urban and Regional Research* 15(2): 269–84.

Goss, Sue. 1988. *Local Labor and Local Government*. Edinburgh: Edinburgh University Press.

Hamnett, Chris and Bill Randolph. 1988. *Cities, Housing, & Profits*. London: Hutchinson.

Harvey, David. 1973. *Social Justice and the City*. Baltimore: John Hopkins University Press.

Healey, Patsy and Susan M. Barrett. 1990. "Structure and Agency in Land and Property Development Processes: Some Ideas for Research." *Urban Studies* 27(1): 89–104.

King, Anthony D. 1990. *Global Cities*. London: Routledge.

Krumholtz, Norman and John Forester. 1990. *Making Equity Planning Work*. Philadelphia: Temple University Press.

Lamarche, Francois. 1976. "Property Development and the Economic Foundations of the Urban Question." In *Urban Sociology*, ed. Chris Pickvance. New York: St. Martin's.

Lawless, Paul. 1990. "Regeneration in Sheffield: From Radical Intervention to Partnership." In *Leadership and Urban Regeneration*, eds. Dennis Judd and Michael Parkinson. Newbury Park, CA: Sage.

Logan, John R. 1992. "Cycles and Trends in the Globalization of Real Estate." In *The Restless Urban Landscape*, ed. Paul L. Knox. Englewood Cliffs, NJ: Prentice-Hall.

Logan, John R. and Harvey Molotch. 1987. *Urban Fortunes*. Berkeley: University of California Press.

Logan, John R. and Todd Swanstrom 1990. "Urban Restructuring: A Critical View." *Beyond the City Limits*, eds. John R. Logan and Todd Swanstrom. Philadelphia: Temple University Press.

London Planning Advisory Committee (LPAC). 1991. *London: World City*. London: LPAC.

Massey, Doreen and A. Catalano. 1978. *Capital and Land*. London: Edward Arnold.

Mollenkopf, John Hull and Manuel Castells (eds.). 1991. *Dual City*. New York: Russell Sage.

Parkinson, Michael and Dennis Judd. 1988. "Urban Revitalization in America and the UK – The Politics of Uneven Development." In *Regenerating the Cities: The UK Crisis and the US Experience*. Manchester University: Manchester University Press.

Peterson, Paul. 1981. *City Limits*. Chicago: University of Chicago Press.

Pickvance, Chris. 1981. "Policies as Chameleons: An Interpretation of Regional Policy and Office Policy in Britain." In *Urbanization and Urban Planning in Capitalist Society*, ed. Michael Dear and Allen J. Scott. London: Methuen.

Sanders, Heywood T. and Clarence N. Stone. 1987. "Developmental Politics Reconsidered." *Urban Affairs Quarterly* 22 (June): 521–39.

Saunders, Peter. 1979. *Urban Politics*. Harmondsworth, Middlesex: Penguin.

Sassen, Saskia. 1991. *The Global City*. Princeton, NJ: Princeton University Press.

Sassen, Saskia. 1994. *Cities in a World Economy*. Thousand Oaks, CA: Sage.

Savitch, H.V. 1988. *Post-Industrial Cities*. Princeton, NJ: Princeton University Press.

Sennett, Richard. 1990. *The Conscience of the Eye*. New York: Knopf.

Simmie, James. 1994. *Planning London*. London: UCL Press.

Sorkin, Michael. 1992. "Introduction." In *Variations on a Theme Park*, ed. Michael Sorkin. New York: Hill and Wang.

Squires, Gregory (ed.). 1989. *Unequal Partnerships*. New Brunswick, NJ: Rutgers University Press.

Squires, Gregory, Larry Bennett, Kathleen McCourt, and Phillip Nyden. 1987. *Chicago: Race, Class, and the Response to Urban Decline*. Philadelphia: Temple University Press.

Sudjic, Deyan. 1992. "Towering Ambition." *Guardian*, April 17.

Weiss, Marc. 1989. "Real Estate History: An Overview and Research Agenda." *Business History Review* 63 (Summer): 241–82.

Zukin, Sharon. 1992. "The City as a Landscape of Power: London and New York as Global Financial Capitals." In *Global Finance & Urban Living*, eds. Leslie Budd and Sam Whimster. London: Routledge.

13 Gentrification, Cuisine, and the Critical Infrastructure: Power and Centrality Downtown

Sharon Zukin

> Two decades of urban restructuring have produced notable changes in the cultural patterns of cities, especially related to the residential and lifestyle choices of upper income groups. Sharon Zukin has studied the "urban pioneers" who transformed New York's SoHo neighborhood from an abandoned warehouse and manufacturing district to a trendy community of artists' lofts. In this reading, Zukin describes the patterns of gentrification of lower Manhattan and relates them to the changing cultural symbols of power in the city. She identifies the symbolic importance of gourmet food in the cultural life of affluent urban groups as a marker of taste and sophistication. In the case of both gentrification and new cuisine, "authentic" buildings and foods are highly valued, even as they are transformed into luxury commodities.

Gentrification as Market and Place

Gentrification refers to a profound spatial restructuring in several senses. It refers, first, to an expansion of the *downtown*'s physical area, often at the expense of the *inner city*. More subtly, it suggests a diffusion outward from the geographical center of downtown's *cultural* power. Ultimately, gentrification – a process that seems to reassert a purely *local* identity – represents downtown's social transformation in terms of an *international* market culture.

Gentrification is commonly understood in a much narrower sense. Not only does it generally refer to housing, especially the housing choice of some members of a professional and managerial middle class, it usually describes this choice in individualistic terms. Yet the small events and individual decisions that make up a specific spatial process of gentrification feed upon a larger social transformation. Each neighborhood's experience of gentrification has its own story – yet every downtown has its "revitalized" South End (in Boston), Quality Hill (in Kansas City), or Goose Island (in Chicago). Regardless of topography, building stock, and even existing populations, gentrification persists as a collective effort to appropriate the center for elements of a new urban middle class.*

The notion of gentrifiers as "urban pioneers" is properly viewed as an ideological justification of middle-class appropriation. Just as white settlers in the nineteenth century forced Native Americans from their traditional grounds, so gentrifiers, developers, and new commercial uses have cleared the downtown "frontier" of existing populations.[1] This appropriation is coordinated, logically enough, with a local expansion of jobs and facilities in business services. While some of these jobs have decentralized to the suburbs, the city's economy as a whole has shifted toward finance, entertainment, tourism, communications, and their business suppliers. Yet neither corporate expansion nor gentrification has altered a general trend of urban economic decline, decreasing median household income, and income inequality. Instead, gentrification makes inequality more visible by fostering a new juxtaposition of landscape and vernacular, creating "islands of renewal in seas of decay."[2]

Reinvestment in housing in the center relies on capital disinvestment since 1945 (or, more accurately, since 1929) that made a supply of "gentrifiable" building stock available. But it also reflects a demand for such building stock that was shaped by a cultural shift. This in turn represents a "reflexive" consumption that is based on higher education and a related expansion of consumers of both high culture and trendy style: these are potential gentrifiers.[3]

The private-market investments of gentrification effectively took over the role of clearing out the center just at the point when public programs of urban renewal ran out of federal funding and alienated supporters from every racial group and social class. Gentrifiers, moreover, often used noninstitutional sources of capital, including inheritance, family loans, personal savings, and the sweat equity of their own renovation work. Gentrification thus constituted a transition in both the mode of downtown development – from the public to the private sector, from

---

* Race poses the most serious barrier to all new private-sector capital investment, including gentrification. During the 1970s, as housing prices continued to climb and the housing supply failed to keep pace with demand, white gentrifiers became "bolder" about moving into nonwhite neighborhoods, or more tolerant of the costs in security and services such residence imposed. Only when gentrification risks displacing people of color – notably, in Harlem – is there even a chance of mobilizing against it. Even then, as in industrial displacement, the victims are either bought out or permitted to buy into the new structure – in this case, the improved housing stock.

large to small-scale projects, from new construction to rehabilitation – and the source of investment capital.

At the same time, the entire political economy of the center city was changing, the result of a long structural process of deindustrialization and cyclical decline in property values. Large manufacturers had moved out of the center since the 1880s, arguing that the multistory arrangement of the buildings and congested streets was functionally obsolete. Dependent on horizontal layout of production processes, truck deliveries, and automobile commuting, manufacturers preferred new green-field plants in suburban locations. Suburban land prices, taxes, and wages also exerted an appeal. But the small manufacturers who remained in the center, often concentrated in late-nineteenth-century loft buildings downtown, paid rents so low they seemed anachronistic. Although they had been hit severely during the 1960s by competition from overseas production and import penetration, such centrally located activities as apparel manufacturing and printing continued to thrive in low-rent clusters near customers, competitors, and suppliers. In New York, they also benefited from mass transit lines that connected downtown and midtown Manhattan to more distant working-class areas where low-wage, often immigrant and minority workers lived.

Despite their economic viability and historic association with downtown areas, these manufacturers lived under the gun. They were perceived as interlopers by the growth machine of landed elites, elected officials, and real estate developers. Their socially obsolete vernacular posed a barrier to expanding the downtown landscape of economic power. During the 1960s, simultaneously with urban renewal programs on the one hand and new office construction in the suburbs on the other, many city administrations turned to reforming mayors who formed a new coalition with corporate business and banking interests. Mayor John Lindsay in New York, for example, shed City Hall's New Deal alliances with small business and labor unions for a more favorable orientation toward the financial sector, including real estate developers. From Lindsay on, New York's mayors backed a growth machine that explicitly focused on service-sector expansion throughout downtown Manhattan.

Provided businesses had a need or desire to be located downtown, the price of property there was by this point relatively low. While a "rent gap" reflected the cyclical loss of economic value at the center, some private-sector institutions – mainly banks and insurance companies, the offices of foreign-owned corporations, and financial services – remained committed to a downtown location for its symbolic value.[4] Yet downtown had never completely excluded "upscale" use. A small number of patrician households had always remained in Boston's Back Bay and Beacon Hill, and Philadelphia's Society Hill and Rittenhouse Square. Small areas such as these, which never lost economic and cultural value, served as springboards of "revitalization" in the center.

With one eye on redevelopment contracts and the other on property values, the patricians who owned downtown land were in an ideal position to direct a new mode of development that increased economic value. They also controlled the sources of investment capital, city government authorizations, and cultural legitimacy that are needed for a massive shift in land use, because they shaped the policies of banks, city planning commissions, and local historical societies. New York may have been an exception, for the patricians with property in downtown Manhattan – who now lived uptown or in the suburbs – pressed only for new building and highway construction until 1973.

In Philadelphia, however, the upper-class residents of Society Hill and their associates in banking and city government started a fairly concerted effort at preservation-based revitalization in the late 1950s. From house tours of Elfreth's Alley, they proceeded to government subsidies for slum clearance of nearby neighborhoods and new commercial construction. Twenty years later, just in time for the bicentennial celebration of the Declaration of Independence, their residential enclave downtown near the Delaware waterfront was surrounded by a large area devoted to historic preservation, tourism, new offices for insurance and financial corporations, and not coincidentally, gentrification in nearby Queen Village. The displaced were small businesses, including manufacturers, and working-class, especially Italian and Puerto Rican, residents.

In downtown Manhattan, by contrast, the displacement of low-rent and "socially obsolete" uses from around 1970 was part of the politics of culture. Specifically, the landscape of downtown Manhattan was shaped by an unexpected triumph on the part of an artists' and historic preservationists' coalition. Formed to defend living and working quarters that cultural producers had established in low-rent manufacturing lofts, artists' organizations protested the demolition of these areas by the growth coalition. They also claimed the legal right to live and work in buildings zoned for manufacturing use alone, on the basis of their contribution to New York City's economy. Since the 1960s, nontraditional forms of art and performance had indeed attracted a larger, paying public. Their gradual concentration in downtown lofts connected these spaces with a downtown arts economy.

In a competition over downtown space between the arts producers, manufacturers, and real estate developers, which lasted until 1973, the artists emerged as victors. Yet they could not have won the right to live in their lofts without powerful allies. Their political strategy relied not only on the growing visibility of artists' clusters, but also on the patronage of some landed and political elite members who otherwise would have supported the growth coalition. Saved by the cultural values of historic preservation and the rising market values of an arts economy, the lofts of downtown Manhattan were transformed from a light manufacturing into a cultural zone. This process ran parallel, we see with hindsight, to gentrification.[5] The legitimation of "loft living" in downtown Manhattan marked a symbolic as well as a material change in the landscape. Cleared of "obsolete" uses like manufacturing by an investment flow apparently unleashed "from below," downtown space demanded a visual, sensual, and even conceptual reorientation. Just as the new mode of development downtown reflected a new organization of production, so many of the gentrifiers' cultural practices related to a new organization of consumption.

At the outset, gentrifiers' fondness for restoring and preserving a historical style reflected real dismay at more than a decade of publicly sponsored urban renewal and private commercial redevelopment, which together had destroyed a large part of many cities' architectural heritage. The photographic exhibit (1963) and book on *Lost New York* (1967), for example, documented the handsome stone, masonry, and cast-iron structures that had dominated downtown Manhattan from the Gilded Age to World War II. Most of these buildings were torn down in successive periods of redevelopment as downtown commerce moved farther north. For a long time, demolition signified improvement. But the destruction in the early 1960s of Pennsylvania Station, a railroad terminal of the grand era whose soaring glass dome was replaced by a mundane office building, dramatized the loss of a collective sense of time that many people felt.

The photographic exhibitions that were mounted for *Lost Boston, Lost Chicago*, and *Lost London* showed a nearly universal dissatisfaction with slash-and-burn strategies of urban redevelopment. Criticism ranged from aesthetics to sociology. The journalist Jane Jacobs, whose family had moved into a mixed residential and industrial area in the oldest part of Greenwich Village, argued for the preservation of old buildings because they fostered social diversity. She connected small, old buildings and cheap rents with neighborhood street life, specialized, low-price shops, and new, interesting economic activities: in other words, downtown's social values. Studies by the sociologists Herbert Gans and Marc Fried suggested, moreover, that for its residents, even a physically run-down inner-city community had redeeming social value.[6]

The rising expense and decreasing availability of new housing in the center worked in tandem with these developing sensitivities. Meanwhile, new patterns of gender equality and household independence diminished the old demand for housing near good schools, supermarkets, and neighborhood stores, at least for those families without children or with adequate funds for private schools. While they couldn't afford Park Avenue, or wouldn't be caught dead on the Upper East Side, highly educated upper-middle-class residents viewed the center in light of its social and aesthetic qualities. Equally well educated lower-income residents – notably, those who had chosen cultural careers and those who lived alone, including significant numbers of women and gays – viewed the center in terms of its clustering qualities. Relatively inexpensive building stock in "obsolete" areas downtown provided both groups of men and women with opportunities for new cultural consumption.

New middle-class residents tended to buy houses downtown that were built in the nineteenth century. They painstakingly restored architectural detail covered over by layers of paint, obscured by repeated repairs and re-partitions, and generally lost in the course of countless renovations. The British sociologist Ruth Glass first noted their presence in the early 1960s as an influx of "gentry" into inner-city London neighborhoods. While the new residents did not have upper-class incomes, they were clearly more affluent and more educated than their working-class neighbors. The neighbors rarely understood what drew them to old houses in run-down areas near the center of town. Since that time, however, gentrifiers have become so pervasive in all older cities of the highly industrialized world that their cultural preferences have been incorporated into official norms of neighborhood renewal and city planning.

With its respect for historic structures and the integrity of smaller scale, gentrification appeared as a rediscovery, an attempt to recapture the value of place. Appreciating the aesthetics and social history of old buildings in the center showed a cultural sensibility and refinement that transcended the postwar suburban ethos of conformity and kitsch. Moreover, moving downtown in search of social diversity made a statement about liberal tolerance that seemed to contradict "white flight" and disinvestment from the inner city. By constructing a social space or *habitus* on the basis of cultural rather than economic capital, gentrification apparently reconciled two sets of contradictions: between landscape and vernacular, and market and place. On the one hand, gentrifiers viewed the dilapidated built environment of the urban vernacular from the same perspective of aesthetics and history that was traditionally used for viewing landscape. On the other hand, their demand to preserve old buildings – with regard to cultural rather than economic value – helped constitute a market for the special characteristics of place.[7]

Yet as the nature of downtown changed, so did gentrification. The concern for old buildings that was its hallmark has been joined, since the early 1980s, by a great deal of new construction. Combined commercial and residential projects near the financial district – like Docklands in London or Battery Park City in New York – exploit the taste for old buildings and downtown diversity that gentrifiers "pioneered." By virtue of its success, however, we no longer know whether gentrification is primarily a social, an aesthetic, or a spatial phenomenon.

Small-scale real estate developers slowly awakened to the opportunity of offering a product based on place. "You find a prestigious structure that is highly visible, and built well, preferably something prewar," says a housing developer who converted a neo-Gothic Catholic seminary in a racially mixed neighborhood near downtown Brooklyn to luxurious apartments. "You find it in a neighborhood that still has problems but is close to a park, a college, good transportation – something that will bring in the middle class. And almost by the time you are through, other buildings around it will have started to be fixed up."[8]

Downtown loft areas formed a more specialized real estate market because they had a special quality. Their association with artists directly invested living lofts with an aura of authentic cultural consumption. If the artist was "a full-time leisure specialist, an aesthetic technician picturing and prodding the sensual expectations of other, part-time consumers," then the artist's loft and the surrounding quarter were a perfect site for a new, reflexive consumption.[9]

Markets are not the only arbiters of a contest for downtown space between landscape and vernacular. The key element is that the social values of existing users – for example, working-class residents and small manufacturers – exert a weaker claim to the center than the cultural values of potential gentrifiers. Gentrification joins the economic claim to space with a cultural claim that gives priority to the demands of historic preservationists and arts producers. In this view, "historic" buildings can only be appreciated to their maximum value if they are explained, analyzed, and understood as part of an aesthetic discourse, such as the history of architecture and art. Such buildings rightfully "belong" to people who have the resources to search for the original building plans and study their house in the context of the architect's career. They belong to residents who restore mahogany paneling and buy copies of nineteenth-century faucets instead of those who prefer aluminum siding.

Gentrifiers' capacity for attaching themselves to history gives them license to "reclaim" the downtown for their own uses. Most of them anyway tend not to mourn the transformation of local working-class taprooms into "ye olde" bars and "French" bistros. By means of the building stock, they identify with an earlier group of builders rather than with the existing lower-class population, with the "Ladies' Mile" of early-twentieth-century department stores instead of the discount stores that have replaced them.

Mainly by virtue of their hard work at restoration and education, the urban vernacular of ethnic ghettos and working-class neighborhoods that were due to be demolished is re-viewed as Georgian, Victorian, or early industrial landscape – and judged worthy of preservation. "In this new perspective [a gentrified neighborhood] is not so much a literal place as a cultural oscillation between the prosaic reality of the contemporary inner city and an imaginative reconstruction of the area's past."[10]

The cultural claim to urban space poses a new standard of legitimacy against the claim to affordability put forward by a low-status population. Significantly, cultural value is now related to economic value. From demand for living lofts and gentrification, large property-owners, developers, and elected local officials realized that they could enhance the economic value of the center by supplying cultural consumption.

In numerous cases, state intervention has reinforced the cultural claims behind gentrification's "market forces." New zoning laws banish manufacturers, who are forced to relocate outside the center. Since 1981, moreover, the US tax code has offered tax credits for the rehabilitation of historic structures. Although the maximum credit was lowered, and eligibility rules tightened, in 1986, the Tax Reform Act retained benefits for historic preservation. Every city now has procedures for certifying "landmark" structures and districts, which tend to restrict their use to those who can afford to maintain them in a historic style. But when landmarking outlives its usefulness as a strategy of restoring economic value at the center – as it apparently did in New York City by the mid 1980s – local government is capable of shifting gears and attacking the very notion of historic preservation.

Gentrification received its greatest boost not from a specific subsidy, but from the state's substantive and symbolic legitimation of the cultural claim to urban space. This recognition marked cultural producers as a symbol of urban growth. While storefront art galleries and "French" restaurants became outposts and mediators of gentrification in specific neighborhoods, cities with the highest percentage of artists in the labor force also had the highest rates of downtown gentrification and condominium conversion.[11]

Yet the aesthetic appeal of gentrification is both selective and pliable. It can be abstracted into objects of cultural consumption that bear only a distant relation to the downtown areas where they were once produced. "Before Fior di Latte," reads an advertisement for a new brand of "fresh" cheese mass marketed by Pollio Dairy Products Corporation, "you had to go to *latticini* [dairy] stores in Italian neighborhoods to buy fresh mozzarella. Store owners made the delicious white cheese daily and kept it fresh in barrels of lightly salted water." The point is that it is no longer necessary to go the ethnic neighborhoods downtown to consume their heritage; international trade and mass distribution can reproduce a historically "authentic" product. "To capture this fragile, handmade essence of fresh mozzarella," the ad continues, "Polly-O uses methods and equipment imported from Italy. We even pack each individual serving of Fior di Latte in water to keep it moist and fresh up to 25 days." No need for *latticini* when fresh mozzarella is sold in supermarkets.

The organization of consumption thus has a paradoxical effect on downtown space. Initially treated as unique, the cultural value of place is finally abstracted into market culture. [...]

Gentrification and Cuisine

Gourmet food – specifically, the kind of reflexive consumption beyond the level of need that used to be called gastronomy – suggests an organization of consumption structurally similar to the deep palate of gentrification.

The labor force that produces gourmet food in new "French" restaurants illustrates the hierarchy of social classes in the new, service-oriented urban population. While they may produce a version of French cuisine more authentic than the "continental" menu that was so popular in the 1950s and 1960s, these restaurants contrast with real French establishments, which are usually French-owned and run according to a traditional professional standard. At the bottom, where French employees would begin an apprenticeship in restaurant management, low-skilled, mainly immigrant, employees work as busboys and sometimes cooks. The kitchen, and even the lesser service stations, which are traditionally the realm of apprentice and master chefs, are staffed by college graduates and degree-holders from culinary arts schools. Generally recruited – in contrast to France – from the middle class, they need restaurant experience to begin a chef's career or open their own establishments. Waiters and waitresses in new "French" restaurants are recruited from the critical infrastructure. So many underemployed actors, artists, and writers have been drawn into part-time restaurant employment, at least in Los Angeles and Manhattan, that the hiring process now resembles a casting call.[12]

Alongside the actual consumption of restaurant food, another set of producers satisfy a need for vicarious consumption. Among the specialized magazines that began publishing in the 1970s and 1980s, a burgeoning "gourmet" press caters to the gentrifier's intellectual curiosity. Over the years these magazines have become more professional, with greater attention to "authentic" ingredients, the careers of chefs, and regions of food production (some of which, like California wine country, have been developed into tourist regions). At the same time, a large number of trade books published for display on the coffee table feature luscious photographs of sushi, grapes, or cheese, organized around exotic themes. (Alexander Cockburn once called this literary genre "gastro-porn.")

Certainly these forms of vicarious consumption are related to older means of communication, especially newspaper journalism and television. We can hardly underestimate the didactic effect of Elizabeth David's and Jane Grigson's writing about food in the English press in the 1950s and 1960s, Julia Child's US television series on French cooking during the 1970s, and the "home," "style," and "weekend" supplements that daily newspapers have published since the 1970s. Increasingly, however, vicarious consumption of gourmet food abstracts, rather than reproduces, cuisine's cultural values: many upper-middle-class devotees of television cooking shows today never go into the kitchen. Restaurant consumers of gourmet food run the same gamut as those who participate in gentrification. New "French" restaurants draw both rich gourmets who know about the food and middle-class pretenders who know about the place. Thus we have a simultaneous increase in restaurants with "four-star" cuisine and those that merely feature modish, trendy, or "theme" menus.

Three main kinds of gentrifiers, moreover, parallel the consumers who patronize gourmet food stores. Gentrifiers are either former urban residents who seek to recapture an old ethnicity, aspirants toward a higher level of cultural consumption, or small-scale investors in housing development. Similarly, "we have a blend of three kinds of customers," the president of a regional chain of discount gourmet food stores says. "Those who grew up where the product was sold and are familiar with it, those who are interested in establishing a higher quality of life for themselves, and those who are the bargain-hunters."[13]

These preliminary notes suggest that, like gentrification, the social organization of gourmet food consumption cannot be adequately explained by demographic changes, the pursuit of positional goods for social differentiation, or the economics of market segmentation. These days, gourmet food takes many forms. Between mass-market prepared dishes and traditional French cooking lies the landscape of nouvelle cuisine. Like the downtown landscape, nouvelle cuisine represents a basic restructuring of socio-spatial power. It also reflects change in a landscape of central power – that is, the production and consumption of classical French cuisine. [...]

A Landscape of Consumption

Both gentrification and new cuisine represent a new organization of consumption that developed during the 1970s. Both imply a new landscape of economic power based, in turn, on changing patterns of capital investment and new relations between investment, production, and consumption. A new international division of labor, greater trade and more travel, the abstraction or removal of traditional activities from local communities: all these consequences of the global economy make available a new range and quality of experience. At the same time, the disappearance of old sources of regional and local identity impoverishes others, leading to a new pursuit of authenticity and individualization.

Shifts in both production and consumption of cultural values create new socio-spatial meaning. Aspirations toward cultural power primarily clear the landscape of socially obsolete, and segmented, vernacular. But this process relies on a shift of perspective that in turn is tied to the social production of a new group of cultural mediators. They enable vernacular to be perceived, appreciated, and consumed as landscape – but then also appropriated, marketed, and exchanged in a more intensive way. This group is a critical infrastructure in two senses. On the one hand, their mediation is *critical* to the social processes of spatial and economic restructuring that are especially visible in modern cities at the center of advanced industrial society. On the other hand, their labor produces *critique* that makes people more aware of consumption and distinguishes reflexive consumers from other social groups.

Members of the critical infrastructure produce the didactic prism through which cultural values are appreciated. They conduct walking tours through seedy neighborhoods, pointing out elements of art and history amid decline. They visit restaurants, writing up reactions to dishes and comparing them with the composite menu of their collective experience. By these activities, the critical infrastructure establish and unify a new perspective for viewing and consuming the values of place – but by so doing they also establish their market values. From this point of view, gentrification – like cuisine – is transformed from a *place-defining* into a *market-defining* process.

Ironically, in either landscape or menu, the key elements are substitutable. The chef's grandmother's stew or Indian spices, red caviar on potato pancakes, tortillas wrapped around foie grass: does it matter, so long as each element is "authentically" part of a culinary landscape? In gentrification, too, appropriation of a homogeneous visual standard of cultural power takes precedence over the social community. "We've reached a point," says the chairman of a local community board on the gentrified Upper West Side of Manhattan, "where the young, middle-class family cannot ever come back here. We are adamant about trying to save *the look of the place* even if we cannot save the population group."[14]

There could be no more devastating indictment of the effects on place of market power.

The "death of downtown" suggests that centrality has its contradictions. For developers, centrality is a geographical space; for gentrifiers, it is a built environment. But for a population that is socially or economically displaced from older cities, centrality is a struggle between their own segmented vernacular and a coherent landscape of power.

Notes

1 Neil Smith, "Gentrification, the Frontier, and the Restructuring of Urban Space," in *Gentrification of the City*, ed. Neil Smith and Peter Williams (Boston: Allen & Unwin, 1986), pp. 15–20.

2 See Peter D. Sahlins, "The Limits of Gentrification," *New York Affairs* 5, no. 4 (1979): 3–12; Brian J. L. Berry, "Islands of Renewal in Seas of Decay," in *The New Urban Reality*, ed. Peter E. Peterson (Washington, DC: Brookings Institution, 1985), pp. 35–55; J. I. Nelson and J. Lorence, "Employment in Service Activities and Inequality in Metropolitan Areas," *Urban Affairs Quarterly* 21, no. 1 (1985): 106–25; Neil Smith, *Uneven Development* (New York: Blackwell, 1984) and "Of Yuppies and Housing: Gentrification, Social Restructuring, and the Urban Dream," *Society and Space* 5 (1987): 151–72.

3 For a detailed review of economic and cultural approaches to gentrification, see Sharon Zukin, "Gentrification: Culture and Capital in the Urban Core," *Annual Review of Sociology* 13 (1987): 129–47.

4 On the rent gap, see Neil Smith, "Toward a Theory of Gentrification: A Back to the City Movement by Capital Not People," *Journal of the American Planners Association* 45 (1979): 538–48; for criticism of the concept, noting that redevelopment by gentrification is only one possible option, see Robert A. Beauregard, "The Chaos and Complexity of Gentrification," in *Gentrification of the City*, ed. Smith and Williams, pp. 35–55; and for defense of the rent gap explanation in terms of opportunity, see Smith, "Of Yuppies and Housing."

5 See Sharon Zukin, *Loft Living: Culture and Capital in Urban Change*, 2d ed. (New Brunswick, NJ: Rutgers University Press, 1989).

6 Jane Jacobs, *The Death and Life of Great American Cities* (New York: Vintage Books, 1961); Herbert Gans, *The Urban Villagers* (New York: Free Press, 1962); Marc Fried and Peggy Gleicher, "Some Sources of Satisfaction in the Residential Slum," *Journal of the American Institute of Planners* 72, no. 4 (1961): 305–15.

7 The work of Pierre Bourdieu seems basic to this analysis, especially his emphasis on the tastes of people with more cultural than economic capital. See Bourdieu, *Distinction: A Social Critique of the Judgement of Taste*, trans. Richard Nice (Cambridge, Mass.: Harvard University Press, 1984).

8 Andree Brooks, "About Real Estate: Brooklyn School Converted to Housing," *New York Times*, March 25, 1988.

9 Quotation on the artist from Meyer Schapiro, quoted in Diana Crane, *The Transformation of the Avant-Garde: The New York Art World, 1940–1985* (Chicago: University of Chicago Press, 1987), p. 83.

10 Quotation from Patrick Wright, "The Ghosting of the Inner City," in *On Living in an Old Country: The National Past in Contemporary Britain* (London: Verso, 1985), pp. 228–9.

11 National Endowment for the Arts study of artists and gentrification cited in Dennis E. Gale, *Neighborhood Revitalization and the Postindustrial City: A Multinational Perspective* (Lexington, Mass.: Lexington Books, 1984), p. 155.

12 John Nielsen, "Even Those Who Serve Must Audition for the Part," *New York Times*, March 2, 1988.

13 Eric Schmitt, "Discount Stores for Fledgling Gourmets," *New York Times*, Feb. 3, 1988.

14 David W. Dunlap, "West Side Sites to Be Weighed as Landmarks," *New York Times*, Nov. 17, 1986; emphasis added.

14 Gazing on History

John Urry

Faced with the decline of manufacturing industries, many local governments have attempted to diversify their economic bases, often through tourism. Both in England and the United States, several older industrial cities have converted their deserted mills to museums of industrial life. In this selection, John Urry describes the development of a new "heritage industry," in which localities recreate the historical sites and activities of workshops, factories, farms, and other environments depicting ordinary life in the not-too-distant past.

Urry examines the architecture and city planning of these tourist-oriented heritage sites, explaining why they can be thought of as postmodern. These heritage towns protect and celebrate the vernacular architecture of ordinary houses and shops to create a distinctive identity, as opposed to encouraging the "placeless" uniformity of modern architecture. Urry finds that communities strive for charm and tourist potential by conserving and marketing their unique or "authentic" features – even if those features must be recreated and sanitized to make them attractive to contemporary audiences.

The Heritage Industry

Tourist sites can be classified in terms of three dichotomies: whether they are an object of the romantic or collective tourist gaze; whether they are historical or modern; and whether they are authentic or inauthentic. Characterising sites in such terms is obviously not straightforward and the third dichotomy, authentic/ inauthentic, raises many difficulties. Nevertheless it is useful to summarise the differences between such sites by employing these dichotomies.

For example, the Lake District in the north-west of England can be character-ised as predominantly the object of the romantic gaze, it is historical and it is apparently authentic. By contrast, Alton Towers leisure park, again in the

Urry, John, "Gazing on History." From *The Tourist Gaze: Leisure and Travel in Contemporary Societies* (Thousand Oaks, CA: Sage Publications, 1990), pp. 104–10, 112–16, 120–2, 123–6, 129–32, 134. © 1993 by Sage. Reprinted by permission of Sage Publications Ltd.

north-west, is the object of the collective gaze, it is mainly modern and it is predominantly inauthentic. These are fairly straightforward characterisations. But more complex are places like the refurbished Albert Dock in Liverpool, the Wigan Pier Heritage Centre in Lancashire and the restored mills in Lowell, Massachusetts, the first industrial town in the USA. These are all examples of the heritage industry, a development which has generated a great deal of debate. Although they are the object of the collective gaze, it is more controversial whether such sites are really 'historical' and 'authentic', as is claimed. There is also much debate as to the causes of this contemporary fascination with gazing upon the historical or what is now known as heritage (generally here see Lowenthal, 1985, especially ch. 1 on 'nostalgia' as a physical affliction dating from the late seventeenth century).

There are indicators of this phenomenon in Britain, where it seems that a new museum opens every week or so. Of the 1,750 museums responding to a 1987 questionnaire, half had been started since 1971. There are now at least 41 heritage centres, including Ironbridge Gorge near Telford, the Wigan Pier Heritage Centre, Black Country World near Dudley, the Beamish Open Air Museum near Newcastle, and the Jorvik Viking Centre in York. In Britain there are now 464 museums possessing industrial material and 817 with collections relating to rural history. The director of the Science Museum has said of this growth in heritage that: 'You can't project that sort of rate of growth much further before the whole country becomes one big open air museum, and you just join it as you get off at Heathrow' (quoted in Hewison, 1987: 24).

Some of the most unlikely of places have become centres of a heritage-based tourist development. Bradford, which once sent most of its holiday-makers to Morecambe, has now become a major tourist attraction in its own right. In the Rhondda valley in South Wales it is planned to locate a museum in the Lewis Merthyr coalmine and to establish a Rhondda Heritage Park (see Halsall, 1986). Almost everywhere and everything from the past may be conserved. In Lancashire environmentalists have sought to preserve the largest slag heap in Britain, which British Coal had wanted to remove. There are now 500,000 listed buildings in Britain, as well as over 5,500 conservation areas. The broadcaster Michael Wood writes: 'Now that the present seems so full of woe...the profusion and frankness of our nostalgia...suggest not merely a sense of loss...but a general abdication, an actual desertion from the present' (1974: 346). The seventeenth-century disease of nostalgia seems to have become an epidemic.

Some museums and heritage centres are, moreover, major developments. For example, in the period January–June 1988 £127.2 million was invested in heritage and museums in Britain. This investment was in a wide variety of sites and activities: such as a chemicals museum in Widnes, the restoration of the West Pier in Brighton, a 'Living Dockyard' attraction in Chatham, a Museum of Nursing in Lambeth, the reconstruction of Coronation Street in the Granada studios in Manchester, a new themed attraction of 'waterfront Poole' in Devon, and a 'Norfolk bygone village' in East Anglia. Until about 1970 or so most museums were publicly owned, normally by local councils. At the same time central government expenditure is considerable. It spends over £100 million a year on conserving the built environment, much of it through increasingly entrepreneurial agencies like English Heritage. One striking feature of these recent developments has been the increased privatisation of the heritage/museum industry, with 56 per cent of recently opened museums being in the private sector (on these various points see Hewison, 1987: 1, ch. 4; White, 1987; Urry, 1988; Thrift, 1989). And these private initiatives have inspired particularly new ways of representing history, as commodifying the past.

Enormous numbers of people visit such places. In 1983–4 more people visited museums and galleries in Britain than visited the cinema, while many more visited heritage buildings than the live theatre (Myerscough, 1986: 292). The proportion of the service class visiting museum and heritage centres in any year is about three times that of manual workers. About two-thirds of the visitors to such places have white-collar occupations (Myerscough, 1986: 303–4). Seventy-five per cent of overseas visitors to Britain visited a museum/gallery during their stay in Britain. By contrast, only 40 per cent went to a theatre/concert and fewer than 20 per cent saw a film at the cinema (Myerscough, 1986: 311).

There is little doubt that similar developments are taking place in many industrial countries (see Lumley, 1988). Lowenthal says of the USA that 'the trappings of history now festoon the whole country' (1985: xv). The number of properties listed in the US National Register of Historic Places rose from 1,200 in 1968 to 37,000 in 1985 (Frieden and Sagalyn, 1989: 201). However, various critics of heritage, such as Hewison or Wright, argue that these developments are more extensive in Britain than elsewhere, although the empirical testing of such a hypothesis is clearly fraught with methodological difficulties (Hewison, 1987; Wright, 1985). What is fair to claim is the following argument.

Since the late nineteenth century in Britain there has certainly been a tradition of visiting/conserving the countryside. This is reflected in the appreciation both of certain kinds of landscape (including villagescapes) and of the grand country houses set in attractive rural settings. On the first of these Raban talks of a recent willingness of people to present a particular impression of village England: 'nowhere outside Africa...were the tribespeople so willing to dress up in "traditional" costumes and cater for the entertainment of their visitors.... The thing had become a national industry. Year by year, England was being made more picturesquely merrie' (1986: 194–5).

Some of these events are now organised as 'costume dramas' by English Heritage, the main body concerned with the protection of heritage sites. The tendency to visit grand country houses also remains immensely popular, with 4.2 million people visiting National Trust houses in 1986 (Thrift, 1989: 29).

There has been a further interest in visiting the countryside, stemming from a widespread interest in the equipment and machinery that was used in farming, and in the patterns of life that developed in agriculture. We noted earlier that there are over 800 museums containing rural exhibits. These have been described as 'pretend farms', with wheelwrights, blacksmiths, horse breeders, farriers and so on (see Vidal, 1988). There are also many restaurants and cafés in rural areas which are in effect small agricultural museums, such as the Tithe Barn in Garstang, Lancashire.

There has been an even more remarkable increase in interest in the real lives of industrial/mining workers. MacCannell points out the irony of these changes: 'Modern Man [sic] is losing his attachments to the work bench, the neighbourhood, the town, the family, which he once called "his own" but, at the same time, he is developing an interest in the "real lives" of others' (1976: 91). This interest is particularly marked in the north of England, where much heavy industry had been located. It seems that it is such industries which are of most interest to visitors, particularly because of the apparently heroic quality of much of the work, as in a coalmine or steel works. However, this should not be overemphasised, since people also appear to find interesting the backbreaking but unheroic household tasks undertaken by women. This fascination with other people's work is bound up with the postmodern breaking down of boundaries, particularly between the front and the backstage of people's lives. Such a development is also part of what I will discuss later, namely, a postmodern museum culture in which almost anything can become an object of curiosity for visitors.

The remarkably rapid de-industrialisation of Britain in the late 1970s and early 1980s had two important effects. On the one hand, it created a profound sense of loss, both of certain kinds of technology (steam engines, blast furnaces, pit workings) and of the social life that had developed around those technologies. The rapidity of such change was greater in Britain than elsewhere and was probably more geographically concentrated in the north of England, South Wales and central Scotland. On the other hand, much of this industry had historically been based in inner-city Victorian premises, large numbers of which became available for alternative uses. Such buildings were either immensely attractive in their own right (such as Central Station that is now the G-Mex Centre in Manchester), or could be refurbished in a suitable heritage style for housing, offices, museums or restaurants. Such a style is normally picturesque, with sandblasted walls, replaced windows and attractive street furniture.

This process of de-industrialisation occurred in Britain at a time when many local authorities were developing more of a strategic role with regard to economic development and saw in tourism a way of generating jobs directly and through more general publicity about their area. A good example is Wigan; this is well represented in a publicity booklet called *I've never been to Wigan but I know what it's like* (Economic Development, Wigan, undated). The first five pictures in black and white are of back-to-back terraced housing, mines and elderly residents walking along narrow alleyways. But we are then asked if we are sure this is really what Wigan is now like. The following twelve photos, all in colour, demonstrate the contemporary Wigan, which is revealed as possessing countless tourist sites, Wigan Pier, a colourful market and elegant shops, excellent sports facilities, attractive pubs and restaurants, and delightful canalside walkways. Selling Wigan to tourists is part of the process of selling Wigan to potential investors, who are going to be particularly concerned about the availability of various kinds of services for their employees. [...]

The preservation of heritage has been particularly marked in Britain because of the mostly unattractive character of the modern architecture produced in the UK. The characteristic modern buildings of the postwar period have been undistinguished office blocks and public housing towers, many with concrete as the most visible building material. Such buildings have proved to be remarkably disliked by most of the population, which has seen modern architecture as 'American'. Yet the contrast with the often striking and elegant north American skyscrapers located in the downstream areas is particularly noticeable. In addition Britain had a very large stock of pre-1914 houses and public buildings suitable for conservation, once the fashion for the modern had begun to dissolve in the early 1970s. An interesting example of this can be seen in the changing attitude towards conservation, particularly of the Regency façades in Cheltenham, which is now one of the prime townscapes being strenuously preserved even though much of it had been scheduled for 'redevelopment' (Cowen, 1990).

So for a number of reasons heritage is playing a particularly important role in British tourism, and it is somehow more central to the gaze in Britain than in many other countries. But what is meant by heritage, particularly in relationship to notions of history and authenticity (see Uzzell, 1989, on the recent professional literature on heritage)? A lively public debate has been raging in Britain concerned with evaluating the causes and consequences of heritage.

This debate was stimulated by Hewison's book on the heritage industry, which was subtitled *Britain in a Climate of Decline* (1987). He begins with the provocative comment that increasingly, instead of manufacturing goods, Britain is manufacturing heritage. This has come about because of the perception that Britain is in some kind of terminal decline. And the development of heritage not only involves the reassertion of values which are anti-democratic, but the heightening of decline through a stifling of the culture of the present. A critical culture based on the understanding of history is what is needed, not a set of heritage fantasies.

Hewison is concerned with analysing the conditions in which nostalgia is generated. He argues that it is felt most strongly at a time of discontent, anxiety or disappointment. And yet the times for which we feel most nostalgia were themselves periods of considerable disturbance. Furthermore, nostalgic memory is quite different from total recall; it is a socially organised construction. The question is not whether we should or should not preserve the past, but what kind of past we have chosen to preserve. Roy Strong wrote perceptively in 1978 that:

> We are all aware of problems and troubles, of changes within the structure of society, of the dissolution of old values and standards. . . . The heritage represents some kind of security, a point of reference, a refuge perhaps, something visible and tangible

which...seems stable and unchanged. Our environmental heritage...is a deeply stabilising and unifying element within our society. (quoted in Hewison, 1987: 46–7)

(Incidentally both Marx and Nietzsche might be said to have a similarly critical attitude to 'nostalgia': see Lowenthal, 1985: 65.) Hewison notes something distinctive about some contemporary developments. Much contemporary nostalgia is for the industrial past. The first major battle in Britain was fought – and lost – in 1962 over the elegant neoclassical arch at the entrance to Euston station. But this gave rise to a survey of industrial monuments by the Council for British Archaeology and a major conference in 1969. Four years later the Association for Industrial Archaeology was founded and by the 1980s industrial museums were developing almost everywhere in the northern half of Britain. Hewison makes much of the contrasts between the development of the industrial museum at Beamish and the devastation brought about by the closure of the steel works at Consett, just ten miles away. The protection of the past conceals the destruction of the present. There is an absolute distinction between authentic history (continuing and therefore dangerous) and heritage (past, dead and safe). The latter, in short, conceals social and spatial inequalities, masks a shallow commercialism and consumerism, and may in part at least destroy elements of the buildings or artefacts supposedly being conserved. Hewison argues that: 'If we really are interested in our history, then we may have to preserve it from the conservationists' (1987: 98). Heritage is bogus history. [...]

What does need to be emphasised is that heritage history is distorted because of the predominant emphasis on visualisation, on presenting visitors with an array of artefacts, including buildings (either 'real' or 'manufactured'), and then trying to visualise the patterns of life that would have emerged around them. This is an essentially 'artefactual' history, in which a whole variety of social experiences are necessarily ignored or trivialised, such as war, exploitation, hunger, disease, the law, and so on.

Overall Lowenthal's judgement on history seems right: 'We must concede the ancients their place.... But their place is not simply back there, in a separate and foreign country; it is assimilated in ourselves, and resurrected into an ever-changing present' (1985: 412).

The following three sections explore certain aspects of heritage in more detail: in relation to its use as part of a local strategy for economic regeneration; in its interconnections with recent trends in design and postmodern architecture; and its role in the development of what I shall term the postmodern museum.

Tourism and the Local State

In the previous discussion of the heritage industry it was noted that there is often considerable local support for conservation. I shall consider more fully here the relationship between local areas and tourism development. In that relation-ship there are three key elements. First, there are local people who are often concerned to conserve features of the environment which seem in some ways to stand for or signify the locality in which they live. Second, there are a variety of private sector owners and potential owners of tourist-related services. And third, there is the local state, which is comprised of local authorities as well as the local/regional representatives of various national-level bodies, including tourist boards.

An interesting example which illustrates this complexity of elements is the Winter Gardens theatre in Morecambe, which has recently been debated in the national press (see Binney, 1988). This theatre closed in the late 1970s and will cost £2–5 million to repair (there is galloping dry rot). It is widely agreed that the theatre, built in 1897, is architecturally superb. English Heritage describes it as 'outstanding', while John Earl of the Theatres Trust has characterised it as the Albert Hall of the north. It may be conserved, although this is by no means certain. If it is, there is little doubt that amongst other uses will be the staging of old-time music hall (as well as pop/classical concerts), hence conveying nostalgic memories of a somewhat imprecise golden age of pre-TV entertainment.

Clearly such a refurbishment would be subject to criticism as yet another example of the heritage industry. However, it should be noted that without a great deal of local support for conservation the theatre might already have been demol-ished. There is an extremely energetic action group convinced that this currently semi-derelict building symbolises Morecambe – that if it is allowed to be demol-ished, that would be the end of the town itself. It is certain that there is wide-spread popular support for increasing the attractiveness of Morecambe, to make it more congested and more subject to the tourist gaze. Indeed potential tourists to any site cannot contribute to environmental concern: that has to be expressed by local residents. Although the building is currently privately owned, it is quite clear that it will only be refurbished with much support from public bodies, including English Heritage, the European Community, Lancashire County Council and Lan-caster City Council. The last of these will almost certainly be involved in putting together an appropriate funding package. The role of the local state may well be crucial.

This example demonstrates two important points about contemporary tourist development: the impact of local conservation groups whose heritage-preserving actions will often increase tourism in an area, sometimes as an unintended conse-quence; and the central organising role of the local state.

On the first of these, it is important to note that the strength of conservation groups varies very considerably between different places. For example, in 1980 while there were 5.1 members of 'amenity societies' per 1,000 population in the UK as a whole, the ratio was over 20 per 1,000 in Hampshire and over 10 per 1,000 in most of the counties around London, in Devon, in North Yorkshire and in Cumbria (see Lowe and Goyder, 1983: 28–30 for more detail). Clearly part of the rationale of such groups is to prevent new developments taking place that will harm the supposed 'character' of the locality (in the south-east especially through low-cost housing schemes). The role of the service and middle classes in such groups is crucial – and is a major means by which those possessing positional goods, such as a nice house in a nice village, seek to preserve their advantages. However, conservation movements can often have fairly broad objectives: not merely to prevent development, but to bring about the refurbishment of existing public buildings and more generally to 'museumify' the villagescape or townscape. Moreover, even if the objectives of the movement have nothing to do with tourism, the effect will almost certainly be to increase the attractiveness of the locality to tourists. [...]

A factor which has helped to strengthen conservation movements is the apparently lower rate of geographical mobility of at least the male members of the service class (see Savage, 1988). As a result such people are likely to develop more of an attachment to place than previously. One can talk therefore of the 'localisation of the service class' and this will have its impact, through the forming of amenity groups, on the level of conservation (see Bagguley et al., 1989: 151–2). To the extent that such groups are successful, this will make the place more attractive to tourists. Thus the preservation of the quaint villagescape or townscape in particular, through middle-class collective action, is almost certain to increase the number of tourists and the resulting degree of congestion experienced by residents. One place where this has been particularly marked is Cheltenham. Because of concerted conservation pressure in the late 1960s the formal development policy was dropped in 1974. Since then a conservation policy has been adopted and there has been wholesale rehabilitation of the Regency housing stock for both housing and prestige office accommodation (see Cowen, 1990).

Before considering the various ways in which local states have responded to such pressures, and more generally how they have in recent years attempted to reconstruct the objects of the tourist gaze, I will note some reasons why local states have recently become centrally involved in both developing and promoting tourism.

As many local authorities moved into local economic intervention during a period of rapid de-industrialisation, so it seemed that tourism presented one of the only opportunities available for generating employment. Indeed it has been estimated that the cost of one new job in tourism is £4,000, compared with £32,000 in manufacturing industry and £300,000 in mechanical engineering (see Lumley, 1988: 22). The chairman of the South-East Tourist Board, for example, concludes that:

> I am heartily encouraged that County Councils are now giving tourism the recognition it deserves. It features strongly in most county structure plans. This is, of course, only right, given that it is one of the few growth elements in our economy. (English Tourist Board, no date: 4)

It was also noted that many such authorities have found themselves with a particular legacy, of derelict buildings, such as the Albert Dock in Liverpool, and/or derelict land, such as that which now comprises the Salford Quays development in Manchester. Converting such derelict property into sites which would have a tourist aspect directly or indirectly has been almost the only alternative available. [...]

Local authorities also play an important role because of the structure of ownership in tourist towns. This is often fragmented and it is difficult to get local capital to agree on appropriate actions from the viewpoint of the locality as a whole. The council is often the only agent with the capacity to invest in new infrastructure (such as sea defences, conference centres, harbours), or to provide the sort of facilities which must be found in any such centre (entertainments, museums, swimming pools). This has led in some of the older resorts, such as those on the Isle of Thanet, to the development of 'municipal Conservatism', a combination of small-scale entrepreneurialism and council intervention (see Buck et al., 1989: 188–9). In the last few years in Britain many Labour councils have enthusiastically embraced local tourist initiatives, having once dismissed tourism as providing only 'candy-floss jobs' (again see Landry et al., 1989, for an example of this argument; Glasgow would be a good illustration).

Finally, local councils have been willing to engage in promoting tourism because in a period of central government constraint this has been one area where there are sources of funding to initiate projects which may also benefit local residents. [...]

It is problematic to assess the economic impact of any particular tourism initiative. This results from the difficulty of assessing the so-called multiplier. If we consider the question of income generation, the impact of the expansion of tourism cannot be assessed simply in terms of how much income is spent by 'tourists' in hotels, camp sites, restaurants, pubs, and so on. It also depends upon what and where the recipients of that income, such as suppliers to the hotel or bar staff in the pubs, spend it, and in turn where those recipients spend it, and so on. There are some further problems in assessing such multipliers for a local economy: the linkages between firms are particularly complex and opaque partly because of the multitude of small enterprises involved; leakages from the economy are often very difficult to assess; there is no clear and agreed-upon definition of just what is a 'tourist' and hence what is tourist expenditure; the definition of the 'local economy' is in any case contentious so that the larger the geographical unit the higher the *apparent* multiplier. For all these difficulties it does seem that tourist expenditure has a fairly high local multiplier compared with other kinds of expenditure that might occur locally. Most studies show that something like half of tourism expenditure will remain in the locality, from its direct and indirect effects (see Williams and Shaw, 1988: 88). However, such income remains highly unequally distributed since tourism areas are notable for their low wages level, even amongst those not even employed in the tourism industry as such. [...]

The inspiration for development in Britain has arisen from the striking ways in which the downtown areas of American cities have been transformed, mainly by private developers but with a fair degree of public co-ordination. The main features found in the USA are the 'festival marketplace', particularly by the developer James Rouse as in Fanueil Hall in Boston; historical preservation, as in Lowell, Massachusetts; the development of new open spaces or plazas, such as Harborplace in Baltimore; waterfront developments, such as Battery City Park in New York; cultural centres, such as a performing arts centre in Los Angeles; renovation of old hotels, such as the Willard Inter-Continental in Washington, DC; refurbished housing, as on Beacon Hill, Boston; and new public transportation systems, even in Los Angeles, the ultimate automobile city (see Fondersmith, 1988; Frieden and Sagalyn, 1989; 210–12).

In the next section I shall consider in more detail the design and architecture of these various developments. Tourism is about finding certain sorts of place pleasant and interesting to gaze upon, and that necessarily comes up against the design of the buildings and their relationship to natural phenomena. Without the right design no amount of local state involvement will attract tourists. It will be seen that much of the architecture of these developments is in different senses *post*modern.

Designing for the Gaze

Given the emphasis on tourist consumption as visual, and the significance of buildings as objects upon which the gaze is directed, it is essential to consider changing patterns and forms that those buildings might take. Moreover, it is of course impossible to consider postmodernism without consideration of the built environment, surely the sphere which many would say best demonstrates such a cultural paradigm.

I shall argue, first, that there are a number of postmodern architectures; second, that the impact of these different architectures depends upon whether we are considering private or public buildings; third, that architects and architectural practices are of major importance in shaping the contemporary tourist gaze; fourth, that tourist practices have to be taken much more seriously by commentators on building design; and fifth, that tourists are socially differentiated and hence gaze selectively upon these different architectural styles.

The first point can be approached by considering what is meant by *post* in postmodern. There are three senses: *after* the modern; *return* to the premodern; and *anti* the modern. I shall now briefly summarise the architectural style associated with each of these (see Harris and Lipman, 1986, for an alternative classification).

After the modern is what one could also term 'consumerist postmodernism'. This takes its cue from Venturi's famous cry to 'learn from Las Vegas' (1972;

Jencks, 1977; Frampton, 1988). Caesar's Palace at Las Vegas or Disneyland are the icons of this architecture, which proudly celebrates commercial vulgarity (see Harris and Lipman, 1986: 844–5). Art and life are fused or pastiched in the playful and shameless borrowing of ornamental style. Previous elements of high culture are mass-produced, and no longer signify anything in particular. This is an architecture of surfaces and appearances, of playfulness and pastiche. It is manner-ist – as if all the historical styles and conventions of architecture are there to be endlessly drawn on, juxtaposed and drawn on yet again. However, a distinction should be made between the literal consumerism of Las Vegas and the manner in which some postmodern architects have hijacked such styles to construct some-thing of an auratic architecture appealing to the cognoscenti (as in James Stirling's Stuttgart gallery). In Britain Ian Pollard is one of the best-known postmodernists. A particularly striking building of his is the *Observer*'s Marco Polo House in Battersea, with its massive porticoes, broken pediments and banded ceramic towers (see Jenkins, 1987). An illustrative controversy has recently occurred over one of his other designs, a do-it-yourself store in west London built for Sainsbury (see Pearman, 1988). At the entrance to this store Pollard had playfully designed a massive Corinthian arch. Sainsbury, however, even before the store was open, found the design, with its abundance of Egyptian motifs and postmodern orna-mentation, far too jokey for a serious retailer. A spokesman for the company condemned it as 'this pastiche of a design' and the arch was demolished before the store was opened. [...]

Much of the debate about postmodernism has tended to concentrate on signifi-cant public buildings, such as Terry Farrell's TV-AM headquarters, Philip John-son's AT-&-T building, and James Stirling's Stuttgart gallery. There is less investigation of the impact of such a style on the everyday architecture of particu-lar towns and cities. This is an important issue, since historically most architecture has been partly eclectic, drawing on earlier traditions, such as the Gothic style favoured by the Victorians, or the Egyptian motifs popular with the Art Deco movement (on the latter see Bagguley, 1990: ch. 5; more generally, see Lowenthal, 1985: 309–21). The one exception was the modern movement and its perhaps unique rejection of all previous architectural mannerisms. Interestingly, even during the heyday of modernism (say 1930–70 in Britain) two other styles were common: red-brick neo-Georgian shopping parades, and neo-Tudor half-timbered suburban housing. [...]

Patrician postmodernism involves a *return* to the premodern. Here what is cele-brated is the classical form, the architecture of an elite. Leon Krier summarises its attraction: 'People never protested against the tradition of classical architec-ture. ... Architecture has reached its highest possible form in the classical prin-ciples and orders ... [which] have the same inexhaustible capacities as the principles which govern nature and the universe itself' (1984: 87, 119).

This reconstructed classicism springs from individuals who believe they have distinct powers of insight, who will be able to return to the aura of the fine building. Architecture here is a self-determining practice, an autonomous discipline able to reproduce the three classical orders. This is linked to the belief that such classicism is really what people want if only their choices were not distorted by modernism. In Britain, Prince Charles in part demonstrates this position, of appearing to speak on behalf of the people who know they do not like modernism and who really want only to gaze on nothing but uninterrupted classical buildings. [...]

The British architect who has become best known for his implementation of the classical tradition is Quinlan Terry, particularly in a series of elegant private houses, which are usually located in pleasant countryside. More recently he has been responsible for the extensive and controversial Richmond development, which consists of fifteen separate buildings built in a variety of classical styles. Terry's properties are expensive since they embody large amounts of craft labour on the exteriors, although the interiors are standardly modern. They are to do with 'an elitist and austere *return* to style and a cult of the unique' and yet compared with a modernist towerblock 'Terry's classy and expensive classical buildings may indeed, in a limited . . . sense, form a "popular" style of architecture' (Wright, 1985: 31). Certainly, to the extent to which such contemporary classical buildings mirror in particular the Georgian style, they will be immensely popular objects of the tourist gaze. If there is a single style of house which tourists in Britain want to gaze upon it is the classical country house (see Hewison, 1987: ch. 3). There is even now a handbook instructing people how to furnish and entertain in such Georgian houses, *The Official New Georgians Handbook* (Artley and Robinson, 1985). [...]

There is a third variant of postmodern architecture. This is not simply after the modern, or involving a return to the premodern – it is *against* the modern. It has much in common with Frampton's concept of 'critical regionalism' (1988) and Foster's notion of a 'critical postmodernism'. The latter defines the critique of modernism as a Eurocentric and phallocentric set of discourses (see Hebdige, 1986–7: 8–9). It is argued that modernism (like of course premodern classicism) privileges the metropolitan centre over provincial towns and cities, the developed world over developing countries, the north Atlantic rim over the Pacific rim, western art forms over those from the 'east' and the 'south', men's art over women's art, the professional over the people, and so on. There is one variant of the postmodern which involves challenging these dominant discourses: in architecture it can be characterised as vernacular postmodernism. [...]

Space in vernacular postmodernism is localised, specific, context-dependent, and particularistic – by contrast with modernist space which is absolute, generalised, and independent of context (see Harvey, 1989, more generally here). Leon Krier talks of the need to create 'localities of human dignity' (1984: 87). In Britain one of the clearest examples of this has been the 'community architecture' movement which Prince Charles has also done much to foster. This movement began with the restoration of Black Road in Macclesfield designed by Rod Hackney. The main principle of such a movement is 'that the environment works better if the people who live, work and play in it are actively involved in its creation and maintenance' (Wates and Krevitt, 1987: 18). This involves much emphasis on the process of design rather than on the end product, on reducing the power of the architecture vis-à-vis clients, on channelling resources to local residents and communities, and on restoration, or where new building is involved, ensuring it is appropriate to local historical context.

The locality is central to such an architecture. And there are important resistances in contemporary societies which have made local vernacular architecture particularly popular, at least outside the metropolitan centres. There is the apparent desire of people living in particular places to conserve or to develop buildings, at least in their public spaces, which express the particular locality in which they live. Such old buildings appear to have a number of characteristics: solidity, since they have survived wars, erosions, developers, town planning etc.; continuity, since they provide links between past generations and the present; authority, since they signify that age and tradition are worthy of preservation; and craft, since they were mostly built using otherwise underrated premodern techniques and materials (see Lowenthal, 1985: 52–63).

And because of the universalisation of the tourist gaze, all sorts of places (indeed almost everywhere) have come to construct themselves as objects of the tourist gaze; in other words, not as centres of production or symbols of power but as sites of pleasure. Once people visit places outside capital cities and other major centres, what they find pleasurable are buildings which seem appropriate to place and which mark that place off from others. One of the very strong objections to modernism was that it generated uniformity, or placelessness, and was therefore unlikely to generate large numbers of buildings attractive to potential tourists who want to gaze upon the distinct. The only exceptions are to be found in major cities, such as Richard Rogers' Lloyds building in London, or his high-tech Pompidou Centre in Paris, which now attracts more visitors than the Louvre. Outside the major cities the universalisation of the tourist gaze has made most other places enhance difference through the rediscovery of local vernacular styles. [...]

Here I have thus shown how the universalisation of the tourist gaze is reaping its postmodern harvest in almost every village, town and city in Britain and in many other western countries as well. I will now turn to one particular kind of building – the museum.

Postmodern Museums

We have seen a spectacular growth in the number of museums in western countries. This is clearly part of the process by which the past has come to be much more highly valued by comparison with both the present and the future. Also, the past has become particularly valued in the UK because of the way in which international tourism in this country has come to specialise in the construction of historical quaintness. And the attraction of museums increases as people get older – thus the 'greying' of the population in the west is also adding to the number and range of museums.

I have strongly argued for the significance of the gaze to tourist activities. This is not to say that all the other senses are insignificant in the tourist experience. But I have tried to establish that there has to be something distinctive to gaze upon, otherwise a particular experience will not function as a tourist experience. There has to be something extraordinary about the gaze.

On the face of it this seems a relatively straightforward thesis. But it is not – because of the complex nature of visual perception. We do not literally 'see' things. Particularly as tourists we see objects which are constituted as signs. They stand for something else. When we gaze as tourists what we see are various signs or tourist clichés. Some such signs function metaphorically. A pretty English village can be read as representing the continuities and traditions of England from the Middle Ages to the present day. By contrast the use of the term 'fun' in the advertising for a Club-Med holiday is a metaphor for sex. Other signs, such as lovers in Paris, function metonymically.[1] Here what happens is the substitution of some feature or effect or cause of the phenomenon for the phenomenon itself. The ex-miner, now employed at the former coalmine to show tourists around, is a metonym for the structural change in the economy from one based on heavy industry to one based on services. The development of the industrial museum in an old mill is a metonymic sign of the development of a post-industrial society.

There have of course been museums open to the public since the early nineteenth century, beginning with the Louvre in Paris, the Prado in Madrid and the Altes Museum in Berlin. And since the *Michelin Guides* first appeared museums have been central to the tourist experience. Horne describes the contemporary tourist as a modern pilgrim, carrying guidebooks as devotional texts (1984). What matters, he says, is what people are told they are seeing. The fame of the object becomes its meaning. There is thus a ceremonial agenda, in which it is established what we should see and sometimes even the order in which they should be seen.

Such museums were based on a very special sense of aura. Horne summarises the typical tourist experience, in which the museum has functioned as a metaphor for the power of the state, the learning of the scholar and the genius of the artist:

> tourists with little or no knowledge of painting are expected to pay their respects solely to the fame, costliness and authenticity of these sacred objects, remote in their frames. As 'works of art' from which tourists must keep their distance, the value of paintings can depend not on their nature, but on their authenticated scarcity. The gap between 'art' and the tourist's own environment is thereby maintained. (1984: 16)

Museums have thus been premised upon the aura of the authentic historical artefact, and particularly upon those which are immensely scarce because of the supposed genius of their creator. Horne argues that what can be especially problematic about museums is their attribution of reverence to objects simply because of their aura of authenticity (1984: 249). How we gaze within museums has changed in three central ways. The sense of aura that Horne describes has been undermined through the development of the postmodern museum. This involves quite different modes of representation and signification. What we 'see' in the museum has been transformed.

First, there has been a marked broadening of the objects deemed worthy of being preserved. This stems from a changed conception of history. There has been a decline in the strength of a given national history, which the national museums then exemplify. Instead a proliferation of alternative or vernacular histories has developed – social, economic, populist, feminist, ethnic, industrial and so on. There is a pluralisation and indeed a contemporarisation of history. This has produced in Britain a 150 per cent increase in the number of museums over the past twenty years (see White, 1987). The British Tourist Authority has calculated that there could be up to 12,000 museum-type venues in Britain (see Baxter, 1989). Museums are concerned with 'representations' of history, and what has happened is a remarkable increase in the range of histories worthy of being represented. I have already noted some of these, especially the development of rural and industrial museums. It is now almost as though the worse the previous historical experience, the more authentic and appealing the resulting tourist attraction (see Urry, 1988: 50). No longer are people only interested in seeing either great works of art or artefacts from very distant historical periods. People increasingly seem attracted by representations of the 'ordinary', of modest houses and of mundane forms of work. Glass-blowing, engine driving, shop working, candle-making, cotton spinning, salt-making, cobbling, chemical manufacture, holiday-making, lace-making, domestic chores, coalmining and so on, are all deemed worthy of being represented in contemporary museums, as are the often mundane artefacts associated with each of these activities (see West, 1988, on Ironbridge Gorge; Bennett, 1988, on Beamish; and Hewison, 1987, on Wigan Pier). There has been a quite stunning fascination with the popular and a tendency to treat all kinds of object, whether it is the *Mona Lisa* or the old cake tin of a Lancashire cotton worker, as almost equally interesting. One could summarise this shift as being 'from aura to nostalgia', and it reflects the anti-elitism of postmodernism (see Edgar, 1987). It should also be noted that all sorts of other phenomena are now preserved in museums, including moving images, radio, television, photographs, cinema, the environment and even the sets of TV soap operas (Lumley, 1988; and see Goodwin, 1989, on the Granada museum of the *Coronation Street* set).

There has also been a marked change in the nature of museums themselves. No longer are visitors expected to stand in awe of the exhibits. More emphasis is being placed on a degree of participation by visitors in the exhibits themselves. 'Living' museums replace 'dead' museums, open-air museums replace those under cover, sound replaces hushed silence, and visitors are not separated from the exhibits by glass. The publicity for the Tyne and Wear museum well expresses this new trend towards participation:

> In our museum, the emphasis is on action, participation and fun. Out are the endless old-fashioned glass cases you pored over in hushed silence. In are professionally designed displays, working models to play with, complete period room settings to browse through and sound effects to complete the picture. (quoted in White, 1987: 10)

Hooper-Greenhill notes a number of further attitudinal changes taking place in Britain's museums which are making them much more aware of the public and of how to improve the experience of visiting the particular museum (1988). In Leicester, for example, some acknowledgement is now made that visitors will come from different ethnic groups and that the museum staff must concern themselves with the various ways in which such visitors may interact with the displays and with the different accounts of histories they present (Hooper-Greenhill, 1988: 228–30).

There are further ways in which the museum display is now far less auratic. It is now quite common for it to be revealed how a particular exhibit was prepared for exhibition, and in some cases even how it was made to appear 'authentic', there are also now a number of museums where actors play various historical roles and interact with the visitors, even to the extent of participating in various historical sketches. At Beamish, for example, there are people acting out various roles in the different shops, while at Wigan Pier visitors are encouraged to experience a simulated school lesson. Elsewhere ex-miners describe mining work to visitors, and people run machinery which does not actually produce anything but simply demonstrates the machinery – 'the working nonworking industry' (White, 1987: 11). Lumley summarises these changes overall by arguing that they involve replacing the notion that the museum is a collection for scholarly use with the idea that it is a means of communication (1988: 15).

In addition there is a changed relationship between what is considered a museum and various other social institutions. Those other institutions have now become more like museums. Some shops, for example, now look like museums with elaborate displays of high-quality goods where people will be attracted into the shop in order to wander and to gaze. In places like the Albert Dock in Liverpool, which contains the Tate Gallery of the North, a maritime museum and many stylish shops, it is difficult to see quite what is distinctive about the shops as such since people seem to regard their contents as 'exhibits'. Stephen Bayley, from the new Museum of Design in the London Docklands, has remarked:

> the old nineteenth century museum was somewhat like a shop...a place where you go and look at values and ideas, and I think shopping really is becoming one of the great cultural experiences of the late twentieth century....The two things are merging. So you have museums becoming more commercial, shops becoming more intelligent and more cultural. (quoted in Hewison 1987: 139)

It has also been suggested recently that 'factory tourism' should be developed in Britain, that factories should in effect be viewed as museum-like. Ministers believe that there would be considerable interest in visiting plants producing cars, planes, processed food, submarines and so on (Jones, 1987). Certainly when factories do organise 'open days' they are very successful. Recently the Sellafield nuclear reprocessing plant in Cumbria has become a major tourist attraction. The English Tourist Board calculates that up to 6 million people visit a factory each year and that this figure will soon rise to 10 million. What is happening is that the factory is becoming more like a museum. Likewise, in the 1980s there has been an extensive 'museumification' of English pubs, many of which have become 'mock Imperial Victorian' and undergone 'ye olde-ing' (see Norman, 1988). Small collections of apparently authentic exhibits are now to be found in many pubs and restaurants.

At the same time, museums have become more like commercial businesses:

> the enterprise and flair of the High St is diffusing in the world of museums.... Packaging means establishing a corporate identity.... Shopping is not just making a purchase, it is about the whole experience, including the ambience of the shop, the style of the staff. (Pemberton, quoted in Lumley, 1988: 20)

This poses particular difficulties for museum staff, who should be trying to fashion an identity for museums different from that of commercial enterprises. The problem has arisen because of the growth of tourist and leisure industries (see Morton, 1988). Theme parks, shopping malls and heritage centres have all forced museums to compete, to become much more market-oriented, certainly to run a prominent museum 'shop' and café, but also to mount spectacular displays as in the exceptional historical reconstructions in the new Canadian Museum of Civilization. The new-style heritage centres, such as the Jorvik Viking Centre in York or the Pilgrim's Way in Canterbury, are competitors with existing museums and challenge given notions of authenticity. In such centres there is a curious mixing of the museum and the theatre. Everything is meant to be authentic, even down to the smells, but nothing actually is authentic. These centres are the product of a York-based company Heritage Projects, whose work is perhaps the most challenging to existing museums who will be forced to adapt even further.

The sovereignty of the consumer and trends in popular taste are colluding to transform the museum's social role. It is much less the embodiment of a single unambiguous high culture from which the overwhelming mass of the population is excluded. Museums have become more accessible, especially to the service and middle classes (see Merriman, 1989, for a recent UK survey, and Heinich, 1988, on the Pompidou Centre). In the leisure of such classes, Merriman (1989) suggests, museum visiting, with its previously high cultural associations, enables the acquisition of a certain cultural capital, an acquisition made possible by the increased degree to which people are now able to 'read' museums. This has helped museums to become important in defining good taste, particularly as we saw earlier, the 'heritage' look. A rural version of this is the 'country decor' look, the parameters of which are partly defined in terms of rural museums and the 'charming' manner in which the various quaint rooms are set out.

It is worth asking whether it is now possible to construct a museum or heritage centre preserving just any set of objects. It certainly seems possible. Some apparently unlikely museums which nevertheless succeed are a pencil museum in Keswick, a museum of the chemical industry in Widnes, a former Gestapo prison cells museum in Berlin, a Japanese prisoner-of-war museum in Singapore, a dental museum in London, and a shoe museum in Street. However, such museums appear to work because some connections between the past and the present are usually provided by place. It may sometimes be provided by occupation, industry, famous person or event. However, some museums/heritage centres do not work, such as a wild West heritage park which was located in the Rhondda Valley in South Wales; it seems that potential visitors did not view this as an appropriate location.

So it is clear that museums cannot be created about anything anywhere. But a museum on almost any topic can be created somewhere. A lot more museums will emerge in the next few years although whether we should still refer to them as 'museums' is increasingly doubtful. The very term 'museum' stems from a period of high art and auratic culture well before 'heritage' had been invented.

Notes

1   [Metonymy: using a related object to substitute for something. –ed.]

References

Artley, A. and J. Robinson. 1985. *The Official New Georgians Handbook*. London: Ebury Press.

Bagguley, P. 1990. "Gender and Labor flexibility in hotel and catering." *Services Industries Journal* 10: 737–47.

Bagguley, P., Mark-Lawson, J., Shapiro, D., Urry, J., Walby, S., and A. Warde. 1989. "Restructuring Lancaster." In *Localities*, ed. P. Cooke. London: Unwin Hyman.

Baxter, L. 1989. "Nostalgia's booming future." *The Daily Telegraph*, 21 July.

Bennett, T. 1988. "Museums and 'the people'." In *The Museum Time-Machine*, ed. R. Lumley. London: Routledge.

Binney, M. 1988. "Will Morecambe be wise?" *The Sunday Telegraph*, 30 Oct.

Buck, N., Gordon I., Pickvance, C., and P. Taylor-Gooby. 1989. "The Isle of Thanet: restructuring and municipal conservatism." In *Localities*, ed. P. Cooke. London: Unwin Hyman.

Cowen, H. 1990. "Regency icons: marketing Cheltenham's built environment." In *Place, Politics and Policy. Do Localities Matter?*, eds. M. Harloe, C. Pickvance, and J. Urry London: Unwin Hyman.

Edgar, D. 1987. "The new nostalgia." *Marxism Today*, March: 30–5.

Fondersmith, J. 1988. "Downtown 2040: making cities fun." *The Futurist*, March/April: 9–17.

Frampton, K. 1988. "Place-form and cultural identity." In *Design after Postmodernism*, ed. J. Thackara. London: Thames & Hudson.

Frieden, B. and L. Sagalyn. 1989. *Downtown, Inc. How America Rebuilds Cities*. Cambridge, MA: MIT Press.

Goodwin, A. 1989. "Nothing like the real thing." *New Statesman and Society*, 12 Aug.

Halsall, M. 1986. "Through the valley of the shadow." *The Guardian*, 27 Dec.

Harris, H. and A. Lipman. 1986. "Viewpoint: A culture and despair: reflections on 'postmodern' architecture." *Sociological Review* 34: 837–54.

Harvey, David. 1989. *The Condition of Postmodernity*. Oxford: Blackwell.

Hebidge, D. 1986–7. "A report from the Western Front." *Block* 12: 4–26.

Heinich, N. 1988. "The Pompidou Centre and its public: the limits of a utopian site." In *The Museum Time-Machine*, ed. R. Lumley. London: Routledge.

Hewison, R. 1987. *The Heritage Industry*. London: Methuen.

Hooper-Greenhill, E. 1988. "Counting visitors or visitors who count." In *The Museum Time-Machine*, ed. R. Lumley. London: Routledge.

Horne, D. 1984. *The Great Museum*. London: Pluto.

Jencks, C. 1977. *The Language of Post-Modern Architecture*. New York: Academy.

Jenkins, S. 1987. "Art makes a return to architecture." *The Sunday Times*, 15 Nov.

Jones, G. 1987. "Factories seen as attractions for tourists." *Daily Telegraph*, 28 Dec.

Krier, L. 1984. "Berlin-Tagel" and "Building and architecture." *Architectural Design* 54: 87, 119.

Landry, C., Montgomery, J., Worpole, K., Gratton, C., and R. Murray. 1989. *The Last Resort*. London: Comedia Consultancy/SEEDS (South East Economic Development Strategy).

Lowe, P. and Goyder, J. 1983. *Environmental Groups in Politics*. London: Allen & Unwin.

Lowenthal, D. 1985. *The Past is a Foreign Country*. Cambridge: Cambridge University Press.

Lumley, R. (ed.). 1988. *The Museum Time-Machine*. London: Routledge.

MacCannell, D. 1976. *The Tourist: A New Theory of the Leisure Class*. London: Macmillan.

Merriman, N. 1989. "Museum visiting as a cultural phenomenon." In *The New Museology*, ed. P. Vergo. London: Reaktion.

Morton, A. 1988. "Tomorrow's yesterdays: science museums and the future." In *The Museum Time-Machine*, ed. R. Lumley. London: Routledge.

Myerscough, J. 1986. *Facts About the Arts. 1986 Edition*. London: Policy Studies Institute.

Norman, P. 1988. "Faking the Present." *The Guardian*, 10–11 Dec.

Pearman, H. 1988. "Setting store by its designs." *The Sunday Times*, 3 Aug.

Raban, J. 1986. *Coasting*. London: Picador.

Savage, M. 1988. "The missing link? The relationship between spatial mobility and social mobility." *British Journal of Sociology* 39: 554–77.

Thrift, N. 1989. "Images of social change." In *The Changing Social Structure*, eds. C. Hamnett, L. McDowell, and P. Sarre. London: Sage, 12–42.

Urry, J. 1988. "Cultural change and contemporary holiday-making." *Theory, Culture and Society* 5: 35–55.

Uzzell, D. 1989. *Heritage Interpretation*, vol. 2. London: Belhaven Press.

Venturi, R. 1972. *Learning from Las Vegas*. Cambridge, MA: MIT Press.

Vidal, J. 1988. "No room here for Mickey Mouse." *The Guardian*, 19 March.

Wates, N. and C. Krevitt. 1987. *Community Architecture*. Harmondsworth: Penguin.

West, B. 1988. "The making of the English working past: a critical view of the Ironbridge Gorge Museum." In *The Museum Time-Machine*, ed. R. Lumley. London: Routledge.

White, D. 1987. "The born-again museum." *New Society*, 1 May: 10–14.

Williams, A. and G. Shaw. 1988. "Tourism: candyfloss industry or job creator." *Town Planning Review* 59: 81–103.

Wood, M. 1974. "Nostalgia or never: you can't go home again." *New Society*, 7 Nov.: 343–6.

Wright, P. 1985. *On Living in an Old Country*. London: Verso.

15 Neo-Bohemia: Art and Neighborhood Redevelopment in Chicago

Richard Lloyd

As the old manufacturing economy disappears or evolves, new industries are taking its place. Chicago, once called the "hog butcher of the world," is rapidly becoming a cultural center for artists, musicians, and internet entrepreneurs. Richard Lloyd argues that analysts and policymakers have focused too much on attracting tourists as a means of economic transformation and have overlooked the grassroots transformations that are occurring spontaneously as young people are drawn to urban lifestyles. He expands on Richard Florida's concepts of bohemianism and creativity as key forces for growth in contemporary cities. One of the paradoxes of this well-educated, neo-bohemian group is that, although they are drawn to the grit and "reality" of city life, their very presence in large numbers threatens to transform their prized edgy, mixed districts into safe and homogeneous middle-class residential neighborhoods.

Culture in New Urban Economies

A growing body of literature in urban studies addresses the role of culture and consumption in contemporary strategies of center city economic development. When addressed to older United States cities like Baltimore, Chicago, or Boston, the emphasis on culture as an economic variable follows from the relative decline in explanatory importance of older variables associated with industrial manufacturing. The steady loss of industrial jobs in older urban cores since the peak period of the Fordist model of economic organization at mid-century led to grave consequences for these cities, and urban entrepreneurs have scrambled to find new strategies to fill the spaces left vacant by the flight of productive capital. These

Lloyd, Richard, "Neo-Bohemia: Art and Neighborhood Redevelopment in Chicago." From *Journal of Urban Affairs* 25(5) (2002): 518–32. Copyright © 2002 Urban Affairs Association and Blackwell Publishing Ltd.

new strategies do not invent so much as rediscover and reconstruct elements of urbanism. Cities have long been sites of trade and cultural innovation; on the other hand, the city as the central space of material production coincides with the industrial revolution and is a relatively recent phenomenon.

Now, we have entered a new period of urbanism in the US, which is referred to variously as informational, postindustrial, post-Fordist, postmodern, or global (Castells, 1989; Dear, 2002; Keil, 1994; Sassen, 1991; Scott & Soja, 1996; Soja, 1989). The theorists of the loosely aggregated LA school of urbanism stress the deconcentration of economic functions and the sprawling growth patterns especially exemplified in the Los Angeles region, a consequence of what Soja (2000) refers to as "the third period of crisis-generated restructuring" of urban form (p. 110). Others demonstrate the importance of tourism and consumption in strategies to redevelop older urban cores left behind by patterns of deconcentration. Generally, this strain of current scholarship has focused on capital intensive developments such as the Disneyfied Times Square, the building of downtown sports stadiums and convention centers, or the injection of cultural centers, theater districts, and museums into decaying areas (Eeckhout, 2001; Euchner, 1999; Hannigan, 1998; Zukin, 1991, 1995). In these studies, the advantages of spatial concentration are reasserted, now as the concentration of cultural amenities rather than blue-collar labor and factories.

But current focus on consumption by urban theorists too often loses sight of everyday life and the spatial practices that link the lived activity of residents to new labor patterns, strategies of accumulation and urban spectacles. Instead, most theories of the city as a site of consumption posit a radical disjuncture between the new spaces of capital and the lives of residents. Judd (1999), for example, poses the formation of tourist bubbles in large cities, which regulate consumption and are cut off from the everyday routes of lived experience. Likewise, Sorkin (1992) argues for a theme park model of urbanism in which the heterogeneity of the old city sidewalk has been progressively replaced by the sanitized venues of consumption. Eeckhout (2001) echoes Sorkin's obsession with Disneyland, characterizing recent redevelopment in midtown Manhattan as the Disneyfication of Times Square. So complete is the disconnect between postmodern urban spaces and the residential practices of the city for some scholars that it seems to make sense when Jameson (1998), the premiere theorist of postmodernism and consumer culture, uses a hotel as the exemplary material manifestation of postmodernism in the city.

These theories make no distinctions among users; locals in such spaces become like tourists, all surrendering to the authority of administered consumption. But city dwellers are active in the production and consumption of cultural amenities in ways that the Disneyfication thesis fails to grasp. To discover the role culture plays in the amenity profile for urban residents, many of whom are young and sport high levels of education and cultural competence, we need to broaden our perspective beyond the signature spaces of postmodernism. The city remains a place where people actually live, not just visit. They also hold jobs; many are involved with the production of culture and consumption opportunities. Neo-bohemia suggests that rather than viewing consumption as the other of productive practice, we need to look at the new intersections of consumption and production in urban space.

Emphasis on big-ticket items like athletic stadiums locates the production of new urban space solely in the hands of developers and political elites. It obscures more evolutionary processes of cultural development, including the expanding role played by traditional patterns of urban subcultural affiliation and artistic innovation in the postindustrial economy – both in terms of local consumption offerings and the concentration of cultural and design enterprises. By approaching the Wicker Park case ethnographically, this study places greater emphasis on the distinctions among the users of urban space than is typical in examinations of what Zukin (1996) calls the city's symbolic economy. The cultural profile of Wicker Park, with its diversity of artistic offerings from popular music to galleries to poetry readings, is responsive to the dispositions of educated young urbanites whose own work may involve aesthetic innovation. Further, the breadth and depth of this local culture contributes directly to conditions supportive of cultural and technological innovation.

Scholarship on the technology-driven economy emphasizes the importance of talent to the success of firms, that is, of the labor of individuals referred to as knowledge workers (Bell, 1973; Drucker, 1995) or symbolic analysts (Reich, 1991) who possess the creative competence required by technology and design enterprises. Many argue that access to such labor has become the key to understanding the location choices of firms, replacing the older spatial variables of fixed capital and transportation that characterized industrial production. These studies emphasize the importance of local amenities as a magnet for highly mobile knowledge workers, employing a number of methods and measures to operationalize quality of life (Clark, Lloyd, Wong, & Jain, 2001; Florida, 2000, 2002b; Lloyd & Clark, 2001; Nevarez, 1999, 2002).

Recently, Florida (2002a) added the concept of bohemia to the analysis of regional amenities. Using a statistical measure called the bohemian index (based on occupational data from the 1990 Decennial Census Public Use Microdata Samples), Florida finds a robust correlation between the presence of artists in a region and the concentration of high technology enterprises.

> The ... presence and concentration of bohemians in an area creates an environment or milieu that attracts other types of talented or high human capital individuals. The presence of such high human capital individuals in a region in turn attracts and generates innovative technology based industries (p. 3).

Florida argues that the driving force behind urban prosperity is the ability to attract members of what he calls the creative class. Members of this class are not necessarily interested in the hermetic spaces focused on by Sorkin and other theorists of theme park urbanism and Disneyfication. "The creative class is drawn to more organic and indigenous street-level culture. This form is typically found . . . in multiuse urban neighborhoods" (Florida, 2002b, p. 182). Both ethnographic informants and media accounts identify the appeal of Wicker Park in this sort of street level diversity, in which even gang activity and homelessness are valued as markers of urban authenticity. [. . .]

Identified as a site of cultural innovation, a tourist destination, and new media hub, Wicker Park has attracted wide attention in the national media. It was selected in 2001 as the location for MTV's popular series *The Real World*, re-affirming its ongoing importance to the generation of hip media images. Wicker Park resembles New York's East Village, probably the best-known new American bohemia of the last 20 years, in which similar intersections between high tech, high art, and consumption are evident. But New York is exceptional in terms of its cultural tradition; it has been a world capital of modern art since World War II shifted the balance of cultural power from Paris (Guilbaut, 1983). Chicago has historically been a backwater of cultural production when compared to New York and Los Angeles, at least in terms of the media and fine arts. Thus, the emergent importance of Wicker Park's art and media presence is especially revealing.

Neo-Bohemia and the Postindustrial Neighborhood

Mired in postindustrial decay during the 1980s, Wicker Park has undergone a striking rehabilitation. By 1993, the local music scene centered in Wicker Park was attracting significant attention nationwide. *Billboard*, the music industry's trade publication declared "Chicago: Cutting Edge's New Capital" in a cover article that featured a detailed map of the neighborhood and its proliferating performance venues (Boehlert, 1993). *The New York Times* followed up with an article in its Living Arts section entitled "Edgy in Chicago: The music world discovers Wicker Park" (Rochlin, 1994). In fact, by the time the music scene was receiving national attention, attention clearly facilitated by the 1990s "indie rock" craze initiated in Seattle, a loosely integrated community of artists operating in a variety of mediums was staking a claim to local spaces in Wicker Park. In addition to the growing popularity of neighborhood venues showcasing up and coming rock bands, the annual "Around the Coyote" art festival, begun in 1989, advertised the work of local artists and simultaneously showed off their rehabbed loft spaces. [. . .]

The once derelict spaces of Chicago's industrial past now house trendy restaurants, boutiques, bars and galleries, and the residential profile features a large number of artists, students, and young professionals. The neighborhood is also attracting participants in design intensive economic activities, including an increasing presence in "media driven Internet companies" (Jaffe, 2001, p. 1). These new economy enterprises benefit from the local ambiance of innovation, as well as from the presence of individuals with creative competence who are available as potential employees (Lloyd, 2001). The association of Wicker Park's gritty spaces with creative energy has helped initiate a new identity and concomitant development. Rather than the hyper-segregation of consumption venues, production sites and residence posed by many theories of contemporary urban morphology, Wicker Park is characterized by the promiscuous mixing of such locales within the neighborhood space. These local trends, linking cultural production to postindustrial development, are important to understanding the continued advantages of dense urban development to postindustrial economic enterprises, and suggest limitations to urban theories that overemphasize deconcentration and sprawl as the characteristic postmodern geographies (Soja, 1989).

Both the blight that afflicted Wicker Park in the recent past and its newfound role as Chicago's neo-bohemia must be understood in the context of global capitalist restructuring. Wicker Park's decline into an obscure and depopulated barrio by the 1980s reflected industrial disinvestment. Once a thriving white ethnic working class neighborhood (Hoekstra, 1994), the neighborhood experienced steady erosion of its economic base in the latter half of the century. In the six-year period from 1977 to 1983 alone, the near West Side lost a staggering 12,543 manufacturing jobs. Although a significant subpopulation of white ethnics remained in Wicker Park, by the 1980s the majority population had become members of the city's newer immigrant groups, mainly Puerto Ricans and Mexicans. Because new immigrants traditionally found employment in Chicago's manufacturing sector, industrial displacement significantly affected employment opportunities for Latinos. While 58% of the Hispanic workforce in Chicago was employed in manufacturing in 1970, that number had declined to 39% in 1991 (Villanueva, Erdman, & Howlett, 2000). Increasingly, Wicker Park evinced characteristics of what Wilson (1987) calls concentration effects, with rising poverty, crime, and other urban ills. The neighborhood population in 1980 had dropped to 40% of its peak in the 1930s, and the median value of single family homes was less than half that of the city as a whole. The poverty rate in 1990 for the larger West Town area in which Wicker Park is embedded stood at 32%, compared to 21.6% for the city (Lester, 2000).

But even in the face of de-industrialization, cities like Chicago continue to evince advantages for some central activities over suburban, exurban and Sunbelt locales. Culture is not incidental. Cities concentrate diversity, and create unique opportunities for cultural production. Neo-bohemia illustrates the importance of neighborhood culture to urban renewal, especially when compared to the perceived cultural homogeneity of the suburban eu-topia (no-place), to borrow Davis's (1990) term describing LA's suburban extensions. These elements create the context necessary to understand the shifting identity of Wicker Park in the 1990s.

The decades following the 1970s saw a resurgence of capital investment in older downtowns, now responding to the demands of an increasingly globalized economy. Global finance and the centralized administration of diffuse economic activities provide part of the answer to center city resurgence. These do not exhaust the economic activities of the postindustrial city, however. Cities like Chicago are still production sites, despite the decline in manufacturing employment. Accounting for the ongoing economic centrality of Chicago requires new categories of production beyond those steeped in industrial capitalism. Sassen (1991) argues that global cities are not only sites of administration but that they also produce innovations, whether in finance, design, technology, or culture. Recent studies by Scott (2000) and Kratke (2002) demonstrate that the production of cultural and media images that may be available for global circulation nonetheless occur within an urban hierarchy of place. As global corporations shed production facilities in exchange for outsourced manufacturing, the emphasis on the aesthetic component in the chain of value added has increased (Klein, 1999). Ironically, former sweatshops in older US cities are now being put to use in the manufacture of images for the aesthetic economy. [. . .]

The built environment is revalorized through what Dickinson (2001) refers to as the "adaptive recycling" of industrial space (p. 47). Historically, artists have proven innovative in their use of space; the spatial practices of artists in New York helped to initiate the market in living lofts (Simpson, 1981; Zukin, 1982) and provide a model for similar strategies in Wicker Park. Beyond residence, these spaces become postindustrial sites for capital accumulation, housing boutiques, restaurants, nightclubs, recording studios, and office space for new media enterprises.

Thus, even with the flight of heavy industry from the city, the spaces and structures of the industrial past need not be seen as a liability. The history embedded in them becomes a source of identification for urban residents, one that is counterpoised to other forms of settlement space. The endlessly reproducible sprawl of tract homes and strip malls cannot provide the depth of history sought in the neobohemian cityspace. Faceless strip malls defy the cognitive mapping described by Lynch (1960) as essential to an integrated urban identity. For the growing number of self-described artistically inclined persons, suburban extensions do not provide adequate inspiration. Place is recovered in the city, as participants incorporate the cumulative culture inscribed on urban spaces into their definition of the situation, including fantasies of urban grit and vice. [. . .]

Artists as Useful Labor

Heading into the 1990s, Chicago ranked third in the United States behind New York and Los Angeles in the number of individuals employed in creative occupations (Zukin, 1995). This corresponds to United States population rankings; what makes the figure more striking is the high rate of growth for this population, a trend evident in a wide variety of cities (Markusen, 2000). New York and Los

Angeles continue to be dominant sites in the geography of cultural production. However, the growing importance of aesthetic production to the economy generally has outpaced the carrying capacity of any one city. While remaining an urban phenomenon, the geography of aesthetic production now incorporates an increasing diversity of cities and neighborhoods.

Chicago has a cost of living much lower than that of New York, while still possessing the cultural advantages of heterogeneity and cosmopolitanism. This combination of relative affordability and cultural diversity makes Chicago particularly well suited to concentrating cultural producers in the nascent periods of their careers. In Chicago, formal arts education is important to concentrating participants. The arts-oriented Columbia College and the School of the Art Institute now enroll over 11,000 students in the South Loop area alone and project high rates of continued growth (Cannon, 2000). The Elevated Train's Blue Line links the South Loop to Wicker Park, and these schools contribute to Wicker Park's cast of aspirants in painting, literature, sculpture, and performing arts. Accordingly, the neighborhood clusters related business activities, including performance venues, galleries, and supply outlets. Although some informants insist that Wicker Park's bohemian moment is over, squelched by gentrification, a recent survey conducted by Chicago's Department of Cultural Affairs (2000) confirms that the area still has the largest concentration of working artists and studio space in the city. Artists, whether living in the neighborhood or simply frequenting it, continue to impact local character and development to an extent disproportionate to their numbers.

In Wicker Park, local artists often articulate their ideological antagonism towards an imago of the privileged urban resident – the yuppie. This antagonism belies the structural similarity of bohemian artists and intellectuals to their object of disdain; a relationship alluded to by Bourdieu (1984) when he refers to them as the "dominated fractions" (p. 176) of the dominant class. While some participants in the local scene are recruited from low-income origins or the ranks of racial and ethnic minorities, many others are pedigreed by middle or upper class birth and elite levels of education. The Chicago Artists Survey 2000 confirms significant educational attainment with 87% of respondents reporting a college degree or higher, compared to a rate of only 25.5% for Chicago as a whole. At the same time, incomes are low; over half of the respondents report total annual household incomes below $40,000, and a significant number report incomes below $25,000. Only a minority makes most of their income directly from art, and most artists are compelled to subsidize their incomes with other work. While there are well-documented cases of artistic practitioners reaping huge financial bonanzas for their efforts, including some who have come out of Wicker Park in the last decade, these are rare exceptions.

However, the poverty of artists is of a distinctive flavor. It does not imply marginality in the new economy. Although artists may forego conventional avenues to material acquisition (enacting the familiar role of the starving artist), their relationship to material scarcity is complicated, not least by the personal insistence that this life was chosen rather than simply foisted upon them. As one neighborhood entrepreneur puts it: "There's a big difference in being poor by choice." While poverty as it is normally experienced inhibits self-determination, the voluntary adoption of relative poverty by bohemians is intended to increase autonomy.

Bohemians may self-select into poor and working class neighborhoods; however, their dispositions are decidedly cosmopolitan. Moreover, they are quite creative in re-imagining the spaces they occupy, often adding significant value by their presence. Despite limited economic means, artists are resourceful urban dwellers. In the past, bohemians in the city may have occupied a marginal space with relation to the mainstream operations of capital acquisition; however, it has always been a kind of privileged marginality. In contemporary Chicago, this condition, supported by the ideology of bohemian self-sacrifice, makes the artistic population available as flexible labor for local enterprises that range from entertainment provision to design subcontracting.

Thus, neo-bohemia incorporates young artists and aspirants into the production of value well beyond that accounted for by formal art markets. In fact, from an economic point of view, most of the artistic activity in the neighborhood produces a trivial amount of direct monetary gain. Few can sustain themselves through pursuits like local theater, musical performance, poetry, or painting; nor do these pursuits in themselves generate much surplus value for others to extract. And yet, the concentration of artistic subcultures is crucial for the new accumulation strategies enacted in the neighborhood space. The paucity of direct economic returns does not make the arts unimportant to the local economy; rather, this importance is complex and mediated.

The relatively large number of young people attracted by the arts community and its associated lifestyle scene often find their creative competence and their colorful personas indirectly valorized. They may toil as bartenders or servers in the hip local nightspots, making the scene as surely as they make drinks. Others divert their talents into media and graphic design, often as freelance contractors. The fact that such jobs usually lack the stability and upward trajectories that were so central in the past to the Fordist social contract is absorbed into dispositions that define fundamental instability as a kind of autonomy. Work in these flexible contexts becomes characterized by mutual non-obligation between employer and employee. Zukin (1995) argues that many artists accept menial and dead end jobs in the service sector because "their 'real' identity comes from activity outside the job" (p. 13).

However, ethnographic work in Wicker Park suggests that artists do not just bracket such employment as a necessary evil supporting authentic creative pursuits. Instead they attempt to construct this labor as continuous with their bohemian lifestyles, even where such efforts are problematic due to the inevitable constraints of wage labor. The ethic of bohemia comes to play a surprising role in incorporating these workers into the flexible relations of the postindustrial service and media economy.

It is easy to dismiss such labor force participation, which is often contingent and temporary, as unimportant. This would be a mistake. With entertainment now Chicago's leading industry (Lloyd & Clark, 2001), and the standardized career trajectories of the Fordist factories and bureaucracies accounting for an increasingly smaller share of the workforce, these flexible labor categories are, in fact, more and more important to new profit generating strategies. This state of affairs is not limited to menial service sector jobs. Even before the bursting of the dot.com stock market bubble, it was apparent that so-called new economy enterprises such as digital design were striving to maximize flexibility in employ-ment relations. Freelancers and highly educated temporary workers provide an important part of their workforce. Under these circumstances, access to a pool of labor possessing appropriate dispositions for flexible labor as well as necessary creative competencies is crucial to the success of many technology-driven enterprises.

Young artists, who generally possess higher than average levels of education and often exceptional technical skills, are practiced in the negotiation of uncer-tainty. A neighborhood concentrating artistic talent, therefore, also concentrates a potentially useful workforce, and thus becomes an attractive location for relevant enterprises. Sure enough, Wicker Park earned a national reputation for its concen-tration of new economy enterprises in digital design by 2000. *The Industry Stand-ard*, a trade publication for the Internet economy, declared Wicker Park the "best new place for media companies" in a recent cover article (Jaffe, 2001). *E-Prairie*, an online publication focusing on the Midwest, echoed the sentiment, noting that "tech artists find Wicker Park great for business" and quoting a local Internet entrepreneur as saying: "I think it's a natural home for creative business" (Littman, 2001). For these firms, individuals with formal arts training become a flexible labor pool, often working as subcontractors. The arts, including small-scale pursuits like poetry readings or experimental visual arts, contribute to a creative milieu that concentrates individuals with diverse competencies and feeds innovative dispositions. As a recent article in the online publication *inc.com* notes:

> When choosing where to locate, companies in these emerging industries are ignoring traditional factors, such as taxes, the cost of doing business, and convenience, which tend to be favorable in the suburbs. Instead, they are considering where creative individuals want to work and environments that foster collaboration (Kotkin, 2000, p. 1).

[...]In contrast to the popular image of media millions, these firms capitalize on the scaled down salary expectations of artists who trade salary and security in order to work in creative occupations and live in a funky neighborhood. Thus bohemia becomes more directly linked to new strategies of capital accumulation in an economy predicated on its aesthetic dimensions. [...]

The Street

Artists' interest in locating in marginal neighborhoods whose majority population is poor and usually non-white involves the desire to occupy inexpensive space adequate to their needs. In the words of Mele (1994), they are a transient population, breaking ground in marginal urban areas that may be targeted for redevelopment. "Because of their limited economic resources and/or preferences for residing in alternative neighborhoods, these groups endure above average levels of crime, noise and drug related problems" (p. 186). But such problems in Wicker Park were not simply endured; in fact, many young artists today lament their increasing disappearance. Street level diversity, even if personal interaction remains superficial, is part of their image of an authentic urban experience, and in keeping with bohemian traditions, the definition of diversity incorporates the illicit elements of an urban underworld. One young sculptor vividly evokes the striking juxtapositions created within the neighborhood in the late 1980s, as the emergent entertainment scene intersected with the seedier elements generated by postindustrial decay.

> I mean, what's really funny is that when the North Side [bar] opened up [in 1988 on Damen just north of the Borderline] there used to be a smack house right across the street, so you could sit at the North Side watching the junkies go get their dope. It was that diverse.

Within three years, the smack house he referred to was also rehabbed into a popular bar. Delia, a film student at the Art Institute, recalls:

> Being a corn fed midwestern girl walking into Wicker Park, I had never seen a six-way intersection before. But it kind of reminded me of how Greenwich Village looked on TV. Kind of gritty inner city, cars, homeless people. So it was pretty much a big culture shock. I had spent most of my time in either rural kind of pseudo suburban area, or a medium sized town like Columbus. So there was nothing like that kind of energy. I loved it. I loved the colors and the people and the sounds and the streets and the whole bustle. It was great.

Residents may even be titillated by increased danger as a part of the "flight from the rationality and sameness of the suburbs" (Allen, 1984, p. 28). One informant notes of Wicker Park during early stages of residential transformation,

> There's a sense of vitality in the streets. Along with danger there's a vitality that you lose – when you're sure of your personal safety there's a certain edge that goes away. And there is something exciting about having that edge.

Given their desire to associate with the fringe, while still having access to galleries, good bars, and school at the Art Institute, it is not surprising that newcomers to Wicker Park soon resented those who followed and upset what appeared to be its ecological balance. Wistfully recalling the arts scene in 1990, a local writer indicated:

> There was a really strong sense of community [among white artists]. I think there was a certain amount of respect...you got balls enough to live here, you must be doing something all right. We were still the extreme minority, the young white suburban artist.

By 1994, such residents were far less quick to give newcomers the benefit of the doubt. A *Chicago Reader* article cataloguing growing anti-gentrification sentiment, entitled "The Panic in Wicker Park," makes clear that the most noisily panicked were usually residents who had themselves been there for only a handful of years at most (Huebner, 1994). The arts scene has endured in an uneasy relationship with its own celebrity. Most recently, the decision of MTV to film its popular program *The Real World* in the neighborhood has given rise to further protest, largely motivated by the media co-optation of a neighborhood aesthetic over which local artists feel proprietary (Kleine, 2001). Given that their own presence is heavily implicated in neighborhood change, such protests suggest what Rosaldo (1989) calls *imperialist nostalgia*, "where people mourn the passing of what they themselves have transformed" (p. 69).

The widely heralded street edge produces benefits for individuals interested in creative pursuits. Diversity and concomitant street level vitality are factors of production in creative enterprises that help us to understand the ongoing association of cities with bohemian activity. The city is not just a container concentrating human capital, but instead distinctly urban arrangements enhance this capital, especially in terms of fostering creativity. Benjamin (1999) provocatively examined the relationship between the observations of the urban stroller and creative dispositions, resolved in the figure of the *flaneur*. Central to the *flaneur* is the diversity of the city street; the *flaneur* encountered not only the dandy on his walks, but also the ragpicker (Buck-Morss, 1997; Gilloch, 1996). "They have little in common save that they jostle each other on the same street," Zorbaugh (1991) wrote of pedestrians on busy Chicago streets in the 1920s. "Experience has taught them different languages" (p. 12).

As Jane Jacobs (1961) observed, the pedestrian on the sidewalk is a key figure in understanding the magical nature of urban life, especially when juxtaposed to "the virgin sidewalks" of suburbia (Duany, Plater-Zyberk, & Speck, 2000). In Wicker Park, local artists emphasize diverse sidewalk life as informing artistic innovation: "It's the difference between having a culture and not having a culture. Culture is you're walking down the street and you see a poster and you read it, it looks interesting to you and you go to see it." Adds another:

> I like the beat of the city. The pace. There are so many things happening in the city on any given thirty seconds that you can add to a story and you can either use those, they

could be some kind of symbol, or hey, maybe they'll just be there ... I believe you can paint a scene just with these little glimpses that a person might see as they're standing on a corner waiting for a cab.

Such sentiments are direct bohemian descendants of the Impressionist street scene or Baudelaire's urban poetry.

The concentration of various forms of cultural production, ranging from pop efforts to more esoteric or folk offerings, are inscribed in the habitus (Bourdieu, 1977) of local participants, whose own creative efforts are inflected by the diversity of the field. As Molotch (1996) indicates:

Local art is a factor of production ... Every designer's hand ... draws from the surrounding currents of popular and esoteric arts and modes of expression – verbal, literate, and plastic – that make up everyday life. These interpenetrations of daily rounds and high culture, ways of life and circulating beliefs, are raw materials of what can come from place (p. 225).

The local creative and lifestyle subcultures are "raw materials of what can come from place" (p. 225) that underlie Wicker Park's strategic advantage as a site for new media enterprises, supporting the image production that feeds what Frank (1997) refers to as hip consumerism.

Analysis of neo-bohemia indicates that artists contribute more than whiteness to neighborhood attraction. The presence of individuals pursuing creative activities is part of the package that new residents view favorably as comprising rich urban life. While sanitized environments like Navy Pier, cut off from any urban residence, are popular, they do not exhaust the urban amenity profile for many educated newcomers. Moreover, cosmopolitanism and creativity are valuable attributes not only for avant-garde artists, but also for professionals in a global economy that increasingly valorizes the creativity of labor force participants (Beck, 2000; Florida, 2002b). The aestheticization of the economy described by Lash and Urry (1994) helps us to understand why many young professionals find the spatial practices of artists so attractive. The trends on the part of small digital firms toward locating in neo-bohemian enclaves in the city, and toward recruiting workers from the artistic community, highlight the surprising and diverse ways that bohemian cityspace can contribute to enterprises in the new economy.

References

Allen, I. (1984). The ideology of dense neighborhood redevelopment. In J. L. Palen & B. London (Eds.), *Gentrification, displacement, and neighborhood revitalization* (pp. 27–42). Albany, NY: State University of New York Press.

Beck, U. (2000). *Brave new world of work*. Cambridge, UK: Polity Press.

Bell, D. (1973). *The coming of post-industrial society*. New York: Basic Books.

Benjamin, W. (1999). Paris, capital of the nineteenth century. In W. Benjamin, *The arcades project*. Cambridge: Harvard University Press.

Boehlert, E. (1993, August). Chicago: Cutting edge's new capital. *Billboard Magazine*.

Bourdieu, P. (1977). *Outline of a theory of practice*. Cambridge: Cambridge University Press.

Bourdieu, P. (1984). *Distinction: A social critique of the judgment of taste*. Cambridge, MA: Harvard University Press.

Buck-Morss, S. (1997). *The dialectics of seeing*. Cambridge: MIT Press.

Cannon, S. E. (2000). *Concentration of study: Area institutions*. Goodman Williams Group Real Estate Research.

Castells, M. (1989). *The informational city*. Oxford: Blackwell.

Clark, T. N., with Lloyd, R., Wong, K., & Jain, P. (2001, September). Amenities drive urban growth. Paper presented at the American Political Science Association.

Davis, M. (1990). *City of quartz: Excavating the future in Los Angeles*. London: Verso Press.

Dear, M. (2002). Los Angeles and the Chicago school. *City and Community*, 1(1), 5–32.

Department of Cultural Affairs. (2000). *Chicago artist's survey*. Unpublished report. Available through the Department of Cultural Affairs: City of Chicago.

Dickinson, J. (2001). Monuments of tomorrow: Industrial ruins at the millennium. *Critical Perspectives on Urban Redevelopment*, 6, 359–80.

Drucker, P. (1995). *Post-capitalist society*. New York: Harper Business Press.

Duany, A., Plater-Zyberk, E., & Speck, J. (2000). *Suburban nation: The rise of sprawl and the decline of the American dream*. New York: North Point Press.

Eeckhout, B. (2001). The Disneyfication of Times Square: Back to the future? *Critical Perspectives on Urban Redevelopment*, 6, 379–428.

Euchner, C. C. (1999). Tourism and sports: The serious competition for play. In D. Judd & S. Fainstein (Eds.), *The tourist city*. New Haven: Yale University Press.

Florida, R. (2000). *Competing in the age of talent: Quality of place and the new economy*. Report prepared for The R. K. Mellon Foundation, Heinz Endowments, and Sustainable Pittsburgh.

Florida, R. (2002a). Bohemia and economic geography. *Journal of Economic Geography*, 2, 55–71.

Florida, R. (2002b). *The rise of the creative class*. New York: Basic Books.

Frank, T. (1997). *The conquest of cool*. Chicago: The University of Chicago Press.

Gilloch, G. (1996). *Myth and metropolis: Walter Benjamin and the city*. Cambridge, UK: Polity Press.

Guilbaut, S. (1983). *How New York stole the idea of modern art*. Chicago: University of Chicago Press.

Hannigan, J. (1998). *Fantasy city: Pleasure and profit in the postmodern metropolis*. London: Routledge.

Hoekstra, D. (1994, February 28). Dancing down 'Polish broadway.' *Chicago Sun-Times*, Section 2, p. 24.

Huebner, J. (1994, August 26). The panic in Wicker Park. *Chicago Reader*.

Jaffe, M. (2001, February 19). Best new place for media companies. *The Standard*. Available: www.thestandard.com [June 2002].

Jameson, F. (1998). *The cultural turn: Selected writings on postmodernism*. New York: Verso.

Judd, D. (1999). Constructing the tourist bubble. In D. Judd & S. Fainstein (Eds.), *The tourist city* (pp. 35–53). New Haven: Yale University Press.

Keil, R. (1994). Global sprawl: Urban form after Fordism? *Society and Space*, 12(2), 131–6.

Klein, N. (1999). *No logo: Money, marketing and the growing anti-corporate movement.* New York: Picador.

Kleine, T. (2001, August 3). Reality bites: The battle for Wicker Park. *Chicago Reader.*

Kotkin, J. (2000, July 1). Here comes the neighborhood. *Inc.com.* Available: http://www.inc.com/magazine/20000701/19549.html [June 2002].

Kratke, S. (2002). *Global media cities in a worldwide urban network.* Globalization and World Cities Study Group and Network, Research Bulletin 80. Available: http://www.lboro.ac.uk/gawc/rb/rb80.html [June 2002].

Lash, S., & Urry, J. (1994). *Economies of signs and space.* Thousand Oaks, CA: Sage.

Lester, T. W. (2000). *Old economy or new economy? Economic and social change in Chicago's west town community area.* Unpublished paper, University of Illinois, Chicago Masters of Urban Planning and Policy.

Littman, M. (2001, February 5). Tech artists find Wicker Park, Bucktown great for business. *E* * *Prairie.* Available: http://www.eprairie.com/news/viewnews.asp?newsletterID=1842 [June 2002].

Lloyd, R. (2001, August). *The digital bohemia.* Paper presented at the annual meeting of the American Sociological Association, Anaheim, California.

Lloyd, R., & Clark, T. N. (2001). The city as an entertainment machine. *Critical Perspectives on Urban Redevelopment*, 6, 359–80.

Lynch, K. (1960). *The image of the city.* Cambridge, MA: The MIT Press.

Markusen, A. (2000, November). *Targeting occupations rather than industries in regional and community economic development.* Presented at the North American Regional Science Association Meetings, Chicago, IL.

Mele, C. (1994). The process of gentrification in alphabet city. In J. L. Abu Lughod (Ed.), *From urban village to east village* (pp. 169–88). Oxford: Blackwell.

Molotch, H. (1996). L. A. as design product: How art works in a regional economy. In A. J. Scott & E. W. Soja (Eds.), *The city: Los Angeles and urban theory at the end of the twentieth century* (pp. 225–67). Berkeley: University of California Press.

Nevarez, L. (1999). Working and living in the quality of life district. *Research in Community Sociology*, 9, 185–215.

Nevarez, L. (2002). *New money, nice town: How capital works in the new urban economy.* New York: Routledge.

Reich, R. (1991). *The work of nations: Preparing ourselves for 21st century Capitalism.* New York: Alfred A. Knopf.

Rochlin, M. (1994, March 14). Edgy in Chicago: The music world discovers Wicker Park. *The New York Times*, p. C1.

Rosaldo, R. (1989). *Culture and truth.* Boston: Beacon Books.

Sassen, S. (1991). *The global city: New York, London, Tokyo.* Princeton, NJ: Princeton University Press.

Scott, A. (2000). *The cultural economy of cities.* London: Sage.

Scott, A., & Soja, E. (Eds.). (1996). *The city: Los Angeles and urban theory at the end of the twentieth century.* Berkeley: University of California Press.

Simpson, C. R. (1981). *SoHo: The artist in the city.* Chicago: University of Chicago Press.

Soja, E. (1989). *Postmodern geographies: The reassertion of space in critical social theory.* New York: Verso.

Soja, E. (2000). *Postmetropolis: Critical studies of cities and regions*. Cambridge, MA: Blackwell.

Sorkin, M. (Ed.). (1992). *Variations on a theme park*. New York: Hill and Wang.

Villanueva, E., Erdman, B., & Howlett, L. (2000). *World city/regional city: Latinos and African Americans in Chicago and St. Louis*. Julian Samora Research Institute: Working Paper No. 46. Available: http://www.jsri.msu.edu/RandS/research/wps/wp46.html [June 2002].

Wilson, W. J. (1987). *The truly disadvantaged*. Chicago: University of Chicago Press.

Zorbaugh, H. W. (1991). *The gold coast and the slum*. Chicago: University of Chicago Press.

Zukin, S. (1982). *Loft living: Culture and capital in urban change*. Baltimore: Johns Hopkins University Press.

Zukin, S. (1991). *Landscapes of power*. Berkeley: University of California Press.

Zukin, S. (1995). *The Culture of Cities*. Oxford: Blackwell.

Zukin, S. (1996). Space and symbols in an age of decline. In A. D. King (Ed.), *Re-presenting the city: Ethnicity, capital and culture in the 21st-century metropolis* (pp. 43–59). New York: University Press.

Part IV

Urban Policy Choices

16 Chaos or Community? Directions for Public Policy

Paul A. Jargowsky

A recurrent theme of recent urban research is the heavily negative impact of economic and social change on low-income minority neighborhoods. In this reading, Paul Jargowsky offers several proposals for public policy that could address the proliferation of concentrated poverty in urban ghettos and barrios. He advocates a combination of approaches both to raise the income levels of low-income groups and to reduce their concentration in isolated, homogeneous communities.

His suggestions include the following: macroeconomic policies to reduce unemployment levels and raise wages; human capital strategies to increase the educational and skill levels of less-educated groups; tax policies to provide additional income to low-wage workers; housing and transportation policies to help low-income residents live near or commute to jobs; city–suburban cooperation rather than increasing fragmentation; and aggressive reduction of housing segregation. Jargowsky is critical of the ways in which some economic and urban policies have been carried out, but he argues that unless public officials take deliberate steps to reduce racial and class isolation it will continue to increase, not only wasting valuable human talent but also threatening the overall fabric of society.

High-poverty neighborhoods, be they black ghettos, Hispanic barrios, or even poor white neighborhoods, have been growing at an alarming rate. Between 1970 and 1990, the number of persons living in ghettos, barrios, and slums in the US grew by 92 percent, and the number of poor people living in them grew by 98 percent. The size of the blighted areas of most metropolitan areas increased even faster. For the more than eight million people who now live in these

Jargowsky, Paul A., "Chaos or Community? Directions for Public Policy." From Chapter 7 of *Poverty and Place: Ghettos, Barrios, and the American City* (New York: Russell Sage Foundation, 1997), pp. 185–6, 193–5, 197–213. © 1997 Russell Sage Foundation, 112 East 64th Street, New York, NY 10021. Reprinted with permission.

neighborhoods, reduced economic opportunities and social isolation add insult to the injury of being poor. Within some of these communities, the deprivation does irreparable harm.

These trends have profoundly negative consequences for our society. The injuries to the residents of high-poverty neighborhoods are apparent in their lower levels of employment and earnings, and in their higher dropout and out-of-wedlock birth rates, even after controlling for individual characteristics and family background. The growth and spread of ghettos and barrios also have more subtle costs, which have to do with the fragile social fabric that keeps anarchy at bay and makes it possible for cities to be communities and not just agglomerations of fearful strangers.

I have argued that the primary factors behind the increasing concentration of poverty are metropolitan economic growth and the general processes that create and sustain segregation by race and class. Metropolitan-level variables for economic opportunity and segregation can explain about four-fifths of the variation among metropolitan areas and about the same proportion of the changes in neighborhood poverty over time. Although such factors as spatial location, neighborhood culture, and social policy may play a role, they are secondary to income generation and neighborhood sorting, which together explain most of the observed variations in ghetto poverty.

The corollary to this finding on the policy side is that neighborhood poverty cannot be "solved" with programs in ghettos and barrios alone. Specifically, the idea that such neighborhoods have become self-sustaining enclaves – with a "culture of poverty" and a separate, totally disconnected underclass – is not supported by the data. A self-sustaining neighborhood culture implies that levels of neighborhood poverty would respond slowly, if at all, to increased economic opportunity. I have, however, documented that ghettos and barrios can decrease sharply in regions experiencing economic booms, as in the Southwest in the 1970s and the Northeast in the 1980s. And my data showed that neighborhood poverty declines as the overall metropolitan mean income rises.

There are a number of implications in this research for ways to reduce neighborhood poverty. Policies that increase productivity and reduce inequality are fundamental to doing so in the long run. Policies that affect the spatial organization of metropolitan areas and reduce racial and economic segregation will also affect the formation of ghettos and barrios. In contrast, policies that aim to alter the culture, values, and behavior of ghetto residents are unlikely to make much difference without larger changes in the metropolitan economy and in rates of segregation. In the context of actual improvements in the opportunity structure, such policies may do some good and help specific individuals. Other policies, such as enterprise zones and local economic development projects that target specific neighborhoods need to be evaluated and implemented carefully, or they too will be ineffective. [...]

Measuring Neighborhood Effects

An increasing body of evidence demonstrates that, even after controlling for personal and family characteristics, neighborhoods have independent effects on individuals that deepen and prolong their poverty. For example, other things being equal, teenagers living in poor neighborhoods are more likely to become pregnant and drop out of school (Anderson 1991; Crane 1991). Males raised in welfare-dependent communities earn less later in life than similar males from other types of neighborhoods (Corcoran and others 1992). Social isolation in high-poverty neighborhoods helps to create and maintain an "oppositional culture" that makes it difficult for children to succeed in school (Anderson 1989, 1994).

On the other hand, research on neighborhood effects has been criticized for not adequately taking into account unmeasured differences between families in ghetto neighborhoods and families outside the ghetto (Tienda 1991). In other words, some effects thought to be attributable to neighborhoods may simply reflect the characteristics of families who end up living in the poorest neighborhoods – those with the greatest personal problems, the lowest employment-related skills, and the weakest motivation or concern for the environment in which their children are being raised. Several studies have suggested that the effects of neighborhoods disappear when appropriate statistical methods are used to account for this "self-selection bias" (Evans, Oates, and Schwab 1992; Plotnick and Hoffman 1993).

Studies of the Gautreaux program in Chicago by James Rosenbaum and his associates have been particularly influential. The Gautreaux program came about as part of the resolution of a lawsuit by Chicago public housing residents against the Department of Housing and Urban Development (HUD) (Rosenbaum 1995). Qualifying public housing residents are offered the opportunity to move to private housing in a variety of different neighborhoods, ranging from low-income black urban neighborhoods to white suburban neighborhoods. Since all the housing opportunities are superior to life in the housing projects, most of the residents accept the first housing opportunity they are offered (Popkin, Rosenbaum, and Meaden 1993).

Rosenbaum and his colleagues used this natural experiment to answer questions about the differences in inner-city and suburban housing locations, both in terms of adults' economic fortunes and in terms of the development outcomes of the program participants' children. Those who moved to the suburbs had higher levels of employment than those who moved to the inner city, though they did not have gains in hours worked or wages. More important, perhaps, the children of suburban movers did better in school and had higher levels of college attendance. Rosenbaum (1995) concludes that there is a "geography of opportunity," meaning that "where individuals live affects their opportunities and life outcomes" (p. 231). These findings have led to the creation of similar programs in other cities, as well as HUD's Moving Opportunity Program.

From Analysis to Policy

My research concludes that income generation had the most dramatic effect overall on ghetto and barrio poverty, and that the neighborhood sorting index plays a secondary role, except perhaps in explaining changes between 1970 and 1980 in the Northeast and Midwest. This does not mean that public policies must follow the same path. The relevant question for public policy is not how large an effect each underlying variable has, but how much public policies can affect neighborhood poverty. [...]

Policies that could potentially affect either income generation or neighborhood sorting are the subject of the following sections. In many cases the goal is clear, but the specific remedies are highly controversial. For example, one way to restore income growth is to increase the rate of productivity growth. Thus, macroeconomic policies promoting productivity will reduce ghetto poverty in the long run. But economists disagree about how to stimulate productivity. These differences include both technical issues and political concerns.

Policies That Primarily Affect Income Generation

As shown previously, an increase in overall income level has more than twice the effect on ghetto poverty than a comparable change in any other income-generation or neighborhood sorting variable. Although the effect was not as large, decreases in either overall income inequality or black inequality would also reduce ghetto poverty. Three types of policies could improve mean income, reduce inequality, or both: macroeconomic policies, human capital policies, and redistributive tax policies.

Macroeconomic policies

Macroeconomic policies have an important impact on ghetto poverty through their effect on income distribution. Basically, policies that increase mean income while reducing (or at least not increasing) the variance of income will help to reduce ghetto poverty. Presumably, if there was consensus on how to manage macroeconomic policy to maximize noninflationary growth, we would already be pursuing such policies, regardless of their side benefits for urban ghettos. Although a review of macroeconomic policies is beyond the scope of this book, a few observations are in order.

First, there is no realistic way to increase the mean household income of metropolitan areas in the long run without increasing productivity growth. Income grew rapidly from 1946 to 1973. Since then, the incomes of American workers and families have grown very little. Between 1960 and 1973, the median earnings of year-round, full-time workers increased from $23,389 to $33,250 (in 1992 inflation-adjusted dollars). Unfortunately, this was the peak; by 1992, two decades later, the figure was $30,358. Household and family incomes have increased over the period, but almost entirely because spouses worked more hours. The consensus of economic opinion is that the slowdown in productivity growth is a major contributor to wage stagnation.

Productivity growth slowed for reasons about which economists differ. Nonetheless, virtually all economists agree that productivity growth is the key to increasing living standards. "Productivity growth is important," write William Baumol and Kenneth McLennan, "because it is the key determinant of a nation's future standard of living.... The failure of a nation's productivity to grow condemns its work force to a stationary income level and forces the society to forgo improvements in its quality of life" (1985, p. 5). The implications for income distribution are clear: real incomes can grow only as fast as productivity.

Second, unemployment has been used as the principal weapon in the war against inflation. Unemployment obviously reduces mean income, but it also increases inequality because it strikes hardest at the lower end of the income distribution. The correct balance between inflation and unemployment cannot be derived from an economic law; both inflation and unemployment generate economic inefficiencies, but the distribution of costs and benefits to various segments of society is quite different (Blinder 1987, chapter 2).

Ultimately, the relative balance between inflation and unemployment reflects a value judgment. Alan Blinder (1987) argues that "America has struck this balance between inflation and unemployment in the wrong place by exaggerating the perils of inflation and underestimating the virtues of low employment" (p. 33). This is a controversial proposal; but it is simplistic (although common) to call for full-employment policies without addressing the employment–inflation trade-off. And if we as a society continue to choose unemployment as the lesser of two evils, we should at least have a full discussion of the value judgments that decision entails, particularly in the current context of relatively low inflation.

Human capital strategies

One approach to raising productivity is to improve the human capital – the basic knowledge, skills, and abilities – of the labor force, particularly those who are now the least productive. Yet, in 1963, Banfield and Wilson wrote: "An...important feature of Negro social structure is the fairly large and growing number of young people who have more education than the job market enables them to use" (Banfield and Wilson 1963, 7). In the context of today's labor market, this is an astonishing remark. Changes over the past thirty years, many of them for the better, have reversed the situation. First, labor market discrimination on the basis of race has been reduced, although by no means eliminated. Educated blacks are far more likely to obtain employment commensurate with their education today than in 1963. Second, the returns to education, especially college, have increased sharply over the period. Such returns increased especially rapidly during the 1980s after a period of stagnation in the late 1970s (Bound and Johnson 1995).

The combination of increasing returns to skill and increasing economic segregation is particularly worrisome. "In the context of locally run schools," argues economist Frank Levy (1995), "growing income stratification by place makes it harder for poor and working class children to acquire large amounts of human capital" (p. 35). This poses a fundamental dilemma and sets up a pernicious feedback mechanism whereby poverty is translated into low skill attainment through geographic variations in the quality of schools and other social and economic resources. If the neighborhood social milieu influences a student's work habits and these work habits determine coursework mastery (Farkas and others 1990), then geographical concentrations of poverty could widen the human capital gap even if ghetto schools were the equal of schools elsewhere.

The sharp wage premium for skills seems to be a permanent feature of the modern economy. In that context, if the goal is to reduce neighborhood poverty by increasing mean income and reducing inequality, one important policy goal should be to dramatically increase the quality of education and opportunities for training and retraining. Special efforts should be made to improve the education and skills of those with the least; if successful, such measures would help reduce inequality.

The growing consensus on the importance of these goals, both as anti-poverty policies and as policies to enhance US competitiveness, is not, however, matched by a consensus on how to achieve them. There is considerable disagreement about how education and training can actually be improved, how much it will cost, who should do it, and how to pay for it. Some see the need for massive new investments in teacher salaries, computers, compensatory education, and longer school days or years. Others believe that current resources could be better applied if competition among schools was fostered by school choice plans, and if educational standards were enforced through more testing programs for teachers and students. Without progress in educating inner-city children, however, it is certain that many of them will fare poorly in the increasingly technological marketplace – in effect, creating the next generation of ghetto and barrio residents.

One significant area of disagreement is about which policies are more effective in reducing poverty – those that improve education and training in general or policies that target poor individuals or the residents of poor neighborhoods. Both could help, but in different ways. Policies to increase the level of human capital across the board ought to lead – other things being equal – to increases in productivity and hence real wages, higher household income, and lower neighborhood poverty. Policies that especially enhance the human capital of those who now have the least should also increase the mean – but only slightly – and, more important, reduce the variance in income, again leading to declines in neighborhood poverty.

The choice hinges on the trade-off between political viability and efficiency in service delivery.

Tax policy

The traditional way for the government to affect income distribution is through the tax code. Recent reforms in the Earned Income Tax Credit have transformed an obscure provision, meant to offset the social security payroll tax for low-income workers, into a large wage subsidy for low-income parents. In tax year 1996, a worker with up to $11,000 of *earned* income and two children could receive a credit of $3,370 from the government, increasing the effective wage rate of the worker by 31 percent (Scholz 1994, 3).

The program receives more widespread support than AFDC and other spending on the poor because it is work related. However, substantial reductions in the EITC were included in the Republican budgets, which President Clinton vetoed. The future of the credit – and, indeed, any redistributive policy – is uncertain at best, given the severe fiscal constraints facing the federal government. Even if the tax code could be made substantially more progressive, a future Congress or administration could easily undo the changes. Thus, in the long run, it would be far better to enable more workers to achieve incomes above the poverty level through education, training, and productivity growth.

Public Policy and Neighborhood Sorting

Although income generation was shown to be the most important factor in determining ghetto poverty, other factors related to neighborhood sorting were relevant. Racial segregation, as measured by the index of dissimilarity, and economic segregation, as measured by the neighborhood sorting index, had significant effects in cross-sectional and longitudinal analyses. Racial segregation has been declining (Farley and Frey 1994). But economic segregation (as measured by the NSI) has been increasing, especially among minority groups (Jargowsky 1996). These changes are taking place in the context of a profound sociodemographic restructuring of metropolitan areas. Any attempt to discuss policies regarding racial and economic segregation must start with a discussion of this restructuring and its correlates.

Changing metropolitan structure

Metroplitan areas are undergoing important sociodemographic changes. Foremost among these is a continuing trend toward decentralization. A dramatic example is the Milwaukee metropolitan area, which showed a uniform pattern of population decline in the central part of the city and uniform population gains in all surrounding areas. Although Milwaukee's experience may be extreme, the general pattern of declining cores and expanding peripheries is very widespread (Waddell 1995). Most large central cities had absolute declines in population. Between 1960 and 1990, central cities' share of the metropolitan population declined from 51 percent to 40 percent (Frey 1993). Without annexation, this relative decline would have been even greater.

In a recent report, *The Technological Reshaping of Urban America*, Congress's Office of Technology Assessment (OTA) describes how new technologies are transforming the nation's metropolitan areas. The OTA's report could well have included the following observation by a noted academic:

> Human geography has been profoundly modified by human invention. [New technologies], by converting the world into one vast whispering gallery, have dissolved the distances and broken through the isolation which once separated races and people... [resulting in] an increasingly wider division of labor. (Park 1926, 14)

Perhaps the OTA cannot be faulted for overlooking this quote, given that it is from an article by the sociologist Robert Park published in 1926. The new technologies *he* was referring to were the telephone, the telegraph, and the radio; the OTA has in mind the explosion of high-speed, high-volume networked communications and a shift from the production of tangible goods to knowledge-based goods. Its report concludes that "the new technology system is creating an ever more spatially dispersed and footloose economy, which in turn is causing metropolitan areas to be larger, more dispersed and less densely populated" (Office of Technology Assessment 1995, 1).

This economic restructuring may be positive and adaptive in an economic sense, but it has profoundly negative implications for inner-city residents. As Mark Alan Hughes (1993) notes, in six of the eight largest metropolitan areas "most if not all job growth during the 1980s was located in the suburbs" (p. 16). He also notes that "there is an extreme pattern in these metropolitan areas: poverty and joblessness are concentrated in formerly central cities while prosperity and job growth are deconcentrating toward the metropolitan periphery" (p. 17).

For every two steps forward, we seem to take at least one step back. Metropolitan areas have transformed in response to residents' demands for spatial amenities and to changing modes of production. From an economic point of view, these are positive adaptations to changes in production technology and business opportunities. But the pooling of poor individuals in urban centers – hardly a new development, since that has always been a function of cities (Hicks 1994, 815) – is no longer a viable means for poor individuals to get connected to the larger economy.

Implications for economic segregation

These large-scale changes in metropolitan organization have provided opportunities for people to sort themselves out in new ways. Deconcentration does not have to lead to more segregation. Indeed, racial segregation has declined slightly as resettlement to the urban periphery has progressed. But economic segregation has risen. "The natural locational forces of US metropolitan areas," writes Peter Salins (1993), "in combination with the effects of their jurisdictional fragmentation, conspire to keep most poor households in the central cities" (p. 92). Whereas suburbs evolved into "fiscal and quality-of-life sanctuaries," the inner cities have been relegated to a role akin to the poorhouse of an earlier era.

As middle-class whites and blacks left inner-city neighborhoods, they were making rational adjustments to a changing economic landscape. But it was not only blacks in the ghetto who were moving. The movement of middle-income blacks out of inner-city neighborhoods is but another manifestation of deconcentration, the "dominant dynamic of advanced urban development" (Hicks 1987, 442). Attempts to halt or reverse the movement of middle-income blacks out of the inner city would probably be futile and, of course, it would be profoundly unfair to deny blacks the same life-improvement paths that earlier generations of middle-class whites took. Such considerations led the 1990 Committee on National Urban Policy to conclude:

> Federal policies and programs should seek to eliminate barriers to residential mobility through full enforcement of fair housing, equal access and other anti-discrimination laws and regulations, enabling people to leave ghettos if they choose, for example through programs of housing vouchers. (Lynn and McGeary 1990, 264)

As Paul Peterson (1985) put it, "the best urban policy...would be directed toward dispersing racial concentrations by increasing the choices available to racial minorities" (p. 26). In essence, the argument is that if we cannot bring jobs to the people, we should bring people to the jobs.

A significant weakness of the ghetto dispersal strategy is its assumption that blacks' low economic status is a function of where they live. The committee recognized this weakness:

> [But] the emptying out of ghettos through residential mobility would not in itself have much impact on the fortunes of the people who had lived there. They would continue to have problems no matter where they lived, because they typically face the liabilities of low levels of education, skills, and work experience; poor health and disabilities; teenage and single parenthood; and racial discrimination. (Lynn and McGeary 1990, 264)

In criticizing ghetto dispersal strategies, Hughes has argued that spatial assimilation follows from economic assimilation, not the other way around (Hughes 1987). This led him to support an economic mobility strategy that would actively assist inner-city minorities to find out about, obtain, and commute to jobs (Hughes 1991). "The whole point," Hughes states, "is to increase the size of the black middle class in order to facilitate the eventual dispersal of the ghetto" (1987, p. 516). But even mobility strategies will not help much if ghetto residents cannot find jobs that pay better than public assistance.

Public policies can help the inner-city poor take advantage of employment opportunities beyond the confines of the ghetto, and even in other cities and regions. The following initiatives could be part of an "economic mobility strategy" (Hughes 1987, 514–17).

Employment information systems that overcome the information barriers to suburban employment;

Restructuring of public transit to promote reverse commuting;

Relocation assistance for workers moving to new jobs;

Subsidies (direct or tax) for commuting costs.

As noted above, measures that connect the poor to employment opportunities can help remove the penalty associated with inner-city location.

If mobility or ghetto dispersion strategies work, however, the more motivated and skilled persons from inner cities will benefit the most. As Wilson argues in *The Truly Disadvantaged*: "As their economic and educational resources improve they will very likely follow the path worn by many other former ghetto residents and move to safer or more desirable neighborhoods" (p. 158). This will further destabilize inner-city communities and *worsen* conditions for those who remain behind.

Neighborhood revitalization

A quite different approach is to bring jobs back to poor central-city neighborhoods and to neighborhoods now in the path of urban blight. The key policy in this area has been the enterprise zone. Enterprise zones take many different forms, but the basic premise is that government policies – zoning, property taxes, pollution regulations, and other forms of "red tape" – have kept the free market from exploiting the economic opportunities of urban neighborhoods, such as proximity to markets and cheap labor (Butler 1981).

Some of the criticisms of enterprise zones are that most direct public subsidies and initial benefits (such as increased property values) may go to firms and non-resident landlords; new jobs may not go to ghetto residents; public subsidies may divert public funds from expenditures that more directly benefit ghetto residents, such as education or police protection; and firms willing to relocate because of public inducements may be the most marginal and provide the weakest base for long-term development (Wilder and Rubin 1988, 2–3). "Urban enterprise zones may resuscitate individual neighborhoods," observed Peterson (1985), "but these kinds of policies only shift problems from one neighborhood to another or from one city to the next" (p. 24). A review of enterprise zones in Great Britain has confirmed that they "have major effects in influencing the location of enterprises and very minor effects in stimulating new economic activities" (Gunther and Leathers 1987, 889). A sample of 140 enterprise zones from across the United States found that only 5 percent of the firms in them were minority owned, and that a disproportionate share of the jobs (relative to the metropolitan economy) were minimum-wage jobs (Glover 1993).

Altering the metropolitan system

Ghetto dispersal, mobility strategies, and enterprise zones have a common flaw: they have little effect on the economic and social systems that give rise to geographic fragmentation of metropolitan areas. Government policies at all levels have contributed to this fragmentation:

> The decentralization of metropolitan regions was made possible by advances in transport and telecommunications technology, but federal and state polices going back to the 1950s have been instrumental in accelerating and expanding the process. Federal highway construction programs have paid for the network of expressways that brought the farflung reaches of suburbia within commuting range of metropolitan job sites, permitting the urbanization of a metropolitan frontier far from the edge of the central city. Federal income tax rules and federal home mortgage programs brought home ownership within the financial reach of millions of middle-income city residents, creating a market for new housing subdivisions at the metropolitan frontier. Federal water and sewer construction subsidies underwrote the infrastructure of newly created (or at least newly populated) suburban jurisdictions, and federal grants paid for the preparation of their land use and infrastructure plans. And not insignificantly, federal corporate tax rules have made it more profitable for manufacturing firms to build new plants in the suburbs than to rebuild their old ones in the central city. (Salins 1993, 97)

State governments also have contributed to decentralization and economic segregation by tolerating exclusionary zoning and "not in my back yard" attitudes on the part of local governments. Federal and state government policies did not create the desire of people to live in neighborhoods segregated by race and income, nor were they the driving forces behind metropolitan decentralization. But these policies have enabled and accelerated these underlying processes; in effect, throwing gasoline on the fire. In contrast, government policy worked against the tendency of people to segregate themselves by race and ethnicity. No one could seriously claim that housing market discrimination has ended, but federal policies since the Fair Housing Act of 1965 have counterbalanced discriminatory attitudes and institutions, resulting in small declines in racial segregation. The situation would be quite different today if the laws passed in 1965 had endorsed, encouraged, and provided financial incentives for segregationary actions.

The worst aspect of current state and federal policies is the way that they encourage spatial tensions while providing ineffective forms of relief to the ghetto and barrio neighborhoods that result. Rather than address this general framework of policies, both explicit urban policies and nonurban policies with urban effects, that exacerbate tensions between the central city and metropolitan periphery, current policies seek to identify neighborhoods that have failed and provide a separate solution for economic development in those areas. Enterprise zones, for example, can never incorporate such areas into the mainstream economy but will only sustain them at a minimal level with a patchwork of subsidies and handouts.

A better approach would be to pressure both state and local government and private developers to move toward more socioeconomically mixed development patterns. Government policy, especially the pervasive practice of exclusionary zoning and other forms of political fragmentation, in many cases *increases* the pressure toward economic fragmentation of metroplitan areas. Rather than funding enterprise zones to clean up after the damage is done, the federal government ought to get strongly behind efforts to strengthen the regional government's capacity (Orfield 1996; Rusk 1993) to break down exclusionary zoning and control the placement of public amenities so as to influence the actions of private developers. The federal government cannot force states and local governments to undertake these actions, but it can work to get local governments to understand that all residents of metropolitan areas ultimately share a common destiny. Less ambitiously, the federal government could structure fiscal incentives so that state and local governments would have to forgo large sums of federal money if they do not at least act as if they believe in sustainable metropolitan development patterns.

Housing policy

Fixed-structure public housing tends to artificially segregate the poor. Through subsidies, such housing anchors the poor to specific neighborhoods. Through density and family selection, an ungovernable and volatile mix of social problems creates a climate of havoc, fear, drug abuse, and violence. For these reasons, in recent years high-rise public housing projects are more likely to be blown up than built. Federal housing policy has evolved into a constellation of programs such as Section 236, Section 202, and Section 8 New Construction and Rehabilitation, which are decentralized or provide "portable" benefits. As a result, public housing was already less concentrated in 1980 than in 1970, as measured by the index of dissimilarity (Warren 1986).

Our single most important housing policy, however, is the home-mortgage interest deduction. The deduction, which reduces taxable income and hence lowers taxes in proportion to a taxpayer's marginal tax rate, is worth substantially more to higher-income individuals. The deduction amounts to a $55 billion subsidy for upscale housing, stimulating demand, raising market prices, and creating higher profit margins for builders. Because housing markets of different levels of quality are intricately related on both the supply and demand sides, the deduction also affects the availability and prices of lower-quality housing. At least partly as a result of the deduction, there is a shortage of affordable housing for low-income renters, and three out of five low-income renters pay more than 50 percent of their income in rent (Lazere 1995, 1–2). For those simply priced out of the market, the last resort is public housing, trailer parks, or – if they can get one – a Section 8 voucher.

Thus, I would argue that housing projects and the mortgage interest deduction are intricately connected. By stimulating the high end of the housing market and providing virtually no support for the lower end of the housing market, conditions of demand and supply result in high prices and constricted supply of low- and moderate-income housing. When, inevitably, the most economically disadvantaged segment of the population is forced out of the private housing market, the federal government becomes the last-resort housing provider, with all its attendant resegregation and poverty-concentrating effects. To change this backward dynamic, it is not *public* housing policy that needs to be revised or expanded but the general framework within which housing markets operate.

A serious effort to improve housing conditions for the poor must include some attempt to level the playing field by adjusting how subsidies are allocated in the nation's largest housing "program." The program is usually considered politically untouchable, and perhaps it is. Nevertheless, in 1996, several presidential candidates and the House of Representatives majority leader have offered flat-tax proposals that change or even totally eliminate the deduction, so the question is at least on the table. Any change would have to be undertaken with extreme caution to avoid wreaking havoc on property values and the loan portfolios based on them. It might be possible to restructure the deduction so that it does not change the amount of the subsidy for most current beneficiaries, improving the proposal's political viability. For example, the current 100 percent *deduction* of mortgage interest could be changed to a 28 percent tax *credit*. The credit could be made refundable, similar to the Earned Income Tax Credit. To the average taxpayer, paying a 28 percent marginal rate, there would be no change in tax liability. Those in higher tax brackets would, of course, pay more taxes, and those in lower brackets who held mortgages would pay substantially less or even receive a refund.

Continuing progress on racial segregation

Racial segregation contributes to ghetto poverty in several ways. First, the historical pattern of segregation combined with inferior service delivery (particularly schools) has impeded the development of human capital in the black community (Kain 1992; Massey and Denton 1993). The powerful effects in my econometric models of the variable for the ratio of black mean income to the overall metropolitan mean are, therefore, partly an indirect effect of past racial segregation. Current racial segregation contributes directly to ghetto poverty.

Racial segregation has been declining, despite inconsistent and lackluster enforcement of the Fair Housing Act. Although consensus exists on the importance of combating overt racial discrimination, the same cannot be said for the goal of proactively encouraging racial integration. The Department of Housing and Urban Development (HUD) has shied away from policies that go beyond preventing overt racial discrimination in housing to actually promote integration (DeMarco and Galster 1993, 145). Policies that seek to stabilize integrated or partially integrated neighborhoods or that encourage individuals to make prointegrative moves are likely to be attacked as social engineering. Such policies may also be attacked as paternalistic by some within the black community, who do not necessarily see integrated neighborhoods as a goal (Leigh and McGhee 1986). Moreover, the goal of creating stable integrated communities may run into explicit conflict with the goal of ending racial discrimination in housing. For example, given the tendency of whites to leave neighborhoods that have reached a certain percentage of blacks (the so-called tipping phenomenon), prointegrative policies often require "occupancy quotas that are designed to limit black population to a specified proportion of the community" (Smith 1993, 117).

Despite these complexities, abundant opportunities to continue breaking down racial segregation exist. HUD should aggressively monitor local public housing authorities to ensure that federally funded public housing does not worsen racial segregation, as it has done in the past (Bickford and Massey 1991). Additional resources could be devoted to investigating and prosecuting overt racial discrimination by private housing providers, real estate agents, and mortgage lenders. Moreover, the federal government should provide incentives for local communities to pursue prointegration policies and should nurture and support communities that have achieved some degree of stable integration.

Chaos or Community?

Neighborhood poverty is the predictable result of two metropolitan processes: income generation and neighborhood sorting. Although a "tangle of pathology" may emerge in such neighborhoods, the pathologies are a symptom of the problem, not its cause. The root causes of the increases in ghettos and barrios in many northern cities are the changing opportunity structure faced by the minority community and, to a lesser degree, the changing spatial organization of the metropolis.

Given the responsiveness of neighborhood poverty to changes in economic opportunity, the potential exists for macroeconomic policies to have a large impact on the problem. To the extent that incomes continue to stagnate or even decline and inequality continues to increase, neighborhood poverty will rise. In this sense, the fortunes of the ghetto and barrio residents are closely allied to the fortunes of the average citizen. The expansion of high-poverty areas is driven by the same economic realities that make it hard for many young families to get by without two incomes and slowly erode their standard of living.

The second most important set of policies for dealing with neighborhood poverty has to do with human capital. With such policies, one could imagine focusing on ghetto and barrio residents alone. To some degree, this can be achieved through programs that are geographically targeted, following the Head Start model. On the other hand, the argument can be made that the failure of the US education and training systems to serve poor neighborhoods is part of a much broader failure of these systems. Moreover, broader reforms may be more likely to win widespread political support and to be sustainable in the long run than intensive remedial efforts in ghettos and barrios.

The endemic social problems of poor neighborhoods have left many residents unprepared to take advantage of new economic opportunities. Thus, programs that emphasize culture, values, and self-esteem are important but only in the context of increasing economic opportunities for the poor. But they must not be stand-alone efforts, because the behavior of the poor is not the cause of neighborhood poverty.

The continuing trend toward metropolitan deconcentration also contributes to neighborhood poverty. Public efforts to reverse fundamental metropolitan transformations would surely be ineffective, inefficient in an economic sense, and ultimately futile. The movement of middle-class blacks out of inner-city neighborhoods is actually positive (for individuals) in the sense that it is part of the overall process of adjustment to changing economic realities. The policy implications of the changing spatial organization of cities are complex. But first and foremost, public policies ought not to make matters worse by exacerbating the natural tendency toward economic segregation. Political fragmentation, restrictive zoning, a skewed housing subsidy, and other federal policies have done just that, and need to be reviewed and fundamentally reoriented. Strategies of economic mobility, such as job-information banks and support for reverse commuting, may help the poor link up to jobs in the metropolitan periphery.

Finally, even though most inner-city neighborhoods will never return to their historical levels of population and economic activity, the public has a responsibility not to abandon such areas. The residents of such neighborhoods need protection from violent crime and appropriate levels of city services. The federal government can play a role in helping financially strained central cities meet these obligations, especially in view of suburb–central city fiscal imbalances. Many inner-city neighborhoods do have very valuable – in some cases, irreplaceable – physical infrastructures and cultural or historical significance, as well as potential for economic renewal. Although it is impossible to generalize about such prospects, because cities and neighborhoods are so different, some inner-city economic development projects that capitalize on existing neighborhood strengths should be pursued. It is important, however, that such projects be carefully considered in light of the economic realities of the city and the neighborhood. They cannot work miracles or reverse fundamental economic changes. To the extent that they can help to anchor economically viable neighborhoods, these public interventions serve important public purposes.

Neighborhood poverty is a complex problem. The hopelessness and despair in many poor neighborhoods is a symptom of broader metropolitan processes. It is quite possible to dramatically reduce levels of neighborhood poverty, as the experience of smaller southern cities in the 1970s has shown. People do react to real changes in the level of economic opportunity, as indicated by the work of Freeman and Osterman. If the nation pursues policies that raise incomes, reduce inequality, and unite rather than divide our society, neighborhood poverty can be significantly reduced and its effects ameliorated. The alternative is to continue blundering down the futile path of letting our cities become hollow shells and allowing our society to divide into two distinct groups – one with access to good neighborhoods and schools and the other warehoused in vast urban wastelands. [. . .]

[W]e must find a new and viable structure for metropolitan areas in the twenty-first century, a larger urban *community* rather than an agglomeration of separate and antagonistic *places*. Martin Buber, the Jewish theologian, argued that the form of community needs to be continuously re-created: "Realization of the idea of community, like the realization of any idea, does not exist once for all and generally valid but always only as a moment's answer to a moment's question" (Buber 1992, 97). The task is difficult and the results of even our best efforts are uncertain, but to continue along our current path is to give the wrong answer to Martin Luther King's question: "Where do we go from here – chaos or community?"

References

Anderson, Elijah. 1989. "Sex Codes and Family Life Among Inner-City Youth." *Annals of the American Academy of Political and Social Sciences* 501: 59–78.

Anderson, Elijah. 1991. "Neighborhood Influences on Inner-City Teenage Pregnancy." In *The Urban Underclass*, eds. Christopher Jencks and Paul E. Peterson. Washington: The Brookings Institution.

Anderson, Elijah. 1994. "The Code of the Streets." *Atlantic Monthly*, May: 81–94.

Banfield, Edward C. and James Q. Wilson. 1963. *City Politics*. Cambridge, MA: Harvard University Press.

Baumol, William, and Kenneth McLennan. 1985. "US Productivity Growth and Its Implications." In *Productivity Growth and US Competitiveness*, eds. William J. Baumol and Kenneth McLennan. New York: Oxford University Press.

Bickford, Adam, and Douglas S. Massey. 1991. "Segregation in the Second Ghetto: Racial and Ethnic Segregation in American Public Housing, 1977." *Social Forces* 69: 1011–36.

Blinder, Alan S. 1987. *Hard Heads, Soft Hearts: Tough-Minded Economics for a Just Society.* Reading, MA: Addison-Wesley.

Bound, John and George Johnson. 1995. "What are the Causes of Rising Wage Inequality in the United States?" *Economic Policy Review* 82: 371–92.

Buber, Martin. 1967. "Comments on the Idea of Community." Reprinted in *On Intersubjectivity and Cultural Creativity*, ed. S. N. Eisenstadt. Chicago: University of Chicago Press.

Butler, Stuart. 1981. *Enterprise Zones: Greenlining the Inner Cities.* New York: Universe Books.

Corcoran, Mary, Roger Gordon, Deborah Laren, and Gary Solon. 1992. "The Association Between Men's Economic Status and Their Family and Community Origins." *Journal of Human Resources* 27: 575–601.

Crane, Jon. 1991. "Effects of Neighborhood on Dropping Out of School and Teenage Childbearing." In *The Urban Underclass*, eds. Christopher Jencks and Paul E. Peterson. Washington: The Brookings Institution.

DeMarco, Donald L. and George C. Galster. 1993. "Prointegrative Policy: Theory and Practice." *Journal of Urban Affairs* 15: 141–60.

Evans, William N., Wallace E. Oates, and Robert M. Schwab. 1992. "Measuring Peer Group Effects: A Study of Teenage Behavior." *Journal of Political Economy* 100: 966–91.

Farkas, George, Robert, P. Grobe, Daniel Sheehan, and Yuan Shuan. 1990. "Cultural Resources and School Success: Gender, Ethnicity, and Poverty Groups Within an Urban School District." *American Sociological Review* 55: 127–42.

Farley, Reynolds and William H. Frey. 1994. "Changes in the Segregation of Whites and Blacks During the 1980s: Small Steps Toward a More Integrated Society." *American Sociological Review* 59: 23–45.

Frey, William H. 1993. "People in Places: Demographic Trends in Urban America." In *Rediscovering Urban America: Perspectives on the 1980s*, eds. Jack Sommer and Donald A. Hicks. Washington, DC: Office of Housing Policy Research, US Dept. of Housing and Urban Development.

Glover, Glenda. 1993. "Enterprise Zones: Incentives Are Not Attracting Minority Firms." *Review of Black Political Economy* 22: 73–99.

Gunther, William D. and Charles G. Leathers. 1987. "British Enterprise Zones: Implications for US Urban Policy." *Journal of Economic Issues* 21: 885–93.

Hicks, Donald A. 1987. "Urban Policy in the US: Introduction." *Urban Studies* 24: 439–46.

Hicks, Donald A. 1994. "Revitalizing Our Cities or Restoring Ties to Them: Redirecting the Debate." *Journal of Law Reform* 27: 813–75.

Hughes, Mark Allen. 1987. "Moving Up and Moving Out: Confusing Ends and Means About Ghetto Dispersal." *Urban Studies* 24: 503–17.

Hughes, Mark Allen. 1991. "Employment Decentralization and Accessibility: A Strategy for Stimulating Regional Mobility." *Journal of the American Planning Association* (Summer): 288–98.

Hughes, Mark Alan. 1993. *Over the Horizon: Jobs in the Suburbs of Major Metropolitan Areas*. Philadelphia: Public/Private Ventures.

Jargowsky, Paul A. 1996. "Take the Money and Run: Economic Segregation in US Metropolitan Areas." *American Sociological Review* 61: 984–98.

Kain, J. F. 1992. "The Spatial Mismatch Hypothesis; Three Decades Later." Housing Policy Debate 3: 371–460.

Lazere, Edward B. 1995. *In Short Supply: The Growing Affordable Housing Gap*. Washington, DC: Center for Budget and Policy Priorities.

Leigh, W. A. and J. D. McGhee. 1986. "A Minority Perspective on Residential Integration." In *Housing Desegregation and Federal Policy*, ed. J. M. Goering. Chapel Hill, NC: University of North Carolina Press.

Levy, Frank. 1995. "The Future Path and Consequences of the US Earnings/Education Gap." *Economic Policy Review*, vol. 1. New York: Federal Reserve Bank of New York.

Lynn, Laurence E., Jr. and Michael G. H. McGeary. 1990. "Conclusions." In *Inner-City Poverty in the United States*, eds. Laurence E. Lynn and Michael G. H. McGeary. Washington: National Academy Press.

Massey, Douglas S. and Nancy A. Denton. 1993. *American Apartheid: Segregation and the Making of the Underclass*. Cambridge, MA: Harvard University Press.

Orfield, Myron. 1996. "Metropolitics: A Regional Agenda for Community and Stability." Unpublished paper.

Park, Robert E. 1926. "The Urban Community as a Spatial Pattern and Moral Order." In *The Urban Community*, ed. Ernest W. Burgess. Chicago: University of Chicago Press.

Peterson, Paul E. 1985. "Introduction: Technology, Race and Urban Policy." In *The New Urban Reality*, ed. Paul E. Peterson. Washington, DC: The Brookings Institution.

Plotnick, Robert and Saul Hoffman. 1993. "Using Sister Pairs to Estimate How Neighborhoods Affect Young Adult Outcomes." Working Papers in Public Policy Analysis and Management, Nos. 93–8. Graduate School of Public Affairs, University of Washington.

Popkin, Susan J., James E. Rosenbaum, and Patricia M. Meaden. 1993. "Labor Market Experiences of Low-Income Black Women in Middle-Class Suburbs: Evidence from a Survey of Gautreaux Program Participants." *Journal of Policy Analysis and Management* 12: 556–73.

Rosenbaum, James E. 1995. "Changing the Geography of Opportunity by Expanding Residential Choice: Lessons from the Gautreaux Program." *Housing Policy Debate* 6: 231–69.

Rusk, David. 1993. *Cities Without Suburbs*. Washington, DC: Woodrow Wilson Center Press.

Salins, Peter D. 1993. "Cities, Suburbs, and the Urban Crisis." *The Public Interest*, 113 (Fall): 91–104.

Scholz, John Karl. 1994. "Tax Policy and the Working Poor: The Earned Income Tax Credit." *Focus* 15: 3.

Smith, Richard A. 1993. "Creating Stable Racially Integrated Communities: A Review." *Journal of Urban Affairs* 15: 115–40.

Tienda, Marta. 1991. "Poor People and Poor Places: Deciphering Neighborhood Effects on Poverty Outcomes." In *Macro–Micro Linkages in Sociology*, ed. Joan Huber. Newbury Park, CA: Sage Publications.

US Congress and Office of Technology Assessment. 1995. *The Technological Reshaping of Metropolitan America*. Washington: US Government Printing Office.

Waddell, Paul. 1995. "The Paradox of Poverty Concentration: Neighborhood Change in Dallas-Fort Worth from 1970 to 1990." Unpublished paper.

Warren, Elizabeth C. 1986. "Measuring the Dispersal of Subsidized Housing in Three Cities." *Journal of Urban Affairs* 8: 19–34.

Wilder, Margaret G. and Barry M. Rubin. 1988. "Targeted Redevelopment Through Enterprise Zones." *Journal of Urban Affairs* 10: 1–17.

Wilson, William Julius. 1987. *The Truly Disadvantaged: The Inner City, the Underclass, and Public Policy.* Chicago: University of Chicago Press.

17 The Missing Link

Douglas S. Massey and Nancy A. Denton

Many analysts have attributed the growth of extreme poverty among African American residents of inner cities to the consequences of economic restructuring and a geographic mismatch between the urban residences of poor workers and the increasingly suburban location of entry-level jobs. Douglas Massey and Nancy Denton argue that economic restructuring, education levels, and job skills by themselves cannot explain the growth of extreme poverty among poor urban African Americans. This reading is the introductory chapter from their book *American Apartheid*, in which they examine the independent role that racial residential segregation has played and continues to play in contributing to the growth of extreme ghetto poverty in cities.

Massey and Denton hold that racial segregation is the fundamental cause of the development of an "urban underclass." Although an increasing number of educated African American households can live in integrated neighborhoods, many lower-income African Americans are trapped in a context of extreme poverty, physical deterioration, and social disorder, with little prospect for geographical mobility, simply because of their race. Massey and Denton show that racial segregation is not simply a holdover from the past but still operates through discrimination and unequal housing opportunities, despite laws to the contrary. Because of its independent role in fostering concentrated urban poverty, any strategies for change must address racial discrimination directly.

It is quite simple. As soon as there is a group area then all your uncertainties are removed and that is, after all, the primary purpose of this Bill [requiring racial segregation in housing].
Minister of the Interior, Union of South Africa legislative debate on the the Group Areas Act of 1950

During the 1970s and 1980s a word disappeared from the American vocabulary.[1] It was not in the speeches of politicians decrying the multiple ills besetting American cities. It was not spoken by government officials responsible for administering the nation's social programs. It was not mentioned by journalists reporting on the rising tide of homelessness, drugs, and violence in urban America. It was not discussed by foundation executives and think-tank experts proposing new programs for unemployed parents and unwed mothers. It was not articulated by civil rights leaders speaking out against the persistence of racial inequality; and it was nowhere to be found in the thousands of pages written by social scientists on the urban underclass. The word was segregation.

Most Americans vaguely realize that urban America is still a residentially segregated society, but few appreciate the depth of black segregation or the degree to which it is maintained by ongoing institutional arrangements and contemporary individual actions. They view segregation as an unfortunate holdover from a racist past, one that is fading progressively over time. If racial residential segregation persists, they reason, it is only because civil rights laws passed during the 1960s have not had enough time to work or because many blacks still prefer to live in black neighborhoods. The residential segregation of blacks is viewed charitably as a "natural" outcome of impersonal social and economic forces, the same forces that produced Italian and Polish neighborhoods in the past and that yield Mexican and Korean areas today.

But black segregation is not comparable to the limited and transient segregation experienced by other racial and ethnic groups, now or in the past. No group in the history of the United States has ever experienced the sustained high level of residential segregation that has been imposed on blacks in large American cities for the past fifty years. This extreme racial isolation did not just happen; it was manufactured by whites through a series of self-conscious actions and purposeful institutional arrangements that continue today. Not only is the depth of black segregation unprecedented and utterly unique compared with that of other groups, but it shows little sign of change with the passage of time or improvements in socioeconomic status.

If policymakers, scholars, and the public have been reluctant to acknowledge segregation's persistence, they have likewise been blind to its consequences for American blacks. Residential segregation is not a neutral fact; it systematically undermines the social and economic well-being of blacks in the United States. Because of racial segregation, a significant share of black America is condemned to experience a social environment where poverty and joblessness are the norm, where a majority of children are born out of wedlock, where most families are on welfare, where educational failure prevails, and where social and physical deterioration abound. Through prolonged exposure to such an environment, black chances for social and economic success are drastically reduced.

Deleterious neighborhood conditions are built into the structure of the black community. They occur because segregation concentrates poverty to build a set of mutually reinforcing and self-feeding spirals of decline into black neighborhoods. When economic dislocations deprive a segregated group of employment and increase its rate of poverty, socioeconomic deprivation inevitably becomes more concentrated in neighborhoods where that group lives. The damaging social consequences that follow from increased poverty are spatially concentrated as well, creating uniquely disadvantaged environments that become progressively isolated – geographically, socially, and economically – from the rest of society.

The effect of segregation on black well-being is structural, not individual. Residential segregation lies beyond the ability of any individual to change; it constrains black life chances irrespective of personal traits, individual motivations, or private achievements. For the past twenty years this fundamental fact has been swept under the rug by policymakers, scholars, and theorists of the urban underclass. Segregation is the missing link in prior attempts to understand the plight of the urban poor. As long as blacks continue to be segregated in American cities, the United States cannot be called a race-blind society.

The Forgotten Factor

The present myopia regarding segregation is all the more startling because it once figured prominently in theories of racial inequality. Indeed, the ghetto was once seen as central to black subjugation in the United States. In 1944 Gunnar Myrdal wrote in *An American Dilemma* that residential segregation "is basic in a mechanical sense. It exerts its influence in an indirect and impersonal way: because Negro people do not live near white people, they cannot... associate with each other in the many activities founded on common neighborhood. Residential segregation... becomes reflected in uni-racial schools, hospitals, and other institutions" and creates "an artificial city... that permits any prejudice on the part of public officials to be freely vented on Negroes without hurting whites."[2]

Kenneth B. Clark, who worked with Gunnar Myrdal as a student and later applied his research skills in the landmark *Brown v. Topeka* school integration case, placed residential segregation at the heart of the US system of racial oppression. In *Dark Ghetto*, written in 1965, he argued that "the dark ghetto's invisible walls have been erected by the white society, by those who have power, both to confine those who have *no* power and to perpetuate their powerlessness. The dark ghettos are social, political, educational, and – above all – economic colonies. Their inhabitants are subject peoples, victims of the greed, cruelty, insensitivity, guilt, and fear of their masters."[3]

Public recognition of segregation's role in perpetuating racial inequality was galvanized in the late 1960s by the riots that erupted in the nation's ghettos. In their aftermath, President Lyndon B. Johnson appointed a commission chaired by Governor Otto Kerner of Illinois to identify the causes of the violence and to propose policies to prevent its recurrence. The Kerner Commission released its report in March 1968 with the shocking admonition that the United States was "moving toward two societies, one black, one white – separate and unequal."[4] Prominent among the causes that the commission identified for this growing racial inequality was residential segregation.

In stark, blunt language, the Kerner Commission informed white Americans that "discrimination and segregation have long permeated much of American life; they now threaten the future of every American."[5] "Segregation and poverty have created in the racial ghetto a destructive environment totally unknown to most white Americans. What white Americans have never fully understood – but what the Negro can never forget – is that white society is deeply implicated in the ghetto. White institutions created it, white institutions maintain it, and white society condones it."[6]

The report argued that to continue present policies was "to make permanent the division of our country into two societies; one, largely Negro and poor, located in the central cities; the other, predominantly white and affluent, located in the suburbs."[7] Commission members rejected a strategy of ghetto enrichment coupled with abandonment of efforts to integrate, an approach they saw "as another way of choosing a permanently divided country."[8] Rather, they insisted that the only reasonable choice for America was "a policy which combines ghetto enrichment with programs designed to encourage integration of substantial numbers of Negroes into the society outside the ghetto."[9]

America chose differently. Following the passage of the Fair Housing Act in 1968, the problem of housing discrimination was declared solved, and residential segregation dropped off the national agenda. Civil rights leaders stopped pressing for the enforcement of open housing, political leaders increasingly debated employment and educational policies rather than housing integration, and academicians focused their theoretical scrutiny on everything from culture to family structure, to institutional racism, to federal welfare systems. Few people spoke of racial segregation as a problem or acknowledged its persisting consequences. By the end of the 1970s residential segregation became the forgotten factor in American race relations.[10]

While public discourse on race and poverty became more acrimonious and more focused on divisive issues such as school busing, racial quotas, welfare, and affirmative action, conditions in the nation's ghettos steadily deteriorated.[11] By the end of the 1970s, the image of poor minority families mired in an endless cycle of unemployment, unwed childbearing, illiteracy, and dependency had coalesced into a compelling and powerful concept: the urban underclass.[12] In the view of many middle-class whites, inner cities had come to house a large population of poorly educated single mothers and jobless men – mostly black and Puerto Rican – who were unlikely to exit poverty and become self-sufficient. In the ensuing national debate on the causes for this persistent poverty, four theoretical explanations gradually emerged: culture, racism, economics, and welfare.

Cultural explanations for the underclass can be traced to the work of Oscar Lewis, who identified a "culture of poverty" that he felt promoted patterns of behavior inconsistent with socioeconomic advancement.[13] According to Lewis, this culture originated in endemic unemployment and chronic social immobility, and provided an ideology that allowed poor people to cope with feelings of hopelessness and despair that arose because their chances for socioeconomic success were remote. In individuals, this culture was typified by a lack of impulse control, a strong present-time orientation, and little ability to defer gratification. Among families, it yielded an absence of childhood, an early initiation into sex, a prevalence of free marital unions, and a high incidence of abandonment of mothers and children.

Although Lewis explicity connected the emergence of these cultural patterns to structural conditions in society, he argued that once the culture of poverty was established, it became an independent cause of persistent poverty. This idea was further elaborated in 1965 by the Harvard sociologist and then Assistant Secretary of Labor Daniel Patrick Moynihan, who in a confidential report to the President focused on the relationship between male unemployment, family instability, and the intergenerational transmission of poverty, a process he labeled a "tangle of pathology."[14] He warned that because of the structural absence of employment in the ghetto, the black family was disintegrating in a way that threatened the fabric of community life.

When these ideas were transmitted through the press, both popular and scholarly, the connection between culture and economic structure was somehow lost, and the argument was popularly perceived to be that "people were poor because they had a defective culture." This position was later explicitly adopted by the conservative theorist Edward Banfield, who argued that lower-class culture – with its limited time horizon, impulsive need for gratification, and psychological self-doubt – was primarily responsible for persistent urban poverty.[15] He believed that these cultural traits were largely imported, arising primarily because cities attracted lower-class migrants.

The culture-of-poverty argument was strongly criticized by liberal theorists as a self-serving ideology that "blamed the victim."[16] In the ensuing wave of reaction, black families were viewed not as weak but, on the contrary, as resilient and well adapted survivors in an oppressive and racially prejudiced society.[17] Black disadvantages were attributed not to a defective culture but to the persistence of institutional racism in the United States. According to theorists of the underclass such as Douglas Glasgow and Alphonso Pinkney, the black urban underclass came about because deeply imbedded racist practices within American institutions – particularly schools and the economy – effectively kept blacks poor and dependent.[18]

As the debate on culture versus racism ground to a halt during the late 1970s, conservative theorists increasingly captured public attention by focusing on a third possible cause of poverty: government welfare policy. According to Charles

Murray, the creation of the underclass was rooted in the liberal welfare state.[19] Federal antipoverty programs altered the incentives governing the behavior of poor men and women, reducing the desirability of marriage, increasing the benefits of unwed childbearing, lowering the attractiveness of menial labor, and ultimately resulted in greater poverty.

A slightly different attack on the welfare state was launched by Lawrence Mead, who argued that it was not the generosity but the permissiveness of the US welfare system that was at fault.[20] Jobless men and unwed mothers should be required to display "good citizenship" before being supported by the state. By not requiring anything of the poor, Mead argued, the welfare state undermined their independence and competence, thereby perpetuating their poverty.

This conservative reasoning was subsequently attacked by liberal social scientists, led principally by the sociologist William Julius Wilson, who had long been arguing for the increasing importance of class over race in understanding the social and economic problems facing blacks.[21] In his 1987 book *The Truly Disadvantaged*, Wilson argued that persistent urban poverty stemmed primarily from the structural transformation of the inner-city economy.[22] The decline of manufacturing, the suburbanization of employment, and the rise of a low-wage service sector dramatically reduced the number of city jobs that paid wages sufficient to support a family, which led to high rates of joblessness among minorities and a shrinking pool of "marriageable" men (those financially able to support a family). Marriage thus became less attractive to poor women, unwed childbearing increased, and female-headed families proliferated. Blacks suffered disproportionately from these trends because, owing to past discrimination, they were concentrated in locations and occupations particularly affected by economic restructuring.

Wilson argued that these economic changes were accompanied by an increase in the spatial concentration of poverty within black neighborhoods. This new geography of poverty, he felt, was enabled by the civil rights revolution of the 1960s, which provided middle-class blacks with new opportunities outside the ghetto.[23] The out-migration of middle-class families from ghetto areas left behind a destitute community lacking the institutions, resources, and values necessary for success in postindustrial society. The urban underclass thus arose from a complex interplay of civil rights policy, economic restructuring, and a historical legacy of discrimination.

Theoretical concepts such as the culture of poverty, institutional racism, welfare disincentives, and structural economic change have all been widely debated. None of these explanations, however, considers residential segregation to be an important contributing cause of urban poverty and the underclass. In their principal works, Murray and Mead do not mention segregation at all;[24] and Wilson refers to racial segregation only as a historical legacy from the past, not as an outcome that is institutionally supported and actively created today.[25] Although Lewis mentions segregation sporadically in his writings, it is not assigned a central role in the set of structural factors responsible for the culture of poverty, and Banfield ignores it entirely. Glasgow, Pinkney, and other theorists of institutional racism mention the ghetto frequently, but generally call not for residential desegregation but for race-specific policies to combat the effects of discrimination in the schools and labor markets. In general, then, contemporary theorists of urban poverty do not see high levels of black–white segregation as particularly relevant to understanding the underclass or alleviating urban poverty.[26]

The purpose of [our research] is to redirect the focus of public debate back to issues of race and racial segregation, and to suggest that they should be fundamental to thinking about the status of black Americans and the origins of the urban underclass. Our quarrel is less with any of the prevailing theories of urban poverty than with their systematic failure to consider the important role that segregation has played in mediating, exacerbating, and ultimately amplifying the harmful social and economic processes they treat.

We join earlier scholars in rejecting the view that poor urban blacks have an autonomous "culture of poverty" that explains their failure to achieve socioeconomic success in American society. We argue instead that residential segregation has been instrumental in creating a structural niche within which a deleterious set of attitudes and behaviors – a culture of segregation – has arisen and flourished. Segregation created the structural conditions for the emergence of an oppositional culture that devalues work, schooling, and marriage and that stresses attitudes and behaviors that are antithetical and often hostile to success in the larger economy. Although poor black neighborhoods still contain many people who lead conventional, productive lives, their example has been overshadowed in recent years by a growing concentration of poor, welfare-dependent families that is an inevitable result of residential segregation.

We readily agree with Douglas, Pinkney, and others that racial discrimination is widespread and may even be institutionalized within large sectors of American society, including the labor market, the educational system, and the welfare bureaucracy. We argue, however, that this view of black subjugation is incomplete without understanding the special role that residential segregation plays in enabling all other forms of racial oppression. Residential segregation is the institutional apparatus that supports other racially discriminatory processes and binds them together into a coherent and uniquely effective system of racial subordination. Until the black ghetto is dismantled as a basic institution of American urban life, progress ameliorating racial inequality in other arenas will be slow, fitful, and incomplete.

We also agree with William Wilson's basic argument that the structural transformation of the urban economy undermined economic supports for the black community during the 1970s and 1980s.[27] We argue, however, that in the absence of segregation, these structural changes would not have produced the disastrous social and economic outcomes observed in inner cities during these decades. Although rates of black poverty were driven up by the economic dislocations Wilson identifies, it was segregation that confined the increased deprivation to a small number of densely settled, tightly packed, and geographically isolated areas.

Wilson also argues that concentrated poverty arose because the civil rights revolution allowed middle-class blacks to move out of the ghetto. Although we remain open to the possibility that class-selective migration did occur,[28] we argue that concentrated poverty would have happened during the 1970s with or without black middle-class migration. Our principal objection to Wilson's focus on middle-class out-migration is not that it did not occur, but that it is misdirected: focusing on the flight of the black middle class deflects attention from the real issue, which is the limitation of black residential options through segregation.

Middle-class households – whether they are black, Mexican, Italian, Jewish, or Polish – always try to escape the poor. But only blacks must attempt their escape within a highly segregated, racially segmented housing market. Because of segregation, middle-class blacks are less able to escape than other groups, and as a result are exposed to more poverty. At the same time, because of segregation no one will move into a poor black neighborhood except other poor blacks. Thus both middle-class blacks and poor blacks lose compared with the poor and middle class of other groups: poor blacks live under unrivaled concentrations of poverty and affluent blacks live in neighborhoods that are far less advantageous than those experienced by the middle class of other groups.

Finally, we concede Murray's general point that federal welfare policies are linked to the rise of the urban underclass, but we disagree with his specific hypothesis that generous welfare payments, by themselves, discouraged employment, encouraged unwed childbearing, undermined the strength of the family, and thereby caused persistent poverty.[29] We argue instead that welfare payments were only harmful to the socioeconomic well-being of groups that were residentially segregated. As poverty rates rose among blacks in response to the economic dislocations of the 1970s and 1980s, so did the use of welfare programs. Because of racial segregation, however, the higher levels of welfare receipt were confined to a small number of isolated, all-black neighborhoods. By promoting the spatial concentration of welfare use, therefore, segregation created a residential environment within which welfare dependency was the norm, leading to the intergenerational transmission and broader perpetuation of urban poverty.

Coming to Terms with American Apartheid

Our fundamental argument is that racial segregation – and its characteristic institutional form, the black ghetto – are the key structural factors responsible for the perpetuation of black poverty in the United States. Residential segregation is the principal organizational feature of American society that is responsible for the creation of the urban underclass. Because this view is so alien to public and academic theorizing, and because beliefs about the voluntary and "natural" origins of black segregation are so deeply ingrained in popular thinking, we build our case step by step, grounding each assertion on a base of empirical evidence.

[We] trace the historical construction of the black ghetto during the nineteenth and twentieth centuries. We show that high levels of black–white segregation were not always characteristic of American urban areas. Until the end of the nineteenth century blacks and whites were relatively integrated in both northern and southern cities; as late as 1900, the typical black urbanite still lived in a neighborhood that was predominantly white. The evolution of segregated, all-black neighborhoods occurred later and was not the result of impersonal market forces. It did not reflect the desires of African Americans themselves. On the contrary, the black ghetto was constructed through a series of well-defined institutional practices, private behaviors, and public policies by which whites sought to contain growing urban black populations.

The manner in which blacks were residentially incorporated into American cities differed fundamentally from the path of spatial assimilation followed by other ethnic groups. Even at the height of immigration from Europe, most Italians, Poles, and Jews lived in neighborhoods where members of their own group did not predominate, and as their socioeconomic status and generations spent in the United States rose, each group was progressively integrated into American society. In contrast, after the construction of the black ghetto the vast majority of blacks were forced to live in neighborhoods that were all black, yielding an extreme level of social isolation.

[W]e show that high levels of black–white segregation had become universal in American cities by 1970, and despite the passage of the Fair Housing Act in 1968, this situation had not changed much in the nation's largest black communities by 1980. In these large urban areas black–white segregation persisted at very high levels, and the extent of black suburbanization lagged far behind that of other groups. Even within suburbs, levels of racial segregation remained exceptionally high, and in many urban areas the degree of racial separation between blacks and whites was profound. Within sixteen large metropolitan areas – containing one-third of all blacks in the United States – the extent of racial segregation was so intense and occurred on so many dimensions simultaneously that we label the pattern "hypersegregation."

[We also] examine why black segregation continues to be so extreme. One possibility that we rule out is that high levels of racial segregation reflect socioeconomic differences between blacks and whites. Segregation cannot be attributed to income differences, because blacks are equally highly segregated at all levels of income. Whereas segregation declines steadily for most minority groups as socioeconomic status rises, levels of black–white segregation do not vary significantly by social class. Because segregation reflects the effects of white prejudice rather than objective market forces, blacks are segregated no matter how much money they earn.

Although whites now accept open housing in principle, they remain prejudiced against black neighbors in practice. Despite whites' endorsement of the ideal that people should be able to live wherever they can afford to regardless of race, a majority still feel uncomfortable in any neighborhood that contains more than a few black residents; and as the percentage of blacks rises, the number of whites who say they would refuse to enter or would try to move out increases sharply.

These patterns of white prejudice fuel a pattern of neighborhood resegregation because racially mixed neighborhoods are strongly desired by blacks. As the percentage of blacks in a neighborhood rises, white demand for homes within it falls sharply while black demand rises. The surge in black demand and the withering of white demand yield a process of racial turnover. As a result, the only urban areas where significant desegregation occurred during the 1970s were those where the black population was so small that integration could take place without threatening white preferences for limited contact with blacks.

Prejudice alone cannot account for high levels of black segregation, however, because whites seeking to avoid contact with blacks must have somewhere to go. That is, some all-white neighborhoods must be perpetuated and maintained, which requires the erection of systematic barriers to black residential mobility. In most urban housing markets, therefore, the effects of white prejudice are typically reinforced by direct discrimination against black homeseekers. Housing audits carried out over the past two decades have documented the persistence of widespread discrimination against black renters and homebuyers, and a recent comprehensive study carried out by the US Department of Housing and Urban Development suggests that prior work has understated both the incidence and the severity of this racial bias. Evidence also suggests that blacks can expect to experience significant discrimination in the allocation of home mortgages as well.

[W]e then demonstrate theoretically how segregation creates underclass communities and systematically builds deprivation into the residential structure of black communities. We show how any increase in the poverty rate of a residentially segregated group leads to an immediate and automatic increase in the geographic concentration of poverty. When the rate of minority poverty is increased under conditions of high segregation, all of the increase is absorbed by a small number of neighborhoods. When the same increase in poverty occurs in an integrated group, the added poverty is spread evenly throughout the urban area, and the neighborhood environment that group members face does not change much.

During the 1970s and 1980s, therefore, when urban economic restructuring and inflation drove up rates of black and Hispanic poverty in many urban areas, underclass communities were created only where increased minority poverty coincided with a high degree of segregation – principally in older metropolitan areas of the northeast and the midwest. Among Hispanics, only Puerto Ricans developed underclass communities, because only they were highly segregated; and this high degree of segregation is directly attributable to the fact that a large proportion of Puerto Ricans are of African origin.

The interaction of intense segregation and high poverty leaves black neighborhoods extremely vulnerable to fluctuations in the urban economy, because any dislocation that causes an upward shift in black poverty rates will also produce a rapid change in the concentration of poverty and, hence, a dramatic shift in the social and economic composition of black neighborhoods. The concentration of poverty, for example, is associated with the wholesale withdrawal of commercial institutions and the deterioration or elimination of goods and services distributed through the market.

Neighborhoods, of course, are dynamic and constantly changing, and given the high rates of residential turnover characteristic of contemporary American cities, their well-being depends to a great extent on the characteristics and actions of their residents. Decisions taken by one actor affect the subsequent decisions of others in the neighborhood. In this way isolated actions affect the well-being of the community and alter the stability of the neighborhood.

Because of this feedback between individual and collective behavior, neighborhood stability is characterized by a series of thresholds, beyond which various self-perpetuating processes of decay take hold. Above these thresholds, each actor who makes a decision that undermines neighborhood well-being makes it increasingly likely that other actors will do the same. Each property owner who decides not to invest in upkeep and maintenance, for example, lowers the incentive for others to maintain their properties. Likewise, each new crime promotes psychological and physical withdrawal from public life, which reduces vigilance within the neighborhood and undermines the capacity for collective organization, making additional criminal activity more likely.

Segregation increases the susceptibility of neighborhoods to these spirals of decline. During periods of economic dislocation, a rising concentration of black poverty is associated with the simultaneous concentration of other negative social and economic conditions. Given the high levels of racial segregation characteristic of American urban areas, increases in black poverty such as those observed during the 1970s can only lead to a concentration of housing abandonment, crime, and social disorder, pushing poor black neighborhoods beyond the threshold of stability.

By building physical decay, crime, and social disorder into the residential structure of black communities, segregation creates a harsh and extremely disadvantaged environment to which ghetto blacks must adapt. In concentrating poverty, moreover, segregation also concentrates conditions such as drug use, joblessness, welfare dependency, teenage childbearing, and unwed parenthood, producing a social context where these conditions are not only common but the norm. [We] argue that in adapting to this social environment, ghetto dwellers evolve a set of behaviors, attitudes, and expectations that are sharply at variance with those common in the rest of American society.

As a direct result of the high degree of racial and class isolation created by segregation, for example, Black English has become progressively more distant from Standard American English, and its speakers are at a clear disadvantage in US schools and labor markets. Moreover, the isolation and intense poverty of the ghetto provides a supportive structural niche for the emergence of an "oppositional culture" that inverts the values of middle-class society. Anthropologists have found that young people in the ghetto experience strong peer pressure not to succeed in school, which severely limits their prospects for social mobility in the larger society. Quantitative research shows that growing up in a ghetto neighborhood increases the likelihood of dropping out of high school, reduces the probability of attending college, lowers the likelihood of employment, reduces income earned as an adult, and increases the risk of teenage childbearing and unwed pregnancy.

Segregation also has profound political consequences for blacks, because it so isolates them geographically that they are the only ones who benefit from public expenditures in their neighborhoods. The relative integration of most ethnic groups means that jobs or services allocated to them will generally benefit several other groups at the same time. Integration thus creates a basis for political coalitions and pluralist politics, and most ethnic groups that seek public resources are able to find coalition partners because other groups can anticipate sharing the benefits. That blacks are the only ones to benefit from resources allocated to the ghetto – and are the only ones harmed when resources are removed – makes it difficult for them to find partners for political coalitions. Although segregation paradoxically makes it easier for blacks to elect representatives, it limits their political influence and marginalizes them within the American polity. Segregation prevents blacks from participating in pluralist politics based on mutual self-interest.

Because of the close connection between social and spatial mobility, segregation also perpetuates poverty. One of the primary means by which individuals improve their life chances – and those of their children – is by moving to neighborhoods with higher home values, safer streets, higher-quality schools, and better services. As groups move up the socio-economic ladder, they typically move up the residential hierarchy as well, and in doing so they not only improve their standard of living but also enhance their chances for future success. Barriers to spatial mobility are barriers to social mobility, and by confining blacks to a small set of relatively disadvantaged neighborhoods, segregation constitutes a very powerful impediment to black socioeconomic progress.

Despite the obvious deleterious consequences of black spatial isolation, policymakers have not paid much attention to segregation as a contributing cause of urban poverty and have not taken effective steps to dismantle the ghetto. Indeed, as [we] document, for most of the past two decades public policies tolerated and even supported the perpetuation of segregation in American urban areas. Although many political initiatives were launched to combat discrimination and prejudice in the housing and banking industries, each legislative or judicial act was fought tenaciously by a powerful array of people who believed in or benefited from the status quo.

Although a comprehensive open housing bill finally passed Congress under unusual circumstances in 1968, it was stripped of its enforcement provisions as its price of enactment, yielding a Fair Housing Act that was structurally flawed and all but doomed to fail. As documentation of the law's defects accumulated in multiple Congressional hearings, government reports, and scholarly studies, little was done to repair the situation until 1988, when a series of scandals and political errors by the Reagan Administration finally enabled a significant strengthening of federal antidiscrimination law.

Yet even more must be done to prevent the permanent bifurcation of the United States into black and white societies that are separate and unequal. As of 1990, levels of racial segregation were still extraordinarily high in the nation's large urban areas, particularly those of the north. Segregation has remained high because fair housing enforcement relies too heavily on the private efforts of individual victims of discrimination. Whereas the processes that perpetuate segregation are entrenched and institutionalized, fair housing enforcement is individual, sporadic, and confined to a small number of isolated cases.

As long as the Fair Housing Act is enforced individually rather than systemically, it is unlikely to be effective in overcoming the structural arrangements that support segregation and sustain the ghetto. Until the government throws its considerable institutional weight behind efforts to dismantle the ghetto, racial segregation will persist. [W]e propose a variety of specific actions that the federal government will need to take to end the residential segregation of blacks in American society.

Ultimately, however, dismantling the ghetto and ending the long reign of racial segregation will require more than specific bureaucratic reforms; it requires a moral commitment that white America has historically lacked. The segregation of American blacks was no historical accident; it was brought about by actions and practices that had the passive acceptance, if not the active support, of most whites in the United States. Although America's apartheid may not be rooted in the legal strictures of its South African relative, it is no less effective in perpetuating racial inequality, and whites are no less culpable for the socioeconomic deprivation that results.

As in South Africa, residential segregation in the United States provides a firm basis for a broader system of racial injustice. The geographic isolation of Africans within a narrowly circumscribed portion of the urban environment – whether African townships or American ghettos – forces blacks to live under extraordinarily harsh conditions and to endure a social world where poverty is endemic, infrastructure is inadequate, education is lacking, families are fragmented, and crime and violence are rampant.[30] Moreover, segregation confines these unpleasant by-products of racial oppression to an isolated portion of the urban geography far removed from the experience of most whites. Resting on a foundation of segregation, apartheid not only denies blacks their rights as citizens but forces them to bear the social costs of their own victimization.

Although Americans have been quick to criticize the apartheid system of South Africa, they have been reluctant to acknowledge the consequences of their own institutionalized system of racial separation. The topic of segregation has virtually disappeared from public policy debates; it has vanished from the list of issues on the civil rights agenda; and it has been ignored by social scientists spinning endless theories of the underclass. Residential segregation has become the forgotten factor of American race relations, a minor footnote in the ongoing debate on the urban underclass. Until policymakers, social scientists, and private citizens recognize the crucial role of America's own apartheid in perpetuating urban poverty and racial injustice, the United States will remain a deeply divided and very troubled society.

Notes

1 Epigraph from Edgar H. Brookes, *Apartheid: A Documentary Study of Modern South Africa* (London: Routledge and Kegan Paul, 1968), p. 142.

2 Gunnar Myrdal, *An American Dilemma*, vol. 1 (New York: Harper and Brothers, 1944), p. 618; see also Walter A. Jackson, *Gunnar Myrdal and America's Conscience* (Chapel Hill: University of North Carolina Press, 1990), pp. 88–271.

3 Kenneth B. Clark, *Dark Ghetto: Dilemmas of Social Power* (New York: Harper and Row, 1965), p. 11.

4 US National Advisory Commission on Civil Disorders, *The Kerner Report* (New York: Pantheon Books, 1988), p. 1.

5 Ibid.

6 Ibid., p. 2.

7 Ibid., p. 22.

8 Ibid.

9 Ibid.

10 A few scholars attempted to keep the Kerner Commission's call for desegregation alive, but their voices have largely been unheeded in the ongoing debate. Thomas Pettigrew has continued to assert the central importance of residential segregation, calling it the "linchpin" of American race relations; see "Racial Change and Social Policy," *Annals of the American Academy of Political and Social Science* 441 (1979): 114–31. Gary Orfield has repeatedly pointed out segregation's deleterious effects on black prospects for education, employment, and socioeconomic mobility; see "Separate Societies: Have the Kerner Warnings Come True?" in Fred R. Harris and Roger W. Wilkins, eds., *Quiet Riots: Race and Poverty in the United States* (New York: Pantheon Books, 1988), pp. 100–22; and "Ghettoization and Its Alternatives," in Paul E. Peterson, ed., *The New Urban Reality* (Washington, DC: Brookings Institution, 1985), pp. 161–96.

11 See Thomas B. Edsall and Mary D. Edsall, *Chain Reaction: The Impact of Race, Rights, and Taxes on American Politics* (New York: Norton, 1991).

12 For an informative history of the evolution of the concept of the underclass, see Michael B. Katz, *The Undeserving Poor: From the War on Poverty to the War on Welfare* (New York: Pantheon, 1989), pp. 185–235.

13 Oscar Lewis, *La Vida: A Puerto Rican Family in the Culture of Poverty – San Juan and New York* (New York: Random House, 1965); "The Culture of Poverty," *Scientific American* 215 (1966): 19–25; "The Culture of Poverty," in Daniel P. Moynihan, ed.,

On Understanding Poverty: Perspectives from the Social Sciences (New York: Basic Books, 1968), pp. 187–220.

14   The complete text of this report is reprinted in Lee Rainwater and William L. Yancey, *The Moynihan Report and the Politics of Controversy* (Cambridge: MIT Press, 1967), pp. 39–125.

15   Edward C. Banfield, *The Unheavenly City* (Boston: Little, Brown, 1970).

16   William Ryan, *Blaming the Victim* (New York: Random House, 1971).

17   Carol Stack, *All Our Kin: Strategies of Survival in a Black Community* (New York: Harper and Row, 1974).

18   Douglas C. Glasgow, *The Black Underclass: Poverty, Unemployment, and Entrapment of Ghetto Youth* (New York: Vintage, 1981), p. 11; Alphonso Pinkney, *The Myth of Black Progress* (Cambridge: Cambridge University Press, 1984), pp. 78–80.

19   Charles Murray, *Losing Ground: American Social Policy, 1950–1980* (New York: Basic Books, 1984).

20   Lawrence M. Mead, *Beyond Entitlement: The Social Obligations of Citizenship* (New York: Free Press, 1986).

21   William Julius Wilson, *The Declining Significance of Race: Blacks and Changing American Institutions* (Chicago: University of Chicago Press, 1978).

22   William Julius Wilson, *The Truly Disadvantaged: The Inner City, the Underclass, and Public Policy* (Chicago: University of Chicago Press, 1987), pp. 1–108.

23   Ibid., pp. 49–62.

24   The subject indices of *Losing Ground* and *Beyond Entitlement* contain no references at all to residential segregation.

25   The subject index of *The Truly Disadvantaged* contains two references to pre-1960s Jim Crow segregation.

26   Again with the exception of Thomas Pettigrew and Gary Orfield.

27   See Mitchell L. Eggers and Douglas S. Massey, "The Structural Determinants of Urban Poverty," *Social Science Research* 20 (1991): 217–55; Mitchell L. Eggers and Douglas S. Massey, "A Longitudinal Analysis of Urban Poverty: Blacks in US Metropolitan Areas between 1970 and 1980." *Social Science Research* 21 (1992): 175–203.

28   The evidence on the extent of middle-class out-migration from ghetto areas is inconclusive. Because racial segregation does not decline with rising socioeconomic status, out-movement from poor black neighborhoods certainly has not been to white areas.

29   See Eggers and Massey, "A Longitudinal Analysis of Urban Poverty."

30   See International Defense and Aid Fund for Southern Africa, *Apartheid: The Facts* (London: United Nations Centre against Apartheid, 1983), pp. 15–26.

18 Fortress LA

Mike Davis

One manifestation of the impact of economic restructuring on the polarization into rich and poor is the physical separation of the rich and poor in cities. Mike Davis shows how property owners, developers, and city officials in Los Angeles have restructured the city to give affluent urbanites and visitors the perception of safety and security by separating them from lower-income and nonwhite residents. He argues that the city has pursued a strategy of "social apartheid" by removing or hiding poverty and elevating security to the top priority for new construction and redevelopment projects.

Davis gives several examples of the strategy of social apartheid, including the destruction of public spaces (e.g., streets, sidewalks) and their privatization (in malls); the forcible removal of poor, homeless, and nonwhite people from view; the creation of gated communities; the proliferation of private security services; and the arming of police with technologically advanced weaponry. In his view, this deliberate isolation of different class and ethnic groups reduces opportunities for the democratic mixing of peoples that is one of the traditional strengths of city life.

The carefully manicured lawns of Los Angeles's Westside sprout forests of ominous little signs warning: 'Armed Response!' Even richer neighborhoods in the canyons and hillsides isolate themselves behind walls guarded by gun-toting private police and state-of-the-art electronic surveillance. Downtown, a publicly-subsidized 'urban renaissance' has raised the nation's largest corporate citadel, segregated from the poor neighborhoods around it by a monumental architectural glacis. In Hollywood, celebrity architect Frank Gehry, renowned for his 'humanism', apotheosizes the siege look in a library designed to resemble a foreign-legion fort. In the Westlake district and the San Fernando Valley the Los Angeles Police barricade streets and seal off poor neighborhoods as part of their 'war on drugs'.

Davis, Mike, "Fortress LA." From *City of Quartz: Excavating the Future of Los Angeles* (New York and London: Verso Ltd., 1992), pp. 224, 226–36, 244, 246, 248, 250–3, 257–8, 260–3. Reprinted by permission of the publisher. Copyright © 1990 by Verso. All rights reserved.

In Watts, developer Alexander Haagen demonstrates his strategy for recolonizing inner-city retail markets: a panoptican shopping mall surrounded by staked metal fences and a substation of the LAPD in a central surveillance tower. Finally on the horizon of the next millennium, an ex-chief of police crusades for an anti-crime 'giant eye' – a geo-synchronous law enforcement satellite – while other cops discreetly tend versions of 'Garden Plot', a hoary but still viable 1960s plan for a law-and-order armageddon.

Welcome to post-liberal Los Angeles, where the defense of luxury lifestyles is translated into a proliferation of new repressions in space and movement, undergirded by the ubiquitous 'armed response'. This obsession with physical security systems, and, collaterally, with the architectural policing of social boundaries, has become a zeitgeist of urban restructuring, a master narrative in the emerging built environment of the 1990s. Yet contemporary urban theory, whether debating the role of electronic technologies in precipitating 'postmodern space', or discussing the dispersion of urban functions across poly-centered metropolitan 'galaxies', has been strangely silent about the militarization of city life so grimly visible at the street level. Hollywood's pop apocalypses and pulp science fiction have been more realistic, and politically perceptive, in representing the programmed hardening of the urban surface in the wake of the social polarizations of the Reagan era. Images of carceral inner cities (*Escape from New York*, *Running Man*), high-tech police death squads (*Blade Runner*), sentient buildings (*Die Hard*), urban bantustans (*They Live!*), Vietnam-like street wars (*Colors*), and so on, only extrapolate from actually existing trends.

Such dystopian visions grasp the extent to which today's pharaonic scales of residential and commercial security supplant residual hopes for urban reform and social integration. The dire predictions of Richard Nixon's 1969 National Commission on the Causes and Prevention of Violence have been tragically fulfilled: we live in 'fortress cities' brutally divided between 'fortified cells' of affluent society and 'places of terror' where the police battle the criminalized poor.[1] The 'Second Civil War' that began in the long hot summers of the 1960s has been institutionalized into the very structure of urban space. The old liberal paradigm of social control, attempting to balance repression with reform, has long been superseded by a rhetoric of social warfare that calculates the interests of the urban poor and the middle classes as a zero-sum game. In cities like Los Angeles, on the bad edge of postmodernity, one observes an unprecedented tendency to merge urban design, architecture and the police apparatus into a single, comprehensive security effort.

This epochal coalescence has far-reaching consequences for the social relations of the built environment. In the first place, the market provision of 'security' generates its own paranoid demand. 'Security' becomes a positional good defined by income access to private 'protective services' and membership in some hardened residential enclave or restricted suburb. As a prestige symbol – and sometimes as the decisive borderline between the merely well-off and the 'truly rich' – 'security' has less to do with personal safety than with the degree of personal insulation, in residential, work, consumption and travel environments, from 'unsavory' groups and individuals, even crowds in general.

Secondly, as William Whyte has observed of social intercourse in New York, 'fear proves itself'. The social perception of threat becomes a function of the security mobilization itself, not crime rates. Where there is an actual rising arc of street violence, as in Southcentral Los Angeles or Downtown Washington, DC, most of the carnage is self-contained within ethnic or class boundaries. Yet white middle-class imagination, absent from any first-hand knowledge of inner-city conditions, magnifies the perceived threat through a demonological lens. Surveys show that Milwaukee suburbanites are just as worried about violent crime as inner-city Washingtonians, despite a twenty-fold difference in relative levels of mayhem. The media, whose function in this arena is to bury and obscure the daily economic violence of the city, ceaselessly throw up spectres of criminal underclasses and psychotic stalkers. Sensationalized accounts of killer youth gangs high on crack and shrilly racist evocations of marauding Willie Hortons foment the moral panics that reinforce and justify urban apartheid.

Moreover, the neo-military syntax of contemporary architecture insinuates violence and conjures imaginary dangers. In many instances the semiotics of so-called 'defensible space' are just about as subtle as a swaggering white cop. Today's upscale, pseudo-public spaces – sumptuary malls, office centers, culture acropolises, and so on – are full of invisible signs warning off the underclass 'Other'. Although architectural critics are usually oblivious to how the built environment contributes to segregation, pariah groups – whether poor Latino families, young Black men, or elderly homeless white females – read the meaning immediately.

The Destruction of Public Space

The universal and ineluctable consequence of this crusade to secure the city is the destruction of accessible public space. The contemporary opprobrium attached to the term 'street person' is in itself a harrowing index of the devaluation of public spaces. To reduce contact with untouchables, urban redevelopment has converted once vital pedestrian streets into traffic sewers and transformed public parks into temporary receptacles for the homeless and wretched. The American city, as many critics have recognized, is being systematically turned inside out – or, rather, outside in. The valorized spaces of the new megastructures and super-malls are concentrated in the center, street frontage is denuded, public activity is sorted into strictly functional compartments, and circulation is internalized in corridors under the gaze of private police.

The privatization of the architectural public realm, moreover, is shadowed by parallel restructurings of electronic space, as heavily policed, pay-access 'information orders', elite data-bases and subscription cable services appropriate parts of the invisible agora. Both processes, of course, mirror the deregulation of the economy and the recession of non-market entitlements. The decline of urban liberalism has been accompanied by the death of what might be called the 'Olmstedian vision' of public space. Frederick Law Olmsted, it will be recalled, was North America's Haussmann, as well as the Father of Central Park. In the wake of Manhattan's 'Commune' of 1863, the great Draft Riot, he conceived public landscapes and parks as social safety-valves, *mixing* classes and ethnicities in common (bourgeois) recreations and enjoyments. As Manfredo Tafuri has shown in his well-known study of Rockefeller Center, the same principle animated the construction of the canonical urban spaces of the La Guardia–Roosevelt era.[2]

This reformist vision of public space – as the emollient of class struggle, if not the bedrock of the American *polis* – is now as obsolete as Keynesian nostrums of full employment. In regard to the 'mixing' of classes, contemporary urban America is more like Victorian England than Walt Whitman's or La Guardia's New York. In Los Angeles, once-upon-a-time a demi-paradise of free beaches, luxurious parks, and 'cruising strips', genuinely democratic space is all but extinct. The Oz-like archipelago of Westside pleasure domes – a continuum of tony malls, arts centers and gourmet strips – is reciprocally dependent upon the social imprisonment of the third-world service proletariat who live in increasingly repressive ghettoes and barrios. In a city of several million yearning immigrants, public amenities are radically shrinking, parks are becoming derelict and beaches more segregated, libraries and playgrounds are closing, youth congregations of ordinary kinds are banned, and the streets are becoming more desolate and dangerous.

Unsurprisingly, as in other American cities, municipal policy has taken its lead from the security offensive and the middle-class demand for increased spatial and social insulation. De facto disinvestment in traditional public space and recreation has supported the shift of fiscal resources to corporate-defined redevelopment priorities. A pliant city government – in this case ironically professing to represent a bi-racial coalition of liberal whites and Blacks – has collaborated in the massive privatization of public space and the subsidization of new, racist enclaves (benignly described as 'urban villages'). Yet most current, giddy discussions of the 'postmodern' scene in Los Angeles neglect entirely these overbearing aspects of counter-urbanization and counter-insurgency. A triumphal gloss – 'urban renaissance', 'city of the future', and so on – is laid over the brutalization of inner-city neighborhoods and the increasing South Africanization of its spatial relations. Even as the walls have come down in Eastern Europe, they are being erected all over Los Angeles.

The observations that follow take as their thesis the existence of this new class war (sometimes a continuation of the race war of the 1960s) at the level of the built environment. Although this is not a comprehensive account, which would require a thorough analysis of economic and political dynamics, these images and instances are meant to convince the reader that urban form is indeed following a repressive function in the political furrows of the Reagan–Bush era. Los Angeles, in its usual prefigurative mode, offers an especially disquieting catalogue of the emergent liaisons between architecture and the American police state.

The Forbidden City

The first militarist of space in Los Angeles was General Otis of the *Times*. Declaring himself at war with labor, he infused his surroundings with an unrelentingly bellicose air:

> He called his home in Los Angeles the Bivouac. Another house was known as the Outpost. The *Times* was known as the Fortress. The staff of the paper was the Phalanx. The *Times* building itself was more fortress than newspaper plant, there were turrets, battlements, sentry boxes. Inside he stored fifty rifles.[3]

A great, menacing bronze eagle was the *Times*'s crown; a small, functional cannon was installed on the hood of Otis's touring car to intimidate onlookers. Not surprisingly, this overwrought display of aggression produced a response in kind. On 1 October 1910 the heavily fortified *Times* headquarters – citadel of the open shop on the West Coast – was destroyed in a catastrophic explosion blamed on union saboteurs.

Eighty years later, the spirit of General Otis has returned to subtly pervade Los Angeles's new 'postmodern' Downtown: the emerging Pacific Rim financial complex which cascades, in rows of skyscrapers, from Bunker Hill southward along the Figueroa corridor. Redeveloped with public tax increments under the aegis of the powerful and largely unaccountable Community Redevelopment Agency, the Downtown project is one of the largest postwar urban designs in North America. Site assemblage and clearing on a vast scale, with little mobilized opposition, have resurrected land values, upon which big developers and off-shore capital (increasingly Japanese) have planted a series of billion-dollar, block-square mega-structures: Crocker Center, the Bonaventure Hotel and Shopping Mall, the World Trade Center, the Broadway Plaza, Arco Center, CitiCorp Plaza, California Plaza, and so on. With historical landscapes erased, with mega-structures and super-blocks as primary components, and with an increasingly dense and self-contained circulation system, the new financial district is best conceived as a single, demonically self-referential hyper-structure, a Miesian skyscape raised to dementia.

Like similar megalomaniac complexes, tethered to fragmented and desolated Downtowns (for instance, the Renaissance Center in Detroit, the Peachtree and Omni Centers in Atlanta, and so on), Bunker Hill and the Figueroa corridor have provoked a storm of liberal objections against their abuse of scale and composition, their denigration of street landscape, and their confiscation of so much of the vital life activity of the center, now sequestered within subterranean concourses or privatized malls. Sam Hall Kaplan, the crusty urban critic of the *Times*, has been indefatigable in denouncing the anti-pedestrian bias of the new corporate citadel, with its fascist obliteration of street frontage. In his view the superimposition of 'hermetically sealed fortresses' and air-dropped 'pieces of suburbia' has 'dammed the rivers of life' Downtown.[4]

Yet Kaplan's vigorous defense of pedestrian democracy remains grounded in hackneyed liberal complaints about 'bland design' and 'elitist planning practices'. Like most architectural critics, he rails against the oversights of urban design without recognizing the dimension of foresight, of explicit repressive intention, which has its roots in Los Angeles's ancient history of class and race warfare. Indeed, when Downtown's new 'Gold Coast' is viewed en bloc from the standpoint of its interactions with other social areas and landscapes in the central city, the 'fortress effect' emerges, not as an inadvertent failure of design, but as deliberate socio-spatial strategy.

The goals of this strategy may be summarized as a double repression: to raze all association with Downtown's past and to prevent any articulation with the non-Anglo urbanity of its future. Everywhere on the perimeter of redevelopment this strategy takes the form of a brutal architectural edge or glacis that defines the new Downtown as a citadel vis-à-vis the rest of the central city. Los Angeles is unusual amongst major urban renewal centers in preserving, however negligently, most of its circa 1900–30 Beaux Arts commercial core. At immense public cost, the corporate headquarters and financial district was shifted from the old Broadway-Spring corridor six blocks west to the greenfield site created by destroying the Bunker Hill residential neighborhood. To emphasize the 'security' of the new Downtown, virtually all the traditional pedestrian links to the old center, including the famous Angels' Flight funicular railroad, were removed.

The logic of this entire operation is revealing. In other cities developers might have attempted to articulate the new skyscape and the old, exploiting the latter's extraordinary inventory of theaters and historic buildings to create a gentrified history – a gaslight district, Faneuil Market or Ghirardelli Square – as a support to middle-class residential colonization. But Los Angeles's redevelopers viewed property values in the old Broadway core as irreversibly eroded by the area's very centrality to public transport, and especially by its heavy use by Black and Mexican poor. In the wake of the Watts Rebellion, and the perceived Black threat to crucial nodes of white power (spelled out in lurid detail in the McCone Commission Report), resegregated spatial security became the paramount concern. The Los Angeles Police Department abetted the flight of business from Broadway to the fortified redoubts of Bunker Hill by spreading scare literature typifying Black teenagers as dangerous gang members.

As a result, redevelopment massively reproduced spatial apartheid. The moat of the Harbor Freeway and the regraded palisades of Bunker Hill cut off the new financial core from the poor immigrant neighborhoods that surround it on every side. Along the base of California Plaza, Hill Street became a local Berlin Wall separating the publicly subsidized luxury of Bunker Hill from the lifeworld of Broadway, now reclaimed by Latino immigrants as their primary shopping and entertainment street. Because politically connected speculators are now redeveloping the northern end of the Broadway corridor (sometimes known as 'Bunker Hill East'), the CRA is promising to restore pedestrian linkages to the Hill in the

1990s, including the Angels' Flight incline railroad. This, of course, only dramatizes the current bias against accessibility – that is to say, against *any* spatial interaction between old and new, poor and rich, except in the framework of gentrification or recolonization. Although a few white-collars venture into the Grand Central Market – a popular emporium of tropical produce and fresh foods – Latino shoppers or Saturday strollers never circulate in the Gucci precincts above Hill Street. The occasional appearance of a destitute street nomad in Broadway Plaza or in front of the Museum of Contemporary Art sets off a quiet panic; video cameras turn on their mounts and security guards adjust their belts.

Photographs of the old Downtown in its prime show mixed crowds of Anglo, Black and Latino pedestrians of different ages and classes. The contemporary Downtown 'renaissance' is designed to make such heterogeneity virtually impossible. It is intended not just to 'kill the street' as Kaplan fears, but to 'kill the crowd', to eliminate that democratic admixture on the pavements and in the parks that Olmsted believed was America's antidote to European class polarizations. The Downtown hyperstructure – like some Buckminster Fuller post-Holocaust fantasy – is programmed to ensure a seamless continuum of middle-class work, consumption and recreation, without unwonted exposure to Downtown's working-class street environments. Indeed the totalitarian semiotics of ramparts and battlements, reflective glass and elevated pedways, rebukes any affinity or sympathy between different architectural or human orders. As in Otis's fortress *Times* building, this is the archisemiotics of class war.

Lest this seem too extreme, consider *Urban Land* magazine's recent description of the profit-driven formula that across the United States has linked together clustered development, social homogeneity, and a secure 'Downtown image':

HOW TO OVERCOME FEAR OF CRIME IN DOWNTOWNS

Create a Dense, Compact, Multifunctional Core Area. A downtown can be designed and developed to make visitors feel that it – or a significant portion of it – is attractive and the type of place that 'respectable people' like themselves tend to frequent.... A core downtown area that is compact, densely developed and multifunctional will concentrate people, giving them more activities.... The activities offered in this core area will determine what 'type' of people will be strolling its sidewalks; locating offices and housing for middle- and upper-income residents in or near the core area can assure a high percentage of 'respectable', law-abiding pedestrians. Such an attractive redeveloped core area would also be large enough to affect the downtown's overall image.[5]

Sadistic Street Environments

This conscious 'hardening' of the city surface against the poor is especially brazen in the Manichaean treatment of Downtown microcosms. In his famous study of the 'social life of small urban spaces', William Whyte makes the point that the quality of any urban environment can be measured, first of all, by whether there are convenient, comfortable places for pedestrians to sit.[6] This maxim has been warmly taken to heart by designers of the high-corporate precincts of Bunker Hill and the emerging 'urban village' of South Park. As part of the city's policy of subsidizing white-collar residential colonization in Downtown, it has spent, or plans to spend, tens of millions of dollars of diverted tax revenue on enticing, 'soft' environments in these areas. Planners envision an opulent complex of squares, fountains, world-class public art, exotic shubbery, and avant-garde street furniture along a Hope Street pedestrian corridor. In the propaganda of official boosters, nothing is taken as a better index of Downtown's 'liveability' than the idyll of office workers and upscale tourists lounging or napping in the terraced gardens of California Plaza, the 'Spanish Steps' or Grand Hope Park.

In stark contrast, a few blocks away, the city is engaged in a merciless struggle to make public facilities and spaces as 'unliveable' as possible for the homeless and the poor. The persistence of thousands of street people on the fringes of Bunker Hill and the Civic Center sours the image of designer Downtown living and betrays the laboriously constructed illusion of a Downtown 'renaissance'. City Hall then retaliates with its own variant of low-intensity warfare.

Although city leaders periodically essay schemes for removing indigents *en masse* – deporting them to a poor farm on the edge of the desert, confining them in camps in the mountains, or, memorably, interning them on a derelict ferry at the Harbor – such 'final solutions' have been blocked by councilmembers fearful of the displacement of the homeless into their districts. Instead the city, self-consciously adopting the idiom of urban cold war, promotes the 'containment' (official term) of the homeless in Skid Row along Fifth Street east of the Broadway, systematically transforming the neighborhood into an outdoor poorhouse. But this containment strategy breeds its own vicious circle of contradiction. By condensing the mass of the desperate and helpless together in such a small space, and denying adequate housing, official policy has transformed Skid Row into probably the most dangerous ten square blocks in the world – ruled by a grisly succession of 'Slashers', 'Night Stalkers' and more ordinary predators. Every night on Skid Row is Friday the 13th, and, unsurprisingly, many of the homeless seek to escape the 'Nickle' during the night at all costs, searching safer niches in other parts of Downtown. The city in turn tightens the noose with increased police harassment and ingenious design deterrents.

One of the most common, but mind-numbing, of these deterrents is the Rapid Transit District's new barrelshaped bus bench that offers a minimal surface for uncomfortable sitting, while making sleeping utterly impossible. Such 'bumproof' benches are being widely introduced on the periphery of Skid Row. Another invention, worthy of the Grand Guignol, is the aggressive deployment of outdoor sprinklers. Several years ago the city opened a 'Skid Row Park' along lower Fifth Street, on a corner of Hell. To ensure that the park was not used for sleeping –

that is to say, to guarantee that it was mainly utilized for drug dealing and prostitution – the city installed an elaborate overhead sprinkler system programmed to drench unsuspecting sleepers at random times during the night. The system was immediately copied by some local businessmen in order to drive the homeless away from adjacent public sidewalks. Meanwhile restaurants and markets have responded to the homeless by building ornate enclosures to protect their refuse. Although no one in Los Angeles has yet proposed adding cyanide to the garbage, as happened in Phoenix a few years back, one popular seafood restaurant has spent $12,000 to built the ultimate bag-lady-proof trash cage: made of three-quarter inch steel rod with alloy locks and vicious outturned spikes to safeguard priceless moldering fishheads and stale french fries.

Public toilets, however, are the real Eastern Front of the Downtown war on the poor. Los Angeles, as a matter of deliberate policy, has fewer available public lavatories than any major North American city. On the advice of the LAPD (who actually sit on the design board of at least one major Downtown redevelopment project), the Community Redevelopment Agency bulldozed the remaining public toilet in Skid Row. Agency planners then agonized for months over whether to include a 'free-standing public toilet' in their design for South Park. As CRA Chairman Jim Wood later admitted, the decision not to include the toilet was a 'policy decision and not a design decision'. The CRA Downtown prefers the solution of 'quasi-public restrooms' – meaning toilets in restaurants, art galleries and office buildings – which can be made available to tourists and office workers while being denied to vagrants and other unsuitables. The toiletless no-man's-land east of Hill Street in Downtown is also barren of outside water sources for drinking or washing. A common and troubling sight these days are the homeless men – many of them young Salvadorean refugees – washing in and even drinking from the sewer effluent which flows down the concrete channel of the Los Angeles River on the eastern edge of Downtown.

Where the itineraries of Downtown powerbrokers unavoidably intersect with the habitats of the homeless or the working poor, as in the previously mentioned zone of gentrification along the northern Broadway corridor, extraordinary design precautions are being taken to ensure the physical separation of the different humanities. For instance, the CRA brought in the Los Angeles Police to design '24-hour, state-of-the-art security' for the two new parking structures that serve the Los Angeles *Times* and Ronald Reagan State Office buildings. In contrast to the mean streets outside, the parking structures contain beautifully landscaped lawns or 'microparks', and in one case, a food court and a historical exhibit. Moreover, both structures are designed as 'confidence-building' circulation systems – miniature paradigms of privatization – which allow white-collar workers to walk from car to office, or from car to boutique, with minimum exposure to the public street. The Broadway Spring Center, in particular, which links the Ronald Reagan Building to the proposed 'Grand Central Square' at Third and Broadway, has been warmly praised by architectural critics for adding greenery and art (a banal bas relief) to parking. It also adds a huge dose of menace – armed guards, locked gates, and security cameras – to scare away the homeless and poor.

The cold war on the streets of Downtown is ever escalating. The police, lobbied by Downtown merchants and developers, have broken up every attempt by the homeless and their allies to create safe havens or self-organized encampments. 'Justiceville', founded by homeless activist Ted Hayes, was roughly dispersed; when its inhabitants attempted to find refuge at Venice Beach, they were arrested at the behest of the local councilperson (a renowned environmentalist) and sent back to the inferno of Skid Row. The city's own brief experiment with legalized camping – a grudging response to a series of exposure deaths in the cold winter of 1987 – was ended abruptly after only four months to make way for construction of a transit repair yard. Current policy seems to involve a perverse play upon Zola's famous irony about the 'equal rights' of the rich and the poor to sleep out rough. As the head of the city planning commission explained the official line to incredulous reporters, it is not against the law to sleep on the street per se, 'only to erect any sort of protective shelter'. To enforce this prescription against 'cardboard condos', the LAPD periodically sweep the Nickle, confiscating shelters and other possessions, and arresting resisters. Such cynical repression has turned the majority of the homeless into urban bedouins. They are visible all over Downtown, pushing a few pathetic possessions in purloined shopping carts, always fugitive and in motion, pressed between the official policy of containment and the increasing sadism of Downtown streets. [...]

From Rentacop to *Robocop*

The security-driven logic of urban enclavization finds its most popular expression in the frenetic efforts of Los Angeles's affluent neighborhoods to insulate home values and lifestyles. [N]ew luxury developments outside the city limits have often become fortress cities, complete with encompassing walls, restricted entry points with guard posts, overlapping private and public police services, and even privatized roadways. It is simply impossible for ordinary citizens to invade the 'cities' of Hidden Hills, Bradbury, Rancho Mirage or Rolling Hills without an invitation from a resident. Indeed Bradbury, with nine hundred residents and ten miles of gated private roads, is so security-obsessed that its three city officials do not return telephone calls from the press, since 'each time an article appeared ... it drew attention to the city and the number of burglaries increased'. For its part, Hidden Hills, a Norman Rockwell painting behind high-security walls, has been bitterly divided over compliance with a Superior Court order to build forty-eight units of seniors' housing outside its gates. At meetings of the city's all-powerful home-owners' association (whose membership includes Frankie Avalon, Neil Diamond and Bob Eubanks) opponents of compliance have argued that the old folks' apartments 'will attract gangs and dope' (sic).[7]

Meanwhile, traditional luxury enclaves like Beverly Hills and San Marino are increasingly restricting access to their public facilities, using baroque layers of regulations to build invisible walls. San Marino, which may be the richest, and is reputedly the most Republican (85 per cent), city in the country, now closes its parks on weekends to exclude Latino and Asian families from adjacent communities. One plan under discussion would reopen the parks on Saturdays only to those with proof of residence. Other upscale neighborhoods in Los Angeles have minted a similar residential privilege by obtaining ordinances to restrict parking to local homeowners. Predictably, such preferential parking regulations proliferate exclusively in neighborhoods with three-car garages.

Residential areas with enough clout are thus able to privatize local public space, partitioning themselves from the rest of the metropolis, even imposing a variant of neighborhood 'passport control' on outsiders. The next step, of course, is to ape incorporated enclaves like Rolling Hills or Hidden Hills by building literal walls. Since its construction in the late 1940s Park La Brea has been a bit of Lower Manhattan *chutzpah* moored to Wilshire Boulevard: a 176-acre maze of medium-rent townhouses and tower apartments, occupied by an urbane mix of singles, retirees, and families. Now, as part of a strategy of gentrification, its owners, Forest City Enterprises, have decided to enclose the entire community in security fencing, cutting off to pedestrians one of the most vital public spaces along the 'Miracle Mile'. As a spokeswoman for the owners observed, 'it's a trend in general to have enclosed communities'.[8] In the once wide-open tractlands of the San Fernando Valley, where there were virtually no walled-off communities a decade ago, the 'trend' has assumed the frenzied dimensions of a residential arms race as ordinary suburbanites demand the kind of social insulation once enjoyed only by the rich. Brian Weinstock, a leading Valley contractor, boasts of more than one hundred newly gated neighborhoods, with an insatiable demand for more security. 'The first question out of their [the buyers'] mouths is whether there is a gated community. The demand is there on a 3-to-1 basis for a gated community than not living in a gated community.'[9]

The social control advantages of 'gatehood' have also attracted the attention of landlords in denser, lower-income areas. Apartment owners in the Sepulveda barrio of the Valley have rallied behind a police program, launched in October 1989, to barricade their streets as a deterrent to drug buyers and other undesirables. The LAPD wants the City Council's permission to permanently seal off the neighborhood and restrict entry to residents, while the owners finance a guard station or 'checkpoint charlie'. While the Council contemplates the permanency of the experiment, the LAPD, supported by local homeowners, has continued to barricade other urban 'war zones' including part of the Pico-Union district, a Mid-Wilshire neighborhood, and an entire square mile around Jefferson High School in the Central–Vernon area. In face of complaints from younger residents about the 'Berlin Wall' quality of the neighborhood quarantines, Police Chief Gates reassured journalists that 'we're not here to occupy the territory. This isn't

Panama. It's the city of Los Angeles and we're going to be here in a lawful manner.'[10]

Meanwhile the very rich are yearning for high-tech castles. Where gates and walls alone will not suffice, as in the case of Beverly Hills or Bel-Air homeowners, the house itself is redesigned to incorporate sophisticated, sometimes far-fetched, security functions. An overriding but discreet goal of the current 'mansionizing' mania on the Westside of Los Angeles – for instance, tearing down $3 million houses to build $30 million mansions – is the search for 'absolute security'. Residential architects are borrowing design secrets from overseas embassies and military command posts. One of the features most in demand is the 'terrorist-proof security room' concealed in the houseplan and accessed by sliding panels and secret doors. Merv Griffith and his fellow mansionizers are hardening their palaces like missile silos.

But contemporary residential security in Los Angeles – whether in the fortified mansion or the average suburban bunker – depends upon the voracious consumption of private security services. Through their local homeowners' associations, virtually every affluent neighborhood from the Palisades to Silverlake contracts its own private policing; hence the thousands of lawns displaying the little 'armed response' warnings. The classifieds in a recent Sunday edition of the Los Angeles *Times* contained nearly a hundred ads for guards and patrolmen, mostly from firms specializing in residential protection. Within Los Angeles County, the security services industry has tripled its sales and workforce (from 24,000 to 75,000) over the last decade. 'It is easier to become an armed guard than it is to become a barber, hairdresser or journeyman carpenter', and under California's extraordinarily lax licensing law even a convicted murderer is not automatically excluded from eligibility. Although a majority of patrolmen are minority males earning near the minimum wage ($4–7 per hour depending on qualifications and literacy), their employers are often multinational conglomerates offering a dazzling range of security products and services. As Michael Kaye, president of burgeoning Westec (a subsidiary of Japan's Secom Ltd), explains: 'We're not a security guard company. We sell a *concept* of security.'[11] (This quote, as aficionados will immediately recognize, echoes the boast of Omni Consumer Products' Dick Jones – the villain of Paul Verhoeven's *Robocop* – that 'everything is security concepts... sometimes I can just think of something and it makes me so horny'.)

What homeowners' associations contract from Westec – or its principal rival, Bel-Air Patrol (part of Borg-Warner's family of security companies, including Burns and Pinkerton) – is a complete, 'systems' package that includes alarm hardware, monitoring, watch patrols, personal escorts, and, of course, 'armed response' as necessary. Although law-enforcement experts debate the efficiency of such systems in foiling professional criminals, they are brilliantly successful in deterring innocent outsiders. Anyone who has tried to take a stroll at dusk through a strange neighborhood patrolled by armed security guards and signposted with death threats quickly realizes how merely notional, if not utterly obsolete, is the old idea of the 'freedom of the city'.

The LAPD as Space Police

This comprehensive urban security mobilization depends not only upon the imbrication of the police function into the built environment, but also upon an evolving social division of labor between public- and private-sector police services, in which the former act as the necessary supports of the latter. As *Police Chief* magazine notes, 'harsh economic realities of the 1980s' – for instance, the tax revolt, rising rates of crime against property, and burgeoning middle-class demands for security – have catalyzed 'a realignment of relationships between private security and law enforcement'.[12] The private sector, exploiting an army of non-union, low-wage employees, has increasingly captured the labor-intensive roles (guard duty, residential patrol, apprehension of retail crime, maintenance of security passages and checkpoints, monitoring of electronic surveillance, and so on), while public law enforcement has retrenched behind the supervision of security macrosystems (maintenance of major crime data bases, aerial surveillance, jail systems, paramilitary responses to terrorism and street insurgency, and so on). The confusing interface between the two sectors is most evident in the overlapping of patrol functions in many neighborhoods and in the growing trend to subcontract jailing (with the privatized supervision of electronic home surveillance as another potentially lucrative market).

In many respects this division of labor is more elaborated in Los Angeles than elsewhere, if only because of the LAPD's pathbreaking substitutions of technological capital for patrol manpower. In part this was a necessary adaptation to the city's dispersed form; but it has also expressed the department's particular definition of its relationship to the community. Especially in its own self-perpetuated myth, the LAPD is seen as the progressive antithesis to the traditional big-city police department with its patronage armies of patrolmen grafting off the beat. As reformed in the early 1950s by the legendary Chief Parker (who admired above all the elitism of the Marines), the LAPD was intended to be incorruptible because unapproachable, a 'few good men' doing battle with a fundamentally evil city. *Dragnet*'s Sergeant Friday precisely captured the Parkerized LAPD's quality of prudish alienation from a citizenry composed of fools, degenerates and psychopaths.

Technology helped insulate this paranoid *esprit de corps*. In doing so, it virtually established a new epistemology of policing, where technologized surveillance and response supplanted the traditional patrolman's intimate 'folk' knowledge of specific communities. Thus back in the 1920s the LAPD had pioneered the replacement of the flatfoot or mounted officer with the radio patrol car – the beginning of dispersed, mechanized policing. Under Parker, ever alert to spinoffs from military technology, the LAPD introduced the first police helicopters for systematic aerial surveillance. After the Watts Rebellion of 1965 this airborne effort became the cornerstone of a policing strategy for the entire inner city. As part of its 'Astro' program LAPD helicopters maintain an average nineteen-hour-per-day vigil over 'high crime areas', tactically coordinated to patrol car forces, and exceeding even the British Army's aerial surveillance of Belfast. To facilitate ground-air synchronization, thousands of residential rooftops have been painted with identifying street numbers, transforming the aerial view of the city into a huge police grid.

The fifty-pilot LAPD airforce was recently updated with French Aerospatiale helicopters equipped with futuristic surveillance technology. Their forward-looking infra-red cameras are extraordinary night eyes that can easily form heat images from a single burning cigarette, while their thirty-million-candlepower spotlights, appropriately called 'Nightsun', can literally turn the night into day. Meanwhile the LAPD retains another fleet of Bell Jet Rangers capable of delivering complete elements of SWAT personnel anywhere in the region. Their training, which sometimes includes practice assaults on Downtown highrises, anticipates some of the spookier Hollywood images (for example, *Blue Thunder* or *Running Man*) of airborne police terror. A few years ago a veteran LAPD SWAT commander (apparently one of the principals in the infamous SLA holocaust in Southcentral Los Angeles) accidentally shot his own helicopter out of the sky while practicing a strafing run with a machine-gun.

But the most decisive element in the LAPD's metamorphosis into a technopolice has been its long and successful liaison with the military aerospace industry. Just in time for the opening of the 1984 Los Angeles Olympics, the department brought on line ECCCS (Emergency Command Control Communications Systems), the most powerful, state-of-the-art police communications system in the world. First conceptualized by Hughes Aerospace between 1969 and 1971, ECCCS's design was refined and updated by NASA's Jet Propulsion Laboratory, incorporating elements of space technology and mission control communications. After the passage of a $42 million tax override in May 1977, the City Council appoved Systems Development Corporation of Santa Monica as prime contractor for the system, which took more than seven years to build.

The central hardware of ECCCS is encased in security comparable to a SAC missile silo in Montana. Bunkered in the earthquake-proofed and security-hardened fourth and fifth sublevels of City Hall East (and interconnecting with the Police pentagon in Parker Center), Central Dispatch Center coordinates all the complex itineraries and responses of the LAPD using digitalized communication to eliminate voice congestion and guarantee the secrecy of transmission. ECCCS, together with the LAPD's prodigious information-processing assets, including the ever-growing databases on suspect citizenry, have become the central neural system for the vast and disparate, public and private, security operations taking place in Los Angeles.

But this is hardly the ultimate police sensorium. As gang hysteria and the war on crack keep the city's coffers open to police funding requests, it is likely the LAPD will continue to win political support for ambitious capital investment programs in new technology. Having brought policing up to the levels of the Vietnam War and early NASA, it is almost inevitable that the LAPD, and other advanced police forces, will try to acquire the technology of the Electronic Battle-field and even Star Wars. We are at the threshold of the universal electronic tagging of property and people – both criminal and non-criminal (small children, for example) – monitored by both cellular and centralized surveillances. Of the latter, ex-Los Angeles police chief, now state senator, Ed Davis (Republican – Valencia) has proposed the use of a geosynclinical space satellite to counter pandemic car theft in the region. Electronic alarm systems, already tested in New England, would alert police if a properly tagged car was stolen; satellite monitoring would extend coverage over Los Angeles's vast metropolitan area. Once in orbit, of course, the role of a law enforcement satellite would grow to encompass other forms of surveillance and control.

The image here is ultimately more important than the practicality of the proposal, since it condenses the historical world view and quixotic quest of the post-war LAPD: good citizens, off the streets, enclaved in their high-security private consumption spheres; bad citizens, on the streets (and therefore not engaged in legitimate business), caught in the terrible, Jehovan scrutiny of the LAPD's space program. [...]

The Fear of Crowds

Ultimately the aims of contemporary architecture and the police converge most strikingly around the problem of crowd control. As we have seen, the designers of malls and pseudo-public space attack the crowd by homogenizing it. They set up architectural and semiotic barriers to filter out 'undesirables'. They enclose the mass that remains, directing its circulation with behaviorist ferocity. It is lured by visual stimuli of all kinds, dulled by musak, sometimes even scented by invisible aromatizers. This Skinnerian orchestration, if well conducted, produces a veritable commercial symphony of swarming, consuming monads moving from one cashpoint to another.

Outside in the streets, the police task is more difficult. The LAPD, true to its class war background, has always hated certain kinds of public gatherings. Its early history was largely devoted to bludgeoning May Day demonstrators, arresting strikers and deporting Mexicans and Okies. In 1921 it arrested Upton Sinclair for reading the Declaration of Independence in public; in the 1960s it indiscriminately broke up love-ins and family picnics in battles to control Griffith and Elysian Park. Subconsciously it has probably never recovered from the humiliation of August 1965 when it temporarily was forced to surrender the streets to a rebellious ghetto.

Whatever the reasons, the LAPD (and the County Sheriffs as well) continue relentlessly to restrict the space of public assemblage and the freedom of movement of the young. But long before the LAPD and the Sheriffs launched their famous anti-gang dragnets, they were operating extensive juvenile curfews in non-Anglo areas and barricading popular boulevards to prevent 'cruising' (in Hollywood this directly abets the current gentrification strategy). And now, of course, they are sealing off entire neighborhoods and housing projects under our local variant of 'pass law'. Even gilded white youth suffer from this escalating police regulation of personal mobility. In the erstwhile world capital of teenagers, where millions overseas still imagine Gidget at a late-night surf party, the beaches are now closed at dark, patrolled by helicopter gunships and police dune buggies.

A watershed in the dual architectural and police assault on public space was the rise and fall of the 'Los Angeles Street Scene'. Launched in 1978 the two-day festival at the Civic Center was intended to publicize Downtown's revitalization as well as to provide Mayor Bradley's version of the traditional Democratic barbecue. The LAPD were skeptical. Finally in 1986, after the failure of the Ramones to appear as promised, the youthful audience began to tear up the stage. The LAPD immediately sent in a phalanx of one hundred and fifty helmeted officers and a mounted unit. In the two-hour mêlée that followed, angry punks bombarded the police cavalry with rocks and bottles, and fifteen officers and their horses were injured. The producer of the Street Scene, a Bradley official, suggested that 'more middle-of-the-road entertainment' might attract less boisterous crowds. The prestigious *Downtown News* counter-attacked, claiming that the 'Street Scene gives Downtown a bad name. It flies in the face of all that has been done here in the last thirty years.' It demanded 'reparations' for the wounded 'reputation of Downtown'. The Mayor's office cancelled the Scene.

Its demise suggests the consolidation of an official consensus about crowds and the use of space in Los Angeles. Since the restructuring of Downtown eliminated the social mixing of crowds in normal pedestrian circulation, the Street Scene (ironically named) remained one of the few carnival-like occasions or places (along with redevelopment-threatened Hollywood Boulevard and Venice Boardwalk) where pure heteroglossia could flourish: that is to say, where Chinatown punks, Glendale skinheads, Boyle Heights lowriders, Valley girls, Marina designer couples, Slauson rappers, Skid Row homeless and gawkers from Des Moines could mingle together in relative amity.

Until the final extinction of these last real public spaces – with their democratic intoxications, risks and unscented odors – the pacification of Los Angeles will remain incomplete. And as long as this is the case, the various insecure elites, like the yuppie-aliens in John Carpenter's *They Live!*, will never know when some revolt may break out, or what strange guise it may wear. On Halloween eve 1988 – a week before the law-and-order climax of the Bush campaign – the LAPD attempted to disperse 100,000 peaceful revelers on Hollywood Boulevard. Police horses charged into crowds while squad cars zigzagged onto curbs, pinning terrified onlookers against storefront windows. Displaying what the police would later characterize as 'a complete lack of respect for the spirit of the holiday', part of the crowd angrily fought back, tossing bottles and smashing the windows of the Brown Derby. By midnight the rioters, mainly costumed, were looting storefronts. The next morning's *Times* carried the following description, evocative of Nathanael West:

> At one souvenir store, the Holly Vine Shoppe, looters smashed windows and took stuffed animals, Hollywood postcards, Hollywood pennants and baseball caps emblazoned 'LAPD'.[13]

Notes

1   See National Committee on the Causes and Prevention of Violence, *To Establish Justice, To Ensure Domestic Tranquility (Final Report)*, Washington, DC 1969.
2   Cf. Geoffrey Blodgett, 'Frederick Law Olmsted: Landscape Architecture as Conservative Reform', *Journal of American History* 62: 4 (March 1976); and Manfredo Tafuri, 'The Disenchanted Mountain: The Skyscraper and the City', in Giorgio Ciucci, et. al., *The American City*, Cambridge, Mass. 1979.
3   David Halberstam, *The Powers That Be*, New York 1979, p. 102.
4   Los Angeles *Times*, 4 November 1978, X, p. 13. See also Sam Hall Kaplan, *L.A. Follies: A Critical Look at Growth, Politics and Architecture*, Santa Monica 1989.
5   N. David Milder, 'Crime and Downtown Revitalization', in *Urban Land*, September 1987, p. 18.
6   *The Social Life of Small Spaces*, New York 1985.
7   Cf. *Daily News*, 1 November 1987; and television interview, Fox News, March 1990.
8   Los Angeles *Times*, 25 July 1989, II, p. 2.
9   Quoted in Jim Carlton 'Walled In', Los Angeles *Times*, 8 October 1989, II, p. 1. The mania for walls has also caught up with the Hollywood Chamber of Commerce who are planning to wall off the base of the famous 'Hollywood Sign' on Mount Lee, as well as installing motion detectors and video surveillance.
10   *Times*, 15 November 1989.
11   Quoted in Linda Williams, 'Safe and Sound', Los Angeles *Times*, 29 August 1988, IV, p. 5.
12   William Cunningham and Todd Taylor, 'A Summary of the Hallcrest Report', *The Police Chief*, June 1983, p. 31.
13   George Ramos, 'Hollywood Halloween: Some Came as Vandals and Looters', Los Angeles *Times*, 2 November 1988, II, pp. 1, 8. Also interviews with eyewitnesses.

19 Economic Inequality and Public Policy: The Power of Place

Todd Swanstrom, Peter Dreier, and John Mollenkopf

The physical separation of different income groups exists not only within cities but throughout metropolitan communities. Since the middle of the nineteenth century, cities of the United States have contained identifiably rich, middle-class, and poor districts. With suburbanization, this pattern of economic segregation has increased and expanded the geographic distances between social classes. In this article, Todd Swanstrom, Peter Dreier, and John Mollenkopf document the increasing economic segregation in American society and its contribution to rising economic and social inequality. They argue that economic segregation not only reduces people's choices of residence but also affects access to jobs, public services (especially education), and retail services. Finally, they question whether democratic political institutions can function when rich and poor live in different communities with different interests and agendas. Thus, they argue that economic segregation deserves attention as a public-policy issue.

Growing class segregation in America's metropolitan areas has had an enormous effect on the daily lives of urban residents, on the nation's efforts to address its urban problems, and on the condition of our democracy. William Julius Wilson's seminal book *The Truly Disadvantaged* (1987) catalyzed a lively scholarly debate on the causes and consequences of concentrated urban poverty. This literature, now grown to considerable proportions, sheds light on how living in a high poverty neighborhood has negative impacts on human development and family life over and above those of simply being poor. At the same time, its focus on ghetto poverty suffers from a kind of tunnel vision. By examining just one extreme, concentrated poverty neighborhoods, researchers working in this vein have failed

Swanstrom, Todd, Peter Dreier and John Mollenkopf, "Economic Inequality and Public Policy: The Power of Place." From *City & Community* 1(4) (2002): 349–57, 359–72. Reprinted by permission of the American Sociological Association.

to appreciate the broader dynamic of how economic classes are distributed across metropolitan space – and why that dynamic undermines efforts to address the needs of those in poverty and near poverty. It is this broader metropolitan dynamic and its effects that we explore here.

Few would dispute that economic inequality has widened greatly in the United States since the 1970s. The Census Bureau reports that between 1980 and 1998, the share of all income going to the lowest fifth of family earners declined from 4.3 to 3.6 percent, while the percent going to the top fifth increased from 43.7 to 49.2 percent (Jones and Weinberg, 2000). A scholarly cottage industry has risen to explain this phenomenon. It has identified five broad, interrelated factors explaining rising economic inequality: (1) the shift from manufacturing to services, which replaces well-paid industrial jobs with less-well-paid service jobs; (2) technological changes that increase the demand for (and the wages of) highly skilled and educated workers at the expense of unskilled and less educated workers; (3) globalization of the economy, which forces American workers to compete with workers around the world, driving down American wages; (4) immigration, which drives down wages among less skilled workers; and (5) decline of unionization, which reduces the bargaining power of workers to raise wages. With a few exceptions, however, these explanations ignore the role of space or geography in widening inequality.

Our thesis is simple: *the sorting of economic classes across space in American metropolitan areas both promotes rising economic inequality and amplifies its effects in ways that do not show up in the income statistics.* We are not arguing that spatial relations are more important than the five explanations noted above. Rather, we argue that spatial relations are an important additional cause of rising inequality, and one that the literature largely overlooks.

Our core argument is that neighborhood and community context have important impacts on life chances over and above individual characteristics and family background. Even when we factor in individual and family characteristics such as gender, race, and family income, we discover that one's access to decent jobs, health care, and good quality food, one's exposure to environmental hazards, and one's opportunities to participate in voluntary groups, or even vote, is partly determined by the kind of place where one lives. These places do not just passively reflect our income (and tastes), as market theory would suggest, but actively shape our ability to earn income in the first place. In short, place matters.

Understanding the power of place not only helps explain income statistics, but also enables us to interpret what role they actually play in people's lives. We draw on the work of Nobel-Prize-winning economist Amartya Sen, who argues that inequality must be understood in broader terms than income or wealth. Drawing on the Aristotelian ideal of the good life, Sen argues that focusing only on income or wealth confuses the means to the good life with the good life itself. He challenges researchers to measure inequality in terms of what he calls human "functionings and capabilities." "[R]elevant functionings can vary from such elementary things as being adequately nourished, being in good health, avoiding escapable morbidity, and premature mortality, etc., to more complex achievements such as being happy, having self-respect, taking part in the life of the community, and so on" (Sen, 1992, p. 39). By capabilities, Sen means our ability to choose what activities to undertake. No matter what our functionings, a life that has more significant choices is a better life.

Sen argues that the ability of people to convert income and wealth into mean-ingful choices about life varies by age, race, gender, and health. A person with kidney disease cannot enjoy the same quality of life as a healthy person because of the large monetary and emotional costs of dialysis. Scholars must take such con-textual factors into account when evaluating economic inequality. We think place of residence should be added to Sen's list of contextual factors. Without an analy-sis of spatial context, or place, no evaluation of economic inequality can be complete.

The literature on the contextual effects of place is large and growing. It seeks to measure the *impact* of economic segregation on the ability of people to meet basic needs and its consequences for the larger society. [...]

We synthesize literature in three areas here – jobs and income, government services, and consumer goods and services. Space limits prevent us from looking at other important topics, such as access to health care services, the quality of the physical environment (including exposure to unhealthy pollution), and the conse-quences of living in a high-crime area. We seek to lay out what we know with certainty, as well as areas where scholarly controversies persist and further re-search is needed. Notwithstanding the significant gaps in our knowledge and op-portunities for further research on contextual effects, we conclude that the evidence is more than sufficient to make a compelling case for policy interventions to address the problem of rising economic segregation. [...]

The Facts of Economic Segregation

The concept of economic segregation has a number of different dimensions. It does not just mean that the poor live isolated from the rest of society, but that the well off and other income strata also live separately from other economic groups in society (Massey, 1996). Moreover, the different economic strata do not just live in different neighborhoods, but in separate local political jurisdictions, particularly municipalities and school districts. Because these local jurisdictions fund and provide many important public services in the United States, economic segregation widens disparities both in the cost to taxpayers and the quality of public services. Also, competition among local governments for tax base distorts metropolitan development, leading to geographical mismatches between where people live and where they work and shop that further exacerbate economic inequalities.

The timing and strength of changes in economic segregation in the United States each support our contention that it is an important component of growing overall inequality. Economic segregation between neighborhoods declined between 1950 and 1970. Throughout most of the 20th century, the economic fortunes of regions in the United States converged. But in the 1970s both trends reversed, at about the same time that wage rates and family incomes also began to diverge. It is also suggestive that the United States not only has the largest amount of income inequality compared to other developed countries, but that it also has the most spatial inequality, to the extent discernable by comparable data (Dreier, Mollenkopf, and Swanstrom, 2001, pp. 53–5).

Jobs and Income

Economic segregation affects both people's ability to get a job and their overall level of income. Living in a concentrated poverty neighborhood undermines workforce participation primarily in two ways: (1) by accentuating the physical distance between place of residence and jobs and (2) by limiting access to networks that link people into job opportunities. (In the next section, we will examine how place of residence also affects economic success by shaping the ability of individuals to acquire various kinds of skills through locally funded public schools.)

In 1968, Harvard economist John Kain wrote a seminal article about what came to be known as the "spatial mismatch" problem. Using simple statistical techniques, Kain argued that Chicago's blacks lost 22,000–24,000 jobs because racial discrimination prevented them from following jobs as they migrated out to the suburbs (Kain, 1968). Most research on the spatial mismatch issue has focused on race, but economic segregation also produces spatial mismatches. Research by John Kasarda and others shows that urban economic restructuring has perverse consequences, with jobs and the workers who could qualify for them moving in opposite directions (Kasarda, 1983, 1985, 1989, 1995; Lang, 2000). Entry-level jobs such as manufacturing, retail, and data entry are leaving central cities and moving to the urban periphery, where rental housing is often in short supply.

At the same time, advanced corporate services jobs, such as in law and accounting, have increased in central business districts. A study of 101 metropolitan areas found that annual pay averaged 10.5 percent higher in the central city than for the same jobs located in the suburbs (US Department of Housing and Urban Development, 2000, p. 2), even though the incomes of central city residents lag well behind those of suburban residents. Indeed, the neighborhoods surrounding central business districts (CBDs) of major American cities are often the poorest in the region, with few residents possessing the qualifications for nearby professional jobs. For young urban professionals, many of whom may have grown up in the suburbs, gentrification of historic neighborhoods around downtowns, which appears to have undergone a resurgence in the 1990s, provides one way to address the mismatch between jobs and housing. This has not been matched with the same kind of new housing opportunities in the suburbs for low-skilled urban workers, however.

To demonstrate a spatial mismatch, one must show not only that people are geographically separated from jobs, but also that this separation impedes success in the labor market. The best way to test for a spatial mismatch would be to conduct an experiment by comparing outcomes between a control group that stays in central city high-poverty areas distant from job centers and an experimental group, alike in all respects, who move to areas closer to jobs in middle-income suburbs. In a free society, such public policy experiments are almost impossible to perform.

Fortunately, a "natural experiment" of this type ensued after a 1976 US Supreme Court decision in the case of *Hills v. Gautreaux*. Public housing residents sued the Chicago Housing Authority and the US Department of Housing and Urban Development for deliberately locating public housing only in poor minority neighborhoods (Rubinowitz and Rosenbaum, 2000). The Court ordered the Housing Authority to give public housing tenants housing vouchers so that they could move to middle-class white neighborhoods throughout the Chicago metropolitan area. When the program ended in 1998, more than 7,000 low-income families (mostly blacks) had participated, with more than half moving to middle-income white suburbs and the rest moving to low-income, mostly black neighborhoods in Chicago. Although not perfect, *Gautreaux* represents the closest thing we have to an experimental test of the contextual effects of place. Analysis of this experience shows that adults who moved to the suburbs had higher rates of employment, though not higher wages or better working hours, compared to those who remained behind in segregated low-income communities. The differences for the suburban children were more dramatic. They were "more likely to be in school, in college-track classes, in four-year colleges, employed, and in jobs with benefits and better pay" (Rubinowitz and Rosenbaum, 2000, p. 189). In the 1990s, the federal government replicated *Gautreaux* in six cities through the Moving to Opportunity program and studied the differences in results for participants and comparable nonparticipants. This study also showed important positive impacts of moving (Goering et al., 1999; Turner, Popkin, and Cunningham, 2000). [. . .]

Finally, research shows that women suffer more from being distant from jobs than men. Women of all classes are much more likely to turn down jobs because they are too far from home or from their children's caregivers (Thompson, 1997). The spatial mismatch is a major stumbling block in moving welfare recipients, most of whom are women with children, into jobs. Not surprisingly, studies of recent changes in welfare policy reveal that welfare recipients who live in low-income central city neighborhoods are least likely to leave welfare and move into the labor force (Leonard and Kennedy, 2002; Fisher and Weber, 2002). Although approximately three-fourths of all welfare recipients live in central cities or rural areas, two-thirds of all new jobs are located in suburbs (Allen and Kirby, 2000).

Nationwide, only one in twenty welfare recipients owns a
notoriously poor at delivering inner city residents to spra
To further complicate things, if a welfare recipient purc
her benefits may be penalized. [...]

Besides physically separating work from home, livin
neighborhood limits access to the social networks
opportunities. Grounded in economic sociology, this asp
match hypothesis argues that markets function most effectively w.
"embedded" in social relations (Granovetter, 1985). According to conven
economics, free markets are driven by rational utility maximizers unencumbered
by attachments to groups or places. By contrast, economic sociologists hold that
social trust, produced in face-to-face relations, is necessary to fair exchanges in the
marketplace.

The role of trust in economic relations has been explored utilizing the concept
of social capital (Putnam, 2000). Early on, it was shown that social networks are
important to career advancement (Granovetter, 1974). More recently, social capital theorists have distinguished between bonding and bridging social capital.
Bonding social capital reinforces group identities through strong ties among similar people. Bridging social capital, by contrast, establishes weaker ties between
insiders and different outsiders. Granovetter has observed that when seeking jobs,
weak ties to distant acquaintances are more important than strong ties to immediate neighbors (Granovetter, 1972). As de Souza Briggs put it, bonding social capital is good for "getting by," but we need bridging social capital to "get ahead"
(Briggs, 1998).

Social capital theory predicts that economic segregation will damage the ability
of poor people to succeed economically. Physical proximity increases social interactions. If poor people live mainly with other poor people, their social networks
will be confined to people who are disconnected from crucial job networks. Poor
people (as well as youths, the elderly, and those with less education) do rely more
on face-to-face networks that are confined to the neighborhoods where they live.
Ethnographic research suggests that this bonding social capital can help poor
people cope with poverty (Stack, 1974; Susser, 1982), but it does not generally
help them to get ahead economically.

From the viewpoint of economic sociology, it makes sense for employers to fill
job openings by relying on social trust accumulated with present employees, who
can guarantee the trustworthiness of their friends and relatives. In fact, research
has shown that more than half of all jobs are found this way, not through want
ads. One survey of Chicago firms reported that 40 percent did not advertise their
entry-level openings in newspapers, but relied on word-of-mouth through present
employees (Wilson, 1996, p. 133). Unfortunately, living in a neighborhood with
many unemployed people means that your friends will be less valuable in helping
you find a job, no matter how skilled, honest, or hardworking you may be. Survey
research shows that jobless blacks in the inner city are more socially isolated than

groups and less likely to have even one employed friend (Wilson, 1996, 65). This may help explain why another study found that blacks and whites living in Atlanta had very poor knowledge of the spatial distribution of job openings in the suburbs (Ihlanfeldt, 1997).

In short, research demonstrates a strong connection between living in areas of concentrated poverty and lack of economic success. Exactly how much economic segregation costs workers will vary according to the context. One study based on census data of 11,000 male workers in Los Angeles County concluded that "moving an individual with exactly the same human capital and demographic characteristics from high-poverty Compton to the more middle-class city of Glendale would raise wages by fifteen percentage points" (Pastor et al., 2000, p. 32). In short, rising levels of concentrated poverty have exacerbated inequality by imposing structural barriers to labor market success of the poor.

Economic segregation has also made economic inequality more entrenched, with families mired in poverty from one generation to the next. The United States has always prided itself on having a fluid class structure. Since the 1960s, however, economic mobility in the United States has declined. One study found that poor people in the United States had the lowest "escape rate" out of poverty of the six industrialized countries studied (Oxley, Dang, and Antolin, 1999, as cited in Mishel, Bernstein, and Schmitt, 2001). Economists have constructed models showing how economic segregation can lead to persistent economic inequalities across generations. The key link in these models is the perpetuation of educational inequalities generated through the local funding of education in the United States.

Public Services

The quality of public services varies widely within metropolitan areas, due primarily to the great variation in fiscal capacity across wealthy and poor municipalities. Though Americans take this reality for granted, it has resulted from three highly unusual facets of the US political system. First, metropolitan areas are highly politically fragmented. Second, local governments must raise most of the revenues to support public services from local sources, primarily real estate taxes. Higher levels of government, particularly the federal government, provide only limited support for local municipalities, mostly state funding for local public education. Third, local governments have considerable autonomy over land use and zoning. The interaction of these three factors produces a competition among local jurisdictions to attract high-value real estate investments and shed "expensive" residents, especially those whose income (and property values) are below the median. Every other major democracy in Europe and Canada provides more central government financing for local public services and exercises more national control over land use than does the United States. [. . .]

Most city governments are perched on the brink of fiscal distress. In the past decade, more suburbs – primarily older, inner-ring suburbs populated by working-class residents and with a limited commercial and industrial tax base – have joined them (Orfield, 2001). Local governments must be prudent in not overtaxing local economic activities, and these revenues fluctuate with local economic conditions. But demand for local services and expenditures tends to be inexorable and difficult to control (as in the case of the local share of Medicaid expenditures). As a result, even economically successful cities face chronic difficulty balancing their budgets. [...]

Urban fiscal conditions improved as the nation's economy boomed in the late 1990s. Urban poverty finally began to decline, residents' incomes rose, and businesses prospered. But cities still could not raise enough revenue to provide everyone with good schools, public safety, and rehabilitated infrastructure, or to compensate their employees at rates that kept up with inflation, much less to lift the incomes of the poor. Their improved bond ratings masked the deeper reality that many cities had already tightened their belts and lowered residents' expectations during the downturns of the mid-1970s, early 1980s, and early 1990s. They closed public hospitals; reduced library hours; deferred maintenance on aging sewers, playgrounds, and parks; and reduced the numbers of public employees. If many cities were able to live within their means in the late 1990s, it is because they attempted to do less than they had in earlier years, especially in addressing the needs of the poor. In early 2000, cities and the nation once more entered a recession, with renewed fiscal difficulty.

The net result of the last several decades is that not only do the well-off live apart from the poor, but they receive strikingly different public services because the poor live in places that lack fiscal capacity, while the rich live in places that can fund high-quality services at relatively low tax rates. In one extreme case, Camden, New Jersey, where almost half the 85,000 residents live in poverty, the city cannot provide even minimal services despite punishingly high tax rates (Hill and Nowack, 2000). Meanwhile, residents of nearby wealthy suburbs receive much better services while paying lower tax rates. Urban disinvestment left central city per capita incomes lower than those of suburbanites in almost every metropolitan area. It also lowered the tax base as the average level of need among city residents was rising. "To compensate, the city must increase tax rates or reduce public spending, further convincing middle-class residents to leave" (Chernick and Reschovsky, 2000, p. 6).

Most cities are still vital centers of culture, entertainment, and other key services within their metropolitan areas. Suburbanites and tourists flock to central city restaurants, museums, sports complexes, concert halls, theaters, and convention centers, as well as to hospitals and universities. But many of these institutions, in particular the nonprofit ones, often do not directly generate tax revenue. One-third of New York City's property is exempt from real estate taxes, compared with 13 percent in suburban Nassau County and 22 percent in suburban Westchester

County (Chernick and Reschovsky, 2000, p. 6). Nor can municipal governments generally tax the incomes of high-earning suburban individuals who commute to jobs in central city corporate service firms. Businesses often threaten to downsize or move from cities that adopt "commuter" taxes; in metropolitan areas with multiple local governments, most public officials are reluctant to test whether such businesses are bluffing. [. . .]

Public education is probably the most important service próvided by local governments. It certainly absorbs the most resources. Public education in the United States is run by 13,726 independent school districts (US Bureau of the Census, 2000, p. 299). Their revenue capacities vary tremendously. In 1973, the Supreme Court ruled, in *San Antonio v Rodriguez*, that the US Constitution does not guarantee education as a fundamental right, and therefore it does not fall under the Fourteenth Amendment's equal protection clause. Eighteen state courts have ruled that fiscal inequalities across school districts do violate state constitutions and have ordered action to reduce them. State equalization grants have lessened the gap in spending between the richest and poorest districts in many states, but expenditures per pupil still vary significantly. In 1997, per pupil expenditures varied from $8,171 in New York City to $12,492 in suburban Nassau County and $12,760 in suburban Westchester County (New York State Education Department, 1999).

As with other public services, the same resources will not produce equal educational outcomes across districts because poor districts have more social disadvantage. State aid only addresses fiscal disparities, not social disadvantages. Wong estimates that only 8 percent of state aid to local school districts is specifically targeted for the socially disadvantaged (Wong, 1999, p. 12). Many have concluded that schools simply reproduce the class inequalities that are present in American society. Children from poor families typically have lower academic performance than do those from middle- and upper-class families. This has nothing to do with their intelligence but much to do with the social conditions that handicap their ability to learn, which are worst when they live in concentrated poverty neighborhoods (Traub, 2000). Poor children move frequently and poor neighborhoods have less stability. Of those children living in families with incomes below $10,000 a year, more than 30 percent have attended three or more different schools by the third grade (US General Accounting Office, 1994). Poor children are more likely to be malnourished and to come to school tired and are less likely to have books at home and parents who read with them. High crime levels in poor neighborhoods lead mothers to keep children inside for their safety and to send them to worse nearby schools rather than have them travel farther to magnet programs.

Equalizing the quality of all public services, particularly education, across these different types of metropolitan jurisdictions would have profound implications. Confronted with the structural disparity between their revenue and their needs and unable to bridge the gap through regional tax sharing, cities have typically looked to federal and state governments for fiscal help. All urban leaders, regardless of political party or ideology, want more state and federal resources. But cities are in a weaker political position than they were even a few decades ago. When the federal government was at its most generous in the 1970s, it filled only part of the gap. Since then, federal aid to cities has dropped dramatically, from 15 percent of municipal revenue in 1978 to less than 3 percent today. State aid did not make up the difference (Kincaid, 1999, p. 136). As a result, locally generated revenue now makes up 70 percent of city budgets (US Bureau of the Census, 2000, p. 13). "Fend-for-yourself federalism" has exacerbated the fiscal stresses and disparities that lead to unequal public services (Hill, 1990).

Proponents of the "free market" – including advocates of public choice theory – celebrate this situation. They view local political competition as creating a marketplace for public services parallel to the market for private goods and services. In this view, consumer choice promotes efficient and effective allocation of resources. Just as shoppers can choose from many brands of toothpaste or television sets, they should be able to choose from a wide array of cities and suburbs, each providing a distinct bundle of amenities and services at a distinct tax price. For public choice theorists, choosing a detergent and choosing a local government have much in common: "Individual choices differ for public goods and services as well as for private. Some consumers want more freeways; others want a rapid transit system instead. Some prefer local parks; others, larger private backyards" (Bish and Warren, 1972, p. 99). Public choice theorists view the competition among local jurisdictions as creating an efficient and responsive market for public services. [...]

Public choice theory justifies economic segregation on the grounds that people with similar tastes for public goods and a similar ability to pay for them will naturally settle in local government jurisdictions that provide those goods. According to Warren, public choice theory "assumes that a metropolitan area is composed of diverse communities of interests which are territorially distinct from one another and which have different preferences for goods and services in the public sector" (Warren, 1964, pp. 198–9).

The public choice perspective has two major flaws. First, it assumes that markets are actually "free" of government influence. Although people do make real choices among alternatives in housing, business location, and other markets, government policies shape every aspect of how they make those choices and what they have to choose from. Indeed, government establishes the regulatory and legal framework that makes it possible for markets to function at all. Markets therefore cannot be isolated from government, public policy, and politics. The "free market" is an abstraction, not a reality. In his celebration of outer-ring suburbs, which he calls "edge cities," Garreau (1991) hardly acknowledges that edge cities have grown up around and depend entirely on publicly funded highways and, in some cases, airports and other government facilities. Local governments compete with each other to attract desirable residents and investments (and to keep out un-wanted facilities), but the rules of the game under which they do so are neither free nor fair. These rules do not give all places an equal chance to succeed. In fact, most federal and state policies – including transportation, tax, housing, and even the siting of defense facilities and contracts – are strongly biased away from central cities and toward suburban jurisdictions.

The second major flaw is that public choice theory seems to work better for middle-class homeowners than for the inner-city poor. It ignores the features of society that constrain or empower people's ability to choose. Most obviously, people with fewer means (or the wrong skin color) have a highly constricted range of choice. The market not only fails people who live in poverty; it punishes them through the negative effects of concentrated poverty.

Retail Services

Surprisingly, the best prices for groceries in metropolitan areas are not found in run-down, dingy inner-city stores but at massive, gleaming supermarkets in the suburbs. Not only do these suburban stores offer lower prices, they also offer many more selections and fresher foods. The basic reason for the difference between the two locations is clear: since almost every household in the suburbs has at least one car, shoppers compare prices in many competing stores, each of which applies the latest technology to remain competitive. In the inner city, on the other hand, many households, lacking a car, are forced to shop in local grocery stores, which, lacking high volume, tend to be technologically backward and less efficient. The situation in groceries is mirrored across the retail sector: retail services are inferior and more expensive for those who live in areas of concentrated poverty in central cities and inner-ring suburbs compared to other parts of the metropolitan area.

Economics 101 teaches us that supply meets demand. The retail sector of major metropolitan areas often violates this truism. Even taking into account reduced consumer spending per household, areas of concentrated poverty have an undersupply of retail outlets – grocery stories, banks, pharmacies, and so forth – and areas of concentrated wealth have an oversupply. One study of retailing in 100 zip codes (averaging 15,000 in population) in seven Ohio cities found a consistent pattern: the number of stores per capita in 10 retail categories fell as the poverty rate rose. Department stores disappeared entirely in the poorest zip codes. Even more revealing, the ratio of retail employees to the population in poor neighborhoods fell even faster than the number of stores (Bingham and Zhang, 1997). In other words, poor central areas export shoppers, and rich outlying areas import shoppers. [. . .]

Unfortunately, the evidence suggests that the problem is rooted more deeply in the environment of concentrated poverty. The main reason why the poor pay more is that different types of stores serve poor neighborhoods than serve well-to-do suburbs. Large, efficient supermarkets serve the suburbs. They are marvels of modern retailing, typically offering over 12,000 separate items and operating on a high volume that enables them to prosper with profit margins of less than 1 percent of sales. They buy in bulk and apply the latest technology, including automated just-on-time inventory systems.

Central cities are losing their large supermarkets. Between 1970 and 1992, Boston lost 34 out of 50 big-chain supermarkets. The number of supermarkets in Los Angeles County fell from 1,068 to 694 between 1970 and 1990. Chicago did worse, losing half its supermarkets (Turque, 1992). One study found that supermarkets with more than 50 employees were nonexistent in the poorest zip codes: "Ghetto residents simply do not have access to chain supermarkets" (Bingham and Zhang, 1997, p. 786).

Why don't modern, efficient supermarkets serve low-income areas? The costs of doing business, including insurance, theft, parking, and land assembly, are indeed higher in poor neighborhoods than in suburbs, but these costs are not the main problem. The main problem is that population densities and rates of car ownership in low-income areas do not generate the required volume of customers. As Adam Smith observed in *The Wealth of Nations*, the division of labor depends on the size of the market. The smaller markets for groceries generated by areas of concentrated poverty are not sufficient to support the modern, specialized, high-volume supermarket. Therefore, areas of concentrated poverty are serviced by small, technologically backward mom-and-pop stores that charge higher prices. The problem cannot be solved until the segregation of the poor is addressed.

The pattern of a two-tiered retail sector, a high-quality, low-price one for well-to-do areas and the opposite for poor areas, is a pattern found throughout the retail sector in American metropolitan areas. One of the best-researched areas is banking. The evidence on redlining by banks and insurance companies is substantial. Residents in low-income areas, especially those with many black and Latino residents, are more likely to be rejected for mortgages, even when they have the necessary income to qualify for them and for homeowner insurance. In many areas of concentrated poverty banks have pulled out entirely, and these areas also suffer from a severe shortage of home insurance agencies (Munnell et al., 1996; Squires and O'Connor, 2001). Children in poor neighborhoods grow up not even knowing what the inside of a bank looks like, reinforcing the isolation of low-income families from the economic mainstream. Fringe banking institutions, such as check-cashing operations and pawnbrokers, have rushed in to fill the vacuum in low-income central city and inner-suburban areas. Check-cashing outlets charge 1.5–2.5 percent to cash a payroll check and pawnshops often charge 200 percent per year for a loan (Caskey, 1994b). In effect, these practices act like a tax on poor people's incomes, lowering them in ways that do not show up in the official income statistics.

Economic Segregation as a Public Policy Issue

Economic segregation is a fact of life, or so it seems. The rich will always distance themselves from the poor in societies with private housing markets. Putting physical distance between oneself and those who are of lower status, primarily the poor and minorities, enhances one's social status, perhaps especially in the United States, where, besides race, fewer outward signs demarcate rank or status. Although many people can afford an expensive suit or fancy car, only a few families can afford to live in exclusive enclaves – whether the Hamptons on Long Island, Ladue in the suburbs west of St. Louis, or Beverly Hills. Living far from the poor is one way of signaling that you have "made it" in American society. In fact, a 1994 a survey by *Town and Country* found that 60 percent of those making more than $400,000 a year felt it was important to live in an exclusive neighborhood (reported in Blakely and Snyder, 1997, p. 76).

Those who defend economic segregation generally see it as an expression of free choice. According to this view, neighborhood composition is determined by a sequential process of bidding in the marketplace. If the rich outbid the poor for a parcel of land, then the rich get to live there. Neighborhood residence is a reflection of one's economic success. Poor families are more likely than the middle class or the wealthy to live in high-poverty neighborhoods. Presumably, under free markets, all the disadvantages discussed above will be reflected in lower land values. Thus, if a neighborhood is distant from jobs and shopping and has poor public services and schools, this will be accurately reflected in land prices. According to this view, people who live in the neighborhood will pay very much lower rents. If the housing market is in equilibrium, then all the utility differences between parcels of land will be eliminated. Everybody, rich and poor, will basically get what they pay for.

In an article attacking the *Gautreaux* experiment, Rockwell reflects this free-market perspective. He argues that "markets mean choice, and with choice comes sorting. People tend to choose to work, socialize, and live with others in their own social, religious, cultural, and economic group. There's nothing wrong with that." He calls segregation "a natural pattern, a product of rational choice," which "makes possible strong communities" (Rockwell, 1994). According to a report for the Heritage Foundation by Howard Husock, sorting people by social rank upholds justice and morality. Those who work hard, defer pleasure, and save to get ahead are able to move into good neighborhoods. Those who lack these virtues are forced to live in bad neighborhoods. The threat of having to live in areas of concentrated poverty, with all the costs we discuss above, provides a constant prod to hard work and good values. For the government to step in and subsidize low-income housing in middle-class neighborhoods, Husock says, gives the poor "an ill-gotten gain," a "reward not commensurate with accomplishment" (Husock, 1991).

From the free market perspective, then, there are many reasons to question whether public policy should even try to address the issue of economic segregation. We may frown on status seeking and deplore the conditions in poor neighborhoods, but if residential sorting is basically the product of consumer choice, then government should not tamper with it. Economic class is not a "suspect classification," like race or religion. It is unconstitutional for local governments to intentionally segregate minorities, but the courts have generally upheld their right to discriminate against people on the basis of incomes (Judd and Swanstrom, 2002, ch. 10). Just as no one has a right to own a Mercedes Benz, no one has a right to live in a privileged neighborhood.

We believe this view is fundamentally wrong. The argument for affirmative policies to address economic segregation has a number of different dimensions.

First, public policies promote economic segregation. Contrary to the contention of free market conservatives that the government has unfairly pushed for economic integration, the overwhelming weight of government policies at the federal, state, and local level has in fact favored economic segregation. These policies range from the interstate highway system, to home mortgage deductions, to the way states have organized local governments, to the zoning decisions of local governments. Government policies have driven "excessive" economic segregation that cannot be justified by free market economics.

Second, economic segregation creates extensive ripple effects, or negative externalities. From the viewpoint of the individual household, it is certainly rational to move into an exclusive suburban enclave. From society's viewpoint, however, economic segregation imposes large costs on the general public. Perhaps the biggest negative externality is suburban sprawl. The problems associated with growing concentrations of poor people, especially crime and poor schools, drive households to move further and further out into the suburbs. This creates inefficient land use patterns and requires the building of massive new infrastructure at the same time that central city and inner-ring suburban infrastructure is being abandoned. It also exacerbates traffic congestion, pollution, the time spent traveling from home to work, and the social and family consequences of long-distance commuting. Another negative externality of economic segregation is school performance. According to a recent study of St. Louis area public schools, two-thirds of the variation of test scores on the Missouri Assessment Program (MAP) can be explained by the percentage of students on subsidized lunches (LaFleur and Hacker, 2002). Reducing economic segregation could boost overall student achievement without spending a single additional dollar on public education (Benabou, 2000).

Third, economic segregation undermines equal opportunity: Even if addressing economic segregation did not make society more efficient, it would still be a way of achieving equal opportunity, or social equity. Far from upholding justice and morality, as many free market conservatives maintain, economic segregation violates the fundamental American value of equal opportunity. We have argued that economic segregation significantly promotes economic inequality in the United

States. The places we live not only reflect our incomes, they help to determine those incomes. Concentrated poverty not only limits people's earnings potential, it limits the quality of life that people can enjoy, whether through public services or private goods. Concentrated poverty imposes other burdens that are impossible to quantify, including exposure to crime, unhealthy environments, heightened stress, and general alienation from society.

Fourth, economic segregation damages democracy. Tocqueville said that "[a] nation may establish a system of free government, but without the spirit of municipal institutions it cannot have the spirit of liberty" (Tocqueville, 1961, p. 55). Economic segregation saps the spirit of municipal institutions. It not only severs economic and social ties between economic classes, it also severs political ties. Economic segregation short-circuits the messy but crucial process of political accommodation and compromise between economic classes. The spread-out nature of suburbs also undermines the sociability that is so directly connected to a healthy civil society. As Putnam noted, "each additional ten minutes in daily commuting time cuts involvement in community affairs by 10 percent" (Putnam, 2000, p. 213). People who cannot drive are remarkably isolated, whether in cities or suburbs, making it difficult for them to participate in community activities, union meetings, or any other form of civic engagement. Those who drive are unlikely to have the kind of chance meetings made possible by the front stoop or sidewalk. As Jane Jacobs put it, "[l]owly, unpurposeful and random as they may appear, sidewalk contacts are the small change from which a city's wealth of public life may grow" (Jacobs, 1961, p. 72).

The political consequences of economic segregation are significant. Economic segregation makes it easier to isolate people with similar economic and social backgrounds in the same legislative districts. As suburbs and cities become more economically homogeneous, and legislative districts more "safe," politics becomes more boring and predictable, driving down levels of civic engagement, including voting. The urban share of the actual electorate is smaller than the urban share of eligible voters, partly because of economic segregation (Sauerzopf and Swanstrom, 1999). The voice of cities in state legislatures and in Congress has become increasingly weaker as the number of congresspersons and state legislators from urban districts has declined more rapidly than their overall population (Wolman and Marckini, 1998). Moreover, economic segregation undermines party competition within legislative districts and especially within central cities. This results in entrenched incumbents and political machines with few incentives to mobilize new groups of voters or develop new issue appeals.

Some scholars have concluded that the evidence for the negative contextual effects of concentrated poverty – and, by extension, economic segregation – is "at best equivocal" (Jargowsky, 2002, p. 443), and therefore the justification for public policy interventions is weak (Jencks and Mayer, 1990; Galster and Zobel, 1998). But when the outcomes examined move from problematic individual behaviors to the broader issues of unequal access and cost examined here, we believe the evidence for the impact of contextual effects is overwhelming. To call for more research is simply an excuse for tolerating the status quo. Indeed, we think urban researchers have a duty to communicate to policy elites and the public the evidence about how place shapes people's lives. Americans tend to believe that each individual is captain of his or her own ship. Advances in technology have fostered the illusion that we have somehow conquered space and that where we live does not matter much anymore. Awareness of the power of place, especially the negative effects of economic segregation, has the potential to alter the agenda of American politics.[...]

Americans believe in equal opportunity. Economic segregation violates that bedrock value. We believe that where people live in relationship to jobs and other opportunities, including education, is an important cause of rising economic inequality in the present period. Moreover, place accentuates inequalities in ways that are not captured by economic statistics. Liberal democracies can tolerate a great deal of economic inequality, but they cannot tolerate the combining of economic, political, and social inequalities into a vicious circle of rising inequality. This is exactly what we believe is happening in American metropolitan areas.

A "secession of the successful," as Robert Reich put it, threatens a central pillar of American democracy: the belief that we are all basically in the same boat (Reich, 1992). In a metropolitan landscape characterized by economic segregation and sprawl, a rising tide does *not* lift all boats. In what is arguably the most prosperous economy ever on the face of the earth, many places (and the people who live in them) are being left behind. Not only are places becoming economically isolated from the mainstream; they are becoming politically cut off as well. The flight to the suburban fringe does not just sever social relations; it also severs political relations. Never before have economic classes sorted themselves into separate governments the way they have in the United States today. The result is a bland politics at the local level that short-circuits the normal processes of political conflict and compromise and undermines civic participation in both cities and suburbs. Stereotypes and mistrust thrive in such an environment, depleting precious stores of social trust that are necessary for democracy to function effectively. The revival of American democracy requires us to address these matters. We all have a stake in this.

References

Allen, K., and Kirby, M. 2000. *Why Cities Matter to Welfare Reform*. Available at www.brook.edu/es/urban/welfarecaseloads/2000report.htm.

Benabou, R. 2000. "Workings of a City: Location, Education, and Production," in M. Sattinger, ed., *Income Distribution: Volume II, Sources of Differences*. Cheltenham, UK: Elgar.

Bingham, R. D., and Zhang, Z. 1997. "Poverty and Economic Morphology of Ohio Central-City Neighborhoods," *Urban Affairs Review*, 32(6), 766–96.

Bish, R., and Warren, R. 1972. "Scale and Monopoly Problems in Urban Government Services," *Urban Affairs Quarterly*, 8, September.

Blakely, E. J., and Snyder, M. G. 1997. *Fortress America: Gated Communities in the United States*. Washington, DC: Brookings Institution Press.

Briggs, X. S. 1998. "Brown Kids in White Suburbs: Housing Mobility and the Many Faces of Social Capital," *Housing Policy Debate*, 9(1), 177–221.

Caskey, J. P. 1994. *Fringe Banking: Check-Cashing Outlets, Pawnshops, and the Poor*. New York: Russell Sage Foundation.

Chernick, H., and Reschovsky, A. 2000. "The Long Run Fiscal Health of Central Cities," *Chicago Policy Review*, 4(1), 1–23.

Dreier, P., Mollenkopf, J., and Swanstrom, T. 2001. *Place Matters: Metropolitics for the Twenty-first Century*. Lawrence, KS: University Press of Kansas.

Fisher, M., and Weber, B. A. 2002. *The Importance of Place in Welfare Reform: Common Challenges for Central Cities and Remote-Rural Areas*. Washington, DC: Brookings Institution.

Galster, G., and Zobel, A. 1998. "Will Dispersed Housing Programmes Reduce Social Problems in the US," *Housing Studies*, 13(5), 605–22.

Garreau, J. 1991. *Edge City*. New York: Doubleday.

Goering, J., Kraft, J., Feins, J., McInnis, D., Holin, M. J., and Elhassan, H. 1999. *Moving to Opportunity for Fair Housing Demonstration Program: Current Status and Initial Findings*. Washington, DC: US Department of Housing and Urban Development.

Granovetter, M. 1985. "Economic Action and Social Structure: The Problem of Embeddedness," *American Journal of Sociology*, 91, 481–510.

Hill, E., and Nowack, J. 2000. "Nothing Left to Lose," *Brookings Review*, 18(3), 22–6.

Hill, R. C. 1990. "Federalism and Urban Policy," in T. R. Swartz and J. E. Peck, eds., *The Changing Face of Fiscal Federalism*, pp. 33–5. Armonk, NY: M. E. Sharpe.

Husock, H. 1991. "Mocking the Middle Class: The Perverse Effects of Housing Subsidies," *Heritage Foundation Policy Review*, Spring, 96–101.

Ihlanfeldt, K. R. 1997. "Information on the Spatial Distribution of Job Opportunities in Metropolitan Areas," *Journal of Urban Economics*, 41, 218–42.

Jacobs, J. 1961. *The Death and Life of Great American Cities*. New York: Random House.

Jargowsky, P. A. 2002. "Review of *Place Matters: Metropolitics for the Twenty-first Century*," *Urban Affairs Review*, 37(3), 442–4.

Jencks, C., and Mayer, S. 1990. "The Social Consequences of Growing Up in a Poor Neighborhood," in L. E. Lynn and M. G. G. McGeary, eds., *Inner-city Poverty in the United States*. Washington, DC: National Academy Press.

Jones, A., and Weinberg, D. *The Changing Shape of the Nation's Income Distribution, 1947–1998*. Available at http://www.census.gov/prod/2000pubs/p60-204.pdf.

Judd, D., and Swanstrom, T. 2002. *City Politics: Private Power and Public Policy*, 3rd ed. New York: Longman.

Kain, J. F. 1968. "Housing Segregation, Negro Employment, and Metropolitan Decentralization," *Quarterly Journal of Economics*, 82(2), 175–97.

Kasarda, J. D. 1983. "Entry-Level Jobs, Mobility, and Urban Minority Unemployment," *Urban Affairs Quarterly*, 19, 21–40.

Kasarda, J. D. 1985. "Urban Change and Minority Opportunities," in P. E. Peterson, ed., *The New Urban Reality*. Washington, DC: Brookings Institution.

Kasarda, J. D. 1989. "Urban Industrial Transition and the Underclass," *Annals, AAPSS*, 501, 26–47.

Kasarda, J. D. 1995. "Industrial Restructuring and the Changing Location of Jobs," in R. Farley, ed., *The State of The Union: America in the 1980s, Volume 1, Economic Trends*, pp. 215–67. New York: Russell Sage Foundation.

Kincaid, J. 1999. "De Facto Devolution and Urban Funding: The Priority of Persons Over Places," *Journal of Urban Affairs*, (21)2, 135–67.

LaFleur, J., and Hacker, H. K. 2002. "Analysis of Income Allows Fair Comparisons Between Schools," *St. Louis Post-Dispatch*, March 14.

Lang, R. 2000. *Office Sprawl: The Evolving Geography of Business*. Washington, DC: Brookings Institution, Center for Urban and Metropolitan Policy.

Leonard, P., and Kennedy, M. 2002. *What Cities Need from Welfare Reform Reauthorization*. Washington, DC: Brookings Institution.

Massey, D. S. 1996. "The Age of Extremes: Concentrated Affluence and Poverty in the Twenty-first Century," *Demography*, (33)4, 395–412.

Mishel, L., Bernstein, J., and Schmitt, J. 2001. *The State of Working America 2000–01*. Ithaca, NY: Cornell University Press.

Munnell, A. H., Tootel, G. M. B., Browne, L. E., and McEneaney, J. 1996. "Mortgage Lending in Boston: Interpreting HMDA Data," *American Economic Review*, 86(1), 25–53.

New York State Education Department. 1999. Statistical Profiles of New York State Schools. http://www.emsc.nysed.gov/irts/ch655_99/D660405.html

Orfield, M. 2002. *American Metropolitics: The New Suburban Reality*. Washington, DC: Brookings Institution Press.

Oxley, H., Dang, T., and Antolin, P. 1999. "Poverty Dynamics in Six OECD Countries." Paper presented at the European Economic Association Annual Congress, September.

Pastor, M., Dreier, P., Grigsby, E. J., and Lopez-Garza, M. 2000. *Regions that Work: How Cities and Suburbs Can Get Together*. Minneapolis, MN: University of Minnesota Press.

Putnam, R. D. 2000. *Bowling Alone: The Collapse and Revival of American Community*. New York: Simon and Schuster.

Reich, R. B. 1992. *The Work of Nations*. New York: Random House.

Rockwell, L. H. 1994. "The Ghost of Gautreaux," *National Review* March, 7, 57–9.

Rubinowitz, L. S., and Rosenbaum, J. E. 2000. *Crossing the Class and Color Lines: From Public Housing to White Suburbia*. Chicago, IL: University of Chicago Press.

Sauerzopf, R., and Swanstrom, T. 1999. "The Urban Electorate in Presidential Elections, 1920–1996," *Urban Affairs Review*, 35(1), 72–91.

Sen, A. 1992. *Inequality Reexamined*. Cambridge, MA: Harvard University Press.

Squires, G., and O'Connor, S. 2001. *Color and Money*. Albany, NY: State University of New York Press.

Stack, C. B. 1974. *All Our Kin: Strategies for Survival in a Black Community*. New York: Harper and Row.

Susser, I. 1982. *Norman Street: Poverty and Politics in an Urban Neighborhood*. New York: Oxford University Press.

Thompson, M. A. 1997. "The Import of Spatial Mismatch on Female Labor Force Participation," *Economic Development Quarterly*, 11(2), 138–45.

Tocqueville, A. 1961. *Democracy in America*, Vol. I. New York: Schocken Books.

Traub, J. 2000. "What No School Can Do," *New York Times Magazine*, January 16.

Turner, M. A., Popkin, S., and Cunningham, M. 2000. *Section 8 Mobility & Neighborhood Health*. Washington, DC: Urban Institute. US Department of Housing and Urban Development.

Turque, B. 1992. "Where the Food Isn't," *Newsweek*, February, 24, 36–7.

US Bureau of the Census. 2000. *Statistical Abstract of the United States*. Washington, DC: Government Printing Office.

US Department of Housing and Urban Development. 2000. *The State of the Cities 2000: Megaforces Shaping the Future of the Nation's Cities*. Washington, DC: US Department of Housing and Urban Development.

US General Accounting Office. 1994. *Elementary School Children. Many Change Schools Frequently, Harming Their Education*. GAO/HEHS 94–45. Washington, DC: US General Accounting Office.

Warren, R. 1964. "A Municipal Services Market Model of Metropolitan Organization," *Journal of the American Institute of Planners*, 30, 193–204.

Wilson, W. J. 1987. *The Truly Disadvantaged: The Inner City, the Underclass, and Public Policy*. Chicago, IL: University of Chicago Press.

Wilson, W. J. 1996. *When Work Disappears: The World of the New Urban Poor*. New York: Knopf.

Wong, Kenneth B. 1999. *Funding Public Schools: Politics and Policies*. Lawrence, KS: University of Kansas Press.

20 The Challenge of Urban Sprawl

Thad Williamson, David Imbroscio, and Gar Alperovitz

The growth of suburbs has been one of the most important features of cities since the 1950s. Early studies documented the negative effects of suburbanization on central cities, such as declining jobs, dwindling tax bases, increasingly expensive services, property abandonment, and the loss of the middle class. More recently, studies have shown that continued growth of the suburbs may create problems for suburban communities themselves.

Thad Williamson, David Imbroscio, and Gar Alperovitz show that unplanned suburban growth ("sprawl") negatively affects the quality of life, hurts the environment, wastes money and land, and hurts small businesses. They review a number of policy initiatives to discourage future sprawl and to address the economic, social, and environmental costs of existing sprawl.

The third aspect of the triple threat to community in the United States consists of the complex of issues pertaining to spatial development and land use, usually connoted by the term *sprawl*. [The two aspects discussed previously are globalization and the mobility of capital. – Ed.] Sprawl refers both to the fact of continuing outward development on the perimeters of metropolitan areas and to the specific form such development has taken, namely, construction of freeways, strip malls, and other car-centered uses of space. A recent Brookings Institution analysis of data from the United States Department of Agriculture's National Resources Inventory found that between 1982 and 1997 the rate of outward land expansion outpaced population increases in 264 of the 281 metropolitan areas they examined.

This trend encompassed both urban areas that grew and cities that declined in population. The population of the Pittsburgh metropolitan area, for instance, declined 8 percent, but its land area, as measured by the National Resource Inventory, increased by some 43 percent. In Atlanta, urbanized land increased by 82 percent, even though the area's population increased by only 61 percent – and even though population in the city of Atlanta itself has actually declined since 1980.[1] Nationwide, urbanized land increased by some 47 percent between 1982 and 1997, while population grew only 17 percent. Consequently, average urban density declined by over 20 percent in just fifteen years.[2] In short, with the exception of those few cities that are hemmed in by physical geographical boundaries, the nation's metropolitan areas have become less dense and more spread out in recent decades.

The explosive growth of suburbia in the United States – the "crabgrass frontier," as historian Kenneth Jackson evocatively calls it – is generally dated from the postwar construction boom. As veterans returned from the European and Pacific fronts, politicians accommodated the huge pent-up demand for modestly priced, reasonable-quality housing by subsidizing the construction of new single-family suburban homes. Specific mechanisms included tax deductions for home mortgages and the public construction of roads connecting urban centers with outlying communities (a construction boom that culminated in the late 1950s with the creation of the interstate highway system). At the same time, private developers, following in the footsteps of the first Levittowns, promoted single-family suburban living as the new ideal of American life. They energetically marketed the new suburb (ironically) as a site of strong community cohesion combined with the amenities associated with escape from the city: less crowding, less crime, less filth. (Just under the surface of this marketing effort was the suggestion that suburbs would have fewer racial and ethnic minorities and poor people.) In time, suburban living became synonymous first with privacy, and then with privatism and disregard for public space and public goods – with the exception of the road system, and, often, public schools. Feminist critics such as Betty Friedan noted the isolation of women in suburbia and the community-debilitating consequences of rigid separations between home, work, and market, while others pointed to the characteristic alienation and occasional antisocial behavior of suburban youth.[3]

Historians and policy analysts generally agree that some degree of suburbanization was probably a reasonable response to problems of overcrowding and housing shortages in central cities in midcentury America. In 1950, as today, the most compelling and most frequently cited argument on behalf of outward expansion from cities was the need to provide additional decent, affordable housing. But the suburban housing boom had almost immediate negative consequences for central cities and their remaining residents: As more affluent citizens left, central city tax bases weakened, even as the poorer residents left behind became more isolated. Today, as road construction and further outward development continue to be practiced as the "solution" to the problem of building desirable, affordable housing in metropolitan regions, a wide range of observers have come to recognize that uncontained sprawl also has a negative impact on the quality of life in the suburbs themselves.

Unplanned Outward Development versus Planned Decentralization

The specific phenomenon of suburban sprawl in the second half of the twentieth century needs to be carefully distinguished from the concept of slowing the growth of cities and encouraging citizens to live in smaller-scale communities. Polls have consistently shown that Americans prefer to live in relatively small communities (100,000 people or less). While there have been few academic studies of optimal city size in recent years, the best extant evidence indicates that smaller cities perform better than large cities with respect to a range of quality of life issues, including environmental quality, crime rates, and traffic congestion.[4] Recent work by Princeton political scientist J. Eric Oliver indicates that smaller cities appear to be more conducive to participation in local politics than very large cities.[5] Such findings in part reflect the damage done to existing big cities by sprawl and associated public policies (as discussed below), but they also suggest that small cities may well be – and be subjectively felt to be – preferable human habitats.

The current form of suburbanization is a distorted reflection of an important line of thinking that originated with Sir Ebenezer Howard and a handful of like-minded thinkers in Britain at the close of the nineteenth century. Howard gave birth to the idea of "garden cities," modestly sized communities organized in circular fashion around the perimeter of large metropolitan agglomerations such as London. Howard's garden city idea helped spawn the "New Towns" movement in Britain and the regional planning movement in the United States of the 1920s and 1930s.

Howard believed garden cities could be the solution to problems of urban poverty and overcrowding. Under his scheme, citizens would leave cities to move to planned new towns located several miles away from the urban core. These new towns would be explicitly designed to accommodate a mix of socioeconomic classes and would be enlivened by visible public spaces and the provision of ecological amenities. Most importantly, in Howard's scheme, land in the new towns would be community-owned, and leased to businesses and residents; as the value of land rose with population growth, the resulting revenue would be used to offset the costs of public goods (thereby also reducing taxes and housing costs). Central to Howard's vision was the notion that the several miles of space between central city and the satellite garden cities would be left undeveloped. Around each garden city, Howard proposed a huge swath of publicly owned, permanent farmland, forests, and pastures, which would demarcate the edge of the city – about 5,000 acres compared with a 1,000-acre town center. Instead of building into this belt, growth would occur only by "jumping over the farm/parklands and "establishing ... another city some little distance beyond its own zone of country."[6]

British followers of Howard succeeded in getting the government to build over two dozen new towns by 1970. None of the new towns maintained Howard's core socioeconomic institution, local community ownership of land, but observers have credited the towns with helping "[establish] what became a distinctive feature of postwar British planning: the system of towns against a backcloth of open country."[7] The new town idea also spread to the United States as well. In the 1930s, New Deal official Rexford Tugwell pushed for the construction of three new "greenbelt" towns in Maryland, Wisconsin and Ohio. In the 1960s developer James Rouse built the new town of Columbia, Maryland, as an explicit attempt to model a multiracial community. The new town experiments in both Britain and the United States enjoyed modest success in providing a relatively high quality of life compared to unplanned suburban development, but even proponents concede that the towns have generally fallen far short of Howard's lofty vision of using local community control over land as a strategy to simultaneously promote social and ecological goals.

The United States in fact never undertook explicit planning aimed at easing urban congestion in a rational manner while also preserving the livability of city centers. Instead, policy makers implemented an array of policies that helped push Americans into suburbia – with little regard either for those left behind in central cities or for the character of the new suburban communities.

The Political Construction of Suburban America

Let us look more closely at the major policy initiatives and public subsidies driving suburban expansion:

The home mortgage tax exemption. The central federal strategy to encourage home ownership, this policy allows homeowners to take a tax deduction on the interest costs of mortgages. The policy is almost untouchable politically, and most strongly benefits the wealthy. As Kenneth Jackson pointed out in 1985:

> The system works in such a way that a $20,000-a-year bank teller living in a private apartment earns no housing subsidy. But the $250,000-per-year bank president living in a $400,000 home in the suburbs has a veritable laundry list of deductions. All $38,000 in interest payments would be subtracted from income, as well as all $7,000 in property taxes. His $45,000 subtraction would save him approximately $22,500 in taxes, or almost $2,000 per month.... Thus, it happens that the average housing subsidy in an elite suburb will exceed by several times the average subsidy to a welfare family in the inner city.[8]

Importantly, as Jackson also notes, the tax subsidy to affluent Americans is so enticing that remaining in the city as a high-income renter is often economically irrational, given the tax savings forgone. The flight of high-income individuals and families into single-family suburban houses in turn has contributed to fiscal problems in American cities. The annual value of the federal mortgage interest deduction now stands at roughly $66 billion, compared to the $32 billion budget of the federal Department of Housing and Development.[9]

Federal Housing Administration (FHA) subsidies and redlining practices. The FHA is the lead federal agency in promoting home ownership and is estimated to have helped finance nearly 11 million new private homes built between 1934 and 1972.[10] FHA offers mortgage insurance, which allows buyers to purchase homes with as little as 10 percent (or even less) down. As preservationists Richard Moe and Carter Wilkie point out, FHA criteria for eligibility for mortgage insurance was substantially biased against African-American neighborhoods for decades. "A single house occupied by a black family in an urban neighborhood, even one tucked away on an inconspicuous side street, was enough for the FHA to label a predominantly white neighborhood as unfit for mortgage insurance," Moe and Wilkie note. "Areas that failed to meet the test were considered too risky and 'redlined' on confidential maps shared with bankers, whose lack of investment in those neighborhoods doomed many of them to eventual decline."[11] The resulting deterioration and decay of urban neighborhoods hastened the flight to suburbia, first by whites and later by moderate-income African-Americans. Although explicit redlining has now been substantially curtailed, much of America's current spatial development can be traced to the widespread use of such discriminatory practices in the past.[12]

Other federally sponsored institutions that support home ownership via the secondary mortgage market include the Federal National Mortgage Association (Fannie Mae), the Federal Home Loan Mortgage Corporation (Freddie Mac), and the federal Ginnie Mae agency, which guarantees mortgages. Until the 1990s, these federally sponsored institutions had no requirements regarding the spatial distribution of its mortgages, meaning they could ignore city homeowners. These institutions, combined with the Farmers Home Administration and smaller federal programs, have a total mortgage portfolio of $1.8 trillion (as of 1995) – most of which has been used to finance single-family homes in suburbs.[13]

The Housing Act of 1949/urban renewal. This act essentially gave a green light for local officials to break up established neighborhoods in favor of new development, usually involving large-scale commercial initiatives near cities' central business districts. Under this authority, Moe and Wilkie note, "city officials with power of eminent domain could seize property in areas identified as 'slums', purchase it with the help of federal funds, then sell the assembled area to a private developer for redevelopment."[14] Over $13 billion in federal money went to directly support urban renewal between 1953 and 1986. Urban renewal policies brought about the outright destruction of many urban neighborhoods and destabilized many others, causing massive dislocation and overcrowding, and replacing working communities with high-rise public housing projects. All too often, David

Rusk charges, "the federal urban renewal program created both dull, lifeless downtown areas that failed to pull suburbanites back into the city and high-poverty, high crime public housing complexes that pushed other households into the suburbs even faster."[15]

Highway construction/National Highway Trust Fund. Hand in hand with the emphasis on establishing middle America in single-family homes in the suburbs was an unprecedented boom in highway expenditures starting in the 1950s. In 1956, the National Highway Trust Fund was established to pay for ongoing highway construction, using revenues generated by taxes on cars and gasoline. US highway construction was thus supported by an autonomous source of revenues not easily touched by other political priorities – a highly unusual mechanism among advanced industrialized democracies. As Pietro Nivola points out, "With a spare-no-expense approach to highway expansions, the size of the US effort became unique. Great distances between cities or states in this country do not wholly account for the magnitude; US interstate plans called for massive expenditures, not just on transcontinental facilities, but also on urban radial and circumferential arteries designed to enhance intra-metropolitan access. These local webs of roadways have sped the dispersal of jobs and housing within metropolitan areas."[16]

Not surprisingly, the percentage of total passenger miles accounted for by public transit in America dropped from 35 percent in 1945 to less than 3 percent today. Between 1977 and 1995 nearly six times as much public funding went to highways and roads as to all forms of mass transit. While critics of Amtrak decry the subsidies needed to keep the intercity rail system in operation, much larger subsidies to highways and automobiles are largely unquestioned politically. Today some 75 percent of federal spending on surface transportation is directed toward highway related projects.[17] Only recently did the 1991 Intermodal Surface Transportation Efficiency Act and the follow-up 1998 TEA-21 legislation begin to take important steps allowing localities some flexibility in promoting mass transit alternatives using federal transportation funds. World Resource Institute economists have estimated that all levels of governments spend over $80 billion a year (1995 dollars) combined on road-related services such as highway patrols.[18]

Low fuel pricing, low taxes on cars, and tax subsidies of parking costs. Suburban growth and sprawl have been driven not only by the massive subsidization of highways but also by direct subsidies to drivers. By international standards, American taxation on gasoline has been exceedingly low: In 1996, gas taxes in the United States totaled 42 cents a gallon, compared with 84 cents in Canada, $2.31 in Great Britain, and over $3 in France, Italy, and the Netherlands.[19] Sales taxes on cars are generally much higher in Europe than in the United States – nine times higher in the Netherlands, thirty-seven times higher in Denmark.[20] American employers are allowed to provide parking as a tax-free benefit, up to $170 a month; the benefit for mass transit users totals just $65 a month.[21] (The parking provision is estimated to cost the United States Treasury over $2 billion a year.)[22]

Tax codes encouraging the discarding of buildings. Other tax laws have also contributed to the decline of cities in favor of new suburban construction and sprawl. On one hand, some observers have complained that building owners receive what is in effect a tax incentive to allow their buildings to decay. Building owners are allowed to depreciate buildings over a period of just 31.5 years. As Moe and Wilkie note, "If property owners could not deduct such losses, they would do more to preserve the value of their property – as well as the value of the surrounding locations that determine the value of their property."[23]

Conversely, other observers have argued that building owners should be taxed *less*. These writers, following the principles of Henry George, have urged a return to land-based, or "site value" taxation. James Howard Kunstler notes that

> our system of property taxes punishes anyone who puts up a decent building made of durable materials. It rewards those who let existing buildings go to hell. It favors speculators who sit on vacant or underutilized land in the hearts of our cities and towns. In doing so it creates an artificial scarcity of land on the free market, which drives up the price of land in general, and encourages ever more scattered development.[24]

Kunstler argues that ending taxation on buildings will encourage the development and preservation of high-quality buildings, while increasing taxation on urban land will discourage speculative activity. This would reduce the costs of urban land by placing more land on the market (as speculators sell) and, by ensuring that all central city land is put to productive use, help undercut pressures toward sprawl. As it is, the existing tax code provides building owners both a disincentive (in the form of building-based taxation) to construct new buildings that appreciate in value over time and an incentive (in the form of accelerated depreciation) to let existing buildings deteriorate. The combined result is increased decay and unattractiveness in center city locations.

High proportion of local property taxes as a source of local revenue. Few Americans realize that in many other advanced countries, such as the United Kingdom and France, national governmental revenues account for the majority of *local* government expenditures. In the United States, only one-third of local government expenditures are funded by federal- and state-level taxes. The reliance of local governments on tax revenues from within their own jurisdictions contributes to the competition between localities for new business investment. However, an additional dimension of the sprawl problem derives from the fact that nearly three-quarters of local taxes are property taxes. As Nivola points out: "Local dependence on property taxation can reinforce a low-density pattern of residential and commercial development. Each jurisdiction acquires an incentive to maximize the assessed valuations of its real estate in relation to the expense of providing local services. One way to defend a favorable ratio [between tax revenue generated and public services provided] is to require through zoning restrictions relatively large parcels of land for buildings."[25] In other words, in order to ensure a strong tax base, suburban localities often seek to bid up taxable land values by promoting not high-density, efficient housing arrangements but large houses and big stores – which in turn implies an auto-dependent design for local communities.

Decreases in federal aid to central cities since 1980. Bruce Katz and Joel Rogers point out that the federal share of municipal budgets declined by over two-thirds between 1980 and 1992 and now stands at less than 4 percent of city budgets. Federal shares of county budgets nationwide have declined even faster, by over 75 percent, since 1980. These cuts in federal aid have taken place at the same time that per capita costs of municipal services have increased. Many state governments also have withdrawn aid for cities. This means local taxes must go up (or city services must be cut back). As Katz and Rogers observe, "The effect of these policies and the resulting income and fiscal dynamics is straightforward. They lower the costs to individuals and firms of living and working outside or on the outer fringes of metropolitan areas, and increase the costs of living and working in the core."[26]

This list of public policies that have contributed to suburbanization and sprawl is hardly exhaustive. It suffices, however, to demonstrate that current spatial patterns in US metropolitan areas are to a substantial degree the result both of political choices and of the peculiar structure of governance in the United States, and not only a result of market processes. To be sure, as Robert Beauregard of New School University has recently argued in detail, the decisions of private economic actors, as well as the overall decline of manufacturing, also played a role in the postwar decline of American cities.[27] In particular, corporate decisions to relocate production in a "cheaper" location have imposed large costs on the cities left behind and have compelled citizens to leave town in search of better economic prospects elsewhere. We agree with Beauregard that it is misleading to blame only specific public policy decisions for damage to cities while ignoring the larger pattern of private-sector disinvestment in older industrial centers – but this does not make reevaluating those policies any less important. Indeed, [we] suggest a two-pronged policy response to urban decay and instability: on one hand, changing public policies (such as the ones noted above) that have explicitly damaged central cities and encouraged sprawl, and on the other hand, developing a strategy to contain and ultimately alter the patterns of private sector disinvestment in cities that characterized the second half of the twentieth century.

Evaluating Urban Sprawl

Sprawl, then, is a product of both public policy and private market choices. But were these the right choices? What exactly is wrong with sprawl, especially from the standpoint of a concern with community economic stability (in both cities and suburbs)? Sprawl has been commonly critiqued on six distinct grounds:

(1) quality-of-life issues, (2) environmental issues, (3) the waste of public resources via increased infrastructure costs, (4) the effect of sprawl upon cities and their residents, (5) the use of new land to facilitate development of giant corporate-owned superstores, and finally (6) the political consequences of suburbanization. We are concerned about all six dimensions of the sprawl problem, each of which is either directly or indirectly connected to prospects for community economic stability and strengthening local democracy.

Quality of life and civic engagement

When sprawl burst onto the national scene as a potent political issue in 1998, it was largely at the behest of suburban residents themselves. Runaway growth, many suburban residents said, was destroying their quality of life – eating up scenic landscapes, crowding schools, worsening traffic (and lengthening their commutes), and raising taxes.[28] Many rural residents, also, feared losing farmland and rural lifestyles to sprawling development.[29] Loss of open space, and the loss of the very sense of isolation and quiet that many suburban residents sought when first moving to the outskirts, is an obvious consequence of sprawl. Moreover, the low-density development encourages automobile dependence – and in fact the number of miles driven per year has doubled since 1970, with annual growth of over 4 percent a year, a rate far higher than annual population growth over the same time span. Consequently, congestion has increased markedly and travel times have lengthened. The average speed of vehicles on the Washington, DC-area Beltway fell, for instance, from 47 to 23 miles per hour over the course of the 1980s.[30] Since low-density areas are not able to support cost-efficient mass transit options such as buses, cars are often the only way for many suburban residents to get around. Hence, there is literally no escaping heavy traffic and the headaches, lost time, and increased number of accidents it involves.

Such tangible negative effects of sprawl may in time be seen as outweighing the advantages of suburban amenities such as (relatively) more open space, larger and cheaper houses, and the like. From our perspective, an even more important consideration involves the degree to which sprawl also diminishes the quality of the nation's *civic* life. Low-density development discourages informal interactions between residents, and many planners believe that such development also discourages residents from joining civic organizations.[31] A recent study by Jack Nasar and David Julian, for instance, found that mixed-use neighborhoods generated stronger feelings of community attachment among residents than single-use neighborhoods.[32] Data collected by Robert Putnam point strongly to a negative relationship between sprawl and civic engagement: "In round numbers," Putnam reports, "the evidence suggests that *each additional ten minutes in daily commuting time cuts involvement in community affairs by 10 percent* – fewer public meetings attended, fewer committees chaired, fewer petitions signed, fewer church services attended, less volunteering, and so on." This finding, added to the fact that large places in general (such as metropolitan areas) are in general less conducive to community life than smaller towns, leads Putnam to conclude that "the residents of large metropolitan areas incur a 'sprawl civic penalty' of roughly 20 percent on most measures of community involvement. More and more of us have come to incur this penalty [by moving to suburbs] over the last thirty years."[33] Finally, it has been widely observed that European cities, with their more compact form of organization, appear to have more vibrant public spaces and a stronger sense of place than comparably sized American metropolitan areas.[34]

The quest for the suburban version of the American dream – including owning a single-family home in a good neighborhood with good schools – is also closely associated with the search for status within American society and the use of consumption as a marker for social status. The corresponding political and cultural ethos of prioritizing the search for one's private dream of suburban comfort over provision of public goods and engagement in public affairs is both symptom and cause of the often hollow practice of local-level democratic governance today.[35] Much more evidence needs to be accumulated to document fully the impact of different kinds of spatial design upon civic life and civic participation. But there is already good reason to believe that sprawl, by undermining central cities (and, increasingly, older suburbs as well), negatively impacts not only community economic stability per se but also the quality of community daily life – and that more-compact, less car-centered spatial designs would probably be more compatible with a strong civic community.

Environmental concerns

It is little surprise that environmental groups such as the Sierra Club have taken the lead in the national antisprawl movement. Sprawl is synonymous with the consumption of open land, including both farmland and forest habitats, as well as with the greenhouse gas emissions and wasted fuel associated with automobile use and traffic congestion.

There are scores of studies of the environmental consequences of sprawl-like development, many of which have been usefully collected in the Natural Resources Defense Council publication *Once There Were Greenfields*. Space permits only a general overview of the picture painted by the drumbeat of scholarly research over the past decade.

Outward development obviously consumes land – lots of land. According to the American Farmland Trust, between 1982 and 1992 alone, over 4.2 million acres of top-quality farmland – and a total of over 13.8 million acres of agricultural land – were lost to development.[36] Land consumption also impacts the overall ecosystem in ways that damage existing wildlife and reduce biological diversity; as existing wildlife habitats are fragmented, they become less capable of supporting a wide variety of species. The phenomenon is especially true of wetlands, which lost a net 117,000 acres between 1985 and 1995, with development responsible for roughly one-fifth of the decline.[37]

Next, there is the environmental impact of suburban driving patterns. A recent HUD report notes that "the average suburban household drives approximately 30 percent more annually than its central city counterpart. That is about 3,300 more miles, which translates to an additional $753 per year per household in transportation costs. Suburban residents spend 110 more hours behind the wheel each year than their urban counterparts – the equivalent of almost 3 full weeks of work."[38] Although many forms of urban air pollution have eased in the past two decades, cars are still a major source of air pollutants, responsible for 62 percent of carbon monoxide releases, as well as 26 percent of volatile organic compound releases and 32 percent of nitrogen oxide releases – two major ingredients in the generation of health-threatening ground-level ozone. A 1998 EPA study estimated that traffic congestion alone generates at least $20 billion a year in health-related costs.[39] While cars have become substantially cleaner in many respects, that gain has been largely offset by the increase in miles driven. Indeed, the trend in Americans' use of cars is negative, not positive – the number of Americans who drive solo to work increased from 64 percent in 1980 to 73 percent in 1990.[40] Moreover, the vehicles now on the road are bigger than ever. Trucks, minivans, and sport-utility vehicles, which are not held to the same fuel efficiency requirements as cars, now account for nearly half of family automobile sales – and, as the NRDC notes, "the 10 most fuel-efficient vehicles in the country today account for only 0.7 percent of all vehicle sales."[41]

A problem potentially even more serious than air pollution is the emission of greenhouse gases by motor vehicles. Mobile sources (i.e., vehicles) now account for 32 percent of all greenhouse gas releases in the United States. Carbon emissions are projected to continue to increase at a rate of 1 percent a year if current habits are maintained, with transportation's share in the total increasing relative to other sources. Simply put, community spatial designs that maximize the amount of driving and gas consumption required to meet the tasks of daily life appear to be fundamentally incompatible with the need to reduce greenhouse emissions in order to forestall or mitigate the potentially disastrous effects of global climate change.[42]

Finally, sprawl increases runoff water pollution. Whereas natural habitats absorb rainfall easily, with runoff into water bodies commonly taking place at a slow, easily absorbable pace, in built-up areas water collects on man-made surfaces such as rooftops and pavements, eventually passing into water sources at higher speeds and in higher quantity. Such runoff causes erosion, generates increased water pollution, and damages underlying water tables. It is estimated that 40 percent of the nation's water bodies are now being damaged by runoff pollution. As sprawl increases the amount of paved area, it contributes more and more to damaging forms of water runoff. Particularly damaging are huge parking lots constructed to service superstores on the suburban fringe. It is little surprise, then, that sprawl-like development has been identified as a causal factor in damage to a number of major water bodies, including perhaps most prominently Chesapeake Bay, along the coast of Virginia, Delaware, and Maryland.[43]

Infrastructure costs associated with sprawl

Quality of community and civic life and environmental well-being have potentially important long-term effects on communities' economic prospects. There are also, however, very direct and immediate costs of sprawl – especially the cost of infrastructure. It is well established that providing roads, water lines, sewers, electric grids, schools, hospitals, police and fire services, and the like to serve low-density development is, in general, more costly than providing such infrastructure to high-density developments. It is also obvious that it is wasteful to allow existing city infrastructure to decay while simultaneously building new developments requiring entirely new infrastructure. Yet that is exactly what sprawl entails. Minnesota legislator and respected scholar Myron Orfield provides but one illustration of an all-too-common (and understudied) phenomenon: "By 1990, 131,488 acres – nearly one-quarter of [the Twin Cities urban areas served by sewers] – remained undeveloped. Yet between 1987 and 1991 at the request of cities and developers the Metropolitan Council provided sewer access for another 18,000 acres, instead of redirecting new growth into areas with adequate sewer capacity."[44]

A number of empirical studies have been conducted that attempt to estimate the infrastructure and fiscal costs of sprawl-driven development. A 1989 study by James Frank, for instance, compared the public capital costs (including streets, utilities, and schools) associated with different densities of development. Total public capital costs per dwelling unit for a suburban single-family home on four acres (a very large lot) amounted to over $77,000 per unit in 1987 dollars. In the more typical single-family-house neighborhood (three homes per acre), costs per unit came to roughly $31,000. As density increased, costs got progressively lower, including $17,000 per unit for apartment buildings with fifteen dwellings per acre and less than $8,000 per unit for high-rise apartments with 30 dwellings per acre.[45]

Another study, by James Duncan and Associates, based on a detailed study of eight communities in Florida, also focused on the public capital costs associated with different forms of development. Duncan calculated the cost to the public per dwelling unit for providing the following services: roads, education, wastewater, potable water, solid-waste disposal, law enforcement, fire protection, and parks. Two communities with scattered development patterns (i.e., low-density and leapfrog) had costs (in 1998 dollars) of $20,158 and $31,534 per dwelling, respectively. In contrast, the downtown area, featuring compact development, had costs of just $12,177 per unit, and two contiguous developments (moderate-density and built contiguously with existing developments) had costs of only $12,855 and $16,706, respectively.[46]

A third study led by Robert Burchell used computer models to project the future costs to the public associated with different types of development patterns in New Jersey. One development pattern built up central-city areas and increased density rates; the other continued sprawl-like development (low-density and scattered). Public capital costs (roads, utilities, and schools) associated with the sprawl-like development were estimated to total $15.64 billion (1990 dollars) over a twenty-year period, compared to costs of $14.21 billion for compact development. As F. Kaid Benfield, Matthew Raimi, and Donald Chen of the Natural Resources De-fense Council observe, if the state had chosen to develop entirely along a compact spatial model starting in 1990, the savings in capital costs would have amounted to $1.79 billion (1998 dollars) over the twenty-year period from 1990 to 2010.[47]

Important qualifications to these studies of the infrastructure costs associated with sprawl have been offered by other researchers, most notably Harvard scholars Alan Altshuler and José Gómez-Ibáñez. Altshuler and Gómez-Ibáñez point out that early studies of sprawl such as the Real Estate Research Corpor-ation's 1973 publication *The Costs of Sprawl* showing higher infrastructure costs for suburban housing did not take into account the fact that suburban housing is often of higher quality and provides more space than urban housing. These scholars also point out that high initial infrastructure costs associated with sprawl may decline if infill development occurs, that retrofitting older areas to accommo-date higher density patterns may be more expensive than suburban developments on vacant land, and that in some cases suburban developments can achieve cost-saving economies of scale.

Even so, Altshuler and Gómez-Ibáñez conservatively allow that sprawl develop-ments typically will be about 5 to 10 percent more expensive than well-planned, more compact developments.[48] Moreover, the most recent wave of research by Burchell and other scholars takes account of Altshuler and Gómez-Ibáñez's criti-cisms of earlier studies and continues to find that compact living patterns are cheaper.[49] Finally, no one disputes that it is almost always wasteful to abandon already-built infrastructure in central cities and inner suburbs at the same time that entirely new developments on metropolitan perimeters are being built.

Central-city decline and the costs of greenfield development

Advocates of outward growth from central cities often cite the need to provide lower-cost housing as a prime justification for sprawl-like development. But when more affluent residents leave cities (and no one replaces them), they also take their property tax payments with them – thus helping push cities into a fiscal crunch that damages their ability to provide even basic government services. A vicious circle is thus often triggered by suburban flight: As residents leave and the tax base declines, it becomes more difficult to pay for social services to city residents. New small businesses expand to – or even relocate to – suburbia in order to directly serve the affluent populace there, making it more difficult for cities to increase their tax base or provide new jobs through business growth. And as the quality of services such as pothole fixing, police and fire, and (perhaps above all) public schools declines in cities, the incentive to move (for both rich and poor) increases. Finally, as jobs move to the suburbs, more inner-city residents, lacking adequate access to transportation and social networks to take advantage of suburban employment opportunities, fall into long-term unemployment, with devastating personal and social consequences.[50] As we have seen, in some cases the destruction of existing center-city neighborhoods has been quite deliberate, as planners razed perceived ghetto areas under the rubric of "urban renewal," substituting higher-income neighborhoods or commercial development in their place. On occasion, neighborhoods were destroyed to provide the very highways that would carry new residents of suburbia back and forth from city jobs to their new, more spacious homes. The move to suburbia also damages existing social networks within the cities and can lead to a widened income gap between rich and poor within cities when middle-class residents move to the suburbs in force – which in turn heightens social tension.[51]

Many defenders of sprawl-style suburbanization point to the tangible private benefits of outward development, holding that the benefits that accrue to business and individuals outweigh these negative social and public costs. However, the most comprehensive and highly detailed cost-benefit analysis to date of the comparative costs of firm location in greenfields (i.e., undeveloped areas on the suburban fringe) versus firm location in cities tells a different story. The recent landmark study *When Corporations Leave Town*, conducted by Joseph Persky and Wim Wiewel of the University of Illinois at Chicago, demonstrates that the *public* and social *costs* of sprawl-like development are roughly equivalent to the *private benefits* created. In other words, sprawl is a redistributive measure, imposing costs on the public and central-city residents while conferring benefits on suburban firms and residents. [. . .]

Superstores versus local business

A fifth dimension of the sprawl problem, nor captured by cost-benefit analyses of the kind utilized by Persky and Wiewel or in studies of the infrastructure costs of different forms of development, is the extent to which sprawl-like development has influenced what *kinds* of firms get access to a critical mass of customers and enjoy favorable prospects of success. Specifically, when residents move to the suburbs from central cities, locally owned city businesses are often not well positioned to follow their customer base. Firms with a greater capacity to adjust to changing geographic patterns gain an advantage over firms reliant on a stable, neighborhood-oriented customer base. In practice, this means that large chains – Wal-Mart, fast-food operators, Circuit City, and the long list of ubiquitous corporate chains – have thrived in strip malls, exurbs, and big box-style superstores located on the edge of town. Suburban shopping centers increased from just 100 in 1950 to 3,000 in 1960 and nearly 40,000 by 1992.[52] As Stacy Mitchell of the Institute for Local Self-Reliance notes, Borders Books and Barnes and Noble alone now account for 25 percent of all book sales, while independent booksellers have seen their market share fall from 58 percent in 1972 to 17 percent (and dropping) as of 1997. Home Depot and Lowe's together control almost 25 percent of the hardware market. Blockbuster Video has 30 percent of the video rental market. Needless to say, locally-owned retailers have not fared as well. Independent office product stores have seen their market share decline from 20 to 4 percent since the mid-1980s, and an estimated 1,000 community pharmacies close annually.[53]

In fact, in a few cases, most spectacularly that of Wal-Mart, chains have deliberately tried to kill off local businesses through predatory pricing, often with the help of state and local subsidies (such as assistance in providing roads and other infrastructure needed to bring large waves of consumers to just-outside-the-city-limits superstores). Developers of new malls and shopping centers often gravitate toward nationally known chains in extending lease offers as a strategy for luring customers as soon as possible. Even in the best-case scenario, where such malls do make homes for local, nonchain businesses, they are commonly anchored by corporate chain department stores. Meanwhile, vibrant downtowns consisting of local businesses owned by local people have become increasingly rare.

What exactly is wrong with chain store development, as compared to locally owned businesses? Certainly the American strip-mall-with-parking-lot scene is often a painful eyesore, an aesthetic nightmare. Moreover, in line with a long tradition of American thought, we believe that the sense of independence and liberty associated with individual or family entrepreneurship is an important value. But local entrepreneurship also has a tangible advantage over the typical corporate chain from the point of view of community economic stability: They are more likely to create purchasing linkages with other local firms, which in turn expands a community's economic multiplier as money gets respent many times in the local economy. Similarly, their profits are not siphoned off to a faraway corporate headquarters, but instead are more likely to be reinvested in the community.[54]

The most detailed studies to date of how superstores affect local communities have been carried out by Kenneth Stone of Iowa State University, who for over a decade has continuously tracked the impact of Wal-Mart on rural communities in Iowa. In a 1997 study, Stone compared thirty-four towns with a Wal-Mart in place for ten years or more with fifteen non-Wal-Mart towns. He found that in a context of overall rural decline, Wal-Mart captured a rapidly increasing share of the shrinking pie – causing damage to independent retailers in Wal-Mart towns. They hurt non-Wal-Mart towns even more by drawing customers away. Overall sales declined by 17 percent in Iowa towns with population between 2,500 and 5,000 in the period between 1983 and 1996, nearly 30 percent for towns with between 1,000 and 2,500 residents, and over 40 percent in towns with fewer than 1,000 people. Shopping at department stores (i.e., Wal-Marts) increased by 42 percent over the same period, whereas drugstores, variety stores, and stores selling automotive parts, groceries, women's apparel, lawn and garden items, hardware, shoes, and men's and boys' wear all suffered significant declines (25 percent or more for all save auto parts and grocery stores) during those years.[55]

These are alarming findings. As Stone concludes, there are strong reasons for seeking to constrict, not accelerate, the growth of superstores – whether the small businesses damaged by the new store are rural or urban. Sadly, it is the fact of widespread economic insecurity that makes low-end retail outlets – whose rise has been predicated not only on sophisticated distribution systems but also on the use of market power to squeeze suppliers – so attractive to many working-class and poor shoppers anxious to save as much money as possible. But the rise of Wal-Mart-type retail only further undercuts the economic security of small towns and their residents. Nor does Wal-Mart compensate for this negative impact by providing good jobs: The retailer considers a 28-hour week full time, virtually all non-management employees earn less than $10 an hour, and there are few benefits (and no unions).[56]

The political consequences of sprawl

Finally, we call attention to the political culture sprawl has helped generate: namely, a city-suburb divide that has weakened public support for efforts to support community development or to provide other forms of assistance to urban areas. As suburbs grow and central cities lose population, the relative political power of city interests in electoral and legislative politics erodes; presidential and gubernatorial candidates court suburban voters, while urban delegations in both national and state legislatures shrink. More importantly, the creation of largely white suburbs, spatially segregated from lower-class minority groups remaining in central cities, has had an inestimable impact on American political culture and the assumptions of ordinary political debate.[57] It has allowed politicians to define suburban life as mainstream America and central-city residents as a "problem," or what some sociologists call "the other." Lost is the idea that all are in it together. Noted "new urbanist" practitioners Andres Duany, Elizabeth Plater-Zyberk, and Jeff Speck make the point this way:

> A child growing up in [a] homogenous environment is less likely to develop a sense of empathy for people from other walks of life and is ill prepared to live in a diverse society. The *other* becomes alien to the child's experience, witnessed only through the sensationalized eye of the television. The more homogenous and "safe" the environ-

ment, the less understanding there is of all that is different, and the less concern for the world beyond the subdivision walls.[58]

Recent research by Juliet Gainsborough of the University of Miami has also demonstrated that suburban residence has a powerful conservative influence on both voters and political attitudes – even *after* controlling for race, gender, age, income, homeownership status, and other standard variables used to predict political orientation. Gainsborough's analysis of National Election Study data found that between 1988 and 1992, living in the suburbs made voters substantially more likely to vote for a Republican congressional or presidential candidate, an effect that cannot be explained by demographic factors. In an even more interesting finding, Gainsborough also found that suburbanites are less likely than others to support aid for cities, government spending, and initiatives to help African-Americans, or to have a sympathetic attitude toward welfare recipients – even *after* controlling for the respondents' party identification as well as other demographic variables. In short, living in the suburbs produces more conservative social attitudes even among self-identified Democrats. Gainsborough's analysis also shows that the strength of this association between suburban residence and conservative social attitudes has intensified in the past two decades – precisely as suburbs have continued to claim a larger share of the nation's population.[59]

We rarely face this issue directly. The problem is not simply that metropolitan areas find it difficult to tax suburbs to pay for the central city – or even to tax commuters enough to pay for the costs of the public goods they themselves consume. It is that our policies systematically create a political-economic reality where inequalities favoring predominantly white suburbs become the rule rather than the exception.[60]

The Turning of the Tide?

For years, environmental activists, preservationists, and urban planners who decried sprawl were lonely voices in the political wilderness. Indeed, it was thought all but impossible to do much about the problem in real political terms. In the late 1990s, however – in a manner suggestive of what we believe might be possible with a number of other issues taken up in this volume – a very substantial grouping of state-level politicians "suddenly" caught wind of the widespread public discontent with suburban sprawl, and began to incorporate concerns about sprawl in their political agendas.

Obviously, something quite powerful had already been quietly building below the radar of the mass media. In November 1998, nearly two hundred state and local ballot initiatives on curbing sprawl won approval, as voters set aside more than $7 billion to purchase land or development rights for preservation.[61] In New Jersey, for example – the only state to be technically defined in its entirety as a metropolitan area,[62] and a state that loses 10,000 acres a year to development – a two-thirds majority of voters approved Republican Governor Christine Todd Whitman's proposal to invest $1 billion over a decade to protect one million acres of undeveloped land, half the state's total.[63] Similarly, Florida voters made permanent the state's land conservation bonding authority – which will likely lead to $3 billion in additional financing for land conservation.[64] In Arizona, a measure to spend $220 million over an eleven year period to buy open space won approval.[65] Programs to preserve farmland and open space were also approved in Minnesota, Michigan, Oregon, and Rhode Island.

At the local level, dozens of cities – including seven in California – passed referendums and other ballot measures to impose clear boundaries on future development. Because of a series of such boundaries approved in Ventura Country, California, about 80 percent of the county has been preserved from further development. On Cape Cod, voters in the fifteen towns of Barnstable County, Massachusetts approved a "local-option three percent property tax assessment to finance community land banks." In Austin, Texas, voters approved a bond issue of $76 million to support parks and greenways; Austin residents had previously voted to pay $65 million in increased water rates to preserve 15,000 acres of land outside the city.[66] And in New Jersey, in addition to the statewide measure, forty-three cities and six counties approved separate tax increases to finance additional preservation measures.[67]

To date, the most committed anti-sprawl elected official at the state level has been Maryland governor Paris Glendening. During his first term (1995–9), Glendening succeeded in passing several antisprawl measures, including the Rural Legacy program (which "earmarks more than $71 million over the next five years to purchase development rights on environmentally valuable land") and the Smart Growth Areas Act (which "restricts state funding for road and sewer projects to those in older communities and areas already slated for growth").[68] Glendening stressed these polices and continued to spread the antisprawl word during his successful 1998 bid for reelection: "We cannot continue to go on with the old patterns of development," he said. "It doesn't make any financial sense. It doesn't make any environmental sense. It destroys the sense of community."[69] In his second term, Glendening moved to tie state assistance to counties to how aggressively each county provides open space and curtails sprawl.[70] State funding for school infrastructure also shifted dramatically in Maryland, as the state now commits 80 percent of the school construction budget to established areas, whereas in the early 1990s over 60 percent of school construction funds were spent in newly developed areas.[71] Other state agencies such as the state Department of Transportation have also undergone major shifts in policy (as well as their internal culture): transportation planners in the state are now encouraged to take into account the needs of pedestrians and the impact of transportation projects on community well-being, instead of bulldozing and laying pavement in every direction.[72]

The antisprawl movement now involves not only environmentalists decrying the loss of habitat and auto exhaust, liberals seeking to stave off inner-city decline, and suburbanites and rural residents seeking to preserve their quality of life, but also members of the business community who believe that sprawl is "bad for business." The Bank of America, for instance, published a comprehensive critique of the impact of sprawl in California in 1996. In 1999 *Governing* editor Alan Ehrenhalt, reporting on Atlanta, noted that antisprawl sentiments there "have spread through [the] entire business community with remarkable speed and intensity.... Everybody in Atlanta seems to be against sprawl now – developers, bankers, utility companies, all the interests that have profited from it for five decades. 'You think back two years,' says John Sibley, chairman of the environmentalist Georgia Conservancy, 'and the change in the mind-set is stunning.'"[73] Another 1999 study by the National Association of Local Government Environmental Professionals documented nineteen business-led "smart growth" initiatives nationwide.[74] For instance, the influential Silicon Valley Manufacturing Group has actively promoted high-density development, public transit, and additional low-income housing both in California and nationally.[75]

Former vice president Al Gore also embraced the idea of smart growth during the second Clinton term. The Clinton administration created a Livable Communities Initiative within the Environmental Protection Agency, and established several modest antisprawl policies, such as a home loan pilot program to encourage housing near mass transit, and a $17 million program to buy 53,000 acres of farmland nationwide.[76] The 2000 Democratic platform endorsed the idea of Better America Bonds, which would have provided tax credits to states and localities on bond issues aimed at building "livable communities" (that is, containing sprawl) by preserving open spaces, farmland, and parks and acquiring more land for preservation and recreation purposes.[77]

Antisprawl momentum continued into the 2000 campaign, as Arizona voters considered a statewide antisprawl proposition (which was strongly opposed by the real estate industry), and a similar measure was proposed in Colorado. The Arizona legislation would have established strong growth boundaries statewide, while the Colorado legislation, following the lead of Oregon, would have mandated that localities develop and receive voter approval for comprehensive land-use plans.[78] Both the Colorado and Arizona measures were defeated by wide margins, but activists in both states have claimed that the initiatives helped alter the public debate about growth in each state.

The Imperative of Community-Controlled Land

We are sympathetic to most of the policy measures now being implemented in Maryland and other localities that aim to contain sprawl. But we remain skeptical about the long-term effectiveness of sprawl-fighting policies that fail to address one of the underlying structural realities driving sprawl, namely, control of land by powerful private actors, not only in rural areas but in urban areas as well. As we have already seen, the principle of using public funds to buy undeveloped, often rural, land for conservation purposes is now broadly accepted across party lines. Equally critical is establishing a measure of community control over *urban* land – not as a means of directly stalling outward development but to ensure that sprawl-stopping measures do not perversely disadvantage low-income city residents by raising housing costs.

Here a major problem must be noted: As already experienced in the growth-boundary city of Portland – which has been rated by the National Homebuilders Association as the second most expensive housing market in the nation – over time we can expect urban land values to rise in cases where outward development is curtailed. The rise in land values translates into increased rents, which in turn make city living unaffordable for low-income renters – who are often replaced by higher-income residents in a gentrification process.[79] While some analysts sympathetic to growth boundaries have noted that housing prices have also risen in fast-growing metropolitan areas without growth boundaries – a recent econometric study concluded that Portland's urban growth boundary is "probably not" primarily responsible for rising housing prices in the city – most acknowledge the theoretical point that limiting the supply of available land on which to build housing is likely to place upward pressure on housing prices.[80] The obvious antidote to this consequence of antisprawl public policy is to make direct provision for low-income housing. This might happen by expanding publicly subsidized housing units or by rehabilitating existing housing stock that has fallen into disrepair. Stable low- and middle-income housing can also be secured by means of urban community land trusts. In the latter, units, blocks, or conceivably entire neighborhoods are placed in a trust. Low-income residents can rent or own units on land controlled by the trust, but owners must resell housing back to the trust, not an outside buyer. This effectively takes the units in question out of the private housing market and guarantees that rising land values and urban rebirth do not displace poor residents. There are over one hundred urban land trusts now operating in the United States, and the number is steadily growing.

It is likely that the next decade will see the further development of land trust mechanisms both to preserve open space and to take increasing increments of urban land off the market. Possibly some cities may experiment with site value taxation of the sort advocated by Kunstler, in which land is taxed more heavily than buildings in urban areas, thereby dampening land speculation activities. In the longer term, we also think it makes sense to reconsider the vision Ebenezer Howard laid out at the end of the nineteenth century – cities (be they old cities or new towns) in which the public directly owns both urban land and immediately outlying areas, and can take effective steps to shape land development. Over time, treating land not as a simple commodity but as a community resource that should be under substantial democratic control will be a crucial lever in a serious long-term attack on sprawl-like development. It will also be critical to the restoration of substantive local-level democracy, in which private developers and other land-oriented businesspeople do not have overwhelming political power, especially with respect to urban planning decisions and the use of public resources in economic development.

Strategies and Solutions

Urban sprawl clearly will have a lasting place on the national agenda. Leaving aside the long-term goal of bringing more land under direct democratic control, which short-term and medium-term policies and strategies hold the best prospect of actually containing fringe development and preserving existing communities (both urban and suburban)? Following Persky, Wiewel, and Sendzik, the available strategies can be summarized and grouped into four categories: policies intended to stall "deconcentration," redistributive policies aimed at mitigating the consequences of sprawl, policies to develop mechanisms of regional governance, and policies aimed at revitalizing urban centers.[81]

Containing deconcentration

Policies to raise the costs of deconcentration include a range of approaches that fall under the rubric of growth management. Specific tactics to limit growth through land-use planning include zoning rules intended to constrain new development, impact fees that charge developers for the public costs incurred by new development, and public intervention into land markets to deliberately limit new development. The paradigmatic example of growth management is Portland, Oregon, which has essentially prevented development in outlying areas by establishing and enforcing a growth boundary. As noted above, a number of states have recognized the obvious fact that buying undeveloped tracts of land for preservation purposes (or arranging for nonprofit preservation groups to do so) can help prevent undesired outward development.

More common than direct intervention into land markets is the use of impact fees: Developers and businesses are charged a fee to help cover the estimated costs to the public (roads, sewers, etc.) of new development projects. Various studies suggest that impact fees appear to be moderately effective, but insufficient empirical evidence exists to make firm judgments. Impact fees have been criticized for essentially providing a windfall to existing residents of a community, since by raising the cost of new housing, such fees also raise the value of existing land and buildings within a community. There is also uncertainty over the best method of calculating how high impact fees should be. Impact fees will almost certainly continue to be used as a check on sprawl, but they are a relatively weak tool and unlikely on their own to seriously constrain or reverse outward growth. (Ironically, as more communities adopt impact fees, their relative effectiveness as an anti-growth measure in any particular place is likely to decline, since the competitive disadvantage of developing in an impact-fee-imposing locality disappears if all localities have such fees. Impact fees would still be defensible and desirable in that eventuality, however, as a way to force private developers to pay a larger share of the costs of new growth, and if *all* suburbs adopted such fees and cities did not, that could increase the attractiveness of cities to developers.)

Another available approach is congestion pricing. Congestion pricing simply refers to increased tolls on rush-hour traffic in congested driving areas, to compel drivers to pay more of the actual social cost of using roads at peak hours. In principle such pricing schemes could raise the cost of travel sufficiently so that firms would be compelled to locate on sites that can be accessed without causing additional traffic. Congestion pricing has been attempted only on a limited basis in the United States, although several cities worldwide have implemented such schemes.[82]

Redistributing costs and benefits

A second set of policies attempt to redistribute the benefits associated with suburban growth. Such policies include:

- "Reverse commuting" policies, which seek to subsidize transportation for central-city residents to suburban job opportunities
- Constructing low-income housing in the suburbs (which implies overturning often exclusionary zoning practices)
- Tax-base sharing in which cities and suburbs effectively share revenue from property taxes, as has been practiced in the Twin Cities area in Minnesota for the past three decades
- Special regional governance bodies, which have authority over a specific issue involving both urban and suburban areas (such as water supply).

None of these policies is capable of seriously redressing urban sprawl; the intent is to make the best of the current situation through modifications that benefit low-income residents. Unfortunately, such programs face the same political obstacles encountered by other programs to help poor citizens, and tax-base sharing is especially unlikely to be accepted politically, since suburban residents by and large do not want to pay for "urban problems."

Regional governance mechanisms

A third antisprawl tactic is the development of formal regional governance authorities, on the model of the Unigov system of combined city and county governance practiced in Indianapolis. Such authorities provide the same benefits as tax-based revenue sharing schemes (allowing suburban tax money to be used to combat urban problems) but may be more efficient in providing public infrastructure and in imposing policies such as impact fees. Regional governance approaches suffer from the same problem of political feasibility that tax-sharing schemes face. Nonetheless, the emergence of regional governance mechanisms would be highly desirable and would make a coordinated antisprawl effort much more plausible. Establishment of such mechanisms, however, would ultimately depend on new city-suburb alliances, based on the realization, as Wiewel and colleagues note, that "suburbs with strong central cities fare better themselves in terms of income and home values."[83] Peter Dreier, John Mollenkopf, and Todd Swanstrom have called upon the federal government to actively promote regional-level governance and cooperation by making metropolitan regions the operational unit for many federal progams.[84]

Revitalizing cities

A final set of strategies focuses less upon changes in the rules governing suburban expansion than upon making central cities more attractive. When urban neighborhoods gain economic stability and become more attractive places to live, some of the distributive effects of sprawl can be countered (such as lack of access by urban residents to suburban jobs). Equally important, there is less impetus for flight to the suburbs on the part of middle-class, high-revenue citizens, as social costs and dysfunctions associated with central-city decline are reduced. As we have noted, making use of existing infrastructure and buildings also has advantages over the construction of new buildings and infrastructure in an effort to escape inner-city decay.

Notes

1   William Fulton, Rolf Pendall, Mai Nguyen, and Alicia Harrison. "Who Sprawls Most? How Growth Patterns Differ Across the United States," July 12, 2001. Report available from the Brookings Institution at www.brookings.edu/es/urban/urban.htm.
2   Ibid.

3 For a well-stated critique, see Betty Friedan, *The Second Stage* (New York: Summit Books, 1981), 282–7. See also Dolores Hayden, *Redesigning the American Dream* (New York: W. W. Norton, 1984). Hayden is an important representative figure in a large literature on the relationship between gender inequality and city and land use planning. See also Leslie Weisman, *Discrimination by Design* (Urbana: University of Illinois, 1992), and Marsha Ritzdorf, "A Feminist Analysis of Gender and Residential Zoning in the United States," in Irwin Altman and Arza Churchman, eds., *Women and the Environment* (New York: Plenum Press, 1994). For a more positive recent assessment of suburban life from a feminist standpoint see Rosalyn Baxendall and Elizabeth Ewen, *Picture Windows: How the Suburbs Happened* (New York: Basic Books, 2000).

4 Richard Applebaum, *Size, Growth, and U.S. Cities* (New York: Praeger Publishers, 1978), 100–1.

5 J. Eric Oliver, *Democracy in Suburbia* (Princeton: Princeton University Press, 2001).

6 Ebenezer Howard, *Garden Cities of To-Morrow*, ed. with a preface by F. J. Osborn, with an introductory essay by Lewis Mumford (Cambridge, MA: MIT Press, 1965), 142.

7 Peter Hall and Colin Ward, *Sociable Cities: The Legacy of Ebenezer Howard* (Chichester, England: John Wiley and Sons, 1998), 67.

8 Kenneth Jackson, *Crabgrass Frontier* (New York: Oxford University Press, 1985).

9 *Federal Budget of the United States 2003 – Analytical Tables* (Washington, DC: Government Printing Office, 2002).

10 Jackson, *Crabgrass Frontier*, 205.

11 Richard Moe and Carter Wilkie, *Changing Places* (New York: Henry Holt & Co, 1997), 48.

12 As Melvin Oliver and Thomas Shapiro have helped show, this in turn limited African-American's accumulation of economic assets in the postwar era. See Oliver and Shapiro, *Black Wealth/White Wealth: A New Perspective on Racial Inequality* (New York: Routledge, 1995).

13 David Rusk, *Inside Game/Outside Game* (Washington, DC: Brookings Institution, 1989). 88–9.

14 Moe and Wilkie, *Changing Places*, 57.

15 Rusk, *Inside Game/Outside Game*, 90–1.

16 Pietro S. Nivola, *Laws of the Landscape: How Policies Shape Cities in Europe and America* (Washington, DC: Brookings Institution, 1999), 13–14.

17 Nivola, op. cit., 15; *Ten Years of Progress* (Washington, DC: Surface Transportation Policy Project, 2001), 11.

18 David M. Roodman, *Paying the Piper: Subsidies, Politics, and the Environment* (Washington, DC: Worldwatch Institute, December 1996), 42.

19 Nivola, *Laws of the Landscape*, 18, Figure 3–3.

20 Ibid., 26, citing John Pucher, "Urban Travel Behavior as the Outcome of Public Policy," *Journal of the American Planning Association* 54 (1988): 513.

21 Nivola, *Laws of the Landscape*, 25.

22 *Federal Budget of the United States 2003 – Analytical Tables* (Washington, DC: Government Printing Office, 2002), 100.

23 Moe and Wilkie, *Changing Places*, 258.

24 James Kunstler, *Home from Nowhere* (New York: Simon and Schuster, 1996), 196–7.

25 Nivola, *Laws of the Landscape*, 26–7.

26 Bruce Katz and Joel Rogers, "The Next Urban Agenda," in Robert Borosage and Roger Hickey, eds., *The Next Agenda: Blueprint for a New Progressive Movement* (Boulder: Westview Press, 2001), 191.

27 Robert A. Beauregard, "Federal Policy and Postwar Decline: A Case of Government Complicity?" *Housing Policy Debate* 12, 1 (2001): 129–51.

28 Jennifer Preston, "Battling Sprawl, States Buy Land for Open Space," *New York Times*, June 9, 1998, A1.

29 Rob Gurwitt, "The Quest for Common Ground," *Governing*, June 1998, 21, 22.

30 Kaid Benfield, Matthew Raimi, and Donald Chen, *Once There Were Greenfields* (Washington, DC: Natural Resources Defense Council, 1999), 35.

31 See William Shore, "Recentralization: The Single Answer to More than a Dozen United States Problems and a Major Answer to Poverty," *Journal of the American Planning Association* 61 (1995): 496–503.

32 Jack Nasar and David Julian, "The Psychological Sense of Community in the Neighborhood," *Journal of the American Planning Association* 61 (1995): 178–84.

33 Robert Putnam, *Bowling Alone* (New York: Knopf, 2000), 204–15. Quoted material from 213, 215.

34 Timothy Beatley, *Green Urbanism: Learning from European Cities* (Washington, DC: Island Press, 2000).

35 For interesting discussions along these lines, see Juliet Schor, *The Overspent American* (New York: Basic Books, 1998), and Jerome Segal, *Graceful Simplicity* (New York: Henry Holt & Co., 1999).

36 Ann Sorenson, Richard Greene, and Karen Russ, *Farming on the Edge*, published by the American Farmland Trust, March 1997, available at www.farmlandinfo.org. See Table 7.

37 Benfield, Raimi, and Chen, *Once There Were Greenfields*, 64–72.

38 HUD Report, *The State of Our Cities* (Washington, DC: Government Printing Office, 1999), iv.

39 Benfield, Raimi, and Chen, *Once There Were Greenfields*, 55, 58.

40 United States Bureau of the Census, "Private Vehicle Occupancy for the United States: 1990 and 1980 Census," undated, cited in Benfield, Raimi and Chen, *Once There Were Greenfields*, 34, Table 2–1.

41 Benfield, Raimi, and Chen, *Once There Were Greenfields*, 51; citing Clay Chandler, "The 60 Watt Mind-Set," *Washington Post*, November 14, 1997, A20, and Warren Brown, "Trucks Are Putting Cars Out of Commission," *Washington Post*, October 7, 1998.

42 Benfield, Raimi, and Chen, *Once There Were Greenfields*, 51. Marc Breslow, "Two Cheers for OPEC," *Dollars and Sense*, May–June 2000, 8.

43 Benfield, Raimi, and Chen, *Once There Were Greenfields*, 78–84.

44 Myron Orfield, *Metropolitics*, rev. ed. (Washington, DC: Brookings Institution, 1998), 72.

45 James E. Frank, *The Costs of Alternative Development Patterns* (Washington, DC: Urban Land Institute, 1989). Cited in Benfield, Raimi, and Chen, *Once There Were Greenfields*, 97–8.

46 James Duncan and Associates, *The Search for Efficient Urban Growth Patterns* (Tallahassee: Florida Department of Community Affairs, July 1989). Cited in Benfield, Raimi, and Chen, *Once There Were Greenfields*, 98–100.

47   Robert Burchell et al., *Impact Assessment of the New Jersey Interim State Development And Redevelopment Plan. Report II: Research Findings* (Trenton: New Jersey Office of State Planning, 1992). Cited in Benfield, Raimi, and Chen, *Once There Were Greenfields*, 101–2.

48   Alan Altshuler and José Gómez-Ibáñez, *Regulation for Revenue* (Washington, DC: Brookings Institution, 1993), 62–76.

49   For a comprehensive literature review on this topic, see Robert Burchell et al., *The Costs of Sprawl – Revisited*, Transit Cooperative Research Program Report 39 (Washington, DC: National Academy Press, 1998).

50   See William Julius Wilson, *When Jobs Disappear* (New York: Knopf, 1996).

51   For further analysis, see Chapters 2 and 3 of Peter Dreier, John Mollenkopf, and Todd Swanstrom, *Place Matters* (Lawrence: University Press of Kansas, 2001).

52   Moe and Wilkie, *Changing Places*, 144; a solid general discussion of this issue can be found in their book on pages 142–77.

53   Stacy Mitchell, *The Hometown Advantage: How To Defend Your Main Street Against Chain Stores . . . and Why It Matters* (Minneapolis: Institute for Local Self-Reliance, 2000), 5–9.

54   See Gunn and Gunn, *Reclaiming Capital*; David Morris, *Self-Reliant Cities* (San Francisco: Sierra Club Books, 1982); David Imbroscio, *Reconstructing City Politics* (Thousand Oaks: Sage Publications, 1997).

55   Kenneth E. Stone, "Impact of the Wal-Mart Phenomenon on Rural Communities," paper presented at National Public Policy Education Conference, Charleston, South Carolina, September 24, 1997.

56   Annette Bernhardt, "The Wal-Mart Trap," *Dollars and Sense*, September–October 2000.

57   See Thomas and Mary Edsall, *Chain Reaction* (New York: Norton, 1991).

58   Andres Duany, Elizabeth Plater-Zyberk, and Jeff Speck, *Suburban Nation: The Rise of Sprawl and the Decline of the American Dream* (New York: North Point Press, 2000), 45–6.

59   Juliet F. Gainsborough, *Fenced Off: The Suburbanization of American Politics* (Washington, DC: Georgetown University Press, 2001). See Appendix for summary tables, 143–69.

60   For an important recent analysis of the consequences of suburban privilege in metropolitan contexts from a political theory point of view, see Iris Marion Young, *Inclusion and Democracy* (New York: Oxford University Press, 2001).

61   Timothy Egan, "Dreams of Fields: The New Politics of Urban Sprawl," *New York Times*, November 15, 1998; Peter S. Goodman and Dan Eggen, "A Vote to Keep Sprawl at Bay," *Washington Post*, November 5, 1998, B1.

62   Robert Geddes, "Metropolis Unbound," *American Prospect*, November–December 1997, 44.

63   Jennifer Preston, "New Jersey Legislature Puts Plan To Conserve Open Land on Ballot," *New York Times*, July 31, 1998, A1; Goodman and Eggen, "A Vote to Keep Sprawl at Bay."

64   Neal Peirce, "Sprawl Control: Now Key Political Issue," *Baltimore Sun*, November 15, 1998.

65   Egan, "Dreams of Fields"; see also Peirce, "Sprawl Control," and " 'Growing Smarter' offers millions to preserve open space," *AP Wire Story*, November 4, 1998.

66 Egan, "Dreams of Fields"; Peirce, "Sprawl Control"; Jennifer Preston, "Battling Sprawl, States Buy Land for Open Space," *New York Times*, June 9, 1998, A1. Quote from Peirce.

67 Egan, "Dreams of Fields."

68 Peter S. Goodman, "Glendening vs. Suburban Sprawl," *Washington Post*, Oct. 6, 1998, B1.

69 Ibid.

70 "Governor Puts Md. Money on Smart Growth," *Washington Post*, August 20, 2000, C1.

71 "Maryland Farmland a Focus In Suburban Sprawl Battle," *New York Times*, June 25, 2001, 10.

72 "Maryland Going 'Beyond the Pavement'; State Shifting Focus From Roads to Pedestrians and Transit," *Washington Post*, September 15, 2000, A1.

73 Alan Ehrenhalt, "New Recruits in the War on Sprawl," *New York Times*, April 13, 1999, A23.

74 John Hughes, "Study: Businesses Fight Urban Sprawl," AP news item, June 14, 1999.

75 See www.smvg.org for an overview of SMVG's activities.

76 Judith Havemann, "Gore Calls For Smart Growth," *Washington Post*, September 3, 1998, A17.

77 2000 Democratic Party Platform Committee Report, 16, available at www.democrats. org.

78 Peter Grant, "Raising Arizona: A Sprawling Battle Nears Vote – Polls Show Strong Support For Measure to Limit Growth Around Cities," *Wall Street Journal*, September 20, 2000, B2.

79 For a solid discussion of the issue in Portland from an activist perspective, see Tasha Harmon "Portland, Oregon: Who Pays the Price for Regional Planning? How To Link Growth Management and Affordable Housing," in *Planners Network* 128 (March–April 1998).

80 See Justin Phillips and Eban Goodstein, "Growth Management and Housing Prices: The Case of Portland, Oregon," *Contemporary Economic Policy* 18, 3 (2000): 334–44; See, also the discussion of Oregon planning consultant Eben Fodor in *Better Not Bigger* (Gabriela, BC: New Society Publishers, 1999), 60–76.

81 Wim Wiewel, Joseph Persky, and Mark Sendzik of the University of Illinois at Chicago have helpfully reviewed a wide range of antisprawl policies in "Private Benefits and Public Costs: Policies to Address Suburban Sprawl," *Policy Studies Journal*, 27, 1 (1999): 96–114.

82 Wiewel, Persky and Sendzik, "Private Benefits and Public Costs."

83 Ibid, 129.

84 Peter Dreier, John Mollenkopf and Todd Swanstrom, *Place Matters* (Lawrence: University Press of Kansas, 2001), 211–12.

Index

productivity: and earnings, 149, 236–7; *see also* economic growth

"progressive" cities, 180*n*

property developers: anti-sprawl measures, 323–5; real estate cycle, 167–81; *see also* gentrification; urban redevelopment

property taxes, 309–10, 324; site value taxation, 322

protohomelessness, 158–9, 161, 164

"proto-postmodern" urban process, 64–8

public agencies and local growth, 23

public choice theory, 293–4

public housing, 36, 164; dispersal strategies, 241–2; federal policy, 154–5, 244–6; Gautreaux program, 235, 288, 296; Moving to Opportunity program, 8, 288; and residential segregation, 244–6; and urban redevelopment, 172

public policy, 7–9, 233–329; and choice, 293–4; and concentrated poverty, 8, 233–48; and economic restructuring, 30–1, 33–4, 35–8, 239–40; and economic segregation, 296–9; homeless deterrent measures, 274–6; and housing, 8–9, 154–5, 164, 244–6; and residential segregation, 241–2, 243–4, 246, 263–5; and suburban development, 9, 293–4, 306–10, 314–15, 323–5; and urban redevelopment, 168, 172–4; *see also* policing; social welfare

public services: and economic segregation, 290–4; ethnic employment, 114

public space: in fortified cities, 269–70, 273–5, 277, 282–3

public toilets, 275

public/private spheres, 76

Puerto Ricans: residential segregation, 255, 261

purdah, 47

Purum houses, 47

Putnam, Robert D., 298, 311–12

quality of life and suburban development, 311–12

quasi-public agencies: and local economic growth, 23

"quaternary sector," 31–2

Raban, J., 197

race riots, 254–5

racial discrimination: anti-immigrant movements in California, 140, 141; and employment of immigrants, 121–3, 141–2; and home-mortgages, 261, 295, 307; and persistent poverty, 256, 257, 258; *see also* residential segregation

racial minorities *see* ethnic minorities

Raimi, Matthew, 315

Reagan administration, 36, 37, 38–9, 152–3, 155

real estate cycle, 167–81

Real Estate Research Corporation, 315

Real World, The (MTV series), 218, 225

Reckless, Walter C., 101

redevelopment *see* gentrification; urban redevelopment

redistribution: people-specific policies, 33; and suburban development, 316, 324; tax credits, 239, 245; and urban redevelopment, 175

"redlining," 307

refugees as migrants, 96, 97

refuse protection, 275

regimes of accumulation, 3, 34

regional governance bodies, 35–6, 324, 325

regulation, 34, 62–3

Reich, Robert, 299

reindustrialization, 33, 149–50

rent burdens, 157

rent gaps, 155–6, 185

residential filtration model, 107

residential segregation, 76, 174; African-American experience, 9, 241–2, 243–4, 246, 252–65; Chinese communities, 101; economic segregation, 8–9, 284–99; fortress communities, 267–83; historical context, 260; hypersegregation, 260; middle-class flight from ghetto, 241, 259, 307, 315–16; and public policy, 241–2, 243–4, 246, 263–5; racial discrimination, 260–1; *see also* economic segregation; suburban development

residential zone, 57

restaurants and gentrification, 190–1

retailers: and apparel industry, 137; and economic segregation, 294–5; and suburban development, 316–18; *see also* shops

"reverse commuting" policies, 324

Rhondda Heritage Park, 196

roads *see* highways

Rockwell, L. H., 296

Rogers, Joel, 310

Rogers, Richard, 207

romantic gaze, 195–6

Rosaldo, R., 225

Rosenbaum, James, 235

Rothschild, E., 149–50

Rouse, James, 204, 306

routinisation of practices, 78

runoff water pollution, 313–14

rural heritage, 196, 197–8, 212

Rural Legacy program, 320

urban–rural migration, 91–8, 106

Rusk, David, 307–8

Salins, Peter, 241, 243

San Francisco, 102

Sanders, Heywood T., 175